Microsoft Resources on the Internet

Name	URL
BackOffice	`http://www.microsoft.com/backoffice/`
Exchange	`http://www.microsoft.com/exchange/`
IIS	`http://www.microsoft.com/infoserv/`
Intranet	`http://www.microsoft.com/intranet/`
Internet Explorer	`http://www.microsoft.com/ie/`
Microsoft Press	`http://www.microsoft.com/mspress/books/b.htm`
Microsoft Training	`http://www.microsoft.com/train_cert/`
NT Server	`http://www.microsoft.com/ntserver/`
NT Workstation	`http://www.microsoft.com/ntworkstation/`
SQL Server	`http://www.microsoft.com/sql/`
Visual Basic Scripting	`http://www.microsoft.com/vbscript/`

D1408167

Mastering Microsoft Internet Information Server

Mastering™ Microsoft® Internet Information Server™

Peter Dyson

SYBEX®

San Francisco • Paris • Düsseldorf • Soest

Associate Publisher: Gary Masters
Acquisitions Manager: Kristine Plachy
Developmental Editor: John Read
Editor: Pat Coleman
Project Editor: Ben Miller
Technical Editor: Mark Edwards
Book Designer: Catalin Dulfu
Graphic Illustrator: Patrick Dintino
Electronic Publishing Specialist: Kris Warrenburg
Production Coordinator: Robin Kibby
Indexer: Ted Laux
Cover Designer: Design Site
Cover Photographer: Mark Johann
Photo Art Direction: Ingalls + Associates
Screen reproductions produced with Collage Complete.
Collage Complete is a trademark of Inner Media Inc.
SYBEX is a registered trademark of SYBEX Inc.
Mastering is a trademark of SYBEX Inc.

Library of Congress Card Number: 96-69668
ISBN: 0-7821-1899-2

Manufactured in the United States of America

10 9 8 7 6 5 4 3 2 1

For my mother and father

ACKNOWLEDGMENTS

The acknowledgments are almost always the last part of the book to be written, and by this late stage in the project, the author really does know who was on his side and who he has to thank.

At Sybex, many thanks to the large team of people who helped to put this book together: Kristine Plachy, Acquisitions Manager; Gary Masters, Associate Publisher; and John Read, Developmental Editor. Thanks to the Project Editor, Ben Miller, who applied just the right amount of lubrication to the wheels, to the Electronic Publishing Specialist, Kris Warrenburg, and to the Production Coordinator, Robin Kibby.

Many, many thanks are owed to the ever-patient Editor Pat Coleman, who steered this book from a rough manuscript into the final form you see between these covers. She brought a wealth of experience to this project, and I think she did an outstanding job.

Special thanks to Peter Denwood, an international trade attorney who has a keen interest in computer-related law, for his expert review of, and suggestions for additions to, chapter eight, *Checking the Fine Print of Legal Issues*.

Thanks to Mark Edwards, Technical Editor and writer, who provided the material that formed the basis for three of the most important chapters: the TCP/IP chapter and the two chapters on internal and external security.

A special thanks to Gene Weisskopf, good friend and fellow author, for stepping in at the very last minute to contribute the chapter on Microsoft's FrontPage as well as material in the *Managing Your Web Site* chapter.

And, as always, thanks to Nancy.

CONTENTS AT A GLANCE

TABLE OF CONTENTS

3   TCP/IP in a Nutshell   61

INTRODUCTION

The Internet is one of the fastest-growing market segments in the history of the computer industry. And the Intranet, the use of Internet technology in a corporate network setting, is going to be every bit as big.

In this book I will tell you everything you need to know about using the Internet Information Server, the latest product from software giant Microsoft, to set up your own external Web site connected to the Internet and your own internal corporate Intranet site.

What This Book Is Not

This book is definitely not just another one of those Yellow Pages listings of the latest cool Internet sites; plenty of books that fall into that category are on the shelves in the bookstores, and I am not the least bit interested in writing another. You will certainly find listings of Internet sites in this book, but each one is there to demonstrate a specific point or because it is an information source, not just because it is on the Internet.

Neither will you find page after page of Hypertext Markup Language listings or scads of Common Gateway Interface scripts or acres of boring C++ code listings that you will never use in a million years. The problems that you have to solve are specific to your site or to your corporate installation; general-purpose solutions are not going to be good enough.

Why This Book?

The documentation available for Microsoft's Windows NT Server is large and very comprehensive, sometimes too large and too detailed, and the documentation that comes with the Internet Information Server is thin and somewhat sketchy. Much of the material for NT Server is written in dense, highly technical language, and many unwarranted assumptions are made about the technical background of the reader.

In writing this book I had three distinct goals in mind:

- To condense the material available for NT Server and tightly focus on only those parts of the system that are of interest to a person setting up a Web server

- To expand and fill out Microsoft's coverage of the Internet Information Server

- To broaden the whole discussion and add material not covered by Microsoft anywhere, including guidelines on connecting to the Internet; planning, designing, and constructing your Web site; how to avoid the most common problems found on many Web sites; and how to get the most out of your corporate Intranet

What you will find in this book is good solid information that will help you to do your job better and faster.

Who Should Use This Book

This book was written for all users, system administrators, and Webmasters who want to get the most out of Microsoft's Internet Information Server. All sorts of readers, from people who run large Internet sites to those who want to use Internet technology to set up a Web server as an Intranet in their department or office, will find this book essential reading.

How This Book Is Organized

There are five different parts to this book and here's a quick rundown:

Part I consists of three chapters. The first gives you some historical background on the growth of the Internet, and the second gives clear guidelines on choosing an Internet Service Provider (ISP) and covers all the different kinds of communications circuits you can use to connect to the Internet. Chapter 3 contains a crash course in the basics of the TCP/IP family of network protocols and describes how you can set up Windows NT Server to use TCP/IP. Remote Access Server (RAS) is also covered for the benefit of users who log in to NT Server from a remote location.

Part II covers the whole process of setting up your Internet Web server in detail. Chapter 4 covers how to install the Internet Information Server on your hardware. Chapters 5 and 6 go together to provide you with sound basics for planning, designing, and constructing your Internet Web site and include warnings for developers of international Web sites. Chapter 7 describes how to create your Web site using Microsoft FrontPage HTML-authoring program. Chapter 8 details some of the legal aspects of publishing on the Internet that you should know about, and Chapter 9 describes the techniques you can use to publicize your new Web site to the rest of the Internet and to the world.

Part III focuses on maintaining your Web site and important security issues. Chapter 10 describes the internal aspects of using NT Server security, and Chapter 11 covers external security issues and firewalls. Chapter 12 contains advice on how best to maintain your Web site, and Chapter 13 covers advanced Web-site administration.

Part IV builds on the discussion in the earlier chapters to cover Intranets, the local application of Internet technology in a department or office. Chapter 14 details the process of creating an Intranet, and Chapter 15 tells you how to put your Intranet to work. Chapter 16 is a look ahead to what the future holds for both the Internet and for corporate Intranets and covers Java, Virtual Reality Modeling Language (VRML), and audio and video applications.

Part V is the reference section of the book and contains three appendices. Appendix A lists the World Wide Web resources I have found useful in the writing of this book and gives the Uniform Resource Locators (URLs) for each of the resources. I am not going to be constantly referring you to this appendix throughout the book; I am going to tell you about it once, here, and then not mention it again. But it is full of good stuff, so check it out. Appendix B is a short tour through the complex and often-confusing world of Web site jargon. Jargon certainly has its place as a kind of shorthand, but it can rapidly become incomprehensible, even to the most seasoned Web surfer. Appendix B is written in plain English and is arranged in alphabetic order so that you can find entries quickly and easily. And Appendix C contains a bibliography of the books and other resources I have found of use during the writing of this book.

A Note about the URLs in This Book

Nothing is more annoying than a dead URL. All the URLs in this book have been individually checked by our Technical Editor; and at the time of writing, they are all active sites, they all work, and they all contain the information that I claim they contain. But that is not to say that some of them won't have changed by the time you try them out.

The better-organized sites will simply post a link to a new site if they make substantive changes, and you can use that link to go right to the new or rearranged site. Other sites, such as the Yahoo site or Microsoft's Web page, reorganize themselves periodically as a part of their housekeeping; the information you want is still available on the site, but you have to look in another place to find it or use the site's built-in search engine to find it.

Some of the sites that contain the most advanced technical information belong to the `.edu` domain, and are usually computer science departments at the major universities. I have tried to keep the number of such sites to a minimum in the book. Although they can be extremely useful, they usually have a lifespan that closely resembles that of the average graduate student. Once the student graduates and leaves that institution, the site becomes neglected and is usually removed soon after. Another dead URL.

And finally, we have tried very carefully not to break a URL across a line; you should be able to type the characters you see in this book without having to worry about whether to type that hyphen or not.

PART I

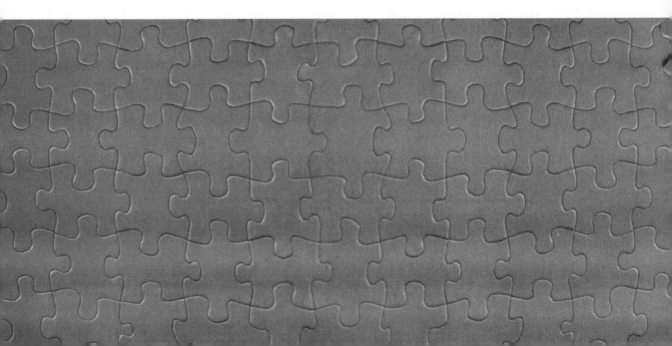

Getting Started on the World Wide Web

CHAPTER
ONE

1

An Introduction to the World Wide Web

In years past, the Internet was for techies and dweebs, computer-science graduates, and university professors and was full of arcane, difficult-to-use commands from the Unix operating system. Connections were difficult to establish and maintain, and you had to learn a mysterious new language to navigate around the system.

Then, the World Wide Web with its graphical browsers was developed, and everything changed, and it seemed to change almost overnight. The Internet went from being a character-based medium to a medium in which all you have to do is point. Now, information is just a click away, and thousands of companies along with millions of people are joining the rush to the Web.

How did all this happen, and how did it happen so fast? To answer these questions, we need to take a short (and I promise it will be very short) look at the recent history of the Internet and the evolution of the World Wide Web in particular. So here goes.

A (Very) Short History of the Internet

You may hear the Internet described as a "network of networks" or as "the world's largest network." Although both statements are true, they do not give you any real indication of how large the Internet actually is.

The Internet was established more than 25 years ago to meet the research needs of the U.S. defense industry, but it has grown into a huge global network serving universities, academic researchers, government agencies, and commercial interests, both in the United States and in more than 100 other countries.

Astonishing as it sounds, no one person runs the Internet, and no single organization pays all the costs; there is no Internet Corporation. The Internet exists as a result of the cooperation of thousands of people all over the world, working in all sorts of organizational and computing environments. The Internet never closes down, mostly because of its decentralized structure, and today the Internet is reliable and predictable. Individual servers may close for upgrades or hardware replacements, but the network is always available without interruption.

From Small Beginnings

In 1969, ARPAnet, an experimental four-computer network, was established by the Advanced Research Projects Agency (ARPA) of the U.S. Department of Defense so that research scientists could communicate among themselves. The first link was between a computer at UCLA's Boelter Hall, home of the Computer Science Department, and another computer hundreds of miles away at the Stanford Research Institute. By 1971, ARPAnet comprised almost two dozen sites, including MIT and Harvard; by 1974, that number had grown to 62, and by 1981, ARPAnet consisted of more than 200 sites.

As more and more computers using different operating systems were connected, the need for a common communications protocol became obvious. The theory required that any computer on the network should be able to talk to any other computer, as a peer. Fault tolerance was designed in at an early stage so that a message from one computer to another could travel by any one of many routes rather than always following a single, unvarying, fixed path. In fact, messages passed between two computers may often take different paths, depending on the availability of the connecting links and the level of network traffic.

Emerging Standards

Eventually, a communications protocol called TCP/IP (Transmission Control Protocol/Internet Protocol) was developed (you will hear much more TCP/IP in the *TCP/IP in a Nutshell* chapter), and in 1983 it became the standard communications protocol on the Internet. The design of TCP/IP was a considerable achievement, solving many nontrivial communications headaches; it is a tribute to the foresight of the original designers that it is still in such common use today.

During the 1980s, many more computer networks were linked to the Internet. Many of them used Ethernet, and many of them ran one variation or another of the Unix operating system—very often BSD Unix (Berkeley Software Distribution, supported by the Computer Science Research Group at the University of California, Berkeley), which included IP networking software.

In 1983, the military portion of ARPAnet was moved onto the MILnet, and ARPAnet was officially disbanded in 1990. By the late 1980s, the National Science Foundation's NSFnet linked five super-computer centers at major universities. At first ARPAnet was tried for communications, but for many reasons this eventually failed. Therefore, NFSnet began its own network, based on the IP technology and using 56Kbps, which was considered very fast at the time.

The most important aspect of the NSF participation was that it allowed everyone to access the network; however, the NSF had a policy known as "acceptable use," which prohibited most commercial activities unless they involved "scholarly communications and research."

Fortunately, this "acceptable use" policy went the way of the dinosaur during 1994 as the U.S. government extracted itself from the Internet and passed control of the NSF backbone to commercial companies such as Sprint and MCI. By 1995, with most of the government involvement removed, commercial activity began to take off in a big way.

Hypertext and Browsers

For the software side of the story we need to go back to 1989, when Tim Berners-Lee, a researcher at the European Particle Research Center (CERN) in Switzerland, and his co-workers proposed a way of formatting documents so that they could be easily transmitted, displayed, and printed on almost any kind of network computer. Berners-Lee also invented the term *World Wide Web* to describe the results of his work, although we usually shorten this to just "the Web."

The World Wide Web was released for internal use at CERN in 1991, where it was used for publishing scientific research papers and the results of experiments. In 1992, the system and the software were made available to the rest of the world.

HTML and HTTP

Berners-Lee's proposal consisted of two separate but closely related parts:

- Hypertext Markup Language (HTML) for formatting the documents

- Hypertext Transfer Protocol (HTTP) for transmitting the documents from one computer to another

Not only did HTML format attractive documents you could look at or print online, but it allowed these documents to contain hypertext links to other documents on other computers on the Internet.

Hypertext is a way of presenting information so that you can look at it in a nonsequential way, regardless of how the original topics were organized by the preparer of the document. Hypertext was designed to allow the computer to respond to the nonlinear way that humans think and access information—in other words, by association, rather than by the linear arrangement of films, books, or recorded speech, for example.

In a hypertext application, you can browse through the information with a great deal of flexibility; you can even choose to follow a different path through the information each time you look at a specific document—something you can't do with video or recorded speech.

A hypertext document can contain a hypertext link to any other document or resource on the Internet, and this link is managed by HTTP. When you select a link, the associated document is displayed, even though it may be on a different computer system, thousands of miles from your location.

Introducing URLs

The computer that requests the document is known as a *client*, and the computer that makes the document available is known as a *server*. Put the two together, and you have the fundamentals of the client-server model for distributed computing.

A Universal Resource Locator, or URL, is a basic HTML element, and when embedded in an HTML document, it points directly to another document somewhere on the Internet that can be retrieved by HTTP. (The process to follow when registering a URL is described in detail in the *Making All the Right Connections* chapter.)

The client software that makes this process happen is called a *browser*, and the first HTML browsers were text-based and somewhat clumsy. They displayed hypertext links followed by a number in brackets; by typing that number, you could follow that link. All this changed with the advent of Mosaic and the other graphical browsers.

Mosaic and Other Web Browsers

Web pages are not transmitted all at once, but are built up over several browser transactions to avoid a long wait as a huge file is downloaded into your system. The text portion of the page is transmitted first, and it contains information about which graphics go where on the page and about where they are located on the server. The browser hides these organizational details from you, and you don't normally see them on your screen.

All this allows your browser to display the text page quickly and easily so that you have something to look at as the graphics are downloaded. You can read this page, wait for the rest of the graphics to arrive, or jump to another page; the browser simply forgets about loading the graphics and instead starts to display the initial text portion of the new page you requested. Figure 1.1 illustrates the process of a Web browser retrieving a page from a Web server.

FIGURE 1.1:

A Web browser retrieving a page from a Web server

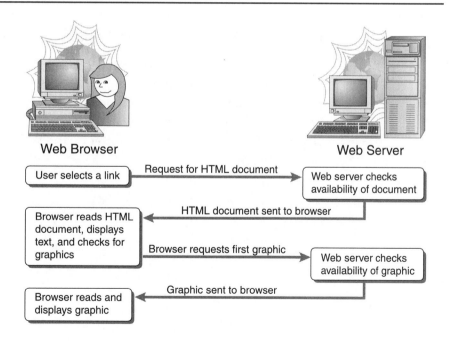

Web Browser   Web Server

| User selects a link | Request for HTML document → | Web server checks availability of document |

| Browser reads HTML document, displays text, and checks for graphics | ← HTML document sent to browser | |

| | Browser requests first graphic → | Web server checks availability of graphic |

| Browser reads and displays graphic | ← Graphic sent to browser | |

Mosaic, written by Marc Andreeson while at the University of Illinois National Center for Supercomputing Applications (NCSA), hid all the HTML elements from the viewer and presented a clear, easy-to-read document containing graphics as well as text. Hypertext links to other documents were displayed as highlighted text; all you had to do was click on a link to display the document. Mosaic also let you add to a list of frequently visited sites and displayed any links you had already visited in a separate color on the screen.

In late 1993, NCSA simultaneously released versions of Mosaic for Microsoft Windows, for Unix systems running the X Window System, and for the Apple Macintosh. Suddenly it seemed that Mosaic was everywhere.

Andreeson left NCSA in 1994 to help co-found Netscape Communications, creators of the popular Netscape browser and one of the computer industry's most oversubscribed initial public offerings. The Netscape browser has been bundled free with all sorts of services from companies such as America Online and CompuServe and is freely available by download from the Netscape Web site; all you pay are the line charges associated with downloading the files.

When a Web browser encounters a type of file that it cannot manage, it checks to see if there is a helper application, or plug-in, for that file type. Common plug-ins include JPEG viewers, sound players, and animation or video viewers and are available for almost all the popular file types you will encounter on the Web. Figure 1.2 shows how all this works.

The architecture of a
Web browser

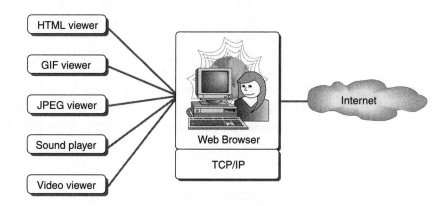

Today, many companies, including such noteworthies as IBM and
Microsoft, offer browser software based on Mosaic, and because they
are all based on the open standards defined by HTML and HTTP,
they all work in pretty much the same way. If you can use one, you
can use them all.

The Web Explodes!

So it was not just one single event that led to the Web taking off in
such a dramatic way, but several related events, including:

- the easy availability of Internet connections
- the removal of restrictions to commercial development of the
  Internet
- access to powerful graphical browsers such as Mosaic and
  Netscape
- the adoption of several important standards

All these elements combined to fuel the Web explosion. During the
last year, the growth in registered commercial names on the Internet
has produced increases in excess of 500 percent, which, taken on a

daily basis, means that hundreds of new sites are being added every day. And this figure does not take into account those small businesses that rent space on third-party Web servers, because you don't have to register those sites with any supervising authority.

Some surveys estimate that there are more than 30 million Internet users today, and of that total, some 8 to 10 million have access to the World Wide Web. Commercial providers such as America Online and CompuServe add new users to this total every day at a phenomenal rate.

Experts put the number of Web pages at somewhere between 30 million and 50 million. Given that an average Web page contains about 500 words, or about 7K of text, the total Web contents must be somewhere between 200 and 300 gigabytes of text, and these numbers are growing at a rate of about 20 percent a month. At this current rate of growth, the Web will soon contain more words than the gigantic Lexis-Nexis database and more words than today's Library of Congress (which contains approximately 29 terabytes) by the end of 1998.

Some of the most successful Web sites, such as those run by Microsoft Corporation (`http://www.microsoft.com/`) or Netscape Communications (`http://home.netscape.com/`), each register several million hits every day (a hit occurs when a user with a Web browser opens a file or a graphic).

Doing Business on the Web

The priorities facing business leaders today are the perennial challenges of reducing costs and time to market, increasing profitability and market share, and being recognized as the leader in what is becoming a global marketplace.

Many corporations are turning to the Web to increase their presence and visibility in today's marketplace; after all, the Web is accessible from well over 100 countries.

Almost all the Fortune 1000 companies have a Web site, a fact that is hard to miss when you hear their Web addresses (or URLs) on the radio and see them on products, in print ads, and on TV. Even the venerable *Wall Street Journal* (`http://www.wsj.com`) is in on the action. You can point your Web browser to the Wall Street Journal's Internet Directory and locate advertisers by name in an alphabetic listing or by category. Simply click on a company name to connect directly to the company's Web site, where you will find company profiles, advertising materials, press releases, and even financial reports.

Advertisers know that making the biggest impact requires the use of techniques specific to each of the traditional media—whether it be print, TV, or radio—and the same is true of the Web. There are ways to make your Web site stand out head and shoulders above those of the competition, and there are some things that you should just not do on a Web site. Large graphics may look flashy, but if the majority of the people accessing your Web site are using relatively slow modems, many of them will never have the patience to wait for the image to load and will move on to the next site before they ever see your prized graphic. And if it is illegal in print or broadcast, it is still illegal when it is on the Web; the laws of copyright also apply on the Internet.

The emergence of secure transactions on the Web, including credit card transactions, makes possible all sorts of business opportunities. Some people are still wary about this aspect of business on the Web, but these same people give their credit cards to all sorts of business owners every day and think nothing of it. The day is rapidly approaching when credit card transactions on the Web will be a standard business procedure.

Internet or Intranet?

All this emphasis on the Internet and the World Wide Web—and the availability of free (or almost free) Web browsers—has led some computer staffs in the corporate world to look at their internal networks in a new light.

The question asked most often is, How can we benefit from this explosion in tools and standards? which is followed very quickly by, What happens if we implement World Wide Web standards in our department or even on our own network?

The answer is an *Intranet*, an internal company network that uses the Web standards of HTML and HTTP and the TCP/IP communications protocol along with a graphical Web browser to support real business applications and provide departmental, interdepartmental, and companywide communications solutions.

An Intranet consists of a Web server connected to a company local area network. The Web server contains electronic copies of important company documents, and as information changes over time, these documents are updated on the server. People in the corporation access this information using a Web browser; thus, they need learn how to use only a single application to access all company information, rather than many applications as in times past. Productivity savings are considerable, and information is up to date and available to everyone on demand.

Intranets are used to publish documents ranging from detailed technical support bulletins all the way to corporate policies and procedures manuals, phone listings, training manuals, new job opportunities, even sales and pricing information. The old barriers of proprietary hardware and software are easily overcome when you adopt the emerging Web standards. Web technology is available for almost all leading operating systems and hardware platforms. Programmers can add links to legacy databases (essential information on mainframe systems that can be considered ancient in computer years) so that information can be viewed and updated quickly and easily. Secure servers can isolate sensitive financial, salary, or sales information and make it available only to those users in, say, the Finance Department. The possible uses for an Intranet are almost endless.

Windows NT Server versus Unix as a Web Server

Most of the computer systems that originally made up the Internet ran one of the variations of the Unix operating system, and so it was only natural that the early Web servers were written to run on Unix; it was simply convenient. But there are few natural advantages to using Unix as a Web server, and in fact there are some very good reasons to avoid using Unix if you possibly can.

Unix has been around for more than 25 years, and many of the security lapses in the operating system and system utilities are well known. But the fact that they are well known does not mean that they have been fixed in all versions and in all installations. Intruders are still exploiting well-known holes in Unix e-mail systems to gain unauthorized access.

Windows NT Server is one of the most stable operating systems around, from any vendor, and the cost of hardware and software is low when compared with the large server hardware appetites usually inherent in Unix. NT Server runs on the Intel series of microprocessors familiar to all PC users, as well as on MIPS RISC, Alpha, and PowerPC platforms, and the operating system is licensed to the Apple Computer Corporation. NT Server can also integrate with all the popular network operating systems available today and supports many networking protocols, including TCP/IP, IPX, SNA, and NetBEUI.

The Microsoft Internet Information Server

In the spring of 1996, Microsoft began shipping the first release of the Internet Information Server, or IIS, which was later incorporated into the BackOffice suite of products. You can also download the software free from Microsoft's own World Wide Web site.

Internet Information Server is a network file and information server that transmits information in HTML using HTTP over a TCP/IP network. The package also includes a Gopher service for publishing information archives and an FTP service for transmitting and receiving files. You will also find copies of Microsoft's own Web browser, Internet Explorer, for a variety of platforms, including Windows NT, Windows 95, Windows for Workgroups, Windows 3.1, and the Macintosh in the Windows NT 4 package and at the Microsoft Web site.

Most people will undoubtedly use IIS primarily as a Web server, providing all the Internet and Intranet services described in this and other chapters of this book. Microsoft believes in putting its money where its mouth is, because it uses IIS running on multiple servers to operate its own Web site, one of the busiest Web sites in the world.

Windows NT Server Version 4

Later in 1996, Microsoft released version 4 of Windows NT Server, containing many additional features, including the famous Windows 95 graphical user interface, already familiar to tens of millions of computer users.

Adding the stability and scalability of Windows NT to the power of the Internet Information Server creates a formidable combination with many advantages over a Unix-based Internet server, including:

- The World Wide Web, Gopher, and FTP services included in IIS are completely integrated with NT's user accounts and file access permissions. This is not an application that runs "on top" of NT, but as an integrated part of NT.

- You can configure your NT Server security in several ways, including physical or protocol isolation, to keep potential intruders at bay.

- Windows NT Server is easy to install, configure, and use. You don't need a department full of Unix gurus and C programmers to establish an Internet presence using NT.

- The security accounts and the tools you use to manage them with IIS are the same tools you use to manage NT security.

- All the software you need to establish an Internet presence is included in the NT package; you won't need to buy other programs later.

- You can extend the reach of the Web server using CGI (Common Gateway Interface) scripts or Microsoft's own Internet Server API (ISAPI).

- A large number of database servers are available for the NT platform, and vendors are showing a great deal of innovation in this arena.

- Windows NT can be configured either as an Internet server or as an Intranet server.

- Windows NT has an inherent scalability that makes changing system components relatively straightforward. Visitors at your site consume resources in the same way as local users do. You can add memory and hard-disk space to NT Server quickly and easily.

Taking all of this together gives a picture of a low-risk, relatively low-cost Internet server running on NT, which is easy to install, configure, and maintain and is eminently capable of providing your company that exclusive presence on the Web.

CHAPTER

TWO

2

Making All the Right Connections

- Looking at Internet connections

- Defining your needs

- Making the choice

- Planning for future expansion

- Finding an Internet Service Provider

- Establishing a domain name

Before you can publish information on the Web or get information from the Web, you must obtain a connection to the Internet. There are two parts to this connection: (1) the communications link itself, and (2) an Internet Service Provider (ISP). The communications link can be one of many kinds, and it is very important that the connection match your anticipated requirements as closely as possible.

On the one hand, you don't want to pay for unused capacity; but on the other, you don't want visitors to your Web site to be put off by too many "port unavailable" or "the server is not responding" error messages.

In this chapter, we'll look at the various types of connections available, as well as the ways you can estimate your requirements, and then look at a checklist of questions to ask of any Internet Service Provider. The aim here is to give you enough information to make your own decisions about the level of service you need now and the level of service that you may need in the immediate future. Finally, we'll look at how to establish a domain name for your corporation.

Looking at Internet Connections

Because no Internet Corporation is in overall charge of the Internet, the connection and service-level choices can seem overwhelming at first. There is no single individual you can contact to order service; instead, you will find a large number of options offered by the phone companies, ISPs, consultants, and contractors. Each organization must assess its needs and then choose a service accordingly.

Your Internet connection will be via a network interface card or other device in your NT Server computer, and this device, along with the bandwidth of the communications circuit to which it is attached, determine the capacity of your Web server. Bandwidth is expressed in terms of megabits per second (Mbps), or millions of bits per second, and determines how many simultaneous users your Web server can process at one time. Put crudely, the higher the bandwidth, the more users your server will be able to support. Figure 2.1 illustrates the main components of a typical local area network (LAN) to Internet Service Provider to the Internet communications connection.

FIGURE 2.1:

The main components of a LAN to ISP to the Internet connection

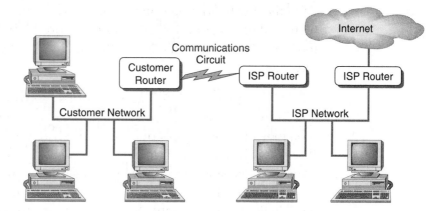

One important thing to remember throughout this chapter is that the Web runs 24 hours a day, every day of the year, and what may well be a suitable access method for a Web browser supporting a single user turns out to be totally inadequate for a major corporation supporting a large Web-server site with hundreds of simultaneous users.

Why Not Lease Web Space?

Sooner or later someone in your organization will ask, Why do we have to have our own Web site? Why don't we just lease Web space from one of these ISPs? There are many answers to these questions, and they all have to do with control and who has it.

If you represent a very small company and want to experiment with a Web presence on a tiny budget, leasing space can be a good way to start. Bear in mind that if you expand your presence to the point where the original site cannot provide adequate levels of support, you will have to move to a new site and change your company URL to reflect this new site. There could be a period of upset as users become accustomed to your new Internet address.

Normally, you will pay for leased space by the megabyte of stored material. Graphics are very popular on most Web sites and can consume a lot of hard-disk space. If your application includes large documents that contain multiple graphics, it will be cheaper to run your own site.

The other aspects of control that you lose when you lease include server response time. You will be sharing the leased space with other users, and you will have no control over server configuration or management or over the type or frequency of hardware or software upgrades. If one of the other sites on the same service turns out to be very popular, your user's response time may suffer as a consequence.

The benefits of leasing Web space are in the initial cost savings; it is relatively cheap to start a small Web site this way. The ISP takes care of all the issues and decisions related to connecting to the Internet and installing and maintaining the host systems, as well as all the administrative and technical details associated with maintaining the site and keeping it running.

Dial-Up or Leased Connection?

The simplest kind of connection to the Internet is via a dial-up connection, sometimes called an on-demand connection. This can be through a conventional modem or through a digital system such as Integrated Services Digital Network (ISDN).

This type of connection is only available part time, as its name suggests, and is not really suitable for a busy Web site that should be available 24 hours every day.

A leased line, also known as a dedicated circuit, on the other hand is always available and can be provided by modem, by ISDN, and by many other kinds of communications circuits. These circuits range in bandwidth from 56Kbps to almost 45Mbps; needless to say, the price of the service rises with the available bandwidth.

SLIP or PPP and Modem

Many Web users will start their explorations using a PC and a dial-up modem connection with a 14.4Kbps V.32 bis or V.42 modem or with a 28.8Kbps V.34 modem. These numbers refer to standards defined by the International Telecommunications Union (ITU), a United Nations umbrella organization that develops and standardizes telecommunications worldwide. The ITU also includes the CCITT (Comite Consultatif Internationale de Téléphonie et de Télégraphie) and several other related organizations. In popular usage CCITT standards are also referred to as ITU standards.

V.32 Modem

A V.32 bis modem (the bis indicates that the original ITU or CCITT standard has been modified and now contains an alternative or an extension to the primary standard) can be used over two-wire dial-up lines or over two-wire or four-wire leased lines. The V.32 standard also includes trellis-coded modulation error correction techniques. The original standard was for 9600 baud, with fallback to 4800; the bis standard extended this to 12.0 and 14.4Kbps.

V.42 Standard

The V.42 standard is not for a modem, but rather for an error-correction technique. V.42 uses LAP-M (Link Access Procedure-Modem) as the primary error correcting protocol, with MNP (Microcom Networking Protocol) classes 2 through 4 as an alternative. An extension to this standard, known as V.42 bis, adds a British Telecom Lempel-Zif data compression technique to this V.42 error correction, usually capable of achieving a compression ratio of 3.5 to 1.

V.34 Modem

The V.34 CCITT standard defines a 28.8Kbps modem for use over dial-up lines using trellis-encoding techniques and advanced data compression techniques to boost effective data-transfer rates well beyond the nominal 28.8Kbps; when V.42 bis compression is added, theoretical data-transfer rates of up to 115.2Kbps are possible.

SLIP

SLIP, or Serial Line Internet Protocol, is used to run the IP protocol over telephone connections using the modems described in the previous paragraphs. SLIP allows you to establish a direct but temporary connection to the Internet, during which your computer appears to the host computer as if it were a port on the host's network. Because it lacks error-correction capabilities, SLIP is slowly being replaced by PPP.

PPP

PPP, or Point-to-Point Protocol, is similar to SLIP, in that it allows you to establish a direct but temporary connection to the Internet using a modem and a phone line.

PPP also provides router-to-router, host-to-router, and host-to-host connections, as well as an automatic method of assigning an IP address so that mobile users can connect to the network at any point.

These modems and protocols are fine for use with Web browsers, but they are certainly not appropriate for use with a Web server, unless you anticipate that you will only ever have two or three simultaneous users. In this kind of low-traffic situation, these connections may suffice, but there is little or no extra bandwidth to allow for future expansion. For most Web servers, one of the following options makes much more sense.

Frame Relay

Frame relay is primarily used in local area networks and in some wide area networks and is offered by most of the RBOC (Regional Bell Operating Companies) and the major carriers such as AT&T, MCI, and Sprint. Bandwidth is in the range of 56Kbps to 1.544Mbps and is suitable for transmitting data only; it is not suitable for transmitting voice or video, because these require constant transmission capabilities.

Frame relay was originally intended as a bearer service for ISDN and is independent of any protocol; therefore, it can transmit packets from TCP/IP, IPX/SPX, and other protocol families. Connections into a frame relay network require a router and a line from the customer site to the carrier's point of entry. After an initial startup cost of somewhere between $1000 and $2500, a connection will cost you between $200 and $500 a month.

ISDN

ISDN is a completely digital service capable of transmitting digitally encoded data, voice, video, and other signals on the same line. ISDN has been popular in Europe for years; although it is slowly gaining ground in the United States, it is still not available in all areas. Table 2.1 shows the approximate number of ISDN lines available in each provider's service area. Most of these providers are working to double or triple the number of lines during the next year.

TABLE 2.1:   ISDN service providers and number of lines installed

Provider	Number of Lines
Ameritech	75,000
Bell Atlantic	150,000
Bell South	30,000
Nynex	90,000
Pacific Bell	70,000
US West	40,000
GTE	25,00

No special wiring is needed for ISDN; it uses the copper twisted-pair wiring of the normal telephone system. ISDN does, however, require a special device to interface between your Web server and the ISDN system. This device is known as a terminal adapter (TA) or as an ISDN modem and can connect normal analog equipment, such as telephones and fax machines, to the ISDN system.

The ISDN Solutions Group, a vendor consortium, has developed a system called ISDN Ordering Codes (IOC) to help simplify ISDN ordering procedures. One group of codes, known as capabilities, is a set of common provisioning profiles, labeled A through S. If your equipment matches one of these profiles, documentation provided by the vendor will tell you to specify that capability when ordering equipment. A second group of codes is equipment-specific, using codes such as Motorola Access 3 to invoke a custom profile for that specific piece of hardware. This IOC system, when used with your ISDN provider, is by far the best way to assemble all the component pieces you will need for your system.

Conventional wisdom says that ordering ISDN is difficult, that you have to be very careful when specifying hardware, and that configuration is painful. Well, that certainly used to be true, but most of the suppliers now have dedicated ISDN ordering lines, and most of the newer equipment is flexible enough to work with almost all ISDN lines. Both Microsoft and Motorola are staging an effort to convert users to ISDN and have posted ISDN specification and ordering forms on their Web sites. Check out Microsoft's site at `http://www.microsoft.com/windows/getisdn/` or the Motorola site at `http://www.mot.com/isdn/`.

ISDN is available in two forms:

- BRI, or Basic Rate ISDN, provides 3 data channels. Two are 64Kbps B (or bearer) channels, and the third is a 16Kbps D (or data) channel that carries call-setup and signaling data between your ISDN devices and the phone company. In some areas, the B channels may run at 56Kbps due to limitation in the phone system. On a BRI line, you can make two separate calls to two different locations at the same time, or you can combine the two channels to give 128Kbps data-transfer rates. Figure 2.2 illustrates a Basic Rate ISDN configuration.

- PRI, or Primary Rate ISDN, provides twenty-three 64Kbps B channels and one 64Kbps D channel for a total bandwidth of up to 1.544Mbps. In Europe and the Pacific Rim countries, where communications standards are slightly different, PRI consists of either thirty or thirty-one 64Kbps B channels, and one 64Kbps D channel, for a total bandwidth of 2.048Mbps. In most areas, one PRI line is much cheaper than the equivalent number of BRI lines. Figure 2.3 illustrates a Primary Rate ISDN configuration.

Each of the B channels operates independently and can carry voice or data.

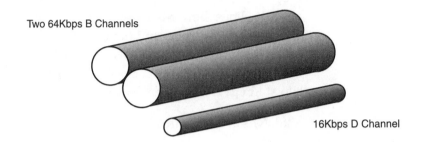

Two 64Kbps B Channels

16Kbps D Channel

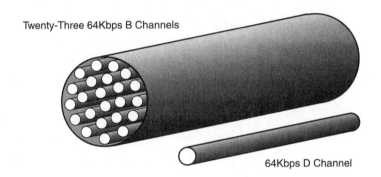

Twenty-Three 64Kbps B Channels

64Kbps D Channel

Prices for ISDN hardware, including ISDN modems, are falling all the time, and connection and line charges are also falling as the services become available in more areas and more popular with users. Rates vary quite a bit from area to area, but in most places, one ISDN line is much cheaper than two normal analog phone lines. Some phone companies offer unlimited calling, others charge by the minute, and others charge only for data calls; check with your provider for details.

Both analog and ISDN phone lines continue to work during a power outage, but your ISDN office equipment will not; consider installing a UPS (uninterruptable power supply) to provide backup power during the inevitable outages.

For more information on ISDN and ISDN-compatible hardware, check out the list of Web sites in *Web Resources on the Internet* appendix under the heading "Modem and Communications Information."

Fractional T1

A fractional T1 (sometimes abbreviated as FT1) line is a subchannel of a full T1 channel, made available at a correspondingly lower price. A full 1.544Mbps T1 line contains 24 fractional T1 lines, each with a bandwidth of 64Kbps. Users can contract for one or more fractional lines without the need to purchase a complete T1 line, and they can add to and expand their stock of fractional T1 lines at any time.

Fractional T1 lines are also made available as packages of 384Kbps (6 fractional T1 lines), 512Kbps (8 fractional T1 lines), and 768Kbps (12 fractional T1 lines).

T1

A T1 is a long-distance point-to-point communications circuit that provides 24 channels of 64Kbps, giving a total bandwidth of 1.544Mbps. T1 is one of the main carriers in the U.S. and Australia and in the Pacific Rim countries, and although it was originally developed to transmit voice, it can also transmit data and images. In Europe and South America, a comparable carrier is designated as E1, with a bandwidth of 2.048Mbps.

T1 services are usually leased on a month-to-month basis and are still quite expensive, especially if they involve two or more phone companies. Installation costs are also high; so T1 services tend to be used for longer-distance links.

To connect your local area network to a T1 line, you will need a:

- Channel Service Unit (CSU), which functions as a certified safe electrical circuit, acting as a buffer between your equipment and the public carrier's network. The CSU prevents faulty equipment from affecting the transmission systems and ensures that all signals placed on the line are appropriately timed and formed.

- Data Service Unit (DSU), which connects data terminal equipment (DTE) to the digital communications lines. The DSU connects to the CSU and converts the local area network signals to T1 signaling formats.

- Multiplexor, which loads multiple channels of voice or data onto the T1 line.

- Bridge or router, which provides the actual connection point between your local area network and the T1 system.

Leased lines such as a T1 circuit have their limitations; they are dedicated lines with a fixed bandwidth. You could, therefore, find yourself paying for bandwidth that you don't use most of the time, but need very occasionally to accommodate short periods of high-burst traffic. Some newer technologies such as SMDS and ATM may actually be more flexible than a T1 line, but you still need the T1 line to connect to the access point of the service. Figure 2.4 illustrates a typical T1 configuration.

A T1 connection will cost on the order of $1500 to $2500 a month; a fractional T1 will be substantially less.

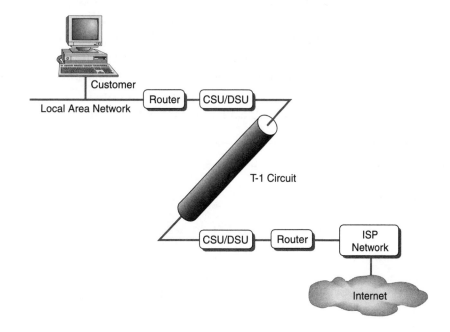

FIGURE 2.4:

A typical T1
configuration

T3

A T3 circuit is a big pipe indeed; equivalent to 28 T1 circuits, it provides a bandwidth of 44.736Mbps and was used originally for transmission between microwave stations.

A T3 line can carry 672 channels of 64Kbps and is usually made
available over high-speed fiber-optic cable. It is used almost exclusively by AT&T and the regional telephone companies, although
certain private companies are using T3 with digital microwave or
fiber-optic networks. Fractional T3 lines are also available to
customers at a lower cost.

Two other T-carrier services are T2 and T4. T2 is a long-distance, point-to-point communications service, providing up to 4 T1 channels. T2 offers 96 channels of 64Kbps, for a total bandwidth of 6.3Mbps. T2 service is not available commercially, although it is used within company telephone networks. T4 provides up to 168 T1 channels, or 4032 channels of 64Kbps, for a total bandwidth of 274.176Mbps. Figure 2.5 illustrates the relationships between the four levels of T-carrier services.

FIGURE 2.5:

The four levels of T-carrier service

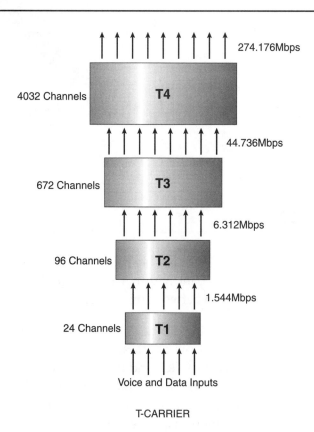

You may also hear a T-carrier service referred to as a DS, an abbreviation for digital signal or digital service, both in the United States and in Europe. DS-0 is equivalent to one 64Kbps circuit, and DS-1 is equivalent to a T1 circuit. Four DS-1 circuits are multiplexed to make a DS-2, equivalent to a T2 circuit, and seven DS-2 circuits are combined to create a DS-3, equivalent to a T3 circuit. Finally, six DS-3 circuits are combined to create a DS-4 circuit, equivalent to a T4 circuit.

SMDS

SMDS (Switched Multimegabit Data Service) is a connectionless, high-speed wide area network service that can transfer data at rates of between 1.544Mbps and 44.736Mbps over T1 and T3 circuits. Figure 2.6 shows an SMDS connection scheme.

FIGURE 2.6:

An SMDS connection scheme

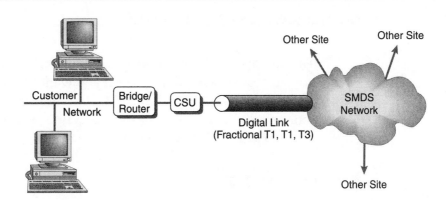

SDMS was developed by Bellcore, and full SMDS services will be made generally available in selected metropolitan areas over a several-year period. Equipment and installation costs are high—approximately five times those of frame relay.

ATM

ATM (Asynchronous Transfer Mode; sometimes called cell relay in order to distinguish it from frame relay) is a relatively new, very high speed digital data transmission circuit capable of data-transfer rates of up to the 2.488 gigabits per second range under experimental conditions. Initial implementations are usually slower, either 155.52Mbps or 622.08Mbps.

Companies such as AT&T and Sprint offer ATM, but the adoption rate has been relatively slow. Because of this, several variations in the basic ATM service have emerged in an attempt to get at least some form of ATM into the market. ATM25 and ATM LAN Emulation are two such attempts.

For more information, check out the ATM forum at `http://www.atmforum.com/`.

Microwave and Satellite

The microwave and satellite options might be worth considering if you are in a very remote area or if you want to transmit a very large amount of data all over the world. For more information, see the International Telecommunications Satellite Organization Web site at `http://www.intelsat.int:8080/`.

SVC versus PVC

Some of the services I have just described can be obtained in two configurations: (1) as an SVC, or Switched Virtual Circuit, or (2) as a PVC, or Permanent Virtual Circuit. Lets take a moment to look at the differences between the two.

An SVC is a connection that is established for a communications session and that is terminated when the session is complete. In this way, a service can provide bandwidth-on-demand as the need for service fluctuates. A different virtual circuit may be established each time a call is made.

A PVC is a logical circuit established between two locations; since the path is fixed, you can think of a PVC as the equivalent of a dedicated line over a packet-switched network.

Figure 2.7 illustrates the differences between PVC and SVC systems. In this figure, each site in the PVC system on the left requires 3 dedicated lines to connect with every other site, for a total of 6 dedicated lines and 12 routers. In the SVC system on the right side, there is only one connection to the network and one router per site.

FIGURE 2.7:

PVC and SVC configurations

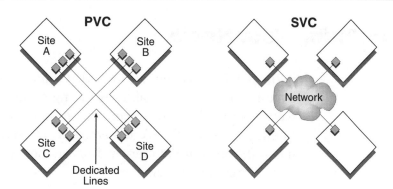

Locating Hardware Compatibility Information

Microsoft runs an extensive hardware testing and qualification system for Windows NT, and you can find a list of all the computer systems and peripherals that have been successfully tested, called the Hardware Compatibility List, at several locations. This list includes modems, ISDN, and other communications devices.

On the Web, see the main Microsoft site at:

```
http://www.microsoft.com/BackOffice/ntserver/hcl
```

You can also get this information by FTP from:

```
ftp.microsoft.com\bussys\winnt\winnt-docs\hcl
```

and in Library 1 of the WINNT forum (GO WINNT) or in Library 17 of the MSWIN32 forum (GO MSWIN32), both on CompuServe.

Microsoft is constantly qualifying new hardware and adding new material to this list; so it is a very good idea to check one of these sites on a fairly regular basis.

Defining Your Needs

In the previous section, we looked at some of the communications circuits commonly available, including frame relay, ISDN, and T1, as well as some of the not-so-common options such as ATM and SMDS. In this section, we'll look at methods you can use to try to estimate the traffic on your Web server. You can then use that number to select a specific communications option.

Using a Stand-Alone Web Server

The quickest and easiest way to establish your presence on the Web is by installing a stand-alone Web server. It is attached to the Internet via an ISP, but there are no other connections to any of your other networks. This approach simplifies estimating traffic and procuring service, because all you have to do is estimate the amount of traffic you expect from the Internet, and it makes dealing with security issues much easier.

The down side of this approach is that you cannot connect your Web site to any other software running on other computers in your company—computers that may contain a customer database or a mailing list that visitors to your Web site might need to update. For most corporations, a stand-alone Web server might be a good place to start, but sooner or later, a corporation will want to connect its Web server to information available elsewhere in the organization, and that means adding the Web server to an existing network or networks.

Adding a Web Server to Your Existing Network

Once you connect your Web server to your existing network, the traffic-estimation problems and security issues become much more complex.

You must spend much more time carefully estimating the incremental network traffic that you expect the Web server to introduce, and you must have adequate hardware in place to ensure that network performance is not degraded for existing users inside the corporation. When you have properly evaluated your needs, you will know whether your site requires a low-, medium-, or high-speed connection to the Internet.

And as soon as you connect your corporate network to the outside world via the Internet, security concerns become much more serious. Some network administrators assume as a matter of course that all visitors to their Web sites are potential intruders, and they plan for this right from the very beginning; others actually try to break into their own networks via the Web server, just to see how hard (or easy) it actually is. We'll look at security issues in much more detail in the *Windows NT Server Operating System Security* and *Security and Firewalls* chapters.

Estimating Your Bandwidth Needs

To assess your bandwidth needs, you must first attempt to measure the amount of data that is likely to flow to and from your Web site. Initially, doing so can be difficult. If you are offering something new and unusual on your site, you may see much more traffic than you expect; some popular sites generate 100,000 hits a day.

Talk to other network administrators in the corporation or in similar corporations to get an idea of how they approached estimating their needs, and then ask how well (or badly) they think they did.

Calculating Web Page Size

If you have already designed your Web page, you can calculate the average size of each page in kilobytes. An average Web text page is about 500 words, or about 7K, but as soon as you add a graphic or two, you must increase this size estimate. A number somewhere between 30K and 50K is probably a reasonable starting point; so use this number if you have not yet designed any of your Web pages.

Then, add in a component for any other services you plan to offer on your Web page, including e-mail, FTP, or Gopher services. These services will probably attract a lower level of interest, and therefore create less traffic, but you should not forget them or exclude them from the picture.

Here are some real numbers to help with this illustration. Table 2.2 shows the times it takes to move a 250K file over various communications links.

TABLE 2.2:   Time needed to transfer a 250K file

Link type	Speed	Transfer time
V.32 Modem	14.4Kbps	2.22 minutes
Frame Relay	56Kbps	34.35 seconds
T1	1.544Mbps	1.24 seconds
T3	44.736Mbps	0.04 seconds

Another useful point of reference you can use to get a handle on your Web-related needs is the speed of your own network. Ethernet usually runs at 10Mbps, and Fast Ethernet and its variations run at speeds of up to 100Mbps. You can also relate the data-communication rates with the data-transfer rates of other familiar devices you will find in your own office, such as your hard-disk systems or SCSI (Small Computer System Interface) hard disk and CD-ROMs. If you plan to use lots of static Web pages with lots of text, your bandwidth requirements will be very different from those of a site that intends to implement video conferencing and real-time audio and video.

Estimating Hit Rates

The next task is to estimate the number of times a day that you think your site will be visited; in other words, how many hits will your site receive each day? This is another quantity that is difficult to estimate, but you can make some sensible assumptions. You will probably see a large number of hits as people discover your new site. Then, as time goes on, you will see the hit rate level off.

To get an idea of the traffic all this involves, multiply the hit rate you expect by the average size of your Web pages; for example, if you expect a hit rate of 10,000 a day, and your average Web page is 50K, your daily server traffic will be on the order of 5000MB of data.

The Internet Is Always Awake

You can take these calculations further and estimate your average hourly traffic, but remember that the Internet pays no attention to time zones; it is always there, not just for an 8-hour workday, but 24 hours every day. You will certainly see peaks and troughs in your hit rates during any 24-hour period, but remember that when it is 8 PM in Europe, and people are accessing your site after a day at work, it is only noon in California, and it is still early in the morning in Alaska and Hawaii.

How Many Users Do You Expect?

The final part in the equation is to estimate how many simultaneous users you want to be able to support. Table 2.3 compares several communications technology circuits in terms of the maximum available bandwidth. I emphasize *maximum available bandwidth* on purpose, as there are many other influencing factors that come into play when you attempt to calculate actual bandwidth rates, including protocol overhead, the speed of intermediate connecting circuits, configuration of intermediate host computer systems, and many others. For these reasons, you will never attain these maximum rates, but you have to start assessing your needs somewhere, and this is a good place.

TABLE 2.3: Comparison of maximum bandwidth and maximum number of users for popular Internet connections

Connection Type	Maximum Bandwidth	Maximum Number of Users
V.32 or V.42 modem	14.4Kbps	1 to 3
V.34 modem	28.8Kbps	1 to 3
Frame relay	56Kbps	10 to 20
ISDN	128Kbps	10 to 55
Fractional T1	64Kbps increments	10 to 20
T1	1.544Mbps	100 to 500
T3	44.736Mbps	More than 5,000

You can check a couple of other places to help build these estimates. If your Web site will be designed primarily to help handle technical support material, ask the existing Tech Support staff how many calls a day they get; if your site will offer customer service information, ask the current staff to describe their workload.

Who's in Charge?

Finally, don't assume that you can add the responsibilities of looking after a busy, evolving Web site to those of your already overburdened network administrator. You can't. You need an additional person or persons with some Windows NT Server administration experience who also have Internet and Web experience and a good eye for attractive design so that they can help lay out the HTML pages you want your Web server to display. Someone will also have to collect, distribute, and perhaps even reply to any e-mail your site collects.

This person should also stay up to date on all matters relating to the Internet and the Web and be prepared to supply that information to others in the corporation, should spend some time surfing the Web looking for sites to link to your own site, and should check that links from other sites lead visitors to the right place on your site. Many links lead to dead ends, and nothing steams visitors like repeated messages that the server is unavailable.

Making the Choice

And as you finally get ready to choose a communications link, here are some rules of thumb:

- Don't even consider dial-up links using conventional PC modems with data-transfer rates of 14.4Kbps or 28.8Kbps. These modems are too slow to support a busy Web server site.

- Frame relay at 56Kbps is really the minimum data-transfer rate that most sites can manage with, giving access to somewhere between 10 and 20 simultaneous users.

- If you anticipate a moderate use of your Web site, say as many as 40 or 50 users at a time, a Primary Rate ISDN service could well turn out to be the best way to go.

- If you think your Web site will attract a great deal of traffic, somewhere up to 500 users at a time, start with a Fractional T1 and then expand as usage grows to a full T1 circuit.

- And if you think that your site will be phenomenally busy, with thousands of simultaneous users, you should establish a 44.736Mbps T3 connection right from the start.

As you will see in the next section, any decision you make today may not last for very long, and this will certainly not be the last time you consider your company's bandwidth needs.

Planning for Future Expansion

You will undoubtedly need to increase both the amount of the hard-disk storage on your Web server, as your site becomes more popular with both visitors and staff within the corporation, and the bandwidth of your communications link in the fairly immediate future, and certainly within a couple of years. Internet applications will continue to grow in terms of computing and storage needs, as well as in terms of the loads they impose on your communications links.

Selecting certain communications options can be expensive when it is time to upgrade your service. Don't put it off; just assume that you will have to upgrade and that you will be upgrading sooner than your current plans indicate. Both ISDN and Fractional T1 services are scalable, and you can work with your provider to add bandwidth as soon as it becomes obvious that you need a little extra.

Finding an Internet Service Provider

Currently, there are approximately 2500 ISPs in the United States, but that number is expected to shrink to about 500 or so during the next two years. ISPs are consolidating in an attempt to cope with the vastly increased competition from the large telephone companies such as Sprint, MCI, and AT&T.

One of the best places to look for information on ISPs is the Web. Check out these Web sites for comprehensive lists of ISPs, and then check out the individual ISP's Web pages for details:

```
http://thelist.com
```

```
http://wings.buffalo.edu/world
```

```
http://www.cybertoday.com.cybertoday/isps/
```

You might also find ISPs listed in the Yellow Pages under *Computers, Networking*, and many ISPs advertise in the Business section of local newspapers.

In choosing an ISP, you must decide the relative importance of several interrelated factors; we look at some of these in the next few sections.

Measuring ISP Performance and Reliability

The most important feature of your Internet connection is that it works and that it works all the time. Check the reliability figures from your ISP, and ask for the names of at least three references; look for references with the same number of comparable systems to the ones you have and in the same or a similar industry if possible. When you get the names, call them and ask them to tell you about their worst day and the nature of the problems encountered. Some ISPs offer service guarantees, and others offer rebates based on down time. All networks fail at some point, and the important factor here is how quickly the ISP isolates the problem and how fast it is fixed and full service restored.

Coping with Power Outages

The most common cause of service loss is one that is not actually under the control of the ISP—a power outage at the customer site. A backhoe on a neighboring construction site can bring the best-made plans crashing. A power outage will either be transient and very, very short, resulting in no loss or virtually no loss in service, or it will last for several hours or even days, depending on the severity. A long power outage is also likely to affect your ISP and also other providers in the area.

Circuit Failure Rates

The next most common failure after a power failure is loss of the communications circuit. Again, this can range from a very brief interruption to a total loss in service that lasts for several hours or even days. Ask your ISP for detailed statistics on its circuit interruptions, and ask what contingency plans are in place to provide an alternative service if the break lasts for longer than expected.

Maintenance Outages

Finally, there are two areas of maintenance to consider. *Unscheduled maintenance* relates to fixing unexpected hardware or software problems and should amount to less than an hour per occurrence. *Scheduled maintenance*, on the other hand, is planned well in advance, and your ISP should be able to give you a list of all scheduled and preventive maintenance operations, the length of time they are expected to take, and their potential impact on services.

Assessing Technical Support

Another way to assess an ISP's ability to provide continuing service is to find out when its network operations center is fully staffed. If you expect Internet access 24 hours a day, for 7 days a week, you need to know if you can call the ISP with technical problems outside normal business hours. The support must be there when you need it. ISPs with people on-site provide better service than those whose support staff are "on call." If staff is on call during the night, ask about average response time and about how many service outages of what duration take place during the night. You should also check an ISP's policies for staffing the Technical Support desk during major holidays; again, those ISPs with staff on call tend to provide terrible support during holidays.

Be sure that the ISP has an adequate supply of spares on hand to be able to cope quickly with common emergencies associated with hardware failures. To determine if the Technical Support desk is adequately staffed, try calling them at odd hours of the day and night before you sign up for service. This way you can make sure that you can get through to a human who can answer your questions, and not just leave a voice-mail message that may or may not ever be answered.

Network Connectivity Bottlenecks

If you decide to install a high-performance link to your ISP, be sure that there are no network bottlenecks or bandwidth restrictions within the ISP's network or in the onward connection between the ISP's systems and the rest of the Internet. Figure 2.8 illustrates how this might happen.

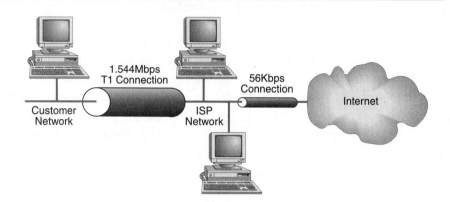

FIGURE 2.8:

Overall network performance is affected by the speed of each connection.

If you install a T3 connection with a bandwidth of 1.544Mbps, but have to pass through a slower 56Kbps link to get from your ISP to the rest of the Internet, your effective bandwidth to all points on the Internet side of your ISP is only 56Kbps. Also, if you have to pass through a very congested network section, your data will be slowed down. The total performance of the network is a result of the available bandwidth of the path your data travels from end to end. The larger ISPs will have several exit points that connect to the Internet; ask about the speed of all these exit points, and be sure that they are all at least as fast as your connection to the ISP, if not faster.

You can use the average round-trip time of data from your network to that of your ISP in an attempt to quantify network performance. Table 2.4 lists typical round-trip times, in milliseconds (ms), for some popular communications links.

TABLE 2.4: Typical round-trip times (measured in milliseconds)

Connection speed	Round-trip time
28.8Kbps	180 ms
56Kbps	45 ms
1.544Mbps	7 ms

You should always keep a weather eye to the future. Ask your ISP about its plans for future upgrades; network technology can be very expensive and takes some careful planning.

Security Concerns

As soon as you connect your network to the Internet via an ISP, the whole security picture changes. Talk with the ISP about what preventive measures are appropriate and what it is doing to protect you against unwanted intruders. We'll be looking at security in much more detail in the *Windows NT Server Operating System Security* and *Security and Firewall* chapters.

Value-Added Services

Many ISPs also provide additional information or services. Many can provide activity statistics for your site, and most publish a newsletter. Ask to see copies of all the reports you will receive as a customer.

Installation and Operational Costs

Any ISP will be able to provide you with information on installation and operating costs, and you should also ask about any charges that might apply in the future if you decide to upgrade your services. High prices do not necessarily mean good service. Typical operating costs for a T1 circuit might run to $1,700 a month; a Basic Rate ISDN connection might cost only a few hundred dollars a month.

Communications is an area where we can look forward to declining costs over the years, as the ISP's costs also fall. Just be sure you understand exactly what you are getting for your money.

Changing to a Different ISP

The world of the ISP is changing from day to day. Competition in the form of the large telephone companies will undoubtedly lead to industry consolidation and a reduction in the number of service providers in any given area. Be very wary of an ISP who asks you to sign a multiyear agreement for services.

Changing to another ISP can be a time-consuming as well as expensive undertaking; so be sure that you evaluate and understand all the steps along the way. But don't let this put you off if you feel that your current ISP is not providing the service level you need or that your company will get significant benefits from changing to another provider.

Questions to Ask Your ISP

To close out this part of the chapter, here is a summary of the questions that you should ask of any ISP whose services you are considering:

- How long has your company been providing Internet services? Which services do you provide?

- Do you give a service guarantee or a rebate against system outages?

- Which service outages do you expect and how long will each last? How do you inform subscribers that the service is down— by phone or by e-mail?

- What kind of network monitoring equipment do you have?

- What are your plans to upgrade your hardware software, and communications circuits?

- When is your operations center staffed and how do we report problems?

- Are there any restrictions on how I can use the Internet connection?

- To which other networks are you connected and at what speeds?

- What security techniques do you use at your site and recommend that I use at mine?

- How will you ensure that my data is kept private?

- Can you provide the names of three references who run sites similar in size and scope to the one I am establishing?

Once you have received satisfactory answers to these questions and understand how costs are charged for the service, you will be in a good position to make an informed decision about each ISP you are considering.

Establishing a Domain Name

To end this chapter, we'll look at the steps involved in establishing your domain name. Unfortunately, the term *domain* is used in several ways depending on the context. In the Internet context here, a domain refers to a collection of network host computers known by the same name. I'll cover what Microsoft considers a domain in NT Server in detail in the *Windows NT Server Operating System Security* chapter.

Many ISPs will register a domain name for you as an additional service, but if your ISP doesn't provide this service, it is not difficult to do yourself. In the *TCP/IP in a Nutshell* chapter, I'll fill in some of the details that I will have to skip here, particularly information about the TCP/IP family of protocols and the IP addressing scheme.

Domain Name System (DNS)

Computers work best with numbers, and people work best with names; to bridge this dichotomy, the Domain Name System (DNS), a distributed database, was invented. A domain name maps or translates the actual numeric IP address used for your Web server into an easy-to-remember alphanumeric name.

An IP address is a set of 4 numbers separated by periods or decimal points and is sometimes known as a dotted decimal address. Such an address might look like this: 198.15.170.10. By now you will have noticed that you don't access your favorite Web site by means of these numbers; a Web site has a name, and this dotted decimal address is translated into a name by the DNS. The process of looking up the domain name to derive the IP address is known as *name resolution*.

But before DNS can do this for you, you must register any name you want to use. A consortium between AT&T and Network Solutions, called InterNIC (Internet Network Information Center) Registration Services, manages the task of assigning IP addresses and domain names to Internet users. In times past, this service was provided free by the National Science Foundation, but now a charge is levied for most services simply because the demand for domain registrations is so high. Since 1993, the NSF has funded the administration of domain name registration through a cooperative agreement with Network Solutions, and this agreement extends through to 1998. Seven domains were established originally:

- `.com`: a commercial organization. Most companies will end up as a part of this domain.

- `.edu`: an educational establishment such as a university.

- `.gov`: a branch of the U.S. government.

- `.int`: an international organization, such as NATO or the United Nations.

`.mil`: a branch of the U.S. military.

`.net`: a network organization.

`.org`: a nonprofit organization.

These so-called top-level domain names are in common use in the United States and the `.gov` and `.mil` domains are reserved strictly for use by the government and the military. In other parts of the world, you will find that the final part of a domain address represents the country in which the server is located; `.jp` for Japan, `.uk` for Great Britain, and `.ru` for Russia, for example.

Here is a quick look at how these domain names are distributed. A January 1996 survey yielded a total of 9.4 million host computers on the Internet, an increase of 2.8 million over the July 1995 total. The `.com` domain is the largest group at more than 2.4 million and has increased its lead over the second largest, `.edu` (at 1.8 million). Hosts with www in their names are by far the most numerous, and at the time of the survey, 129 countries were connected to the Internet. Table 2.5 lists the domain breakdown by percentage in each category. Of the organizations collected in the final 10.9 percent in Table 2.5, no single organization has more than 1.6 percent of the total.

If you think that most of the new `.com` sites are in the Pacific Northwest close to Microsoft and other high-tech companies, think again. The largest number of registered commercial site names is in San Francisco. The Puget Sound area is actually seventh after Manhattan, San Jose, Boston, Los Angeles, and the Boulder-Denver area. Completing the top ten list are Vancouver in British Columbia, Anaheim in California, and Oakland, also in California.

TABLE 2.5: Internet domain breakdown

Domain name	Domain type	Percentage
com	U.S. Commercial	25.7
edu	U.S. Educational	18.9
net	Networks	8.0
de	Germany	4.8
uk	United Kingdom	4.8
ca	Canada	3.9
gov	U.S. Government	3.3
au	Australia	3.3
jp	Japan	2.8
org	U.S. Nonprofit	2.8
mil	U.S. Military	2.7
us	United States	2.5
fi	Finland	2.2
nl	Netherlands	1.8
se	Sweden	1.6
	Total Others	10.9

Registering Your Own Domain Name

Your domain name should reflect your organization or corporation; many companies use their own names to capitalize on any name recognition that they already have in the mind of the consumer. The name you choose will then have a top-level domain name type added to the end of it. For example, if my company name is Dyson Industries, I might use dyson as my domain name, which would have .com added to the end to become dyson.com. Alternatively, I might choose `dyson-industries`, which would become `dyson-industries.com`.

It is possible that someone else has already reserved or may even be actively using a domain name that you are interested in using for your company. If this is the case, you can either choose a new name or an unused variation on your original choice, or you can seek legal advice. Responsibility rests with the applicant to ensure that a domain name is not a trademark that already belongs to or is legally protected by someone else.

Contact InterNIC at this URL:

`http://rs.internic.net`

or by e-mail at:

`hostmaster@internic.net`

If you are not connected to the Internet yet, you can send mail to this address:

Network Solutions
InterNIC Registration Services
505 Huntmar Park Drive
Herndon, VA 22070

or you can phone or fax:

Telephone (703)742-4777
Fax (703)742-4811

InterNIC lets you apply for any domain name you like, regardless of your company name; the only restriction is that the name must be available and not already reserved by someone else. Several names are reserved, but do not appear on any Web sites, at least not yet; both MacDonalds Corporation and Burger King have reserved names, but neither company (at the time of writing) has a Web site.

To see if a domain name is available, use the InterNIC Whois service at:

```
http://rs.internic.net/cgi-bin/whois
```

To use the Whois service, type your proposed name in the Query box, for example, `dyson.com`, and press Enter when you are ready to search the database. When the search is complete, you will find out if anyone has already reserved the name you entered. If no one has registered your chosen name, you will see a message similar to the following:

```
No match for "DYSON.COM".
```

To register your new name, go to:

```
http://rs.internic.net/help/domain/new-domain-reg.html
```

as a good starting point. Here you will be guided through the many steps in the process, and you can fill in your application form right here using your favorite Web browser. Here is a summary of the steps:

1. Review the appropriate policies.

2. Determine whether your selected name is already in use.

3. Coordinate for primary and secondary DNS service for the name.

4. Obtain a Domain Name Registration Template. You fill in information on this screen, and an application is sent to you by e-mail. Complete the application and send it back to InterNIC; otherwise, your domain name will not be registered.

5. Review the template.

6. Review the most common errors made in the process.

7. Submit the template.

You can also apply to modify, transfer, or delete a domain name, and a help desk is always available if you need to ask a question or two.

When you are done, you can track the process of your application, and an invoice will be mailed to you automatically. The whole process can take several weeks, depending on the size of the current backlog. A commercial domain name costs $100 (`.edu` or `.org` domain names are still free), so plan ahead. The $100 fee covers the cost of your domain name for two years; InterNIC charges $50 a year to maintain an already existing domain name.

CHAPTER

THREE

3

TCP/IP in a Nutshell

- The Transmission Control Protocol

- The Internet Protocol

- The application protocols

- Benefits of using TCP/IP

- Understanding IP addressing

- Using DNS

- Using WINS

- Configuring TCP/IP with Windows NT

- Introducing RAS

- Using a Windows NT Server as an Internet gateway

- Using TCP/IP on your Intranet

Transmission Control Protocol/Internet Protocol is used on the Internet, as well as on many other networks, and Microsoft recognized the importance of this protocol by including TCP/IP support in the Windows NT Server operating system. Before you can do anything on the Internet, you need to understand TCP/IP and configure it on your server.

This chapter starts by describing the TCP/IP family of protocols, continues with a description of IP addressing, and concludes with a discussion of how to set up and configure TCP/IP on Windows NT Server. It is a completely self-contained chapter; all the TCP/IP information you are ever likely to need is concentrated here, rather than being spread through several other chapters in this book. If you are not interested in learning about how TCP/IP works and how to set up Windows NT Server to use TCP/IP, you can safely skip this chapter. If however, you are a network administrator coming from a Novell IPX/SPX background or if you will be setting up a Web server yourself, this chapter contains important technical and background information that you will be able to use to make your job easier.

Introducing TCP/IP

TCP/IP actually refers to a whole family of protocols, with its name coming from only two of them: the Transmission Control Protocol and the Internet Protocol. As you will see as in the next few sections of this chapter, there are many more members of the TCP/IP family.

A Brief History of TCP/IP

The TCP/IP protocol was first conceptualized and proposed in 1973, but it was not until 1983 that a standardized version was developed and adopted for wide area use. In that same year, TCP/IP became the official transport mechanism for all connections to ARPAnet, a forerunner of the Internet.

Much of the original work on TCP/IP was done at the University of California at Berkeley, where computer scientists were also working on the Berkeley version of Unix (which eventually grew into the Berkeley Software Distribution [BSD] series of Unix releases). TCP/IP was added to the BSD releases, which in turn was made available to universities and other institutions for the cost of a distribution tape. Thus, TCP/IP began to spread in the academic world, laying the foundation for today's explosive growth of the Internet.

During this time, the TCP/IP family continued to evolve and add new members. One of the most important aspects of this growth was the continuing development of the certification and testing program carried out by the U.S. government to ensure that the published standards, which were free, were met. Publication ensured that the developers did not change anything or add any features specific to their own needs. This open approach has continued to the present day; use of the TCP/IP family of protocols virtually guarantees a trouble-free connection between many hardware and software platforms.

TCP/IP Design Goals

When the U.S. Department of Defense began to define the TCP/IP network protocols, their design goals included the following:

- It had to be independent of all hardware and software manufacturers. Even today, this is fundamentally why TCP/IP makes such good sense in the corporate world; it is not tied to IBM, to Novell, to Microsoft, or to any specific company.

- It had to have good built-in failure recovery. Because TCP/IP was originally a military proposal, the protocol had to have the ability to continue operating even if large parts of the network suddenly disappeared from view, say after an enemy attack.

- It had to handle high error rates and still provide completely reliable end-to-end service.

- It had to be efficient with a very low data overhead. The majority of data packets using the IP protocol have a simple, 20-byte header, which means better performance in comparison with other networks. A simple protocol translates directly into faster transmissions, giving more efficient service.

- It had to allow the addition of new networks without any service disruptions.

As a result, TCP/IP was developed with two main elements. Each component performs unique and vital functions that allow all the problems involved in moving data between machines over networks to be solved in an elegant and efficient way. In the next two sections, we'll look at both of them. First, though, let's see where TCP/IP fits into the broader world of network protocols and particularly how it compares to the theoretical reference model published by the International Standards Organization (ISO) as the Open Systems Interconnection (OSI) model.

TCP/IP and the OSI

The OSI model divides computer-to-computer communications into 7 connected layers; TCP/IP uses 5 layers, as Figure 3.1 shows. Each sucessively higher layer builds on the functions provided by the layers below.

In the OSI model these layers are as follows:

- **Application Layer 7.** The highest layer; defines the manner in which applications interact with the network, including databases, e-mail, and terminal-emulation programs.

- **Presentation Layer 6.** Defines the way in which data is formatted, presented, converted, and encoded.

- **Session Layer 5.** Coordinates communications and maintains the session for as long as it is needed, performing security, logging, and administrative functions.

- **Transport Layer 4.** Defines protocols for structuring messages and supervises the validity of the transmission by doing some error checking.

- **Network Layer 3.** Defines protocols of data-routing to ensure that the information arrives at the correct destination node.

- **Data Link Layer 2.** Validates the integrity of the flow of the data from one node to another by synchronizing blocks of data and controlling the flow of data.

- **Physical Layer 1.** Defines the mechanism for communicating with the transmission medium and the interface hardware.

FIGURE 3.1:

A comparison of the 7-layer OSI model and the 5-layer TCP/IP protocol

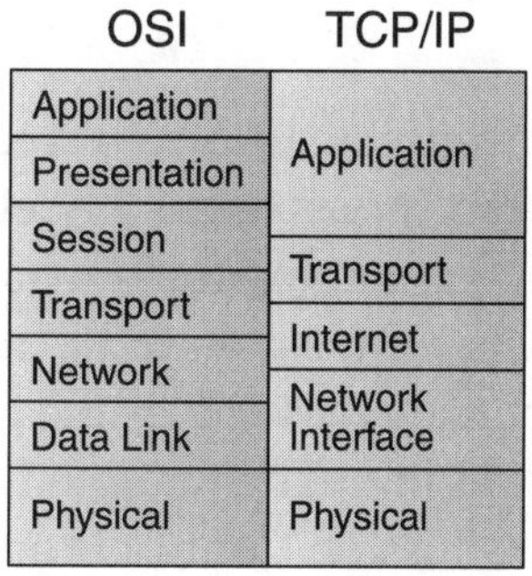

OSI	TCP/IP
Application	Application
Presentation	
Session	Transport
Transport	
Network	Internet
Data Link	Network Interface
Physical	Physical

Although no networking protocol follows this model exactly, most perform all the same functions.

In TCP/IP the five layers are as follows:

- **Application Layer 5.** The highest layer; applications such as FTP, Telnet, and others interact through this layer.

- **Transport Layer 4.** TCP and other protocols add transport data to the data packet.

- **Internet Layer 3.** Adds IP information to the packet.

- **Network Interface Layer 2.** Interfaces with the physical layer.

- **Physical Layer 1.** Defines the mechanism for communicating with the transmission medium and the interface hardware.

Each layer adds its own header and trailer data to the basic data packet and encapsulates the data from the layer above. On the receiving end, this header information is stripped, one layer at a time, until the data arrives at its final destination. Now let's look at how TCP and IP work together.

The Transmission Control Protocol

Transmission Control Protocol is the transmission layer of the protocol and serves to ensure reliable, verifiable data exchange between hosts on a network. Transmission Control Protocol breaks data into pieces, wraps it with the information needed to route it to its destination, and reassembles the pieces at the receiving end of the communications link. The wrapped and bundled pieces are called *datagrams*. Transmission Control Protocol puts a header on the datagram that provides the information needed to get the data to its destination. The most important information in the header includes the source and destination port numbers, a sequence number for the datagram, and a checksum.

The *source port number* and the *destination port numbers* allow the data to be sent back and forth to the correct process running on each computer. The *sequence number* allows the datagrams to be rebuilt in the correct order in the receiving computer, and the *checksum* allows the protocol to check whether the data sent is the same as the data received. A checksum totals the contents of a datagram and inserts that number in the header. The receiving computer performs the same calculation, and if the two calculations do not match, an error occurred somewhere along the line, and the datagram is resent.

Once the header is in the datagram, TCP passes the datagram to IP to be routed to its destination. Figure 3.2 shows the layout of the datagram with the TCP header in place.

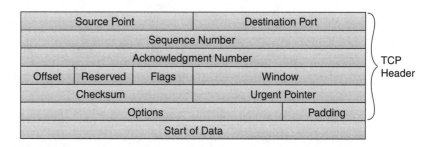

In addition to the source and destination port numbers, the sequence number, and the checksum, a TCP header contains the following:

- **Acknowledgment number.** Indicates that the data was received successfully. If the datagram is damaged in transit, the receiver throws the data away and does not send an acknowledgment back to the sender. After a predefined time-out expires, the sender retransmits data for which no acknowledgment was received.

- **Offset.** Specifies the length of the header.

- **Reserved.** Variables set aside for future use.

- **Flags.** Indicates that this packet is the end of the data or that the data is urgent.

- **Window.** Provides a way to increase packet size, which improves efficiency in data transfers.

- **Urgent pointer.** Gives the location of urgent data.

- **Options.** A set of variables reserved for future use or for special options as defined by the user of the protocol.

- **Padding.** Ensures that the header ends on a 32-bit boundary.

The data in the packet immediately follows this header information.

Transmission Control Protocol communications can be summarized as follows:

- Flow control allows 2 systems to cooperate in datagram transmission to prevent overflows and lost packets.

- Acknowledgment lets the sender know that the recipient has received the information.

- Sequencing ensures that packets arrive in the proper order.

- Checksums allow easy detection of lost or corrupted packets.

- Retransmission of lost or corrupted packets is managed in a timely way.

The Internet Protocol

The Internet Protocol is the network layer portion of TCP/IP, and it actually moves the data from Point A to Point B, which is called routing. Internet Protocol is sometimes described as unreliable because it contains no error detection or recovery code. Internet Protocol is also connectionless; that is, it does not swap control information (or handshaking information) before establishing an end-to-end connection and starting a transmission.

Internet Protocol must rely on TCP to determine that the data arrived successfully at its destination and retransmit the data if it did not. The only job of IP is to route the data to its destination. In this effort, IP inserts its own header in the datagram once it is received from TCP. The main contents of the IP header are the source and destination addresses, the protocol number, and a checksum. Without this header, intermediate routers between the source and destination, commonly called gateways, would not be able to determine where to route the datagram. Figure 3.3 shows the layout of the datagram with the TCP and IP headers in place.

FIGURE 3.3:

A datagram with TCP and IP headers

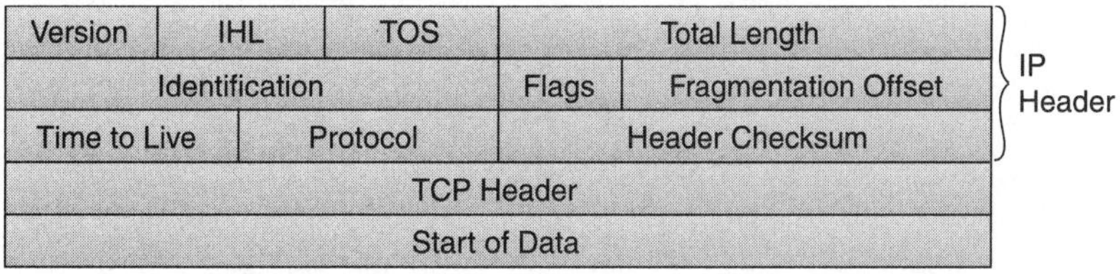

Version	IHL	TOS	Total Length	
Identification			Flags	Fragmentation Offset
Time to Live		Protocol	Header Checksum	
TCP Header				
Start of Data				

IP Header

Let's take a look at the fields in the IP header:

- **Version.** Defines the IP version number. Version 4 is the current standard, and values of 5 or 6 indicate that special protocols are being used.

- **IHL (Internet Header Length).** Defines the length of the header information The header length can vary; the default header is five 32-bit words, and the sixth word is optional

- **TOS (Type of Service).** Indicates the kind or priority of the required service.

- **Total Length.** Specifies the total length of the datagram, which can be a minimum of 576 bytes and a maximum of 65,536 bytes.

- **Identification.** Provides information that the receiving system can use to reassemble fragmented datagrams.

- **Flags.** The first flag bit specifies that the datagram not be fragmented and therefore must travel over subnetworks that can handle the size without fragmentation; the second flag bit indicates that the datagram is the last of a fragmented packet.

- **Fragmentation Offset.** Indicates the original position of the data and is used during reassembly.

- **Time to Live.** Originally, the time in seconds that the datagram could be in transit; if this time was exceeded, the datagram was considered lost. Now interpreted as a hop count and usually set to the default value 32, this number is decremented by each router through which the packet passes.

- **Protocol.** Identifies the protocol type, allowing the use of non-TCP/IP protocols. A value of 6 indicates TCP, and a value of 17 indicates UDP.

- **Header Checksum.** An error-checking value that is recalculated at each stopover point; necessary because certain fields change.

- **TCP Header.** The header added by the TCP part of the protocol suite.

The data in the packet immediately follows this header information.

The Application Protocols

The following applications were built on top of the TCP/IP protocol suite and are available on most implementations:

- Simple Network Management Protocol (SNMP), which allows

network administrators to collect information about the network.

- File Transfer Protocol (FTP), which provides a mechanism for file transfers between computer systems. File Transfer Protocol uses TCP to actually move the files.

- Simple Mail Transfer Protocol (SMTP), which allows a simple e-mail service.

- Telnet, which is a terminal emulation package that provides a remote logon over the network.

- TN3270, which is a special version of Telnet specifically designed for use on IBM mainframes using 3270 series terminals and which also provides a remote logon over the network.

- ICMP (Internet Control Message Protocol), which works at the IP network layer level and provides the functions used for network-layer management and control.

- ARP (Address Resolution Protocol), which helps to reference the physical address of a node to its IP address.

- UDP (User Datagram Protocol), which is a transport-layer connectionless protocol that also uses IP to deliver its packets.

Figure 3.4 shows how some of these components fit together.

FIGURE 3.4:

The components in a TCP/IP block diagram

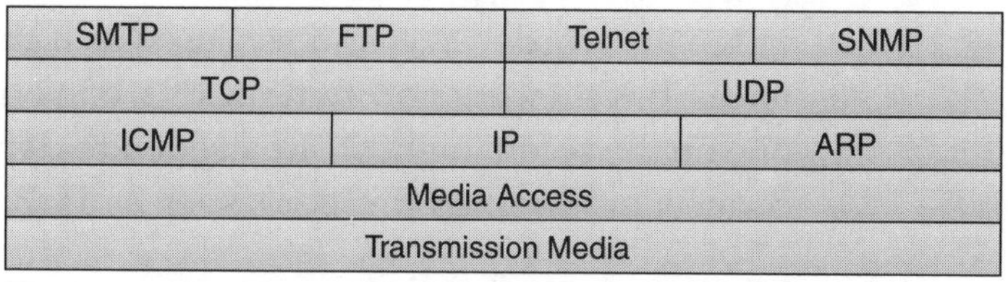

SMTP	FTP	Telnet	SNMP
TCP		UDP	
ICMP	IP		ARP
Media Access			
Transmission Media			

Ports and Sockets Explained

On a TCP/IP network, data travels from a port on the sending computer to a port on the receiving computer. A *port* is an address that identifies the application associated with the data. The *source port number* identifies the application that sent the data, and the *destination port number* identifies the application that receives the data. All ports are assigned unique 16-bit numbers in the range 0 to 32767.

Today, many ports are standardized. Thus, a remote computer can know which port it should connect to for a specific service. For example, all servers that offer Telnet services do so on port 23, and Web Servers normally run on port 80. The TCP/IP protocol uses a modifiable lookup table to determine the correct port for the data type.

In multiuser systems, a program can define a port on the fly if more than one user requires access to the same service at the same time. Such a port is known as a *dynamically allocated* port and is assigned only when needed, for example, when two remote computers dial into a third computer and simultaneously request Telnet services on that system.

The combination of an IP address (more on IP addresses in a moment) and a port number is known as a *socket*. A socket identifies a single network process in terms of the entire Internet. You may hear or see the words *socket* and *port* used as if they were interchangeable terms, but they are not. Two sockets, one on the sending system and one on the receiving host, are needed to define a connection for connection-oriented protocols such as TCP.

Sockets were first developed as a part of the BSD Unix system kernel, in which they allow processes that are not running at the same time or on the same system to exchange information. You can read data from or write data to a socket just as you can do with a file.

Socket pairs are bidirectional so that either process can send data to the other.

In the Novell NetWare world, a socket is part of an IPX internetwork address and acts as a destination for the IPX data packet. Most socket numbers are allocated dynamically, but a few are associated with specific functions.

Benefits of Using TCP/IP

So now that I have described how TCP and IP are used, let's take a look at the major benefits of using TCP/IP over other networking protocols:

- TCP/IP is a routable protocol, which means that it can send datagrams over a specific route and thus reduce traffic on other parts of the network.

- TCP/IP has reliable and efficient data-delivery mechanisms.

- TCP/IP is a widely published open standard and is completely independent of any hardware or software manufacturer.

- TCP/IP can send data between different computer systems running completely different operating systems, from small PCs all the way to mainframes and everything in between.

- TCP/IP is separated from the underlying hardware and will run over Ethernet, Token Ring, or X.25 networks and even over dial-up telephone lines.

- TCP/IP uses a common addressing scheme. Therefore, any system can address any other system, even in a network as large as the Internet. (We will look at this addressing scheme in the next section.)

The popularity that the TCP/IP family of protocols enjoys today did not arise just because the protocols were there or even because the U.S. government mandated their use. They are popular because they are robust, solid protocols that solve many of the most difficult networking problems and do so in an elegant and efficient way.

Understanding IP Addressing

As you saw in an earlier section, IP moves data between computer systems in the form of a datagram, and each datagram is delivered to the destination port number that is contained in the datagram header. This destination port number, or address, is a standard 16-bit number that contains enough information to identify the receiving network as well as the specific host on that network for which the datagram is intended.

In this section, we'll go over what IP addresses are, why they are so necessary, and how they are used in TCP/IP networking.

Ethernet Addresses

You may remember that in an earlier section I mentioned that TCP/IP is independent of the underlying network hardware. If you are running on an Ethernet-based network, be careful not to confuse the Ethernet hardware address and the IP address required by TCP/IP.

Each Ethernet network card has its own unique hardware address, known as the Media Access Control (MAC) address. This hardware address is predefined and preprogrammed on the network interface card (NIC) by the manufacturer of the board as a unique 48-bit number.

The first three parts of this address are called the OUI (Organizationally Unique Identifier) and are assigned by the Institute of Electrical and Electronics Engineers (IEEE). OUIs are purchased in blocks by the manufacturers who then assign the last three parts of the MAC address, making each assignment unique. Remember, the Ethernet address is predetermined and is hard-coded onto the network interface card.

Understanding IP Addresses

Transmission Control Protocol/Internet Protocol requires that each host on a TCP/IP network have its own unique IP address. An *IP address* is a 32-bit number, usually represented as a 4-part number, with each of the 4 parts separated by a period or decimal point. You may also hear this method of representation called *dotted decimal* or *quad decimal*. The network address is made up from the higher-order bits of the address, and the host address constitutes the rest. In addition, the host part of the address can be divided further to allow for a subnetwork address, as you will see in a moment.

Each individual byte (or *octet* as they are sometimes called) can have a usable value from 1 to 254. The term *octet* is the Internet community's own term for an 8-bit byte and came into common use because some of the early computers attached to the Internet had bytes of more than 8 bits; some of DEC's early systems had bytes of 18-bits.

Some host addresses are reserved for special use. For example, in all network addresses, host numbers 0 and 255 are reserved. An IP host address with all bits set to zero identifies the network itself; so 52.0.0.0 refers to network 52. An IP address with all the bits set is known as a *broadcast address*. The broadcast address for network 204.176 is 204.176.255.255. A datagram sent to this address is automatically sent to every individual host on the 204.176 network.

InterNIC assigns and regulates IP addresses on the Internet ; you can get one directly from the InterNIC, or you can ask your ISP to secure an IP address on your behalf. If you are setting up an Intranet and you don't want to connect to the outside world through the

Internet, you don't need an address from InterNIC. Another strategy is to obtain your address from InterNIC and only use it internally until you are ready to connect to the Internet.

Multihomed Hosts

A host may have more than one IP address, and hosts that do are known as *multihomed*. Normally, hosts have a single IP address. Today, with the popularity of the World Wide Web and its explosive growth, more and more Web servers are becoming multihomed. Multihoming is necessary for several reasons, including the ability to establish virtual Web servers.

Virtual Web servers allow one single Web server to act as if it were actually several Web servers. Without the virtual Web server capability, a single Web server that houses several Web sites would have to use URLs that include the Web server's domain name.

For example, the Bigco Corporation has a Web server whose fully qualified domain name is `www.bigco.com`. Its URL is `http://www.bigco.com`. If Bigco decides to host a Web site for the Widget company whose Web server is called Widget, Widget's URL might wind up being something like `http://www.bigco.com/~widget`. It's easy to associate the Widget identity is with the Bigco identity through the URL, and this may not be acceptable to a firm seeking to establish it's own unique identity on the World Wide Web.

If, however, Bigco's Web server is configured with IIS, which coincidentally makes it a multihomed host, Widget can use its own domain name. Thus, its URL is `http://www.widget.com`, and it now has its own unique identity on the exact same Web server as Bigco. Virtualizing Web servers is probably today's most common reason for making a server multihomed.

Gateways and Routing

Routing is the process of getting your data from Point A to Point B. Routing datagrams is similar to driving a car. Before you drive off to your destination, you determine which roads you will take to get there. And sometimes along the way, you have to change your mind and alter your route.

The IP portion of the TCP/IP protocol inserts a header that contains the source and destination addresses for a datagram. Before the datagram begins its journey, however, IP determines whether it knows the destination. If it does know, IP sends the datagram on its way. If it doesn't know and can't find out, IP sends the datagram to the host's gateway.

Each host on a TCP/IP network has a gateway, an off-ramp for datagrams not destined for the local network. They're going somewhere else, and the gateway's job is to forward them to that destination if it knows where it is. Each gateway has a defined set of routing tables that tell the gateway the route to specific destinations.

Because gateways don't know the location of every IP address, they have their own gateways that act just like any TCP/IP host. In the event the first gateway doesn't know the way to the destination, it forwards the datagram to its own gateway. This forwarding, or routing, continues until the datagram reaches its destination. The entire path to the destination is known as the route.

Datagrams intended for the same destination may arrive via different routes. Many variables determine the route. For example, overloaded gateways may not respond in a timely manner or may simply refuse to route traffic and thus time out. That time-out causes the sending gateway to seek an alternate route for the datagram. The route can also vary because network links are down or because servers or gateways are down and because of many other factors that we won't get into in this book.

Routes can be predefined and made static, and alternate routes can be predefined, providing a maximum probability that your datagrams travel via the shortest and fastest route.

IP Address Classifications

In the 32-bit IP address, the number of bits used to identify the network and the host vary according to the network class of the address. The several classes are as follows:

- Class A is used for very large networks only. The high-order bit in a Class A network is always zero, which leaves 7 bits available to define 127 networks. The remaining 24 bits of the address allow each Class A network to hold as many as 16,777,216 hosts.

- Class B is used for medium-sized networks. The 2 high-order bits are always 10, and the remaining bits are used to define 16,384 networks, each with as many as 65,535 hosts attached.

- Class C is for smaller networks. The 3 high-order bits are always 110, and the remaining bits are used to define 2,097,152 networks, but each network can have a maximum of only 254 hosts.

- Class D is a special multicast address and cannot be used for networks. The 4 high-order bits are always 1110, and the remaining 28 bits allow access to more than 268 million possible addresses.

- Class E is reserved for experimental purposes. The first 4 bits in the address are always 1111.

Figure 3.5 illustrates the relationships between these classes and shows how the bits are allocated among the classes.

FIGURE 3.5:

The IP address structure

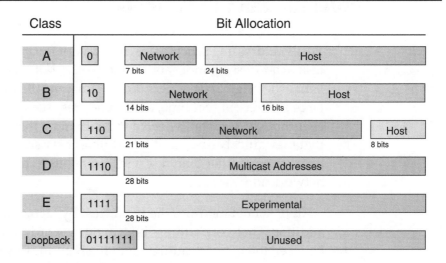

Because the bits used to identify the class are combined with the bits that define the network address, we can draw the following conclusions from the size of the first octet, or byte, of the address:

- A value of 126 or less indicates a Class A address. The first octet is the network number, the next three, the host addresses.

- A value of exactly 127 is reserved as a loopback test address. If you send a message to 127.0.0.1, it should get back to you unless something is wrong with your network. Using this number as a special test address has the unfortunate effect of wasting more than 24 million possible IP addresses.

- A value from 128 through 191 is a Class B address. The first two octets are the network number, and the last two are the host address.

- A value from 192 through 223 is a Class C address. The first three octets are the network address, and the last octet is the host number.

- A value greater than 223 indicates a reserved address.

Understanding IP Subnets

The IP addressing scheme provides a very flexible solution to the task of addressing thousands of networks, but it is not without problems. The original designers did not imagine the Internet growing as large as it has; at that time, a 32-bit address seemed so large (Who ever thought we would need a PC with more than 640K of memory?) that they quickly divided it into different classes of networks to facilitate routing rather than reserving more bits to manage the growth in network addresses.

An IP subnet modifies the IP address by using host address bits as additional network address bits. In other words, the dividing line between the network address and the host address is moved to the right, creating additional networks, but reducing the number of hosts that can belong to each network.

An IP address can be subnetted on an even-byte boundary or on a bit boundary. The solution depends on how you want to manage your address space.

When IP networks are subnetted, they can be routed independently, which allows a much better use of address space and available bandwidth. To subnet an IP network, you define a bit mask known as a *subnet* mask, in which a bit pattern cancels out unwanted bits so that only the bits of interest remain.

The subnet mask is similar in structure to an IP address, in that it has 4 parts, or octets, but now it defines 3 elements (network, subnet, and host) rather than two (network and host). If a bit is on in the mask, that equivalent bit in the address is interpreted as a network bit. If a bit in the mask is off, the bit is part of the host address. The 32-bit value is then converted to dotted-decimal notation. A subnet is only known and understood locally; to the rest of the Internet, the address is still interpreted as a standard IP address. Table 3.1 shows how this all works for the standard IP address classes.

TABLE 3.1:   Default subnet masks for standard IP address classes

Class	Subnet Mask Bit Pattern				Subnet Mask
A	11111111	00000000	00000000	00000000	255.0.0.0
B	11111111	11111111	00000000	00000000	255.255.0.0
C	11111111	11111111	11111111	00000000	255.255.255.0

Subnetting has many advantages, including reducing the size of routing tables, minimizing network traffic, isolating networks from others, maximizing performance, optimizing IP address space, and enhancing the ability to secure a network.

Internet Host Names

Internet host names are used because they are easier to remember than long dotted-decimal IP addresses. Host names are typically the name of a device that has a specific IP address and on the Internet are part of what is known as a fully qualified domain name. As you saw in the *Making All the Right Connections* chapter, a fully qualified domain name consists of a host name and a domain name. For example, in the fully qualified domain name www.dyson.com, the host name is www, and the domain name is dyson.com.

Although I also have a Social Security number and I can certainly recall that number when I need it, I wouldn't like to have to remember the Social Security numbers of all my friends and associates. Likewise, it's easier to remember www.microsoft.com than it is to remember 198.105.232.6.

HOSTS Explained

Several automatic conversion systems are available to translate an IP address into a host name, and HOSTS is one of the simplest. You create a file called HOSTS and enter a line into it for every system, like this:

```
198.34.56.25 myserver. com
198.34.57.03 yourserver.com
```

Now comes the nasty part. You must store this ASCII file on *every single workstation*; when you make a change, you must change the contents of the HOSTS file on *every single workstation*. Simple but painful inside a network, but what happens if you want to go out to other networks or to the Internet? Fortunately, there are better solutions to this problem, as you will see in the next two sections.

Using DNS

The abbreviation DNS stands for Domain Name Service. You use DNS to translate host names and domain names to IP addresses, and vice versa, by means of a standardized lookup table that the network administrator defines and configures.

Suppose you are using your browser to surf the Web, and you enter the URL http://www.microsoft.com to bring up the Microsoft home page. Your Web browser then asks the TCP/IP protocol to ask the DNS server for the IP address of www.microsoft.com. When your Web browser receives this address, it connects to the Microsoft Web server and downloads the home page.

DNS is an essential part of any TCP/IP network, simplifying the task of remembering addresses. You may recall that humans think best with words, and computers work best with numbers. DNS provides the human a simple way to relate numeric addresses without having to remember them all. You simply remember the host name and domain name instead.

DNS Tables are composed of records. Each record is composed of a host name, a record type, and an address. There are several record types, including the address record, the mail exchange record, and the CNAME record.

The address record, commonly known as the A record, maps a host name to an IP address. The example below shows the address record for a host called `mail` in the `company.com` domain:

```
mail.company.com.          IN        A        204.176.47.9
```

The mail exchange record points to the mail exchanger for a particular host. DNS is structured so that you can actually specify several mail exchangers for one host. This feature provides a higher probability that e-mail will actually arrive at its intended destination. The mail exchangers are listed in order in the record, with a priority code that indicates the order in which the mail exchangers should be accessed by other mail delivery systems.

If the first priority doesn't respond in a given amount of time, the mail delivery system tries the second one, and so on. Here are some sample mail exchange records:

```
hostname.company.com.      IN        MX       10 mail.company.com.
hostname.company.com.      IN        MX       20 mail2.company.com.
hostname.company.com.      IN        MX       30 mail3.company.com.
```

In this example, if the first mail exchanger, `mail.company.com`, does not respond, the second one, `mail2.company.com` is tried, and so on.

The CNAME record, or canonical name record, is also commonly known as the alias record and allows hosts to have more than one name. For example, your Web server has the host name www, and you want that machine also to have the name `ftp` so that users can easily FTP in to manage Web pages. You can accomplish this with a CNAME record. Assuming you already have an address record established for the host name www, a CNAME record adding `ftp` as a host name would look something like this:

```
www.company.com.         IN      A       204.176.47.2
ftp.company.com.         IN      CNAME   www.company.com.
```

When you put all these record types together in a file, its called a DNS table, and it might look like this:

```
mail.company.com.        IN      A       204.176.47.9
mail2.company.com.       IN      A       204.176.47.21
mail3.company.com.       IN      A       204.176.47.89
yourhost.company.com.    IN      MX      10 mail.company.com.
yourhost.company.com.    IN      MX      20 mail2.company.com.
yourhost.company.com.    IN      MX      30 mail3.company.com.
www.company.com.         IN      A       204.176.47.2
ftp.company.com.         IN      CNAME   www.company.com.
```

You can establish other types of records for specific purposes, but I won't go into those in this book. DNS can become very complex very quickly for the novice, and entire books are dedicated to the DNS system. For an in-depth and thorough understanding of DNS, you might want to seek out a complete manual on the subject. Several are available, including the O'Reilly and Associates Nutshell Series, which you will find very informative.

Using WINS

WINS, or Windows Internet Naming Service, is an essential part of the Microsoft networking topology. Before I get into a discussion of WINS, however, I need to define a few new terms including these two horrors: NetBIOS and NetBEUI.

- NetBIOS (pronounced net-bye-os) is an acronym formed from *network basic input/output system*, a session-layer network protocol originally developed by IBM and Sytek to manage data exchange and network access. NetBIOS provides an API with a consistent set of commands for requesting lower-level network services to transmit information from node to node, thus separating the applications from the underlying network operating system. Many vendors provide either their own version of NetBIOS or an emulation of its communications services in their products.

- NetBEUI (pronounced net-boo-ee) is an acronym formed from *NetBIOS Extended User Interface,* an implementation and extension of IBM's NetBIOS transport protocol from Microsoft. NetBEUI communicates with the network through Microsoft's NDIS (Network Driver Interface Specification). NetBEUI is shipped with all versions of Microsoft's operating systems today and is generally considered to have a lot of overhead, making it a poor choice for large networks.

WINS is used in conjunction with TCP/IP and maps NetBIOS names to IP addresses. For example, you have a print server on your LAN that you have come to know as PrintServer1. In the past, to print to that server you needed only to remember its name and to select that name from a list. Because TCP/IP is a completely different protocol, it doesn't understand NetBIOS names; it therefore has no way of knowing the location of those servers or their addresses. That's where WINS comes in. When you install TCP/IP on your Windows NT Server, you'll probably find that things work a lot better, and more seamlessly, if you also install WINS.

Each time you access a network resource on a Windows NT network using TCP/IP, your system needs to know the host name or IP address. If WINS is installed, you can continue using the NetBIOS names that you have previously used to access the resources because WINS provides the cross-reference from name to address for you.

When you install and configure TCP/IP, as described later in this chapter, you'll see a place to specify the WINS server addresses. These addresses are stored with the configuration, and TCP/IP uses them to query for host names and addresses when necessary. WINS is similar to DNS in that it cross-references host names to addresses; however, as I mentioned earlier, WINS references NetBIOS names to IP addresses, and DNS references TCP/IP host names to IP addresses.

Another major difference between WINS and DNS is that WINS builds its own reference tables, and you have to configure DNS manually. When a workstation running TCP/IP is booted and attached to the network, it uses the WINS address settings in the TCP/IP configuration to communicate with the WINS server. The workstation gives the WINS server various pieces of information about itself, such as the NetBIOS host name, the actual username logged on to the workstation, and the workstation's IP address. WINS stores this information for use on the network and periodically refreshes it to maintain accuracy.

The Microsoft DNS Server software currently ships with Windows NT. The value in the Microsoft DNS Server is a new type of DNS record called a WINS record, which allows the DNS server to work in perfect harmony with a WINS server. When a DNS query returns a WINS record, the DNS server then asks the WINS server for the host name address. Thus, you need not build complex DNS tables to establish and configure name resolution on your server; Microsoft DNS relies entirely on WINS to tell it the addresses it needs to resolve. And because WINS builds its tables automatically on the fly, you don't have to edit the DNS tables when addresses change; WINS takes care of this for you.

You can use both WINS and DNS on your network, or you can use one without the other. Your choice is determined by whether your network is connected to the Internet and whether your host addresses are dynamically assigned. When you are connected to the Internet, you must use DNS to resolve host names and addresses because TCP/IP depends on DNS service for address resolution.

Configuring TCP/IP with Windows NT

Now that the discussion on TCP, IP, and IP addressing is out of the way, we can take a look at how you can configure Windows NT 4 to use TCP/IP. I'll assume that you already have Windows NT 4 installed and that you are installing TCP/IP on a machine that will have a TCP/IP host name of www and a domain name of company.com. Additionally, I'll assume that this server uses an IP address of 204.176.47.2, a subnet mask of 255.255.255.0, and a default gateway of 204.176.47.1 and that it has only one network card installed. And finally, I'll assume that there is a WINS server on your network with an IP Address of 204.176.47.11.

To begin installing TCP/IP, follow these steps:

1. Click on the Start button, select Settings, and then select Control Panel. Windows NT displays a window that contains icons for all installed objects, as shown in Figure 3.6.

FIGURE 3.6:

The Windows NT
Control Panel

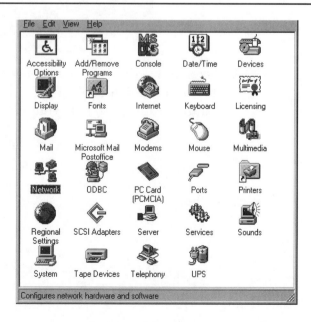

87

2. Scroll down until you locate the Network icon and click on it. In the Network dialog box (see Figure 3.7), select the Protocols tab, and then click on the Add button. Windows NT displays the Select Network Protocol dialog box (see Figure 3.8).

FIGURE 3.7:

The Network dialog box

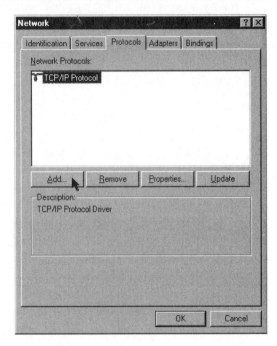

3. Scroll down the list of available protocols until you see TCP/IP Protocol. Double-click on TCP/IP Protocol, or click on the Add button to add TCP/IP to your network configuration.

FIGURE 3.8:

The Select Network
Protocol dialog box with
TCP/IP selected

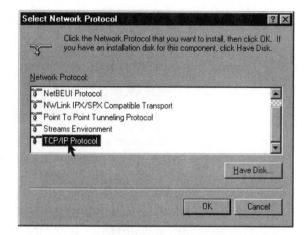

4. Windows NT displays the TCP/IP Setup dialog box, as shown
   in Figure 3.9, which asks if you have a DHCP Server on your
   network and if you want to use it for dynamic IP address assignment. Because you want a static IP address for your Web server,
   click on the No button even if you have a DHCP server on your
   network. Windows NT displays the Windows NT Setup dialog
   box, as shown in Figure 3.10.

FIGURE 3.9:

A filled-in TCP/IP
Setup dialog box

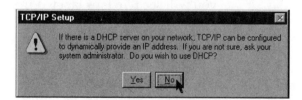

FIGURE 3.10:

The Windows NT
Setup dialog box

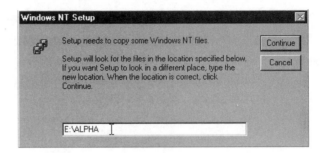

5. In the text box, select or enter the drive and path of the Windows NT installation files. These files should be on the CD-ROM from which you installed Windows NT; so insert your CD-ROM in the appropriate drive, enter its drive letter in the dialog box, and click on Continue. TCP/IP Setup then copies the necessary files to your hard drive.

6. Click on the Close button. Windows NT begins rebuilding the registry entries and bindings for the network. It detects that TCP/IP has not been configured yet and displays the Microsoft TCP/IP Properties dialog box, as shown in Figure 3.11.

   Across the top of the Microsoft TCP/IP Properties dialog box you will see five tabs labeled from left to right as follows:

   • IP Address
   • DNS
   • WINS Address
   • DHCP Relay
   • Routing

FIGURE 3.11:

Configuring the IP
address, subnet mask,
and gateway in the
Microsoft TCP/IP
dialog box

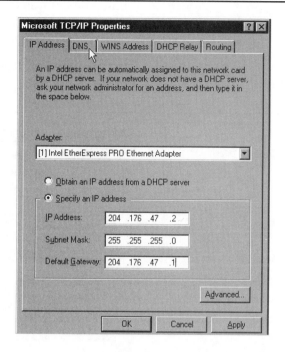

Each tab controls the settings associated with a specific aspect of using TCP/IP under Windows NT Server; and in the sections that follow, we'll look at all the settings you can configure on all these tabs. The settings that you use on your system will obviously depend on the configuration of that system and exactly how you intend to use it.

7. In the Microsoft TCP/IP Properties dialog box, select the IP Address tab to bring it to the front. Be sure that your network card is the one displayed in the Adapter list.

8. Click on the Specify an IP Address radio button, and fill in the IP Address, Subnet Mask, and Default Gateway text boxes. (If you click on the Advanced button, Windows NT displays the Advanced IP Addressing dialog box in which you can add other IP addresses and gateways and manage certain aspects of TCP/IP security. I'm assuming that this host has only one gateway and one IP address; so I won't go into the Advanced IP

Addressing dialog box at this time. This aspect of Windows NT TCP/IP security is covered in the *External Security and Firewalls* chapter.) Now click on the DNS tab.

9. Windows NT displays the DNS section of the Microsoft TCP/IP Properties dialog box, as shown in Figure 3.12.

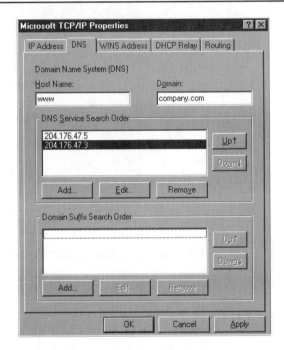

In the Host Name text box, type www, and in the Domain text box, enter your domain name or the domain name of your ISP. Remember, we're using the domain name company.com for this example installation.

10. Now click on the Add button beneath the DNS Service Search Order list box. Windows NT displays the TCP/IP DNS Server dialog box. In the DNS Server text box, enter the IP address of your first DNS server, and click on the Add button. Windows NT displays the DNS section of the Microsoft TCP/IP Properties dialog box. Click on the Add button in the Microsoft TCP/IP

Properties dialog box to add the IP address of your second DNS server, if you have one. You can specify a maximum of three DNS servers.

11. If you specify only a host name in step 9 above, Windows NT displays the Domain Suffix Search Order list box, shown in the lower half of Figure 3.12. This provides a list of domain names for NT Server to use when you specify only a host name in a command. For example, if you want to use the `ping` command with a host named `mail.company.com`, you can open a command-line window and enter this command:

```
ping mail
```

As long as the domain `company.com` is listed in the Domain Suffix Search Order list box, Windows NT can combine this with your original command, making it equivalent to the complete name, as though you had originally typed:

```
ping mail.company.com
```

In this example, `mail` is called the prefix, and `company.com` is the suffix. To take advantage of this feature, enter the name you want to use into the Domain Suffix Search Order list box.

Installing WINS

Now that we're finished with the DNS properties, we'll install WINS. To do so, follow these steps:

1. In the Microsoft TCP/IP Properties dialog box, click on the WINS Address tab. Windows NT displays the WINS Address section, as shown in Figure 3.13.

FIGURE 3.13:

The WINS Address
section of the Microsoft
TCP/IP Properties
dialog box

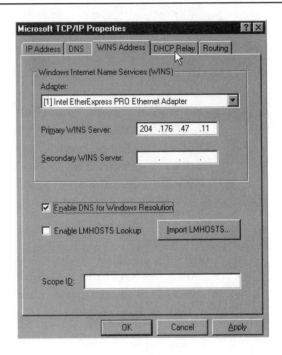

2. In the Primary WINS Server text box, enter the IP address of
your WINS server. In the Secondary WINS Server text box, enter
the IP address of your secondary WINS server.

3. Because we want Windows NT to use DNS to look up hosts and
addresses, check the Enable DNS for Windows Resolution
checkbox.

4. By default, the Enable LMHOSTS Lookup checkbox is checked.
In this example installation, we want to rely only on DNS for
lookups; so uncheck this box. LMHOSTS Lookup is another
method of name resolution. It is quite different from DNS in that
it maps IP addresses to NetBIOS computer names, which is similar to the way that WINS operates.

So that DHCP can manage IP addresses, it must know which IP
addresses it can give out. You give IP this information with a

scope, which is simply a range of IP addresses. You use a scope for two reasons:

- You can assign at least one scope to each subnet serviced by your DHCP server.
- You might also want to divide a subnet's IP addresses for reasons associated with fault-tolerance planning.

5. In the Scope ID text box, enter a name for your scope.

Dynamic Host Configuration Protocol, or DHCP, is a service that allows workstations and servers to be assigned IP addresses automatically.

The primary reason for using DHCP is to centralize the management of IP addresses. When the DHCP service is used, pools of IP addresses are assigned for distribution to client computers. The address pools are centralized on the DHCP server, allowing all IP addresses on your network to be administered from a single server. It should be apparent that this saves loads of time when changing the IP addresses on your network. Instead of running around to every workstation and server and resetting the IP address to a new address, you simply reset the IP address pool on the DHCP server. The next time the client machines are rebooted, they are assigned new addresses.

DHCP can manage much more than the IP addresses of client computers. It can also assign DNS servers, gateway addresses, subnet masks, and much more. For purposes of our example installation, we'll assume that no DHCP servers are in use on your network. If you want to look at or change any of the DHCP settings, however, click on the DHCP Relay tab in the Microsoft TCP/IP Properties dialog box. This screen is shown in Figure 3.14.

FIGURE 3.14:

The DHCP settings in the
DHCP Relay section of
the Microsoft TCP/IP
Properties dialog box.

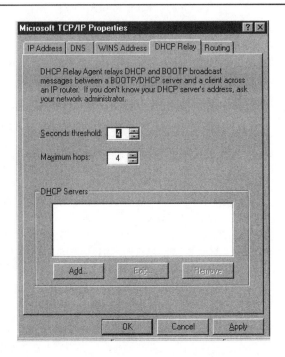

The DCHP Relay agent allows a computer to relay messages from one network to another. Normally, you would have a DHCP server on both networks, but with NT Server, you can install a DHCP Relay agent on any computer on a network, and it will relay messages through the router that connects the two networks to the DHCP Server on the other network.

When you install the DHCP Relay agent, you can accept the default values displayed in the DHCP Relay dialog box shown in Figure 3.14, or you can set new values for Seconds Threshold, Maximum Hops, and DHCP Servers addresses. To specify the address of the DHCP Server to which DHCP messages will be relayed, click on the Add button in the DHCP Relay dialog box to open the DHCP Relay Agent dialog box. Enter the server's IP address in the DHCP Server field, and click on the Add button. To return to the DHCP Relay dialog box without adding the server's IP address, click on the Cancel button.

The DHCP Relay agent is installed as an NT service and is enabled automatically.

6. Finally, to complete our tour of the TCP/IP settings under Windows NT Server, click on the Routing tab in the Microsoft TCP/IP Properties dialog box, and you will see the Routing section as shown in Figure 3.15.

FIGURE 3.15:

The Routing section of the Microsoft TCP/IP Properties dialog box

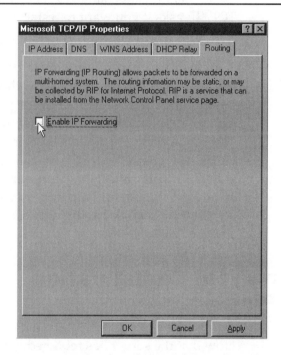

Internet Protocol forwarding allows datagrams to be forwarded on a multihomed host. In some multihomed hosts, you need datagrams to be able to route between the network cards to other parts or segments of the network. If you have more than one network card installed in a server and you want Windows NT to be able to send datagrams between them, check the Enable IP Forwarding checkbox in the Routing section of the Microsoft TCP/IP Properties dialog box. Otherwise, leave it unchecked. This setting can also be key in establishing a secure network segment.

Now that you have looked at and configured all the settings in the five sections of the Microsoft TCP/IP Properties dialog box, click on the OK button at the bottom of this dialog box to continue with our original mission, which, if you can still remember, was to configure TCP/IP on Windows NT Server.

Windows NT continues the installation process, and, as you have made a significant change to NT's configuration by installing TCP/IP, asks if you want to restart the system. Click on Yes to reboot Windows NT and to load and use the TCP/IP protocol on your system.

All this TCP/IP configuration information is stored in the Windows NT Registry database, along with other hardware-specific information. You can change most of the TCP/IP parameters by using either the Control Panel or the Administrative Tools. Certain parameters, such as Time to Live and the default Type of Service, can only be changed using the Registry Editor. If you change some of these Registry parameters, you may affect the performance of TCP/IP on your system in an adverse way; to find out more, see the REGENTRY.HLP file on the *Microsoft Windows NT Resource Kit* CD-ROM.

Testing Your Configuration with Ping

Now that the server has rebooted, you can log on and test your configuration using the `ping` command. To do so, open the Command Prompt window, and enter this command:

```
ping 127.0.0.1
```

as shown in Figure 3.16.

FIGURE 3.16:

Testing the local host
with Ping

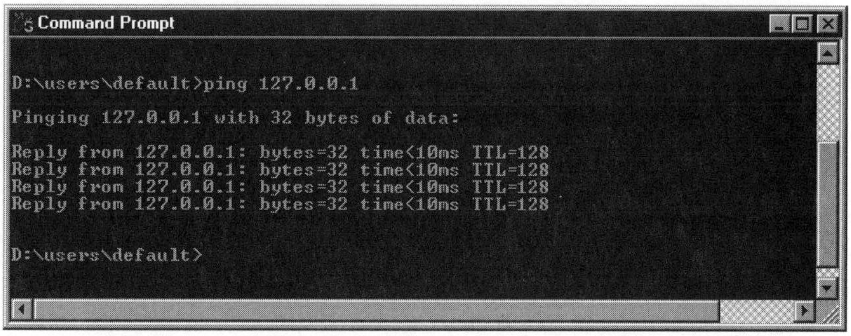

```
Command Prompt

D:\users\default>ping 127.0.0.1

Pinging 127.0.0.1 with 32 bytes of data:

Reply from 127.0.0.1: bytes=32 time<10ms TTL=128
Reply from 127.0.0.1: bytes=32 time<10ms TTL=128
Reply from 127.0.0.1: bytes=32 time<10ms TTL=128
Reply from 127.0.0.1: bytes=32 time<10ms TTL=128


D:\users\default>
```

The ping command (ping stands for packet internet groper) transmits a special diagnostic packet (an ICMP echo request) to a specific node on the network, forcing that node to acknowledge that the packet reached its destination. You will often hear people use ping as a verb; they will say something like, "Ping that workstation to see if it's awake."

In this example, which uses the special loopback test IP address, the ping command sends 4 packets to the server itself and shows the turnaround time of the responses. Pinging the server simply ensures that the TCP/IP protocol is actually working at the basic levels.

If there is a problem with your TCP/IP configuration, you may receive time-out errors instead of a valid response. In that case, the transmission rate for the packets of data was too long, and the receiving host did not respond. The ping command uses a default time-setting that tells ping how long to wait for responses. You can adjust this time-setting with a command line switch; however, the default setting is usually sufficient for testing most TCP/IP-based network devices. If the host received none of the 4 packets successfully, a time-out error from `ping` might look something like this:

```
C:\USERS\DEFAULT> ping 127.0.0.1

Pinging 127.0.0.1 with 32 bytes of data:

Request time-out.
Request time-out.
Request time-out.
Request time-out.

C:\USERS\DEFAULT>_
```

After you `ping` the special loopback test address, try to `ping` another host on your network. For example, if you have another host on your network with the IP address of 204.176.47.31, `ping` that address. Or, if your network has a DNS or a WINS server, `ping` another machine by name. Additionally, if your network is attached to the Internet and you have set the correct gateway address to your network's Internet gateway, try pinging a popular Web server, such as `www.microsoft.com`. In any event, when you `ping` these other machines, the response should be similar to that you receive when you `ping` your server.

Introducing RAS

RAS is an acronym for Microsoft's Remote Access Service, an NT Server feature that lets mobile or remote users connect to the main NT Server network by means of a dial-up connection. Remote users run a RAS client application on their computer and then open a connection to the RAS server using a modem, using an X.25 or using an ISDN connection.

The RAS server, running on NT Server, authenticates the user and services the communications session until it is terminated by the originating user or by the system administrator. Everything that a conventionally connected user can access on the NT server is also available to someone using RAS, given the usual user and account permissions. Windows NT logon and domain security, support for security hosts, data encryption, and callback provide secure access for remote users.

Without RAS, you would have no way to connect NT-based systems via dial-up connections, and you would simply be stuck using physically wired networks. RAS supports several local-area networking protocols that can be used when establishing a connection between the client and the server, including NetBEUI, IPX/SPX, and TCP/IP. In addition, several other remote-access protocols are also supported, including PPP, SLIP, the proprietary Microsoft RAS protocol, and the new Point-to-Point Tunneling Protocol (PPTP).

NT's RAS supports a maximum of 256 remote clients and can be configured to give a remote client access to an entire network or to only the RAS server itself.

By means of RAS, Windows NT can provide a range of services to Internet users. You can configure a Windows NT Server system as an ISP, offering dial-up connections to any PPP client. You can configure the ports on a RAS server as:

- Dial Out Only
- Receive Calls Only
- Dial Out and Receive Calls

These settings affect only the specified port; you can configure other ports individually.

Errors and other significant events are stored in the NT Server Event Log, and you can use the Event Viewer to look at the log to determine the cause of any problems. You install and configure RAS using the Control Panel Network option, and you use the Control Panel Services icon to establish startup options. When you install and configure RAS, any protocol already installed on the NT Server (such as TCP/IP in our example in the last section) is enabled for RAS use automatically on in-bound and out-bound calls.

Each remote computer connecting to the RAS server by means of PPP is automatically provided with an IP address from the range of addresses set up by the system administrator when configuring RAS. Windows RAS clients can also use preassigned IP addresses specified in their RAS PhoneBooks. In this latter case, you have to configure the RAS server to allow a RAS client to request this specific address.

As well as an IP address, a RAS client will also need access to one of the name resolution services we looked at earlier in this chapter. RAS clients attaching to a small network on which IP addresses do not change can use HOSTS or LMHOSTS; on larger systems, RAS clients can use the same WINS and DNS servers that the RAS server uses. The Windows NT RAS server also allows remote RAS clients to share subnet addresses with other computers on the network and thus conserve IP addresses.

Using a Windows NT Server As an Internet Gateway

Each workstation on your network that needs access to the Internet has to either connect itself directly to the Internet or route to the Internet through a gateway. The most cost effective and popular way to connect a LAN to the Internet is by using a gateway that routes the entire LAN.

You can easily configure Windows NT Server as an Internet gateway. How you go about doing so depends on how you are connecting Windows NT Server to the Internet. One of the most common ways today is ISDN, which provides 56Kbps, 64Kbps, and 128Kbps connections; these connections are significantly faster than a 28.8Kbps modem. RAS and Windows NT treat a modem as they would treat any other network interface. Therefore, with an actual network card to connect the server to the rest of the LAN and with an ISDN modem to connect the server to an Internet Service Provider, you can configure TCP/IP routing to forward datagrams, and each workstation on your network can access the Internet by using the Windows NT Server as its gateway.

You can also use Windows NT Server as an Internet gateway if portions of your LAN are connected in different ways. For example, one portion of your LAN might be connected to the Internet via Windows NT Server and RAS, another portion might be connected with a standalone ISDN router, and still other portions of your LAN might not have direct access to the Internet. You can configure Windows NT to route to the Internet gateway by placing it on both parts of the network and giving it routes to that destination. Once Windows NT has routes to the Internet gateway, workstations on that portion of the LAN can use the Windows NT router's IP address as their default gateway. Windows NT then forwards workstation traffic destined for the Internet straight to the Internet gateway.

Configuring Two Network Protocols on One Server

One of the design goals of the Windows NT Server developers was to make the integration of multiple network protocols seamless. As a result, configuring Windows NT with more than one networking protocol is easy, as compared with doing so on other operating systems. Once you have installed TCP/IP, you can install additional networking protocols in essentially the same manner; the only difference is in how you configure the new protocol's parameters.

As an example, let's take a look how to install Novell's IPX/SPX protocol on our Windows NT Server running TCP/IP. In summary, here are the steps:

- Select the protocol and load the appropriate files from your original NT Server CD.

- Restart Windows NT Server to install the new protocol.

- Configure the operating parameters that are specific to this new protocol.

To begin, open the Control Panel, and double-click on the Network icon. Now follow these steps:

1. In the Network dialog box, click on the Protocols tab. Windows NT displays the TCP/IP protocol in the Network Protocols list box. Now, click on the Add button. The Select Network Protocol dialog box displays a list of the available protocols. Scroll down the list and find NWLink IPX/SPX Compatible Transport, and double-click on it. This is the Windows NT implementation of Novell's IPX/SPX protocol.

2. In the Windows NT Setup dialog box, enter the location of your Windows NT installation files in the text box, and click on the Continue button. Setup copies the appropriate files to your hard drive.

3. If you installed RAS, the Setup dialog box will ask you if you want to enable IPX/SPX for RAS.

4. The protocol list in the Network Protocol list box now includes NWLink NetBIOS Compatible Transport and NWLink IPX/SPX Compatible Transport. Click on the Close button.

   NT Server knows that you have not yet loaded or configured the protocol and suggests that you reboot the server so that this can be done. Click on the Restart button to reboot NT Server. Once NT has restarted, open the Control Panel, double-click on the

Network icon, and follow the rest of the steps below:

5. In the Network dialog box, choose the Protocols tab.

6. In the Network Protocols list box, select NWLink IPX/SPX Compatible Transport. Windows NT displays the NWLink IPX/SPX Properties dialog box, as shown in Figure 3.17.

FIGURE 3.17:

The NWLink IPX/SPX Properties dialog box

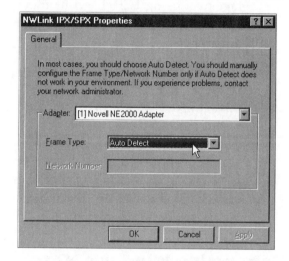

7. In the Adapter text box, enter the name of the network card to which you want the IPX/SPX protocol bound. In the Frame Type text box, you can leave Frame Type set to the default of Auto Detect. If Auto Detect does not work on your network, you can enter an Ethernet Frame Type and Network Number manually. The Network Number is a hexadecimal number used to assign a logical number to a NetWare server. Using the network number allows you easily to uniquely identify a NetWare server on a multi-NetWare server network.

Using TCP/IP on Your Intranet

Using TCP/IP on your Intranet has all the advantages of using TCP/IP to connect to the Internet. When using TCP/IP on an Intranet with Windows NT, however, you gain one distinct advantage over using TCP/IP with other types of network operating systems: ease of configuration and use. And here are some other advantages.

Hundreds and hundreds of vendors are creating software for the Windows NT operating system. This increases the likelihood of finding software that does what you need.

Transmission Control Protocol/Internet Protocol is available for almost every operating system in production today. Because TCP/IP is a standardized family of protocols, connecting dissimilar operating systems is a breeze. You can also connect new systems to your older legacy systems in a snap.

Connecting Windows NT to Novell NetWare

In the previous section, I discussed installing multiple protocols on Windows NT platforms. The most common instance of this is adding Windows NT to a network composed mainly of Netware servers running IPX/SPX. You can use the Windows NT NWLink IPX/SPX Compatible Transport (NWLink) as a protocol between NT Server systems, to connect NT Workstation computers to NT Server systems, or to add NT Server-based networks to a Novell NetWare network.

In addition, you can use Gateway Service for NetWare to connect a computer running NT Server to NetWare servers and to create a gateway to other NetWare resources. Doing so allows computers running Microsoft software to access NetWare resources through the gateway.

Remember that IPX/SPX is a much more traffic-intensive protocol than TCP/IP, and if you need to connect Windows NT to Novell, you should uninstall Novell's IPX/SPX and convert your entire network to TCP/IP. You'll find that network traffic goes down and network performance goes up.

Sites that run databases on Unix, NT Server, or OS/2 may depend on Novell NetWare for print and file services. And when the company decides to add Intranet services, this same network must also support a Web server and Web browsers. The only protocol that can do all this and connect all these disparate systems is TCP/IP.

This move toward TCP/IP has certainly not gone unnoticed by the software developers at the major companies that provide networking operating systems. Novell's NetWare now includes NetWare/IP, a NetWare Loadable Module (NLM) that almost adds IP to a Novell server. NetWare/IP adds a 40-byte header to an IPX packet; so the protocol is certainly not pure TCP/IP, but Novell has promised to add a real implementation of TCP/IP in the near future. And along with Novell go Apple, IBM, Banyan, and many other companies, all working to improve their TCP/IP offerings.

Connecting Windows NT to Unix

Connecting Windows NT to a Unix network environment is easy, since TCP/IP is the standard protocol for Unix networks. As it does with any other TCP/IP-based networking systems, Windows NT integrates seamlessly into a Unix networking environment.

And these days, the large and growing Unix world includes versions and variations of Unix running on hardware from a PC to a Cray supercomputer; Cray offers Unicos, DEC offers Ultrix, IBM offers AIX, Apple Computing offers A/UX, Silicon Graphics offers Irix, and Hewlett-Packard offers HP-UX.

Commercial versions of Unix for the Intel series of processors include SCO Unix, Solaris from Sun Microsystsems, UnixWare originally from Novell and now from SCO; free versions of Unix include the Free Software Foundation's GNU Project, FreeBSD, NetBSD, and the ever-popular Linux.

If your network comprises Apple Macintosh systems, minicomputers, mainframe computers, Unix systems, IBM PCs running Novell, and IBM PC compatible systems running some version of Windows, these computers normally couldn't communicate. But with TCP/IP installed on each of them, they are all capable of communicating and transferring data back and forth with the greatest of ease. This is simply not possible with any other networking protocol in existence today.

PART II

Designing and Building
Your Web Site

CHAPTER
FOUR

Installing Microsoft Internet Information Server

- Hardware requirements for your Web server

- Components of the Internet Information Server (IIS)

- Installing IIS on Windows NT version 4

- Installing IIS on Windows NT version 3.51

- Testing your IIS installation

In this short chapter we'll go through the steps to install the Microsoft Internet Information Server family of programs under Windows NT Server version 4 as well as take a quick look at how to install it on Windows NT Server version 3.51. Installation is straightforward and takes only a few minutes, assuming you are installing from a CD-ROM. I will close the chapter with a brief demonstration of how Internet Information Server (IIS) works. But first, a word or two about hardware.

Hardware Requirements for Your Web Server

Before starting the installation process, let's look at the hardware requirements of a Windows NT Server running as a Web server. As a general guideline, plan to spend as much as your budget will allow, especially on the processor, memory, and hard disk space—all the items that will make your Web server run as fast as possible.

You can spend less on the video system, although in the Intel world, you will need at least a VGA card; the days of installing an old monochrome monitor on the server are (fortunately) long gone. You will also need a tape drive for backups and a CD-ROM for software installations. A 3.5 inch floppy disk is always a good idea. Let's take a look at the individual components in detail.

CPU

In the Intel world, you should use a Pentium processor running at 100 MHz or faster. A large number of $x86$ multiprocessor machines are also capable of running NT Server. If you are using a DEC Alpha AXP RISC system, you'll want one of the faster AlphaServers, and the same applies if you are using a PowerPC or a MIPS RISC system. The minimum Intel system supported is an 80486 processor running at 33 MHz; NT Server no longer supports the Intel 80386.

RAM

According to Microsoft, the minimum amount of RAM required on the Intel platform is 12MB, and on other systems at least 16MB is required. You shouldn't think about running NT Server with less than 16MB of RAM. As you add users and applications to NT Server, you will need to add more memory. A good place to start for a Web server is 32MB, and even then you may have to add as your site attracts more visitors.

Internal Bus

Any system running NT should have one of the advanced 32-bit buses; EISA, PCI, and MicroChannel are all good choices. The important thing is that the bus support mastering, which makes a VESA-bus system a poor choice.

Video

You will need at least a VGA video card to load NT Server, but you don't need the latest all-turbo PCI video accelerator board. Boards based on the S3 chip set give good performance; they have been around for a long time and so are generally well supported. The S3 systems are also available for a good price these days.

The amount of RAM on the video card determines the maximum resolution and the number of colors you can display on your monitor. These days, most cards come with at least 1MB installed, which normally gives you 256 colors at 1024 by 768 pixels. As no one will be using any fancy image-manipulation software or looking at very high quality graphical images actually on the file server itself, there is no need to go to a higher resolution, and specifying more colors may actually slow screen painting and video response.

CD-ROM

You will definitely need a CD-ROM with NT Server; no one loads large software packages from floppy disks any more if she or he can possibly help it. In fact, some server software is not available on floppy disks—only on CD-ROM. A SCSI interface is usually better supported than any of the proprietary interfaces, and NT supports the newer SCSI II interface with an additional feature called SCSI parity. The Adaptec SCSI cards, such as the 16-bit 1542C or the 32-bit EISA 2742T, are good performers, well supported, and often used; some of the cheaper cards perform less well and are not as well supported by their vendors.

Tape Drive

It is absolutely essential for every NT Server installation to have a tape drive available for system backup and for reloading software in the event of a system or hardware failure. The tape can also use the SCSI interface; just make sure that the tape is big enough to back up the whole file server at one go. No one likes doing attended backups and waiting around to swap tapes.

Vendors such as Archive, Conner, Hewlett-Packard, and Sony distribute 4 mm DAT (Digital Audio Tape). Other tape drives are available from DEC, Exabyte, Tandberg, Colorado, and Tecmar.

There are also several alternatives to a tape drive, including removable media from Sony, Bernoulli, and Syquest; 100MB zip drives from Iomega; and 4.6 optical drives from Pinnacle.

Hard Disk

Again, a SCSI-based disk system is a good idea with NT Server because NT supports a wide variety of SCSI products. Consult the most recent Hardware Compatibility List for information on newly qualified hardware. Another excellent reason to use a SCSI-based hard-disk system is that fault tolerance mechanisms such as RAID (Redundant Array of Inexpensive Disks) and disk mirroring require properly working SCSI systems. You certainly can create a mirrored set of non-SCSI hard disks, but they will not have sector-remapping capability.

NT relies heavily on paging information out of memory onto the hard disk, in effect, using hard-disk space as the equivalent of RAM, and this mechanism requires a fast and reliable hard disk.

NT Server occupies a minimum of 115MB of hard-disk space on Intel-based systems and as much as 150MB on RISC-based systems. And remember that this is the minimum amount of room needed for the operating system files; if you use large applications or create large data files, you will need more room.

Suggesting an appropriate size for a server hard disk is almost impossible; the right size for you depends on the size and nature of the other applications you want to run on or from the server. As you start to assemble the HTML pages and graphics files you will be using on your Web server, you can begin to put together a better size estimate. Common these days are 1.2GB hard disks; they are cheap, and they represent good value for money. Larger drives are also easy to find, so why not install two?

Note that 5.25 inch floppy disks are no longer supported by NT Server.

Mice and Serial Ports

You will often need three serial ports on your server: one for the mouse, one to attach to the UPS system (more on this item in a moment), and one for the modem to support the RAS (Remote Access Services). Sometimes using three serial ports can be a problem, and using a parallel mouse such as a PS/2 or InPort mouse can partly solve this. Multiport serial adapters are available from Consensys and DigiBoard.

Modems

If you use or plan to use RAS, you will need a modem so that remote users can access the server. NT supports more than 300 models of conventional modems from all the major modem manufacturers, as well as more than 20 PCMCIA modems.

UPS

A UPS (or uninterruptible power supply) takes over and continues to provide power when the main power to the server fails. You will want your Web server available at all times, and so a UPS is an excellent way to ensure this. Be sure that all the equipment you need for continued operation, not just the server itself, has UPS support, including all the communications equipment. UPS systems suitable for use with NT Server are available from American Power Conversion and from Best Power Technology.

Because NT Server tries to detect all the hardware attached to the system, including the serial ports, during the installation process, disconnect the UPS devices before you start installing the software.

Communications Equipment

You will also need the appropriate communications equipment to support the type of link you have chosen. This can be small and compact in the case of an ISDN TA (terminal adapter) assembly, or it can be a whole room full of equipment for some of the larger data-communications connections; in some instances, most of the communications equipment may be located on the phone company's premises. The larger the communications requirement, the more equipment you will need, and the more crucial proper air-conditioning becomes, even in northern climes and in Europe—areas that don't normally use air-conditioners at any time.

And depending on the final configuration you choose for your Web site, you may well find yourself looking for a location for a firewall system, as well as a router or two.

Adding a Web Server to an Existing Network

The preceding list defines the main hardware components for your Web server, but what should you do if you are adding a Web server to your existing NT Server network, which already has certain hardware installed and a population of users?

Do not underestimate the impact that Web traffic may have on the performance of your server, and be ready to upgrade your hardware if the existing installation proves inadequate. If you insist on running with the existing systems, you will not only alienate new visitors to your site as they wait for a slow server to respond, but you will also make your existing corporate users very angry indeed as they watch their previously speedy applications grind to a halt.

Part of the system administrator's job is to monitor system performance and make the appropriate recommendations and upgrades as they are needed.

Components of the Internet Information Server

The Microsoft Internet Information Server (IIS) consists of several components. Here's the list:

- Internet Service Manager, an administrative program for managing all your Internet services

- World Wide Web Services, a set of programs with which you create and publish you own Web pages

- Gopher Service, a set of programs with which you create your own Gopher service

- FTP Service, programs with which you create your own FTP site

- ODBC (Open Database Connectivity) drivers and administrative programs

- Microsoft FrontPage, a Web-authoring and site-management tool

- Search Server, a search engine

- Microsoft Internet Explorer version 2, a Web browser for Windows 95, Windows NT Server, Windows NT Workstation, Windows 3.1, and Windows for Workgroups

- Windows NT Workstation also contains Peer Web Services, a personalized web server optimized for use on Windows NT Workstation 4.

Microsoft first offered IIS as beta software that you could download from the main Microsoft Web site. The package was formally released in early 1996 and is now distributed free, as a part of the NT Server system. It also plays an important role in Microsoft's BackOffice product line.

If you downloaded the beta software or if you have a version that is dated earlier than March 1996, be sure to get the latest version. This earlier version contained a bug that could compromise system security. This bug has been fixed, and later versions do not have this problem. Another update was made avilable in June 1996.

Internet Information Server runs as a Windows NT Service on all the Windows NT Server hardware platforms on versions of NT Server 3.51 and later. If you are still running version 3.51, be sure that you install Service Pack 3 before you install IIS. The Internet Service Manager component of IIS will not run on NT Workstation, but must run on NT Server.

Installing IIS on NT 4

Installing Microsoft Internet Information Server is straightforward; all you have to do is run the Setup program from the compact disc. If you already have your connection to the Internet via your ISP or if you are publishing on an Intranet, you can accept many of the default settings during installation, and your Web site will be up and running in no time. Your ISP will tell you the IP address to use with your Web server, as well as the subnet mask and the IP address of the default gateway system through which your server will route all traffic to the Internet.

The installation process can be summarized in these four steps:

1. Installing and configuring Windows NT Server

2. Running the Setup program to install IIS and all its component parts

3. Setting up all the HTML files that you want to use on your Web server

4. Testing your Web server

We will go through all these steps in the next few sections.

Installation Requirements

To install Microsoft Internet Information Server, you must have:

- A computer with at least sufficient hardware to support Windows NT Server.

- A copy of Windows NT Server, version 3.51 or later. If you are using version 3.51, you will also have to install Service Pack 3, which is included on the IIS compact disc.

- TCP/IP networking protocol installed on the server. You can use the Network application in the Control Panel to install or configure both the TCP/IP protocols and also several related items. See the *TCP/IP in a Nutshell* chapter for details.

- Sufficient free hard-disk space to load IIS and to install the HTML files that constitute your Web server content. It is a good idea to format the hard disk using the Windows NT File System (NTSF) for security reasons. More on this in the *Windows NT Server Operating System Security* chapter.

Internet Requirements

To publish on the Internet, you will also need the following items:

- A suitable communications link to the Internet, provided by your selected ISP.

- The appropriate hardware and device drivers to connect your server to that communications circuit.

- An IP address, also provided by your ISP.

- A DNS-registered name for that IP address, from InterNIC. (See the *Making All the Right Connections* chapter for more information on how to get a DNS name.) A DNS-registered name is not mandatory, but it sure makes things a lot simpler; visitors to your Web site can use this easy-to-remember name when accessing your site rather than the 4-figure dotted decimal IP address.

Intranet Requirements

If you plan to publish Web content using an Intranet instead, the requirements are just a little different:

- An appropriate network interface card and a suitable connection into your local area network.

- The WINS (Windows Internet Name Service) or DNS (Domain Name System) installed on a computer attached to your Intranet. Again, this is an optional step, but it means that users of your Intranet can use a friendly name rather than the dotted decimal IP address when they access the server and your Web content.

Completing the Preinstallation Checklist

Before you install IIS, you must configure the NT Server networking environment so that you can connect to the Internet's TCP/IP networks. Several security-related issues (which I'll take up in detail in the *Windows NT Server Operating System Security* chapter) will prevent other Internet users from accessing or tampering with your server.

You can use the Network application in the NT Server Control Panel to perform all the configuration options described in the following section. Here are the steps to follow through the preinstallation checklist:

1. Install Windows NT Server on the appropriate hardware.

2. Obtain a communications link to the Internet through an ISP. Your ISP will also provide an IP address, a subnet mask, and the default gateway's IP address for you to use in step 3.

3. Install and configure the TCP/IP protocol on NT Server. If you are using any beta Internet software from Microsoft or Internet-related software from any other company, you must remove it now before going any further.

4. Close any applications that use ODBC before you start the installation; otherwise you will generate an error message that one or more ODBC components are in use when you try to install the ODBC drivers from the Internet Information Server compact disc.

5. Register your domain name with InterNIC.

6. Use one of the naming systems—DNS, WINS, or HOSTS—depending on whether you plan to connect to the Internet or to a local Intranet, to resolve the IP address into a name.

7. Assign multiple IP addresses to the network interface connected to the Internet if you want to host multiple domain names such as www.dyson_1.com and www.dyson_2.com.

You can also take several steps to enhance system security if you plan on connecting your NT Server to the Internet, including:

- Review the rights and permissions associated with the IUSR_*computername* account.

- Select appropriate passwords.

- Define and implement strict account policies.

- Limit membership of the Administrators group to those people who genuinely need such access.

- Install the NTFS file system rather than the FAT file system. NTFS has important security aspects that you should take advantage of.

- Enable Auditing so that you can track events more effectively.

- Check your network protocols and run only the network services that you need. This will allow you to tighten security controls and also set an appropriate network performance baseline. You should unbind any network protocols that are unused or prove unnecessary.

- Check permissions on network shares.

All these topics as well as several other important aspects of NT operating system security are covered in more detail in the *Windows NT Server Operating System Security* chapter.

Installing Internet Information Server

After you complete the appropriate sections of the preinstallation checklist, you are ready to install Microsoft Internet Information Server on your NT Server system. Before you can start the installation, you must first log on with system administrator privileges, and if you want to configure the Internet Information Server services using the Internet Service Manager, your user account must also be a member of the Administrators group on the target machine.

Here are the steps to follow:

1. Insert the Microsoft Windows NT Server CD into the CD-ROM disk drive.

2. On the Desktop, click on the Install Internet Information Server icon.

3. The Setup program begins, and after the copyright notice is displayed, Select OK to start the installation. You can use the Setup program to add, modify, or remove Internet Information Server components later if you wish.

4. If you are installing IIS onto version 3.51 and you have yet to install Service Pack 3, you will see a dialog box offering to install the Service Pack for you at the end of Setup. Click on Yes to install the Service Pack; IIS will not operate without it. When the installation of the Service Pack is complete, you will have to shut down and restart your server.

5. The Microsoft Internet Information Server dialog box opens. Click on OK to open the next dialog box shown in Figure 4.1.

FIGURE 4.1:

The IIS Installation
dialog box

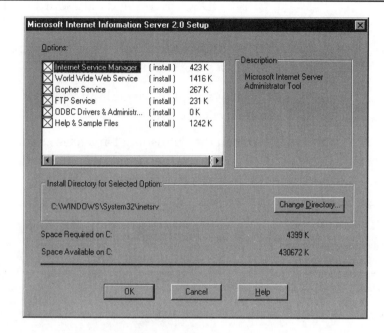

All the items in the dialog box are checked by default, and the
hard-disk space they will each occupy is shown on the right side
of this list. The total amount of hard-disk space required and the
amount of space available is shown at the bottom of this dialog
box. If you prefer not to install one of the options, click on the
box to the left of that option. Your choices are:

- **Internet Service Manager**, an administration tool.
- **World Wide Web Services**, which you use to create a Web
  site.
- **Gopher Services**, which you use to create a Gopher server.
- **FTP Services**, which you use to create an FTP server.
- **ODBC Drivers and Administration**, which installs the
  ODBC drivers you will need for logging on to ODBC files
  and turning on ODBC access from the Web server. To pro-
  vide access to a database through IIS, you can set up the

ODBC drivers and data sources using the ODBC application in the NT Server Control Panel.

- **Help and Sample Files**, which installs the IIS help files and a set of sample HTML files.

6. Either accept the default directory or enter a new name, and then click on OK.

7. When the Publishing Directories dialog box opens, as shown in Figure 4.2, either accept the default directory names or enter new ones, and then select OK.

FIGURE 4.2:

Enter the names of the default directories in the Publishing Directories dialog box.

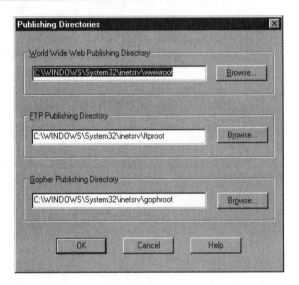

8. When prompted to create the service directories, click on Yes. The default names for these directories are WWWROOT for the Web service, GOPHROOT for the Gopher service, and FTPROOT for the FTP server.

9. When the Create Internet Account dialog box opens, enter and then confirm a password. This account is used for all anonymous access to the Internet Information Server. Meanwhile, Setup copies the remaining IIS files to your hard disk.

10. If you checked the ODBC Drivers and Administration checkbox, the Install Drivers dialog box opens next. To install the SQL Server driver, select it from the list displayed in the Available ODBC Drivers list box, and then click on OK.

11. The Setup completion dialog box opens; click on OK to complete the installation.

12. If you were prompted about Service Pack 3 during the installation and you answered Yes, the Service Pack is installed next. When it completes, remember to shut down and restart your server.

And that is all there is to it; you are now ready to publish information on the Internet or on your own internal Intranet. You don't have to start the Internet Service Manager unless you want to look at or change the advanced configuration options.

Installing Internet Explorer or Internet Service Manager

Two other Setup programs are on the compact disc, one in the \CLIENTS directory, used to install only the Internet Explorer, and another in the \ADMIN directory, used to install only the Internet Service Manager. These programs work in just the same way as the Setup program covered in the last section; simply follow the directions on the screen, or click on Help once the Setup program starts running.

These two versions of the Setup program are useful when you want to use Internet Information Server on your local area network. You can copy the contents of the \CLIENTS directory to a shared network directory and allow clients to install Internet Explorer over the network.

You can also copy the contents of the \ADMIN directory to a shared network directory and let administrators install the Internet Services Manager and use it for remote administration of IIS from any system on the network running Windows NT Workstation or Windows NT Server.

Making an Unattended Installation

When using Internet Information Server on a network, you can copy the contents of the compact disc to a directory on the network and then install from that directory. This can be very useful when making several server installations or when using over-the-network techniques to install Internet Explorer. You can make an unattended installation directly from the compact disc, but only of the default configuration.

In each of the directories containing the Setup program, you will find a sample unattended installation configuration file called UNATTEND.TXT. This file contains the settings you need with the value 1 equal to TRUE and the value 0 equal to FALSE. Copy this file into the appropriate directory, and modify the settings as needed to meet your specific installation requirements.

Installing IIS on NT version 3.51

Installing IIS on Windows NT Server 3.51 is essentially the same as the process I have just described in the section above. The only difference is that you must install Service Pack 3 onto version 3.51 before you try to install the IIS package. If you don't have Service Pack 3, you can install it from the IIS compact disc; in fact the Setup program will install it for you automatically.

You must start an unattended installation from the command prompt with this command:

```
setup -b unattend.txt
```

where UNATTEND.TXT is the name of the file you modified to meet your own needs.

Testing Your IIS Installation

When you have completed the installation, you can test your Internet Information Server quickly indeed to be sure that everything is working. If you have files in HTML format, simply copy them into the default home directory; if you are using the Web server, copy your files into the \WWWROOT directory. We will look at publishing on the Web in great detail in the next few chapters; the following steps are just for the purposes of this test.

Testing a Server on Your Intranet

To test a server attached to an internal Intranet, follow these steps:

1. Be sure that the server is connected to the local area network and that the WINS server service or any other name resolution service is running.

2. Start Internet Explorer or another browser on one of the workstations attached to the network.

3. Enter the URL (Uniform Resource Locator) for the default home directory of the newly installed server, and press Enter. The URL will be:

   ```
   http://
   ```

   followed by the Windows Networking name of the server, which is followed by the name of the file you want to see. If your server is registered with the WINS server as Wallaby and if the HTML file you want to view is called `homepage.htm`, the URL becomes:

```
http://Wallaby/homepage.htm
```

The home page will be displayed on your screen.

Testing a Server Connected to the Internet

The steps to test a server connected to the Internet are similar:

1. Start Internet Explorer on a workstation or on the server—it doesn't matter; however, the computer must have an active connection to the Internet.

2. Enter the URL for the home directory of the server. If your server is registered as `www.company.com` and if the name of the file you want to view is `homepage.htm`, type:

```
http://www.company.com/homepage.htm
```

and press Enter.

The home page will be displayed on your screen.

CHAPTER

FIVE

5

Planning Your Web Site

- Doing business on the Web

- Looking at different kinds of Web sites

- Making a Web site plan

Before you start slinging HTML pages all over the place, you will find that it is a good idea to pause for a moment and ask a few fundamental questions about what you want your Web site to do. What do you want your Web site to achieve? How will you create the effect that you are looking for? Does the company already have advertising material that you can use or at least base your initial Web pages on? In this chapter, I'll help you answer all these questions, as well as raise a few more. We'll also look at some real-life examples of how some companies have solved these and other problems by thinking creatively about how best to use their Web sites. We'll look at the types of Web sites set up by others and then consider some of the more important planning issues.

Doing Business on the Web

No matter what your service or product, you can use a Web page to disseminate information to your visitors. A recent survey by Web Track shows that in the last quarter of 1995 advertisers paid about $12.5 million to buy ad space on Web sites. Top advertisers included AT&T, American Airlines, Honda, MCI, and Sprint.

Add to this the more than $85 million that an ActivMedia study indicates that companies spent worldwide on Web site development, and the sums are getting to be very impressive. Forrester Research predicts that spending for online media will hit $75 million this year and will grow to more than $2.6 billion by the year 2000. Now that's getting to be some serious money.

Eventually, of course, the Web will take its place alongside the more traditional advertising media of print, radio and TV, and Yellow Page listings, as well as play a part in the communications arena along with the phone and fax, e-mail, and voice mail.

Who Uses the Web?

No one really knows how many people regularly access the World Wide Web; the surveys published so far show widely divergent results—the *Wall Street Journal* says 24 million people. Both Arbitron and Nielson Media Research have recently introduced packages that attempt to actually measure Web usage.

But we can make a few generalizations based on the results of these surveys, particularly the survey from the Graphics, Visualization, and Useability Center of the Georgia Institute of Technology. Find it at:

```
http://www.cc.gatech.edu/user_serveys/survey-04-1996.
```

The results of this survey were first published in 1994 and are updated every six months. This survey does not count Web servers, but attempts to characterize the users of the Web, and is in general agreement with other surveys. Here is a summary of its most recent results:

- The average age of both male and female Web users is 33.

- The estimated average income is $59,000.

- Overall, slightly more than half are married, with 40 percent single and 6 percent divorced.

- The number of women users is climbing rapidly and now stands at almost 32 percent.

People accessing the Web spend their time as follows:

- More than 80 percent use their browsers at least once a day.
- More than 40 percent use their Web browsers from 6 to 10 hours a week.
- More than 28 percent use their browsers from 11 to 20 hours a week.

And this is what they do with their browsers:

- More than 33 percent have used their browsers for shopping.
- Fifty-one percent use their browsers in work-related tasks.
- Sixty-four percent use their browsers for entertainment purposes.
- More than 80 percent report that they spend their time just browsing the Web, seeing what's out there.

The demographics and purchasing power of this group are hard to ignore, and the survey shows that although the percentages in each group may change between, say, U.S. and European respondents, there are actually very few differences between the response profiles.

Opening Your Digital Storefront

Most companies start out with a Web site as a source of information for the customer and only move to a Web site that sells their products once their Web presence is well established.

A digital storefront is a way of selling goods and services over the Web, and we'll look at some examples in a moment. You might also hear the terms *virtual malls*, *cybermalls*, even *online malls*; they are all the same thing—a Web site that sells real merchandise (nothing virtual about that)—and they really will take your credit card number.

A digital storefront should be a natural extension of your current business, not something tacked onto the side. Everyone in the company—marketing, sales, and shipping—should be involved. As a natural outgrowth of your core business, the digital storefront will look and feel like your other marketing materials; don't confuse customers by sending them one message online and a different message in your traditional media.

For most people, shopping on the Web is a new thing, and many people are very cautious about trying it, mostly because of fears fueled by the media that someone will steal their credit card number. People who routinely hand over their cards to stores and restaurants to pay for goods and services, or who give them out over the phone, are very reluctant to send them over the Internet. To help calm these fears, Internet Commerce Providers have been hard at work designing secure standards.

An Overview of Internet Commerce Providers

A great deal of time and effort has been put into designing secure Internet protocols that can protect sensitive banking and financial information from prying eyes. Several companies and standards are emerging as leaders in this field, and each system has its advantages and disadvantages. New companies are making important announcements almost weekly; so the picture is constantly changing.

DigiCash

Companies such as Amsterdam-based DigiCash are running pilot schemes based on electronic cash, or ecash, which is designed for secure payments from a PC to any other workstation—by e-mail or over the Internet. To load up on ecash, you must establish an account with one of the participating banks. The digital money used in this scheme is known as Cyberbucks and is stored locally on your PC. It is transferred to the merchant by public-key encryption and can be used to buy a rather eclectic range of goods and services from certain merchants.

CyberCash

On the other hand, CyberCash serves as a secure method of transporting payments between buyers and their banks, and it generates fees from these banks rather than from individual consumers. CyberCash is working with several major companies in the encryption field as well as with the Wells Fargo Bank to provide a secure way to encode and transmit credit card numbers.

Start by downloading the Wallet software, developed by CheckFree. Once you have a CyberCash account, you can look for Web pages belonging to participating merchants who display a special CyberCash "buy" icon. You can then select the item you want to purchase, choose the buy icon to launch CyberCash, and select the credit card icon. The program sends your encrypted CyberCash ID number via RSA's public-key encryption directly to CyberCash, who decodes the transaction and submits it to a participating bank for authorization and processing.

Open Market

Open Market manages real-time transactions, both in order processing and in credit card payments. Open Market has a series of tools, including StoreBuilder, which generates and manages Web site content, and TransactionLink, which adds the software needed for electronic transactions.

First Virtual

First Virtual is a financial company and is the first merchant bank to offer online payment services on the Internet. Several important features separate the First Virtual effort from those described above. First, the system is not encrypted, but carefully managed so that no proprietary information passes over the Internet. Second, it is a try-before-you-buy system, and merchants do not get paid until after they deliver the products.

To use the system, you must first open a First Virtual account with an ID number, which usually costs $2. After this initial charge, no other fees are charged to the buyer, only the costs of the goods and services you purchase.

To make a purchase, you give your ID number to the merchant, who forwards this number and information about your transaction to the First Virtual server. First Virtual then sends you e-mail requesting approval; when you approve, your credit card is billed. Lots of participating stores are on the Web, and First Virtual's site includes links to all of them.

CheckFree, NetCash, and NetChex

Other companies—such as CheckFree, NetCash, and NetChex—are pursuing the goal of the virtual checking account, providing electronic coupons that you can use to pay for goods and services. In Europe, SmartCards, which look like normal credit cards but have a tiny microprocessor and some flash memory, are becoming something of a success story. You can use SmartCards at normal retailers, and you can connect them to a PC with special hardware so that you can make transactions over the Internet.

This field is rapidly changing; and once the major credit card companies really get involved, there will be something of a shakeout, with some smaller companies being swallowed up by the bigger ones. Eventually, the appropriate standards and protections will be in place, and commerce over the Internet will be commonplace. See the *World Wide Web and Windows NT Resources Available on the Internet* appendix for more information on these companies.

Understanding Secure Transactions on the Web

Many of the world's best mathematicians have spent considerable effort in designing systems that will encrypt information so that if it is intercepted by an intruder, it is impossible for the intruder to decode that information and use it for personal advantage. Another way of saying this is that encryption schemes make breaking the code so difficult that the intruder could not use the decoded information in a timely way, perhaps not even in his or her lifetime, even utilizing a whole lab full of high-powered computers. Here is a quick overview of the current standards.

DES (Data Encryption Scheme)

Developed by the U.S. National Bureau of Standards, DES is a standard method of encrypting and decrypting data that works by combining transposition and substitution. It is used by the U.S. government and by most banks and money-transfer systems to protect all sensitive computer information.

Despite years of use, DES remains unbroken. The method completely randomizes the information so that it is impossible to determine the encryption key even if some of the original text is known.

Although difficult to crack, DES is not immune to common fraud by the sender or the receiver; there is no way to identify a sender who has learned the key and is imitating the real sender.

RSA

A patented, public-key, or asymmetric, encryption scheme, RSA was invented by and named after three mathematicians—Ron Rivest, Adi Shamir, and Len Adlemen—who went on to found a company of the same name based on the technique. RSA has also been used with digital signatures, a technique used to ensure that the recipient of a message knows the identity of the sender.

When implemented in software, DES has been estimated to be 100 times faster than RSA; when implemented in hardware, DES may show even greater speed advantages over RSA.

For more information and a good collection of FAQs on the subject of cryptography, see RSA's Web site at:

`http://www.rsa.com/rsalabs/`

PEM

An abbreviation for privacy enhanced mail, PEM is an e-mail system that uses RSA encryption to provide a confidential method of authentication. PEM messages are encapsulated in ordinary mail messages, and the PEM portion of the message contains a special code indicating the PEM message type.

PEM has not been widely adopted, perhaps because PEM and MIME (Multipurpose Internet Mail Extensions) are currently incompatible, and so PEM may eventually disappear.

PGP

An abbreviation for Pretty Good Privacy, PGP is a popular, easy-to-use shareware public-key encryption program, written by Phil Zimmermann. For noncommercial use, it is available at no cost from certain Internet sites.

This is the package that caused all the trouble when the U.S. government decided that Zimmermann had violated weapons-export laws because the scheme uses a key-length of more than 40 bits. The U.S. government classifies all encryption schemes that use more than 40 bits as munitions, and they are therefore subject to very strict export and national security controls. The case against Zimmermann caused an outcry and was eventually dropped. The discussion over the export of encryption schemes, however, continues.

Today, a secure Web server will feature either S-HTTP or SSL, and some feature both. Fierce competition continues between developers of Web servers to set the standards for secure service.

S-HTTP

A secure version of the HTTP protocol, S-HTTP is a nonproprietary standard that provides three levels of security service:

- Encryption, to ensure that only the person authorized to receive the message can do so. S-HTTP supports both PGP and PEM.

- Digital signature, to prevent message forgery and to verify the message source.

- Authentication, to test the integrity of the file and to verify that the sender is actually the author.

S-HTTP servers can communicate with both secure and nonsecure HTTP servers, but they will not provide secure information to a nonsecure server. Instead of simply replacing HTTP, S-HTTP creates a new layer between TCP/IP and HTTP. Instead of calling TCP/IP library routines to open connections and transmit or receive data, HTTP browsers and servers call SSL library routines, which handle the task of setting up a secure communications channel.

SSL

An abbreviation for Secure Sockets Layer, SSL was developed by Netscape to encrypt data traveling between a Web server and a Web browser and has become something of an industry standard. This may be due to the current popularity of the Netscape browser.

Because SSL is protocol-independent, it can encapsulate any of the application-level protocols, including FTP, Telnet, Gopher, and HTTP, and actually uses two different protocols:

- The SSL Record Protocol encapsulates everything that comes through, including SSL Handshake Protocol packets.
- The SSL Handshake Protocol negotiates and establishes security methods and parameters.

Shen Protocol

The Shen protocol, created by Phillip Hallam-Baker of CERN, is similar to S-HTTP in that it replaces HTTP with a more secure protocol, but the big difference is in how it provides for various levels and types of security, including the following:

- Public data, readable by anyone
- Copyright data, readable for a pay-per-view fee
- Confidential data, readable by certain authorized individuals
- Secret data, whose very existence should not be known

Shen also uses public-key encryption for messages and for digital signatures.

STT

An abbreviation for Secure Transaction Technology, STT is an effort from Microsoft and Visa, aimed at providing a secure method for encoding credit card information.

PCT

An offshoot of the STT work, PCT (Private Communication Technology), which is also from Microsoft and Visa, is aimed at securing all kinds of financial transactions, not only credit card transactions.

Some of the protocols and techniques discussed above are popular and well used; others are standards waiting in the wings for a wider acceptance and more general use. Time alone will select the winners.

Looking at Different Kinds of Web Sites

There are as many kinds of Web sites as there are individuals and corporations on the Web. You can categorize the sites by size:

- *Individual.* Created and managed by a single person; likely to be quirky and to contain odd information about the person's likes and dislikes.

- *Small company.* Created by or for a small company; likely to be highly individualistic and creative in presentation and outlook, with splashy graphics and clever effects. May not be viewable by all browsers.

- *Large corporation.* Created and managed by a large corporation; likely to be very well done, with a great deal of careful thought in the design and layout of the material. May be based on or strongly echo existing marketing materials so as to present a united front across all advertising media.

- *Intranet.* A special kind of internal Web site, often with no connection at all to the Internet. (The chapters in Part 4 of this book discuss Intranets in detail.)

A more useful breakdown is to look at the kinds of sites by function, and in the next few sections, we'll look at the whole range of functions now being performed on the World Wide Web.

You may find that a site, such as a search engine, for example, uses only one of the functions listed below but uses it several times; on the other hand, a site belonging to a large corporation may have several areas, each one providing a different function. Let's take a look.

A Typical Home Page

The home page is often the starting point for a visitor's explorations of your Web site. When you publish a URL in print or in other marketing material, it points to the location of your home page. Your home page sets the tone for the rest of your site, both by way of an introduction and as a gateway; it acts as a combination of a magazine cover, a billboard, and the main headlines on the front page of a newspaper. The better your home page looks, the more likely a visitor is to stay and investigate the rest of your site.

The most popular home pages reflect the personality of the sponsoring organization or corporation. Some are flashy and attention grabbing; others are subdued. If the company has a specific tone or approach in other advertising materials—print, catalogs, TV, and radio—that feel should carry over to the Web site. No one would ever confuse L. L. Bean's corporate identity with that of MTV, and there should be no confusion between their Web sites either.

Keep the initial home page short and to the point; users do not want to have to scroll down to see material that was initially out of sight and hidden from view. And be sure that your home page itself contains or points to valuable content; visitors will return to a site that contains good solid information rather than just a sales pitch.

One of the first elements that visitors should see is a collection of navigation buttons they can use to jump to other pages. What each button actually does depends on the needs of your site, but some common applications might include the following:

- *Contents button.* Displays an organized view of your whole site.

- *Map button*. Displays a graphical overview of your site. Be careful when using large graphics, and remember that they take time to download to a visitor's browser.

- *Search button*. Opens a search engine that allows visitors to specify a word or a phrase in which they are interested.

- *Previous and Next buttons*. Allow a visitor to move around your site quickly and easily, even on an initial visit.

- *Icon buttons*. Site-specific buttons that give visitors access to the main content of your site.

Your home page should begin to answer some of the following questions:

- What is the main focus of your business?

- What is your business philosophy?

- Who is in charge of your organization?

- How long has the corporation been in business?

- Do you have an association with a larger business unit?

- In what ways are you and your products better than those of your main competitors?

You should also include a signature at the bottom of your home page. The signature should always include a copyright statement (more on this in the *Checking the Fine Print of Legal Issues* chapter), the date when the page was last revised, an e-mail address, your phone number (including the area code, of course), and the physical address of your company so that visitors can contact your corporation if they wish. If you have an 800 number, also include that, remembering that it may not be accessible to all visitors at your site.

A Table of Contents or an Index Page

Another popular function offered on many sites is a table of contents or an index. A table of contents is similar to the table of contents in a book; it indicates the kind of information your site provides and how it is organized. The items in an index are arranged in strict alphabetic order.

On a contents page, be sure that the Next and Previous buttons operate in the order suggested by the table of contents.

An index can be especially useful if the terminology used in Web page titles is particularly technical or complex, making it difficult for the average visitor to use a table of contents. Even if you do not have entries for all the letters in the alphabet, leave all the letters in place. Just think how disorienting an alphabet that only contains 12 letters will appear to most of your visitors.

And always remember the indexer's golden rule: Use entries that the reader (or in this case, the visitor) will recognize. If your site uses many graphical elements or icons, consider adding them to your index. If your index grows too long and becomes unwieldy, place the entries for a single letter or for a group of letters on a new Web page and provide links from these pages back to the main index page.

A Catalog Entry

Visitors to your site can use a catalog entry to collect information about a product and to order the product. A catalog entry is one way for a company to grow worldwide sales quickly and easily.

Include a picture of the item with each entry, as well as a short written description indicating why the visitor should buy this product now; you can even link to an online demonstration of the product in use in a typical environment. Follow up with lists of features, applications, benefits, and technical specifications for the product. If the technical specifications are long and detailed, consider dividing them by major headings and linking each heading to a new page.

You can even include testimonials from existing customers; these can be simple text or audio and video clips.

A Glossary or Dictionary Page

If you have a glossary or dictionary page, visitors can look up the meaning of specific technical words or jargon. You can even let users jump from normal Web pages into the glossary, right to the definition of any term you have linked to the glossary. Again, even if you don't have entries for all the letters of the alphabet, be sure that all the letters remain in place.

A Technical Support Page

A technical support page might include instructions on how to perform a specific operation, such as an upgrade, or it might contain a trouble-shooting chart designed to help users identify and then fix specific problems.

For a how-to operation, include an initial brief summary of the operation and then list all the items and tools that will be needed during the upgrade. The content in this case will consist of the steps of the procedure; describe what each specific step will accomplish and include photographs or other illustrations where appropriate. If you need to include warnings, be sure to place them immediately before the related step. And be sure to provide information or a short test that lets users evaluate whether they have performed the operation correctly.

When providing trouble-shooting information, be sure that each step in the process is well thought out, well written, and at the right technical level for the majority of your users. After all, they are visiting your site because they already have a problem; if your Web pages are badly laid out and are difficult to follow, you are compounding their problem and increasing their irritation at the same time.

A Technical Report Page

Many companies use their Web sites to present new or updated technical information to interested parties. Sun Microsystems, the inventors of the Java scripting language, is a good example of a company using this approach.

Sun engineers prepared technical information papers for those interested in Java and for applications developers and made them readily accessible and available on Sun's Web site. Microsoft manages its white papers in a similar way, making then available over the Web.

A technical report page is one instance in which you can violate the rule about only using short pages. Generally speaking, very long Web pages are considered a bad idea; they require a visitor to scroll through the document several times to go from beginning to end. Visitors might want to print out a technical report, however; and if it is a self-contained document (all on one long page), they do not have to chase down related pages to see the whole thing.

You can also provide many kinds of links on a technical report page, including the following:

- Original raw data, from which your conclusions are drawn
- Statistically derived tables of data
- Text or audio of interviews with subjects in the study or with other experts in your field
- Audio and video clips
- Text of other papers by the same author or authors
- Reference works cited and the bibliography

- The author's biography
- Web sites and newsgroups that provide more information on these and related topics

A Biography Page

A biography page is a useful way to introduce important players in your organization, people who have recently joined your company, or people whose jobs or responsibilities have changed. You will find that a biography page can give your site a warm, personal tone and can add credibility. Include photographs and audio or video clips, if you can; even a cartoon or a short animation segment adds spice. All these elements can help humanize the subject or subjects.

A Press Release Page

A press release makes new information available to users of your products; you can use it to announce new, upgraded, or revised products, new staff, even new research and development projects. Very often, the bulk of the information contained in a press release on your Web page will rely very heavily indeed on the original written press release sent to radio, TV, and print media. But there is a major difference: The information on your Web page communicates directly with your users and is aimed at them rather than at news editors.

In fact, other sites may not bother to quote your release; instead they will provide a link to your site so that interested visitors can jump there and can read the information for themselves.

A Sampler Page

A sampler page is similar in organization to a glossary or to a catalog page, but is different in several important ways. A sampler page lets visitors view pictures and graphics, listen to audio clips, and watch video or animation sequences. The overall intention might be to sell CDs or tapes, to establish a sound archive or a museum, or to use multimedia to sell your existing products.

For all this to work, of course, visitors to your site must have the appropriate helper applications available with their Web browsers; a helper application processes and "displays" the audio or video file when it arrives from the server. Some visitors will not have the appropriate helper application and will become frustrated; that is the time to link to a download menu page on which they can locate the appropriate helper free of charge.

A Download Menu Page

A download menu page gives your visitors a quick and easy way to download documents, read-me files, device drivers, technical support bulletins, bug fixes, service packs, software revisions, compressed file archives such as zipped files, and so on.

You can use icons to indicate the range of file types available for download, including text files, executable files, PostScript files, game files, and zipped files. Along with each filename, include the file format, the size of the file in bytes, and the revision level so that visitors know exactly what they are letting themselves in for.

This information lets visitors make intelligent choices, including whether they can run or use the file after they have spent the time downloading it, how long the download is likely to take, and whether they will have sufficient hard-disk space to store the file after they have received it from your site.

A Registration Form or Survey Page

From the design point of view, a registration form and a survey page have a lot in common. The registration page lets users all over the world register their purchase of one of your products; a survey page collects information about their likes, their dislikes, and demographic background. You can use both kinds of pages to collect information and opinions that may help your company market new or similar products in the future, build up a mailing list of interested visitors, and even let users order products or request product information.

When asking questions of visitors to your site, remember these guidelines:

- Test your survey offline on real users before putting it on your Web page, and incorporate any relevant feedback. This will help to iron out any unanticipated kinks in the questions so that when you post the questions on your Web site, you won't receive unexpected responses.

- Time how long it takes to answer all the questions.

- Try to keep the questions simple, and try to be brief. Remember that scrolling from one page to the next in order to read a long complex question will likely turn most visitors off very quickly.

A Search Engine

A search engine, which uses a keyword to locate specific Web resources, is a very specialized kind of Web application. We'll look at search engines and how you can get the best out of them in the *Announcing Your Web Site to the World* chapter; we'll even look at how you can incorporate one into your own Web site.

A Web Case Study: Offering Stock in a Brewery

I will end this section by describing a real-world example of a unique kind of Web site, one that is likely to catch the eye of the financial staff in every small company in the country.

The Spring Street Brewing Company, a microbrewery in New York City, was caught in a typical fund-raising trap: The company was too small to attract major Wall Street underwriters, but was reluctant to sell itself to venture capitalists. To solve this conundrum, they set up a Web site with a very specific function: to create a place where people interested in buying and selling its stock could meet and do deals. The site was called Wit-Trade, named for the Wit beers that Spring Street brews, and the Spring Street Brewing Company launched its own initial public offering (IPO) from this site, raising $1.6 million without paying a single penny to underwriters. The company posted contracts that buyers and sellers completed from their home computers using a Web browser. Buyers then mailed a check to Spring Street, which processed the transaction the same way that a Wall Street broker would and then sent the seller's stock certificate to the buyer.

Spring Street was initially investigated by the Securities and Exchange Commission (SEC), who reviewed the legal implications of what Spring Street was doing. The SEC suggested several changes in procedure that Spring Street implemented, including arranging for a bank or other escrow agent to process the transactions rather than the brewery itself.

From this case, we can draw several important conclusions:

- The Internet has the power to free small companies from some of the more traditional limitations they face every day all over the country.

- The SEC is ready, willing, and able to apply a soft touch when dealing with innovative trading techniques but, at the same time, can continue to protect the participants and ensure that they operate in ways that are consistent with securities trading legislation.

- Using the Internet for trading and underwriting securities will increase rapidly; it is a natural for small- to medium-sized companies, allowing them to market more or less directly to the investing public.

- Securities trading laws usually observe geographical boundaries; but the Internet is a global phenomenon, and the technology shows no respect for these boundaries. One way around this might be to exempt Internet offerings from registration with a state body unless the issuers try to sell a security to residents of that particular state, in which case, registration would certainly be appropriate.

A company called Direct Stock Market offers an Internet service called Scor-Net, which lists securities information for several hundred small issuers and currently receives well over a thousand hits a day. More than a dozen similar systems are currently in development; they specialize in small security offerings not normally traded on the major exchanges.

The discount brokerage house Charles Schwab has announced that it is currently planning an Internet trading system, and it will not be long before the other major brokerage companies follow suit and establish their own Internet trading presence.

The potential explosion of Internet trading must be a daunting prospect for the SEC. Self-regulating organizations such as the National Association of Securities Dealers and the New York Stock Exchange police the trading that takes place in conventional markets; if trading on the Internet increases, there isn't anyone else but the SEC to perform the monitoring functions.

Making a Web Site Plan

In this part of the chapter, we'll look at some of the planning issues you will have to deal with before you start building your Web site. These issues fall neatly into two groups: Internal issues that you have some degree of control over, and external issues that are driven by your customer base and the Internet itself.

Internal issues include the following:

- Forming the project team
- Setting goals and objectives
- Developing a business strategy
- Developing content
- Designing, building, and testing your Web site
- Tracking results and responding to visitor feedback
- Defining success
- Revising your site

External issues include the following:

- What do your customers want to see on your Web site?
- How will people visit your Web site?
- How can you make sure that people stay to explore your site?

In the sections that follow, we'll look at all these issues, and I'll suggest ways that you can avoid some of the pitfalls inherent in the Web site planning process.

Forming the Project Team

The first step in establishing a Web presence is to form the project team. This team will cross traditional boundaries in your organization and should include members from several departments, including the following:

- Technical Services, sometimes called IS (Information Systems), DP (Data Processing), or MIS (Management Information Services)

- Marketing

- Sales

- Product Research and Development

- Customer Service

- Public Relations

Technical Services people will focus on the technical aspects of setting up the Web site, but in most corporations, this is one of the least important aspects. You will find that establishing business strategies, deciding what the site will actually do, defining the appropriate level of system security, and defining rules for maintaining the site will generate much more discussion and will turn out to be much more important issues than which hardware to use in your installation.

Give each member of the team a copy of your favorite Web browser, and be sure that they all spend some time surfing the Web and looking at all sorts of sites: the good, the bad, and the ugly. And this should be a part of their ongoing, continuing education.

Companies that already have some sort of centrally focused computer system will find that it is relatively easy to adapt their approach to developing a Web site. Federal Express, for example, has more than 10 years experience with its Powership program, which allows customers to use FedEx software to track any individual package.

When the people at Federal Express decided to develop a Web presence in 1994, they found it to be a relatively easy process, because all key departments were already well used to working together, and the usual office politics and turf wars did not surface.

Setting Goals and Objectives

Simply being on the Web is not an appropriate goal for your corporation; you must do better than that. Saying that you want to "use the Internet for marketing" or to "offer technical support and education" won't do either. You must establish a set of clearly defined, specific, detailed goals and then get the members of the project team to sign off on them as a group. If you ignore this step, your Web site will end up unfocused and vague and confusing to the visitor.

Why Do We Need a Web Site?

Corporations often establish Web sites for one or more of the following reasons:

- Research, surveys, and information collection
- Online ordering of goods and services
- Global exposure and market presence

and it is up to your team to decide where your company fits in this scheme. Here are some questions you should be asking:

- Why is the company creating this Web site?
- What is the purpose of the site? What is its mission statement?
- What does the company want to get out of this site?
- Who will manage technical issues and keep the server running?
- Who will manage the content on the site and keep the site fresh, updated with new content, and, above all, technically accurate?
- Who will monitor the competition?

Looking at Specific Case Studies

Let's take a look at how several kinds of organizations might express their goals and objectives for their own Web sites:

A small consultancy or service bureau can use a Web site to:

- increase name recognition.
- take a more prominent position with relation to peers and competitors.
- gain access to new and international markets.
- build a prospect database and generate new sales leads.
- provide technical upgrades, order status information, and customer support at a lower cost.
- make specialized resources available to a wider audience.
- provide unique goods and services.
- maintain the appearance of a large company.

A community or nonprofit organization can use a Web site to:

- increase name recognition.
- stimulate interest in new programs.
- educate the public on important topics.
- provide support to the community.
- extend its sphere of influence beyond the local community.

A public or government agency can use a Web site to:

- provide administrative information quickly and easily.
- speed internal processes and reviews.
- conduct opinion polls on current issues.

- educate the public on important topics.

- publicize job vacancies or purchasing contracts.

- advertise decisions and actions of prominent people within the organization.

Within each of these types of organizations are individual departments that can also set goals for their own Web sites.

A marketing, an advertising, or a sales department can use a Web site to:

- generate new sales leads.

- keep up to date with competitors.

- improve competitive positioning.

- conduct polls and surveys.

- create online sales.

- cut catalog print and mailing costs.

- direct Internet demographic groups to other marketing options.

- publicize discounts, freebies, competitions, and other sales incentives.

A technical support or customer service department can use a Web site to:

- reduce the number of telephone calls to the department.

- provide faster response times to users.

- allow users to download the latest version of a device driver, software upgrade, service pack, or software beta release.

- provide online product registration.

- display warranty and service contract information.

- distribute new FAQs, technical research papers, or position statements.
- distribute up-to-the-minute trouble-shooting information.
- publicize important product changes.

A human resources or training department can use a Web site to:

- reduce the number of telephone calls to the department.
- standardize policies and procedures information online.
- speed processing of forms, paperwork, and training evaluations.
- provide equal access to training materials irrespective of geographic location.
- provide simple, spare-time training on safety and environmental topics or on legal or technical issues specific to your company.
- provide accurate and up-to-date policies and procedures information 7 days a week, 24 hours a day (sometimes abbreviated as 7*24).

Prioritizing Your Goals

You may well find that you end up with a list of several goals, in which case, you will have to impose a priority on them. You can do this by asking:

- What will give the biggest return (depending on how you choose to define this) on the effort invested?
- What will generate real, tangible results most quickly?

Once you have set the goals, keep them in mind as you continue through the design process by asking questions such as:

- What am I trying to achieve on this page?
- Why is this page here?

- What is the best way to present this information? As a table, as text, or as a graphic?

- How does this page advance our goals?

One or more negative answers indicates that your site is heading toward trouble, and it is time to apply a course correction before things get too far out of line.

Only by establishing appropriate goals will you be able to determine a suitable return on investment for the company.

Developing the Right Business Strategy

The Web site business strategy motivates any decisions you make about your Web site, and it should be consistent with the strategy used throughout the rest of the company, although it does not have to be identical.

Two key points to remember when developing this strategy are:

- Your Web site must be integrated with the rest of your business; it cannot and must not exist in a vacuum. People from all departments in the company must be involved.

- Materials published on the Web site must be consistent with material published by the company in other ways, in both look and in feel. Don't confuse existing customers by sending one message online and another through more traditional media.

Some key business decisions you will have to make include:

- What strategic information will your Web site include, and what will happen when a competitor gains access to that information? (They surely will; they read your other advertising literature, don't they?)

- Will you offer items for sale online?

- Will you offer any special promotional products or give-aways?

- Will you offer discounts? If so, to whom, and how deep will these discounts be? Will they conflict with discounts offered to customers through other marketing channels?

- What forms of payment will you accept?

- Do you plan to enter into partnership with other companies?

Be sure that your Web site offers something out of the ordinary so that visitors have a good reason to patronize it.

CHAPTER
SIX

6

Designing and Constructing Your Web Site

- Developing content

- A Web case study: Amazon.com

- Tracking results and responding to visitor feedback

- Defining success

- How much will it cost?

- Implementing your Web site

- Tips for optimizing Web site performance

- Notes for international sites

- Avoiding the most common mistakes

In the previous chapter we looked at all the decisions you will face when planning your Web site. In this chapter we will concentrate on the next two parts of the process, designing your Web site and then putting that design into place as you construct your Web site.

You need to progress through several individual steps, in sequence, in designing and building your Web site. First, you will have to decide on the content you want to offer; then proceed to designing individual pages. When your design is complete, the next step is to code the pages in HTML and add any CGI scripts you need. The final stage involves testing your new pages individually and collectively.

Developing Content

A good starting point is to examine existing marketing material and print-based product information. The content you offer will be determined, at least in part, by the business strategy that you adopt. You should also identify external sources, including other Web pages, to which you want to link. Review everything before it is put up on the Web server; be sure that only good, solid information gets the worldwide distribution that the Web brings.

If you don't have good information to offer, you are exposing your organization unnecessarily, and visitors will stop taking you seriously; you might even end up on one of the "Worst-of-the-Web" sites as a subject of ridicule. Remember, the Web is all about content, content, and then more content.

Designing Individual Pages

I will greatly expand on this topic in a later section in this chapter, but I want to raise a few general questions here as a part of the ongoing wider discussion:

- Does your Web site integrate well with existing material and systems? People will form an opinion of your company based on what they see. Remember, you only get one chance to make a first impression; so don't blow it.

- Do you have a mechanism in place to correct any errors in content within one business day? Your site may be accessed by thousands of people; if a page contains an error, they will find it for you.

- Are the security elements in place to protect both your Web site as well as any other connected networks? (See the *Windows NT Server Operating System Security* and *External Security and Firewalls* chapters for more on internal and external security issues and how to deal with them.)

Programming Each Page

Once you have the content in place, what remains is the task of converting the material to a form suitable for display on the Web site. Anything you can do to automate that process should be given serious consideration, particularly if your content is likely to be volatile and to change frequently.

Take an incremental approach when making changes; this allows you to retain material that can be reused, and it minimizes the amount of discarded material.

Testing, Testing, Testing

You will hear me say this more than once in this book: Test your pages, and then test them again, and then test them some more. My background in software development has given me a healthy respect for careful testing of any kind of software. You should make absolutely sure that the people who do the testing are not the same people who developed the content or who programmed the pages. These people will be too close to the original material, and they will see exactly what they expect to see; if you use someone who has no such preconceived notions as your tester, you will create a product of a much higher quality.

A Web Case Study: Amazon.com

The creators of Amazon.com Inc, Internet booksellers (find them at `http://www.amazon.com` and see Figure 6.1 for Amazon's opening page), say they can provide any book in print (and that is a very impressive claim considering that there are well over one million books in print at any one time). The developers took testing their Web site very seriously indeed. And that approach is somewhat unusual in a world in which it is possible to open a Web site in only a few days.

Amazon is a completely Web-based business and one of the most successful of the newer startups, well on the way to $5 million in sales this year. It does no non-Web business and does virtually no advertising.

Once they completed the construction phase, workers at Amazon tested the site for a 4-month beta period, during which time they sold books only to a small pilot population. This group found many of the bugs in the system during this test phase and also provided much

FIGURE 6.1:

The opening page at Amazon.com

Welcome to Amazon.com Books!

One million titles, consistently low prices.

We've picked our first winner!
Now you've got another chance to
~ Win a Book a Week for a Year ! ~

SPOTLIGHT ! -- JULY 9TH

Go to extremes: from firewalls to falling snow, from sunspots to cold snaps, from bucking the sun to paddling to the arctic. Books for any temperature, all **30% off.**

FEATURED ON NPR AND IN THE NEW YORK TIMES BOOK REVIEW

The best books from the bottom of the FM band and from the pages of the Sunday New York Times.

CALLING ALL WEB SITES

useful feedback on the operation of the site in general; many of their comments were incorporated into the site during this beta phase.

But the long beta test period was also useful from another important point of view: It allowed Amazon to look at its site using all the browsers anyone could find. And the developers made several changes based on these findings. These were not bugs, as such, but glitches in the way that different browsers interpreted specific HTML statements. Amazon realized quickly that if something appears to be wrong or off-putting in some way, a visitor is unlikely to want to repeat what was after all an unpleasant experience and revisit the site in the future.

When you access the Amazon site, you will notice an almost complete absence of graphics. Instead you will find content, content, and more content. You can search for a specific book, author, or topic, or you can browse through 23 subject categories to locate the book that you want from a database of 1.1 million books—five times as many as the typical Barnes and Noble or Borders superstore. When you select a book, Amazon displays several related titles that you might also find interesting. Editors select books for special promotions and prepare capsule synopses, selections from reviews, and even author interviews for these promotional items. Amazon will even send you e-mail when a specific book appears for the first time in paperback. If you give Amazon a list of your favorite authors and lists of topics in which you are interested, Amazon will send you a stream of recommendations of other books and authors you might like to try.

Since Amazon doesn't actually order most books until after it sells them, it can turn over its inventory—mostly consisting of bestsellers—more than 150 times a year, compared with 3 or 4 times for conventional booksellers, and most books are discounted between 10 and 30 percent. Amazon has a staff of 33 people, occupies a 17,000 square-foot building in an industrial setting, has no expensive furnishings, no sales staff, and virtually no inventory. It is open for business 24 hours a day and accepts orders from all over the world; Amazon currently ships books to more than 65 countries. More than half of current orders come from repeat customers. This is all in sharp contrast to traditional book retailing with its need for quality real-estate, large inventory, and lots of people.

Tracking Results and Responding to Visitor Feedback

Once your Web site is linked to the Internet and you start getting hits, you will also get e-mail and comments from people and other sources, including demographic information and hit counts, telling you who is accessing your site and what they are doing once they get there.

You must be ready to deal with these comments in an effective manner; after all, every contact is a potential customer. With the speed of electronic communications these days, you should have a mechanism in place to provide a reply to queries within one working day at the outside, and faster is better in this case. If it takes you a week to reply to a customer, you can bet that your reply is too late and that customer has already gone somewhere else.

Defining Success

You will compare these tracked results against your original goals to help in the next step of the process, which is to reach a definition of how successful you consider your site. Keep this definition to reasonable proportions, and add specific, quantifiable results.

Avoid statements such as, "I want our site to attract lots of quality visitors," and instead use a statement containing elements that you can actually measure, such as, "Our site is successful when the typical visitor adds our URL to a Hot list, visits our site regularly (four or more times a year), and buys two of our products during those visits." Here are some basic questions you can start with:

- How many people visit our Web site during a normal week?
- How long do people stay connected to our site?
- What do visitors do when exploring our Web site?
- How frequently do visitors return to our Web site?
- How many pages or links on our site do visitors typically explore?

Consider using a short survey page to collect some of this information from your visitors.

You can measure three main areas of operation as elements of success:

- Raw data
- Internal benefits

- External benefits

The applicability of each of these categories will depend on your organization and the original goals that you set. Let's look at each one in turn.

Raw Data

Raw data are data that can be measured easily, including the number of hits each day and other usage statistics. It is relatively easy to generate some big numbers that sound very impressive when budget-review time rolls around. You can also use changes in these raw data over time to measure changes you make in your Web site structure, page layout, and content.

Internal Benefits

Internal results show the effect that your Web site or Intranet is having on your own organization. These results might appear as fewer telephone calls to your Customer Service, Technical Support, or Human Resources departments or as an increase in contacts from overseas. These are real benefits that you can measure and, perhaps more important, can quantify and express as dollars and cents.

Companies such as L. L. Bean and Land's End have cut the printing and mailing costs associated with their traditional catalog by offering the same goods for sale from their Web sites, which is a real benefit that they can measure precisely. Federal Express uses its Web site to allow customers to track individual packages; thus, it can express savings in terms of fewer telephone calls to its customer support centers. And the makers of a particular spaghetti sauce or soup might measure the success of their site by counting the number of visitors who download a coupon and redeem it at the supermarket.

External Benefits

External benefits demonstrate the effect that your Web site is having outside your organization. These benefits can include increased awareness of your products and services, particularly newly developed or newly announced products, increased customer satisfaction, or increased public discussion of an important topic or issue if you represent a government agency or nonprofit organization. These benefits are usually much harder to quantify, but are real and tangible, nonetheless.

Developing Content and Revising Your Site

One of the Web's most attractive features is the ease with which you can change content and revise your site as new products appear or in response to customer feedback. This might include:

- Adding new information to existing pages. Preserve and reuse as much of the original material as possible to keep costs down.

- Analyzing user hit patterns to decide which Web pages are working and which are not and then revising those pages that are not working.

- Automating the production of new pages or revisions to existing pages, perhaps using output from a database to create new price lists every month.

- Developing templates to establish the look and feel of your site, particularly for background colors and placement of major elements on the page.

Your visitors will certainly expect to see new content each time they visit, and one way to keep them coming back is to keep your site as up to date as you can.

A Web Case Study: 1-800-FLOWERS

A good example of the need to keep revising content to ensure that visitors return is shown by the managers of 1-800-FLOWERS (find it at `http://www.1800flowers.com` and see Figure 6.2 for the home page). They are constantly revising their pages and displaying fresh and new information on plant care and new varieties of flowers, as well as providing promotional materials and specials appropriate to the season. Their site is always fresh, bright, and full of good ideas; other Web-site managers would do well to copy this philosophy and extend it to their Web sites.

FIGURE 6.2:

The Web site of 1-800-FLOWERS does indeed say it with flowers.

What Do Your Customers Want to See?

So far we have concentrated on the information that you want to present to a visitor to your Web site, but you might also ask, What do our customers want to see on our Web site? According to a recent survey, customers want to see several things when they visit a Web site:

- Applications to help them find and download software updates, service packs, and bug fixes

- Specific, factual information, including technical information of all kinds

- Customer service, including online bulletin boards that are monitored or staffed by customer service personnel

The survey also emphasized the importance of being able to customize generalized product information to answer specific customer questions, rather than present the same static information to each visitor.

Here are some questions you should be asking:

- Who are your customers and how extensive is your customer base?

- How important will first-time drop-in visitors be to your overall Web strategy?

- What do you think your users want to see on your Web site?

- How often do you expect visitors to return to your Web site?

- Do you have to attract new users, or do you have an existing captive audience? Are you planning an Intranet purely for internal consumption?

- How does the typical visitor access your site—by dial-up modem, by ISDN, or by some other means?

In planning your site, look for ways to reduce the volume of material presented to each visitor, and increase the value of content they do see. If you don't address users' needs, they won't stay long, and they will never come back.

A Web Case Study: Frito-Lay, Inc

Farmers have been using computers to help run their businesses for years, and recently, some have started using the Internet in their never-ending search for information on commodity prices and markets for what their farms produce.

At Frito-Lay's Web site at the Midwest Corn Handling Facility in Sidney, Illinois, farmers can check on their supply contracts any time it is convenient, rather than phoning during normal office hours, and they find that to be a time-saver. Frito-Lay also likes using the Web site this way, because as more farmers use the system, the number of phone calls to the office decreases, which in turn frees the employees who used to answer the phones to do other tasks.

Managers of the Frito-Lay Web site deliberately decided not to make their site too flashy, but to make it simple to look at and easy to understand. Most material on the site is presented in simple black text against a solid-color background, but the Web pages are packed with information. Farmers can enter their name and a password and get a complete breakdown of how much corn they have delivered to Frito-Lay, as well as information on how much that corn is worth.

How Will People Visit Your Site?

People will discover your Web site in a finite number of ways, and in this section, we'll look at the most common ways.

By Direct Invitation

People will access your site by direct invitation when they see your Web site address, or URL, in your advertising material, in print, or on TV or when they ask, Do you have a Web site? If your company name already has a strong association with your products in the mind of the consumer, you can enhance this by using the company name or product name as part of your site's domain name, as you saw in the *Making All the Right Connections* chapter. For example, a site called `chevrolet .com` will not be misinterpreted by anyone; whereas a site called `car-maker.com` might be.

Once your Web site is established, all advertising materials, press releases, and other publications should include your URL, along with the usual telephone numbers and fax numbers. People who visit your Web site as a result of seeing a press release in a magazine article are likely to be among your most qualified visitors.

By Links from Search Engines

A common way for visitors to access your site is as a result of a keyword search of one of the popular Web search engines, such as Yahoo or AltaVista.

When using a search engine, a visitor enters a keyword; the search engine looks in its database for sites where that keyword appears and then displays the list of sites. The visitor then chooses one to visit.

People who use these search engines are often the most qualified and important visitors to your site, because they are not idly surfing the Web; they are actively searching for information as part of a research effort or other project. We'll look at search engines in more detail in the *Announcing Your Web Site to the World* chapter.

By Links from Other Sites

Another way for a visitor to arrive is as a result of a link from another site; that's why they call it the World Wide Web, after all. This might be a site run by a different part of your corporation or a site concerned with a similar product or service. The creators of the other site have added a link to your site because they think you have something on it that their visitors will value, and it makes then look pretty good to be associated with you in this way.

By Mention in a Newsgroup

A mention in a Usenet newsgroup can send visitors your way, particularly if the mention is subtle. Be sure to add a brief signature to any e-mail you send to Usenet newsgroups, and be sure your URL is included as a part of your signature.

Large-scale advertising through Usenet newsgroups is always a bad idea, and you should not do it unless you like getting a lot of hate mail and flames, as those who have tried it can tell you. The Web site is the best place on the Internet for this sort of commercial activity, because you can provide a place where people can linger and look at what you have to offer at their leisure.

They Are Coming, but How Do You Make Sure They Stay?

You have visitors coming to your site as a result of product announcements and advertising, but how do you make sure they stay and browse for a while or even make further contact by e-mail or by calling? We will look at the major Web site design issues in the next section, but first, bear in mind two things.

Keep It Short and Sweet

Your opening page should be an attention grabber and make visitors want to explore the rest of your site. You can do this in several ways, and we'll look at them in detail in the next section. You should not try to show a visitor too much on this first page, and you should always consider the mechanism that your average visitor is using to access your site. Is it over a 14.4Kbps dial-up connection to the Internet, or is it a 10Mbps local area network using an Intranet?

Bandwidth always makes a big difference; for example, at 14.4Kbps, an HTML page will arrive in just over 1K per second under good conditions. If your page does not appear on a visitor's browser in a fairly short time, you've lost him; he is gone.

Use the Best Designers You Can Get

You should use the best design help that you can afford. You can hire a Web site designer yourself, or you can use one of the up-and-coming ad agencies who specialize in Web design. Alex Brown & Co estimates that Web-related advertising revenue will rise from about $20 million today to $1.4 billion by 1998. So many Web sites are out there that you have to do something striking to catch your customer's eye and hold her attention. In the next section we'll look at how you can do this.

Designing and Constructing Your Web Site

In this section we'll look at some of the most important topics related to Web site design and at how you can design Web site elements to your advantage.

When you first view a Web page, you do not look at it in the same way that you would look at printed material such as a book or magazine page; instead, you look at it as if it were a picture or a photograph. You see the page as a whole, and your eye wanders all over the page, pausing or coming to rest at the most visually important elements. The arrangement of individual design elements on the page is much more important than you might think at first and is the primary influence on what you pay attention to and read; either that, or you click on the Stop button and go somewhere else.

On the Web it's easy to wander off the subject on a tangent and to lose track of your original place; this is particularly acute for visitors who access your site through a search engine. This can deposit them at almost any point in your site hierarchy, rather than at your home page.

A Web Style Guide

Before you jump into the process of writing copy and collecting graphics to use on your Web site, you will want to consider a number of important design issues. In this section, we'll look at all these issues, and I'll provide you with as much direction as possible so that you can avoid repeating the mistakes of many sites you see on the Web today.

In order for this next section to make sense, I will have to introduce some elements of HTML, but I will try to keep these as brief and as self-explanatory as possible; we will look at HTML in more detail in a later section.

In many ways, the best design advice I can give you is the ancient adage of "keep it simple"; just because you can do it on the Web, it isn't necessarily a good idea.

Writing for the Web

Writing for the Web is not the same as writing for the book or magazine page. The Web opens up enormous opportunities for incorporating sound and video, but at the same time, you face all sorts of difficulties in controlling some of the most elementary aspects of page formatting, such as font size and precise positioning. These limitations can also be something of a blessing in disguise, because if you can't fiddle with something, you probably won't.

The greatest challenge is in keeping the visitor oriented and providing a structure in which the relationship of one page to another is clear and precise. If your site is easily recognizable, has clearly marked entrances and exits, and is easy to navigate, there is no doubt that visitors will return. If your site appears confusing, is hard to navigate, and contains links that look local but that can deposit a visitor on the other side of the globe, visitors will never return.

People don't read Web pages in the same way they read a book; they like to skip all over the screen, and all those links are mighty powerful temptations to leave this page altogether and go off on some fun tangent or other. What this means, of course, is that you should keep all this in mind as you write your Web pages:

- Keep it simple. This is a theme I will return to again and again in this book, but here it applies doubly; reading from a computer screen is not particularly easy, and the resolution is much poorer than that of the printed page.

- Keep it short. People like to skim most Web pages (unless your site specializes in some sort of extremely technical subject) rather than read the whole page from top left to bottom right. If you discover you have written a very long sentence, divide it into two or more shorter ones.

- Keep it focused. Don't wander off the subject or write woolly and vague prose. Say what you mean and move on to the next topic. Use energetic prose, and don't ever use the passive voice. What's the passive voice? This is: *The circuit board should be inserted into the 8-bit bus.* How should you rewrite that sentence? Like this: *Insert the circuit board into the 8-bit bus.* Simple, isn't it?

Providing a Site Overview

One way to add this important element of clarity is to provide an overview of your site on your home page and to provide links that indicate clearly what is going to happen when a visitor chooses one of them. Let people get in, do what needs to be done, and then get out quickly, much as they would in a convenience store; your site may include the most up to date features, but if it doesn't do what people expect, they won't come back.

Rules for Using Graphics

The designers of many Web sites use graphics with little or no thought about what value these graphics add to the page. Designers tend to use large graphical elements without considering how long they will take to download to a browser and without concern for the visitor who either cannot or does not want to run with graphics turned on. If your page does not make sense without the graphics, redesign the page. Don't get me wrong—graphics can be useful; but if you use them, do so because they add something of value to the page rather than simply increasing the download time.

Managing Inline Graphics

Using inline graphics is a major part of the Web's attraction. Here are a few short rules to help you use them effectively:

- Don't assume that all graphics on a page will always be displayed. Some users will be using text-only browsers, and others will turn off graphics options to gain speed.

- Use a graphical element on a page only when it adds value to the page; don't use a graphic just because you happen to have a file in the right format. Space on a Web page is always at a premium; so don't waste it with unnecessary graphics.

- Keep all graphics small to minimize download time.

- Limit the number of colors in all graphics to minimize download time.

- Standardize on the same number of colors for all graphics. If you place two images with different color resolutions on the same Web page, the visitor's Web browser will be forced to compromise their display. This can result in images that look posterized and cartoonlike—not very attractive.

Using Icons

Don't use daft little icons when a simple bullet will do the job just as effectively. Much application software these days is loaded with hordes of icons for all sorts of obscure operations. If you do decide to use icons, be absolutely sure that a text label is associated with each one. Web sites are not like the word processors or spreadsheets that people use every single day; they are not visited often enough for anyone to remember how the icons you have chosen work on your site. And if you must use icons, be sure that you always use the same icon to perform the same function throughout your site.

Using Imagemaps

An imagemap is a graphical element that can point to several links at the same time, depending where the visitor clicks inside the image. For example, a travel agent might present an imagemap of a whole country and then ask a visitor to click on a state to visit. Each part of the imagemap points to a different link, and so the Web site appears to offer custom service irrespective of the potential traveler's choice of destination.

The problems arise when something goes wrong, and the imagemap becomes completely useless. Often you will find that the site does not offer an alternative route to the data if the imagemap isn't working.

Allowing Searching

Any Web site that has more than just a few simple pages should also allow visitors to search for specific keywords so that they can find the information they want quickly and easily.

If your Web site is a result of the work of several departments within your company, it may well reflect that organization to a visitor. The trouble is that the visitor does not care about or understand your internal organization, which may often appear to be complete nonsense to someone outside your company. Searching can help solve this particular problem; so be sure to include a Search button on each page. The search can be simple; it does not have to offer full Boolean operators and lots of fancy options to get the job done.

Packaging Information in Right-Sized Pieces

One of the most important tasks in designing Web pages is to divide the content into reasonable pieces so that the visitor can look at a full and interesting screen, but does not have to wait an inordinately long time for the page to load. Striking the right balance is sometimes difficult because there is no theoretical limitation on page length; it can be anywhere between one word and several megabytes.

So, do you cram everything into one giant page, or create lots of little pages all linked together? Here are some points to consider:

- If a page is larger than one screen full, a visitor will have to scroll down to read the second half of the page. This is not much of a problem with graphical browsers, but can take a long time in a text-based browser.

- Long pages take longer to load and display; some visitors to your site will be using slow dial-up links to the Internet.

Very short pages make loading and reading feel choppy; every time a visitor tries to follow a link, there is a pause as the next page loads from the server. Also, the visitor may feel cheated after waiting for a new page to load and then finding that it contains only two short paragraphs at the top of the page.

Organizing information into predefined pieces is not always an easy task, but it is one that copy writers, advertisers, and print journalists have to deal with all the time. It is a problem that can be solved. How else do you think that there is always just enough news to fill the newspaper every morning? If this task seems too daunting for you to handle alone, get help, because it is too important to be left to chance.

Placing the Most Important Material First

To capture a visitor's attention, always place the most important elements at the top of the page. If you move this material to the bottom of the page (on a long page, this will be way off the bottom of most normal screens) or on a page nested deeply in your site, chances are good that no one will ever find it.

Don't waste time and real estate stating the obvious, such as, "This important site is part of the international World Wide Web." Every visitor to your site already knows this and does not need to be reminded of it.

Obviously, not everything will fit on the top page; it is inevitable that slightly less important material will end up lower down in your structure. Try to keep track of how many links a visitor will have to complete to reach this material. Any more than about three links is probably too many, and you should consider redesigning your structure to give more visibility to important information.

Laying Out Individual Pages

Hypertext Markup Language is good at describing the internal structure of a Web page, but it does not offer many formatting commands that you can use to control the appearance of that page. That said, you can do several things to influence the display of your content. Here are some suggestions:

- Many Web browsers flow both text and graphics against the left margin, which results in funny-looking, long, thin pages that waste lots of space. To read the complete page, visitors must scroll vertically. You can get around this if you:

  - avoid long series of short lines.
  - use wide graphics instead of tall graphics.
  - use swashes that point toward the left side of the screen. A swash is a graphic bar of a graduated color rather than a solid color.

- Some designers divide the page into several sections, (somewhere between three and five, and certainly no more than seven) and group similar information into each zone on different pages. Users quickly catch on to where the content is on the page, and this helps them to navigate through your site with confidence because it makes your site more predictable.

- You can use four main devices to divide a page into different zones:

  1. A horizontal rule created with the <HR> tag. You can use two different thicknesses to indicate major divisions and minor divisions.

  2. A swash of graduated color. Keep swashes small because they are considered graphics and so take extra time to load. Reuse the same swash if you can; many browsers can cache items and therefore avoid reloading them.

3. A blank line created with the `<BR>` tag. Use breaks between horizontal rules or swashes because they are much less prominent on the screen.

4. Text flowed around graphics (in some browsers). Use the `<ALIGN>` tag within the image tag. `ALIGN=LEFT` anchors the graphic on the left margin, and `ALIGN=RIGHT` anchors it on the right.

- HTML version 3.0 defines tables that can contain both text and graphics, but tables are not compatible with older browsers; the individual text and graphics elements they contain are displayed along the left margin of the page by default.

Choosing Page Banners

Most Web pages that you see start with a page banner or title across the top of the page. You can combine text and graphics on a banner and use it to perform several important functions, including:

- Identify the subject material treated on this page

- Indicate this page's importance

- Set the tone for the material on this page

- Evoke a sense of continuity from one page to the next

- Establish a sense of place or of identity (more on this in a moment)

You can create a banner in many ways. Here are some suggestions to get you started:

- Text with a bright underline or swash

- Text as graphics

- An icon with associated text

- Text on a photographic background

Remember that although a large banner may look impressive and may contain lots of good information, the bigger it is, the longer it takes to load. If you are dealing with a set of related pages arranged in a hierarchy, use a larger banner on the pages dealing with major topics and smaller banners on pages dealing with minor topics.

Choosing Titles

You should also take care when selecting titles for your pages; titles should be short and should identify the page origin as well as the content on that page. Users can add titles to their Hot lists to identify frequently accessed pages. Some search engine sites on the Web also use them; so you have to make them able to stand alone from the rest of your site.

Don't use a general term such as *Bibliography* by itself; it will mean nothing to a visitor who looks at it again in six months. By then, a visitor could have collected a "Bibliography" entry from several sites. Instead, be sure to use a title that continues the theme of the other related Web pages, such as "Dog Training: A Bibliography" or "Intergalactic Industries: Corporate Biography"; these make much more sense.

Some popular browsers can sort their Hot lists in alphabetic order. I'm not suggesting that all your titles should start with the letter *A*, but by using a common theme in your titles, you can at least be sure that all your pages will appear next to each other in this list.

There are several ways to do this. If you have a product with a characteristic name, be sure that all your titles feature this name in the same way. For example, the first might be "New Wonder Snibbo and Septic Tanks: The Truth at Last"; and thus the next would be "New Wonder Snibbo Sticks Like Glue," and so on. If you are promoting an activity rather than a product, you can do much the same thing. For example, the first title might be "Fly Fishing: The Latest Gear," and the next one might be "Fly Fishing: The 100 Best Locations." You get the idea.

Establishing a Sense of Identity

One of the odd and unexpected problems found on the Web is that the limitations of HTML and Web browsers often make every page look similar. This is compounded by the increasingly common use of search engines to navigate the Web; you choose a link, and suddenly you find yourself on another site half way around the world.

To avoid this problem, be sure that every page on your site displays the name of your organization and that it has a link back to the home page. You can do this in two ways:

- In text, by choosing appropriate page titles
- In graphics, by including a small (and I do mean small) graphic of the company logo, perhaps in only two or three colors

This technique accomplishes two objectives:

- It establishes a sense of place so that visitors knows exactly where they are on the Web, even if they arrived by search engine.
- It places your corporate symbol in a place where it is most visible on the page and where it will be seen by every visitor to your site.

How to Link Pages Successfully

Hypertext links are both a blessing and a curse; they let you connect related pieces of information in all sorts of creative ways, but they can also be a major distraction to a visitor because of the constant temptation to find out where the next link goes and what the next page holds.

If you try really hard, you can create a highly linked site like the one shown on the left side of Figure 6.3 in which every page points to every other page, and the impression given to a visitor is one of completely unnecessary complexity. When visitors begin to explore a site such as this one, they get the feeling that they are getting nowhere and are just going around and around in circles. If they even find an exit, they will be gone, never to return.

The other extreme to this highly linked site is shown in the middle of Figure 6.3. This site is simple and shows a linear progression from one page to the next. A visitor arrives at some point in the chain and moves, page by page, along the chain to the end. This is not a very exciting presentation, but may be suited to sites specializing in very technical information, and it is easy to maintain: Simply drop in a new page and update the links in the page before and in the page that follows.

FIGURE 6.3:

Various types of links

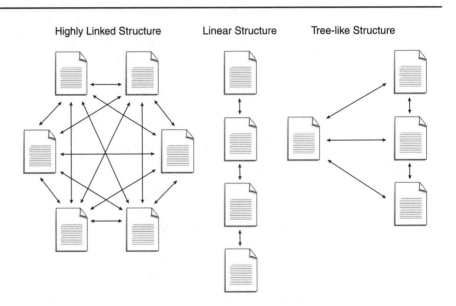

Highly Linked Structure   Linear Structure   Tree-like Structure

As with so many things, the most useful organization lies somewhere in the middle between these two extremes, as demonstrated by the site shown on the right side of Figure 6.3. In this site, a single page is used as a jumping-off point to get to the other pages, forming a treelike structure. Each page contains three links: one pointing to the next page, one to the previous page, and one pointing back to the table of contents page. This design is easy to maintain and expand

and works for everything from a single document all the way to a whole site.

Try to keep the number of links modest rather than linking everything to everything else, and certify that every link counts. If the link doesn't add value, get rid of it; if it points somewhere irrelevant, your visitor will just get annoyed. It is a cruel fact of the Web that once a visitor to your site selects a link, chances are good that this person will never return to that original page.

If your intention is to keep people on your site for as long as possible—so that they might be tempted to buy something, perhaps—be *very* careful about providing links, especially to other Web sites. After all, do you think that the Ford Web site includes a link to Volvo's home page?

Creating Links

Make your links obvious; they should not be mysterious, but be careful how you indicate them. In most browsers, a link is displayed as underlined or highlighted text, and you should be careful how you construct the sentence. Here is an example of what not to do:

```
Choose here to learn absolutely everything there is to
know about our new discount structure.
```

The link is too far away from the description of what it does to make any sense, and highlighting the link word merely makes things worse. Using the word *link* isn't any better either:

```
Choose this link to learn absolutely everything there
is to know about our new discount structure.
```

This example is not much better either:

```
Click here for more information.
```

More information on what exactly? Don't use the word *click* either; use *choose* or *select* for those users of text browsers or those visitors who run with graphics turned off.

Make all your links self-explanatory, like this:

```
Want to know more about our new discount structure?
```

You should also try to differentiate between internal links, those to other pages on your own site, and links that point to completely different sites; consider using a word such as *jump* to make it plain that your visitors are going to a new site:

```
All proud new owners of black-tailed ferrets will want
to jump to the Australian Ferret Fanciers Web site.
```

If you do provide links to other sites, check them from time to time, first, to make sure that they are still there and, second, to make sure that the link still makes sense and that the linked material has not changed in any substantive way.

Linking to Nontext Documents

Be very careful when linking to documents that are not simple text and graphics pages, such as sound, video, or animation that require a specific helper application. Make it crystal clear what will happen when a visitor selects that link, because any visitors who wait for a megabyte-sized file to download only to realize that they don't have the right helper application to process the file are likely to end up very angry indeed.

Including a Signature

Don't let your pages remain anonymous; add a signature at the bottom, and be sure that your signature contains at least the following elements:

- *Copyright symbol.* In HTML use the character code &#169: or the entity name &copy:. For more on this and other legal issues, see the *Checking the Fine Print of Legal Issues* chapter.

- *Date.* Use the date that the page or site was last updated. This gives a visitor a good sense of how old your content is.

- *E-mail address.* Give visitors a way to contact you easily. You can also add fax numbers and telephone numbers.

The usual convention is that the signature appears at the bottom of the first page below a horizontal rule.

A Final Checklist

Designing effective, useful, and good-looking Web pages is not that difficult if you keep a few simple rules in mind as you proceed:

- Be sure that the design of a particular page advances the goals of that page; do not use clever design for its own sake.

- Use a consistent approach when designing a group of related pages.

- Add a banner to the top of a page.

- Establish a sense of place by using a small graphic on each page.

- Divide complex pages into different, quite separate zones by function so that each zone contains only one specific kind of information, such as identification, navigation aids, or technical content.

- Prepare routes through your site for users of nongraphical browsers and for those visitors who have purposefully turned off their graphics options in the interest of increasing speed.

- Create templates for others to use that impose a single look-and-feel to all the pages on your site.

Using a Designer

If your company typically uses an outside agency to create advertising materials, you should at least consider using an outside agency to design your Web pages for you, rather than trying to do everything yourself.

The traditional ad agencies have lagged behind in the technical skills needed in the development of Web pages, and you are far more likely to get a suitable response from a company that does nothing but design Web pages.

Some of the most innovative Web sites around are those related to the entertainment industries, in which advertising budgets are often large, but also in which the products they are selling (movies, CDs, and software) are all easily digitized and displayed on a Web page. Products such as stainless steel or horse trailers are harder to get a feel for over a computer.

How Much Will It Cost?

The sooner you start work on your Web site, the better, because costs are rising all the time. Initial hardware and software costs, content development costs, and personnel costs for a medium-sized installation can quickly run to a $1 million or more for the first year; a large site might cost $3 to $4 million. You will find that approximately 60 percent of this figure is made up of personnel costs, spent in developing content, services, and marketing.

The two most expensive types of sites are promotional sites and those that let visitors perform some sort of transaction. The content on promotional sites requires constant revision; otherwise, people will not make a second visit, and you will fall victim to the "been there, done that" response. The transaction sites are often more expensive because of the increased security and testing that must be done to ensure that the site is as secure as possible. There are also the more mundane costs of maintaining, updating, and improving Web sites.

As new technology arrives, you will have to be prepared to revise both the content and the way in which your site actually works so that you can stay abreast of developments and ahead of your competition. The later you delay your entry to the Web, the more you will have to do to stay in the same place with respect to what others, including your competition, are doing on their Web sites.

When you consider that the average print ad costs $75,000 to develop—never mind a place in a national or an international publication—it is absurd to limit spending on a Web site that has such enormous potential.

Implementing Your Web Site

In this part of the chapter, I want to introduce you (and I can do no more that) to the main Web-preparation techniques you can use to prepare the content of your Web pages. I will cover the various HTML standards, describe some of the HTML creation and translation tools, and cover some of the Common Gateway Interface (CGI) programming techniques you can use to interface existing back-end applications and your Web site. All this, by necessity, will be brief; there are many excellent books and Web sites on using HTML and CGI and other scripting languages, many of which are mentioned in the appendices of this book.

Introducing HTML, the Language of the Web

Hypertext Markup Language, HTML, is the basic language used to post content on the Web, and it specifies the form and function of your documents. Using HTML you can specify how Web browsers will display your Web pages, create links between different documents and different sites, and display inline graphics, sound, and other multimedia elements.

HTML began life as a portion of SGML (Standard Generalized Markup Language), an ISO standard mechanism for describing document markup languages. Other page definition languages, such as PostScript or T_EX, apply extremely detailed descriptions to prescribe how the text is presented; HTML takes the opposite approach and uses much more abstract styles to describe the portions of a document. Thus, HTML can hand off the messy details of how the document is actually displayed to the Web browser software, and you, the content creator, are free from decisions such as what to do if your visitors do not have a particular font loaded on their machine. You don't care about that level of detail; the visitor's browser takes care of the implementation details. We'll take a look at HTML versions 0 and 1 next and then look at versions 2 and 3.

Form versus Structure

If you are new to HTML, the basic premise you need to remember is that you are not describing the format of a document, but you are specifying its structure, such as paragraphs, lists, headings, and so on. For people who have used WYSIWYG word processors for many years, this concept comes as something of a surprise, and often as an unpleasant one. HTML allows a separation between the definition of the document and the software (or Web browser) used to view that document. The point behind this is that HTML lets you define the structure of your document or Web page so that *any* current or future Web browser, running on any hardware/software combination will be able to read it and display it in a way that makes most sense for the browser.

An additional benefit is that an HTML file is a plain ASCII text file with no special control characters or embedded binary codes; this makes it portable to any computer that can process ASCII and means that you can send Web pages as e-mail and work on them using the simplest of text editors, even Notepad or Write.

There are formal published definitions of the various HTML standards, but some browser manufacturers are promoting extensions to HTML that are not yet a part of these standards. Many of the extensions are moving toward a page-definition language and away from the portable concepts of HTML as a purely structural definition of the document.

HTML Tags

Users of HTML create a text file and use *tags* to define the structural elements of the document; this is something like creating a source code file when using a programming language, but HTML is much simpler in concept that any programming language. Let's look at a short example:

```
<HTML>
<HEAD>
<TITLE>An example of an HTML document</TITLE>
</HEAD>
<BODY>
<P>
This is an example of the internal structure found within an
HTML document.</P>
</BODY>
</HTML>
```

The elements contained within the < and > symbols are the tags that mark the beginning and the end of the structural elements within the document. Tags often occur in pairs, as in:

```
<TITLE>An example of an HTML document</TITLE>
```

The first <TITLE> tag signals the beginning of the structural element, and the second </TITLE> tag signals the end of that same element. Capitalization inside a tag is not important; <TITLE>, <Title>, and <title> will all produce the same effect. And you don't have to start every new tag on a new line, although by doing so, you can make the document more legible for others and make it easier to understand.

These tags are never (normally) displayed, and they guide the Web browser behind the scenes. Once you understand what these tags do, you can quickly add them to any text file or interpret the structure of a previously prepared HTML document. Remember, though, you cannot determine how the document will appear in someone's Web browser by looking at the HTML tags alone.

Some elements are defined by a single tag, for example, the line-break element, <BR>. Others require a beginning tag, for example the paragraph element, <P>, and let you use an optional end tag </P> to delimit the paragraph. And some elements such as the <TITLE> element we just looked at require both a start tag and an end tag; the end tag is identified by the / immediately before the tag name.

The placement of elements in your document must obey the HTML nesting rules, which define where you can and cannot place HTML elements. For example, a heading element <H1> cannot contain a list or another heading. Also, HTML elements cannot overlap. We can only look at a very small number of HTML tags in this section, and there really isn't enough room to cover all the rules of HTML syntax.

HTML Template

Three elements will appear in every HTML file:

- <HTML> </HTML>: This element contains the entire file. The first tag appears at the very beginning of the file, and the second appears at the end as the final element. Together they define the enclosed text as an HTML document.

- <HEAD> </HEAD>: This element defines the header and contains information about the document that is not part of the viewable text.

- `<BODY> </BODY>`: This element contains all the other elements in your document, and is normally the largest part of the file.

These three elements create a template that all HTML documents follow:

```
<HTML>
<HEAD>
   header elements
</HEAD>
<BODY>
   body elements
</BODY>
</HTML>
```

Certain elements can also have attributes. For example, the image element used to place a graphic in a document, looks like this:

```
<IMG Src="http://home/dir/filename.gif">
```

The image element uses the `Src` attribute to define the location of the graphic file to use.

Linking to Other Web Sites

Links are an essential component of the Web and are created using an anchor tag `<A>`. When selected, the text between the opening `<A>` and the closing `</A>` is the link that takes the visitor to a new location in the current document or in a new document. Most browsers underline or highlight links or display them in a contrasting color to make them stand out from the surrounding text.

You specify where a link points to by using the HREF attribute. A link might look something like this:

```
<A HREF="page2.html">Jump to page 2</A>
```

where the HREF attribute is set to the name of the document called `page2.htm`. Using quotes around the filename is good standard HTML practice, although you don't need them unless the filename contains spaces or other odd characters. The text between the `<A>` and `</A>` tags Jump to page 2 becomes the link, and selecting it takes the visitor to the new document. The HREF attribute can reference another HTML document, a graphic, or anything else that can be addressed using a URL. The anchor can also enclose an <IMG>, or image tag, allowing graphics such as icons to become links.

For even finer control over your links, you can attach a label to a block of text in the destination document and set up the link so that you jump right to that location. The label looks like this:

```
<H2>
<A NAME="Section12">
Section 12 Lawn Tractors
</A>
</H2>
```

and links in other documents can now refer directly to this section by using a pound sign (#) in the HREF to separate the filename from the anchor name, like this:

```
<A HREF="page2.html#Section12">
```

When someone selects this link, the document opens at the specified section.

HTML Limitations

There are several things that HTML versions 0 and 1 can't do, such as make tables, present mathematic formulas, specify multiple columns of text or graphics, use tab characters, or include an external HTML file; some of these features are included in HTML version 2 or higher.

HTML 2

All browsers can interpret the basic HTML levels 0 and 1, but the widespread acceptance of graphical browsers such as Mosaic and Netscape Navigator led to the addition of new HTML features for user interaction.

One of these features, known as forms, is now available to many browsers. Forms are used to present graphical user interface features such as fill-in-the-blanks boxes, checklists, radio buttons, and so on and can be used for a huge variety of tasks relating to an interactive interface. Forms can be used for everything from specifying the stock market symbol of a security to filling in the results of a marketing survey on galvanized deck screws.

A form sets up a group of related variable name fields and their associated value fields. The variable name is supplied in the form, and the user supplies or selects the variable value; you can even code appropriate default values into the form. Here is a simple example designed to collect text input to a maximum of 20 characters:

```
<INPUT TYPE="TEXT" NAME="User_Name" SIZE=20>
```

This tag creates a text field 20 characters wide and stores the information that a user enters in the variable called User_Name.

Netscape Extensions and HTML

The makers of Web browsers are constantly pushing for more and better HTML elements and in many ways seem to be trying to turn HTML into the page-definition language that it was never intended to be. As HTML grows and changes, as it surely must, you will find that you have even more choices about how to structure your Web documents.

Netscape extensions to HTML add graphical backgrounds, different colors on links, and extensions to other elements that control border widths and spacing specifications.

You can use tables to line up items on an HTML page. A TABLE element allows you to create tables containing rows and columns, headers, and data. These data cells can extend across several columns or rows and can contain graphics, forms, or other tables. The Microsoft Internet Explorer browser supports tables.

Frames are an extension to tables that let you divide a Web page into regions that can remain static (containing titles, headings, or buttons) and regions that can be updated simultaneously (containing content). Each frame can be an independently scrollable region on a single Web page with its own distinct URL.

The Netscape extensions are often considered the same as the HTML 3 standard, but that is not quite true. There are indeed large areas of overlap, but there are still major differences. You may well see a short note like this on some Web sites:

```
This Web site uses the Netscape extensions and is best viewed
using a Netscape-compatible browser.
```

You just hope that the creators of this site know how horrible their content looks when it is viewed with a non-Netscape compatible browser.

Any standardized additions to HTML in the future will be backward compatible with current existing standards; too many documents would stop working if this were not done. Future extensions to HTML may allow browsers to display complex mathematic symbols and add document-management features such as style sheets.

Web browsers are currently changing so fast that they give you the feeling of the *browser du jour*. Upgrades are appearing at the rate of four or more a year from each vendor; any organization of substantial size must be prepared to do some major planning just to keep up with it all. All this version trauma can lead to some large and unexpected support costs, but the way to cope seems to be to recognize that the rate of change is not going to slow any time soon. Plan your strategy accordingly.

HTML Tools

As more people work to create Web pages, the software companies are offering better and better tools to help in this process. To create an HTML page in times past, you wrote the content, added the HTML tags using a text processor, and then used your favorite browser to look at the results. This was not only tedious and time consuming, but it is quite possible to make a mistake in HTML that prevents the document from displaying in the browser.

FrontPage and Other HTML Editors

HTML editors make the creation of Web pages much simpler, and you can get add-on products for most word processors, including Microsoft Word, that make Web page production a breeze. You can download the Microsoft Word add-on called the Internet Assistant free from Microsoft's own Web site.

Microsoft also offers a complete Web authoring product called FrontPage (originally developed by Vermeer Technologies, Inc) that eases the process of creating HTML code, supports GIF and JPEG file types, offers GIF file editing, and has hot keys for common HTML tags, easy-to-use templates, and many other features designed to make structuring Web page content easier. (See the *Creating Your Web Site with FrontPage* chapter.) Creating imagemaps and links is straightforward, and the Link, Outline, and Summary views make content management easy. FrontPage also includes Bots which make it very easy to create custom applications for your Web server. These Bots are preprogrammed CGI scripts that let the Webmaster set up discussion groups, forms, search engines, or other services on your Web server. For more information, see "Managing Your Web Site with FrontPage Explorer" in the *Managing Your Web Site* chapter.

HTML Syntax Checkers

Many HTML errors are subtle and occur when two tags overlap in a way that makes no sense, or an error may occur because you forgot to terminate a tag properly. The result is a page that does not display as you expected or that perhaps does not display at all.

When you write HTML from scratch, it can be especially prone to these complex errors, and the currently available syntax checkers can both catch errors and advise against using poor HTML technique in much the same way as the program language syntax checkers based on the Unix `lint` utility work on programs written in the C language.

Format Converters

An alternative to creating your HTML files from scratch is to use a word processor to do the job for you and then convert the file into a simple text file with the appropriate HTML tags inserted where they are needed. Yahoo is a major source of information on converters at:

```
http://www.yahoo.com/Computers/World_Wide_Web/HTML_Converters
```

Working with Imagemaps and Multimedia

Graphical images and icons go a long way toward adding sizzle to your Web site, and imagemaps, in which different portions of a single large graphic are linked to different documents, are growing ever more popular. For example, on a medical site, a visitor might choose different portions of the human anatomy to see information on diseases, or on a commercial site, a visitor might choose one region from a map of the whole country to see where the local dealers or distributors are located. Special software helps make the creation of imagemaps quite straightforward.

The imagemap is referenced by a map file that contains definitions of the various areas on the image; these areas can be defined as rectangles, circles, or polygons. Once a visitor selects a particular area of the image, the server software checks this map file to determine which area was chosen.

Once that is known, the browser can load the appropriate linked document and display it. It does so by using the `ISMAP` attribute in the <IMG> tag. The HTML that activates the file mypic.gif as an imagemap might look something like this:

```
<A HREF="http://mysite.com/imagemap/mymap.map">
<IMG SRC="http://mysite.com/mypic.gif" ALT=""ISMAP"></A>
```

The mymap.map file contains the coordinate map, and the mypic.gif file is the imagemap graphic. The ALT attribute is used here to specify text as an alternative to the graphic for those working with graphics turned off or with text-based browsers.

The technical basis for much of the multimedia use on the Web is based on MIME (Multipurpose Internet Mail Extensions), a standard that encompasses non-ASCII character sets, images, sounds, movies and animation, binary files, PostScript files, and many other file formats. Depending on the filename extension of the document, your browser will interpret and display the contents of the file if it can, or it will invoke a helper application to do the job if the browser can't do it alone. For more information, see "Configuring Mime Tyes" in the *Managing Your Web Site* chapter.

Gateway Programming with CGI and ISAPI

So far we have looked at how to publish mostly static information on a Web site, but how do you create truly interactive applications for the Web? Fortunately, here are several answers to that question. You can write scripts, or external programs, using almost any 32-bit programming language such as Perl (more on Perl in a moment), or the C or C++ programming languages, or even REXX or Visual Basic; you can also use NT batch files, although I would not recommend that you do. You just have to make sure that you use one of the two standard server interfaces:

- CGI (Common Gateway Interface) is the traditional definition of how server and browser interact. Despite what you might hear,

CGI is not a programming language, but a definition of how server and browser communicate. A CGI script is simply a script that conforms to this CGI standard.

- ISAPI (Internet Server API). This is a new Microsoft API (application programming interface) released with IIS; for information on the details of how to use this interface, see Microsoft's Web site, contact the Microsoft Developer Network (MSDN), or see the BackOffice Software Development Kit (SDK). Look for details on how to access the BackOffice series of products from Microsoft using this programming interface. Applications that use ISAPI are compiled as DLLs (dynamic link libraries) and are loaded by the IIS service at startup. Because they are compiled and are memory resident, programs using ISAPI can appear to run faster than interpreted programs using CGI. You can create extremely complex ISAPI programs to perform any task that it is possible to program.

The term *script* originates in the Unix world, where it describes programs written in and interpreted by one of the Unix shells. Scripts are external programs that the Web server runs in response to a request from the browser. When a visitor requests a URL that points to a script, the server executes it, and any output that the script creates is sent back to the browser for display. Figure 6.4 shows the basic information flow.

FIGURE 6.4:

Information flow through the CGI or ISAPI interfaces

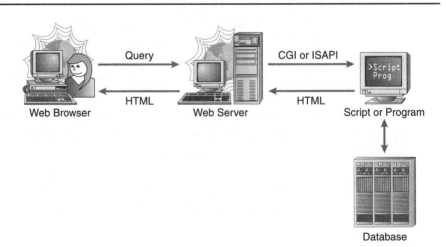

You can use a script for tasks as varied as creating an interface to a relational database system or creating your own search engine, and anything in between; there are really no limits. CGI also allows the server to create new documents on the fly, that is, at the moment the browser requests them.

The truly major benefit of using CGI is that any CGI-compliant script will run on any CGI-compliant Web server, including IIS, and that simple fact can save you a whole lot of time. There is a very good chance that someone somewhere has already solved a problem similar to yours and created a CGI script to do it. He or she may well have posted the solution on one of the many Web sites that carry lots of CGI scripts. Start your search at one of these sites:

```
http://wsk.eit.com/wsk/dist/doc/libcgi/libcgi.html
http://www.boutell.com/cgic/
```

You should always bear in mind that much of the early work with CGI scripts was done in a Unix environment; some of the scripts might work on Windows NT, others almost certainly won't. Always check first before you run anything on your own system. A disadvantage of using CGI is that scripts can be inefficient and can slow server performance in some cases.

The newer generation of Web servers, such as IIS, promise to increase the flexibility and add new functions to the server side by using APIs such as ISAPI. Using this sort of approach over the conventional CGI approach has several advantages, including:

- APIs can be more efficient in their use of memory, because initialization occurs only once.

- APIs let a server application stay connected to the Web browser without losing important information. In CGI scripting, the browser disconnects from the server after each request and has no memory of any previous transactions between browser and server.

- APIs let you plug in custom applications such as user authentication routines or database logging applications.

And the major disadvantage to using an API is that it is bound to a specific server or group of servers; whereas CGI scripts are, in theory at least, portable to any environment.

The ISAPI is currently available for Microsoft's IIS and Process Software's Purveyor WebServer on the Windows NT Server, Open-VMS, and NetWare platforms. To help convince software developers that ISAPI is the way to go, Microsoft plans to provide a simple wrapper for ISAPI applications that will make them CGI-compliant. That way, software developers can have their cake and eat it too.

Undoubtedly, the increasing use of ISAPI will lead to the addition of new functions to IIS as third-party software developers create new applications to improve performance and add security and logging functions currently not available.

Programming with Perl

Perl, an acronym formed from either Practical Extraction and Reporting Language or Pathologically Eclectic Rubbish Lister, depending on your bias, is an interpreted language created by Larry Ward and is used in the Unix world to manipulate text, files, and processes and to print reports based on extracted information.

Perl looks something like the C programming language, but it also includes text-manipulation features originally found in the Unix utilities awk and sed. Perl's strengths—powerful text-manipulation capabilities—are exactly what CGI programmers need, and so Perl has become very popular indeed.

You will find two popular versions of Perl commonly available, Perl 4 and Perl 5. Perl 4 is a straightforward implementation of Perl, and Perl 5 adds object-oriented extensions and allows classes and inheritance. You can embed Perl 5 code in a C or C++ application, and you can embed C or C++ code in a Perl 5 application.

You can get Perl 4 for Windows NT from:

`ftp://ftp.intergraph.com/pub/win32/perl/`

Look for the file `ntperlb.zip` if you want only the compiled version; look for the file `ntperls.zip` if you want the source code.

You can get Perl 5 for Windows NT from:

`ftp://ntperl.hip.com/ntperl/`

You will find source code, binary executables, and documentation on this site.

Several quite large libraries of Perl CGI scripts are available on the Web. For Perl 4, try:

`http://www.bio.cam.ac.uk/web/form.html`

and for Perl 5, try:

`http://wwwgenome.wi.mit.edu/ftp/pub/software/WWW/cgi_docs.html`

Hip Inc, the independent software vendor that developed Perl for Win32 platforms, is developing a version of Perl that runs as an ISAPI. This means that Perl server scripts run much faster than before by taking advantage of ISAPI's in-process model.

An unsupported prerelease of ISAPI Perl is available from:

`http://www.perl.hip.com/ntperl/`

and you can use the e-mail address:

`perlis@mail.hip.com`

to ask questions and to send feedback.

Tips for Optimizing Web Site Performance

The best-looking Web site in the world is completely useless if it takes too long to load and people bale out before loading completes. People have a relatively short attention span and want to see something happen 10 seconds or so after selecting a link; if they are really interested in what they think you have to offer, they might wait for 30 seconds, but certainly they will not wait any longer.

The best way to understand how your pages behave is to test them from a remote location using a link of the same type that you expect most of your visitors will use. Use the same browser that you expect them to use too, or, even better, use several browsers and get a much broader picture.

The main idea behind performance optimization is to keep everything as small and as simple as possible; simply put, the larger the page, the longer it takes to download to a browser. Text-heavy screens download quickly, but as you add graphics, or even worse, an imagemap, things slow down in a hurry.

When designing pages, you have to balance the benefits of displaying that large graphic of the company logo against the possibility that a portion (perhaps a significant portion) of your visitors will never see it, because they will abort downloading before the graphic ever arrives at their computer.

Keep graphics small, and use simple images with bold areas of just a few colors rather than complex scanned photographs. Try to limit the number of graphics to between three and five on each page, as their effect on download time is accumulative. Some browsers cache inline images; so reusing an image can make your pages appear to load faster.

An image in JPEG format tends to be smaller than the same image in GIF format; so if you are using a group of thumbnail images, consider using JPEG format for your inline images. On the other hand, you can display GIF images using the interlaced option, in which the image is built up over successive passes. This at least gives the visitor the impression that something is actually happening.

And keep an eye on overall Web server performance; listen to users' complaints about how the system seems to be slower than it was and that response is poor. These are all signs that your site is a success and is attracting visitors in large numbers; it is also a sign that you should start thinking about upgrading your system in the near future. A couple of short-term measures might help: reducing the number and size of inline graphics, and turning off Internet Information Server features that you don't need or use. But sooner or later the time will come when you will have to look at both system hardware and the bandwidth and expandability of your network and communications circuits. Be ready with a plan in place to allow a smooth transition to a more powerful system.

Notes for International Sites

The World Wide Web really is a global phenomenon. You can connect to it using a modem, a local area network, or a wide area network. You can run your browser on almost any hardware and operating system combination you can think of. Did you know that there is even a Web browser for the Apple Newton?

Although most current users of the Web seem to be in the United States and in Canada, other parts of the world are catching up rapidly, particularly Eastern Europe, South America, and Asia. As in the rest of the computer industry, English is the language spoken most often on the Web, although English will be the second (or third) language for many Web users.

Because many Web users are not native readers and speakers of English, you may have to modify your Web pages for a truly international audience. Language is only part of the problem; the other component is culture. The first thing to decide is whether you want your site to be easily accessible by a truly global audience or by an audience of people with English as their first (and often only) language. If you want to target a global audience, you may have to think about translating your Web pages.

Translating Web Pages

Translation is often necessary, but it can also be expensive and add considerably to your overhead. Here are some issues to mull over as you decide whether to translate:

- How often will the content on your Web site change? This will give you an indication of how often you will need to translate material.

- What proportion of your visitors do not read English, and which language or languages do they read?

- How expensive is the translation process, and can you find qualified, conveniently located translators who are familiar with the technical aspects of the content on your Web pages? We are all familiar with those phrase-book translations that turn a simple phrase into the Latvian equivalent of "Please help. The hair on my grandfather's chest is caught in the lawnmower."

- Can you avoid the need for translation by clever use of graphics or by some other organizational changes?

- Are Web browsers available in the target language? The answer to this question is almost certain to be yes.

Text originally written in English has an interesting habit of growing by 20 or 30 percent when it is translated into one of the other common worldwide languages such as Spanish or Portuguese. This means that you may have to redesign your Web pages after the translation is complete; since this seriously compounds your configuration management and system update problems, proceed with caution.

Making Web Pages Universal

If you decide not to translate your Web pages into a language other than English, you can do several simple things do to make your content less ambiguous to a worldwide audience. Here are some suggestions:

- In date formats, spell out the name of the month, as in 5th October 1997. Because different cultures swap the day and the month around, a date written as 10-05-97 is interpreted as the 5th of October 1997 in some places, but as the 10th of May 1997 in others.

- In telephone numbers, add the country code and the area code so that overseas visitors can call quickly and easily. Because 800 numbers are often limited in scope and range, always provide a toll number that everyone can use to contact you.

- In time formats, remember that most of Europe and Asia uses a 24-hour clock, rather than dividing the day into AM and PM.

- In units of measure, remember that much of the world uses the metric system; to be truly international, you should provide both imperial and metric measures.

- When you create a form on which a visitor will enter an address, be sure that the form always has a box for the country, and remember that postal formats differ from country to country.

- When you include a list of your overseas offices or distributors on your Web page, be sure to include addresses and telephone numbers. Many times, language-barrier problems simply disappear if someone can talk to a company representative using his or her original language.

Finally, check your Web pages for specifically local content that might confuse people unfamiliar with your country, particularly in the United States. Examples include references to the IRS, which in the United States refers to the Internal Revenue Service; in Great Britain the same function is performed by the IR (Inland Revenue). International confusion will also arise over the use of CDC, FCC, and SEC.

Avoiding the Most Common Mistakes

In an earlier section of this chapter, we looked at some of the tricks you can use to optimize the performance of your Web pages. In this final section, we'll look at the other side of that same coin and list some of the most common mistakes made on Web sites so that you will be able to avoid making them on yours.

Avoid Giant Graphics

By far *the* most common mistake on many major sites is the use of a giant graphic or imagemap on the first page. You may like that picture of a sunset, or your chairman may want the company logo to be BIG, but think of your poor visitors. And then think again of those visitors with a 14.4Kbps modem and a VGA monitor who have to sit still and wait for several minutes while that giant logo downloads to their system. What is it going to tell them that they didn't know before? Absolutely nothing; so don't do it.

You can use some of the editing features found in many image-manipulation programs such as Photoshop to reduce the size of the graphic and also to reduce the number of colors. Both these changes will help to reduce transmission time from the server to the Web browser, but will not affect the final displayed image quality.

If your site is solely concerned with big images, perhaps a stock photography site, display a thumbnail of the photograph in the document so that a visitor can identify the image. Post a text warning about the size of the image file and the download time to be expected over communications circuits of various kinds and speeds.

Focus your use of graphics where they will add the most value; use them as a masthead or as a corporate logo. And never rely on graphics alone to get your message across. Any important information—such as messages, menu choices, and titles—should also appear somewhere in the text.

Don't Be Too Wordy

And of course it is possible to go too far the other way and end up with a page covered in dense, hard-to-read text. A Web page is not a book, and visitors' expectations are colored more by video games and what they see on TV than by the printed page. Look at the content in detail, and turn some of it into a table. Add some graphical elements and move some of that text onto a second page.

Provide Navigational Aids

In the recent past, visitors always accessed a Web site by starting at the top of the structure of your home page. That is no longer the case, as more and more people use search engines to navigate the Web. They can search on a keyword, and then, using a dynamic link, they can access your site at the page that contains the keyword, perhaps somewhere near the middle of your structure. They can find themselves on a page that they have never seen before, with no idea of what lies on adjacent pages and with no idea of how they got there.

Add navigational icons to your pages to give these visitors a clue about how they can navigate your site and see the content on the other pages on your Web site. If you are using special terms or icons, be sure to make them self-explanatory, and as a minimum provide buttons to move up, down, to the next and previous relevant topics, and to your site's home page.

Remember the World Wide Part of the World Wide Web

It is not called the World Wide Web for nothing; just remember that what you publish can be accessed by millions of people in well over one hundred countries spread all over the world. That two-fingered gesture, indicating victory to people living in the United States, will be considered obscene by people in England and Australia. Similarly, the gesture of a circle made with thumb and forefinger indicating that a thing is very good means something very different to a South American, and in Japan it is a reference to money.

Try to avoid colloquialisms and sports jargon; expressions such as "the whole nine yards" or "It's the bottom of the 9th, the bases are loaded, and you're up next" don't mean a thing outside a very restricted circle of visitors. Even people who speak and read English quite well will take down the dictionary and try to analyze phrases such as these one word at a time, and of course they will end up with nonsense and a deepening sense of frustration.

Don't Do It Just Because You Can

The World Wide Web is a very creative place, and some Web creation tools are very exciting, but you should never put the use of a neat feature before your user's need for information. That is why your Web site is out there and why you have a job, after all. Resist the temptation.

Don't automatically assume that all your visitors will be using the latest, all-singing, all-dancing Web browsers, because they won't. Visitors in the United States will have the most up to date software; users in other countries can be as much as a year or 18 months behind.

And just because the latest proposed addition to the HTML standard says that you can use a tag that lets the screen violently pulsate, you don't have to use it on every page or even at all.

Use Only Valid HTML

It may be very tempting to use the latest and greatest HTML extension proposed by a browser manufacturer, but remember your audience and the level of support that the extension has in the other browsers that people are likely to use.

Some of these new elements may create fabulous effects on your browser; their appearance may vary wildly on other browsers, and some will just ignore the tags in your carefully crafted page and line everything up on the left margin. And that leads us neatly to the next topic, testing.

Test and Test Again

You should test your Web site, accessing each page in turn, using several of the most popular browsers, to make absolutely certain that you are getting the effect that you want. Different browsers behave in subtly different ways; what is bold text in one browser will be displayed in a slightly different way in another.

Test your content pages offline at first, to squeeze out the largest and most obvious errors and to make sure that everything displays as you expect and that all the internal links operate as you anticipate.

Then place the file on your server as a part of your Web site structure and test again using several of the most popular browsers.

You should also test your site at a variety of times during the day and night so that you can see what happens as the network traffic changes. Also access your site using different communications links, if that is possible, to gauge the differences that speed and bandwidth produce.

Keep Your Content Up to Date

Work hard to keep the content of your Web site current and topical. How old is the date in the signature at the bottom of the first page? Three months? Six months? Longer?

Check any links you have included to other sites from time to time, because sites come and go, and nothing frustrates visitors more than finding an expired link that looks promising but that leads nowhere.

Don't provide links to sites that are still under construction either; nothing is more frustrating that waiting for the page to load and then finding that the site doesn't actually contain anything useful.

Don't Try Too Hard

You can use your Web site to advertise your goods and services, but you should show some restraint and not blow your own trumpet too much. The idea of the site is to inform, and perhaps to entertain, your visitors, but a full-blown sales pitch is not likely to entice them back for a second visit. Give them a reason to want to make that second visit.

Don't Open Before You're Ready

Avoid announcing your Web site before it is finished, and by finished, I mean completely finished. Designed, coded, tested, tested, and tested again. Construction site signs are a complete waste of time and can be very annoying for the casual visitor. After visitors have wasted their time waiting for the site-under-construction graphic to download to their browser, they will never visit your site again, no matter how good it is.

Use Files of the Right Size

When you create a paper document, it usually consists of a single file and is distributed as a stack of paper. On the Web, divide your material into right-sized chunks and put each chunk into its own file. You can then add the links to reference appropriate material later.

Some visitors will certainly want to print some of your documents and will get very frustrated very quickly if you have divided a major topic into a whole fleet of tiny files that they have to locate and then access one by one. You will have to decide on an individual basis what makes most sense for each of your Web pages.

Creating Your Web Site with FrontPage

- Introduction to the components of FrontPage

- Creating new Web pages in the FrontPage Editor

- Editing Web pages in the Editor

- Adding structure to Web pages with lines, headings, and lists

- Setting the format properties of characters and pages

- Creating links and bookmarks

- Inserting images into your Web pages

- Creating clickable hotspot links in images

- Automating your pages with WebBots

- Using tables, forms, and frames

Once you have planned and designed your Web site, as discussed in the last two chapters, you are ready to get to work constructing it. The good news is that you already have a set of first-rate Web publishing tools in Windows NT 4—Microsoft FrontPage.

Introducing FrontPage

FrontPage consists of 4 components that together make a comprehensive Web publishing package: (1) the Personal Web Server, (2) the Explorer, (3) the Editor, and (4) the To Do List. With these components, you can create and maintain a Web site, build and edit new Web pages, and manage the links in your pages.

In this section, you will be introduced to these 4 parts of FrontPage. The rest of the chapter will concentrate on the component you will probably use the most—the FrontPage Editor. Later, in the *Managing Your Web Site* chapter, you will learn more about using the FrontPage Explorer for site-management and administration tasks.

The Personal Web Server

You use the FrontPage Personal Web Server (let's call it PWS for now) to build and test your Web site locally on a single PC, without having to access the server that will ultimately host your Web site. Thus, you are free to work on your Web site from a laptop computer, for example, seated comfortably in a beach chair miles from any telephone lines.

The PWS works hand in hand with the other components in FrontPage. For example, it lets the FrontPage Explorer access any of the Web sites that are located under the PWS, and it provides password security.

With the PWS acting as the server, you can use a Web browser to test your Web site on your local PC. The PWS will check a user's access authorization, fetch requested pages, and respond to FrontPage WebBots when they are activated (WebBots are automated services similar to CGI scripts and are discussed later in this chapter).

You don't have to use the PWS when you edit pages in the FrontPage Editor. But to take advantage of all that the FrontPage package has to offer, you will generally open the PWS, Explorer, and Editor so that they can all work in concert.

The FrontPage Server Extensions

FrontPage can work hand in hand with Windows NT 4 Server and the IIS so that you can, for example, do the following:

- Automate common Web page and Web site chores with FrontPage WebBots, which are discussed later in this chapter

- Enable Web-site security for browsers and authors

- Copy an entire Web site and all its FrontPage facilities from one FrontPage-aware server to another

- Import a Web site into the FrontPage environment from a non-FrontPage–aware server

FrontPage comes with versions of the Server Extensions for several servers, and you can find more versions on Microsoft's Web site where they are available free of charge:

```
http://www.microsoft.com/frontpage/freestuff/
fs_fp_extensions.htm
```

You will also find there an updated list of operating systems and Web servers for which the FrontPage Server Extensions are available.

If your server cannot support the FrontPage Server Extensions, keep the following in mind:

- FrontPage uses the naming convention `index.htm` for the home page in a Web site; you may need to configure your server to match this convention.

- You can still include many of the WebBots in your Web pages, but you should avoid those that require server interaction. These include the WebBots named Confirmation Field, Discussion, Registration, Save Results, and Search.

- Create client-side clickable imagemaps, not server-side ones, as discussed later in this chapter.

- When you copy a Web site you've created in FrontPage to the server where it will reside, do not include any folders whose names begin with `_vti_`. These are FrontPage-related and are not needed when a server does not have the FrontPage Server Extensions.

To use the FrontPage extensions, you must first install IIS and FrontPage, and you must be logged on to Windows NT Server as an administrator during the installation and usage of the FrontPage Server Extensions.

The FrontPage Explorer

The tool for creating, managing, and maintaining a Web site is the FrontPage Explorer. It works in conjunction with either the Front-Page Personal Web Server or the Web server you will ultimately be using, such as Windows NT 4 with the IIS.

You can open any Web site to which you are allowed access on any of the servers available to the Explorer. You work on only one Web site at a time, which is called the *current* or *active Web site*. Figure 7.1 shows the FrontPage Explorer with an active Web site.

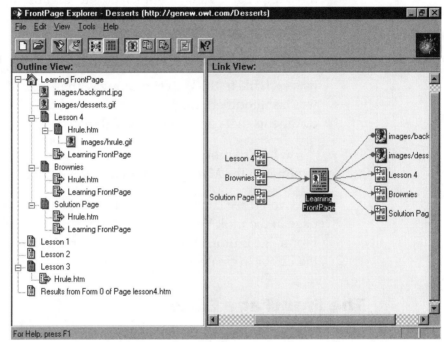

The left side of the Explorer is the Outline View. It lists all the pages and other files that are part of the current Web site. It uses either their HTML page title or, in the case of graphic files, their filenames. The pages and other files are arranged in a hierarchical manner, based on the links each page contains. A Web site has only one home page, which, by definition, is named `index.htm`. That page always appears at the top of the list in the Outline View. Figure 7.1 shows this file as Learning Front Page, which is its title.

You can manipulate the outline in the usual manner—click on the plus sign to expand a level of the outline to show more detail, or click on the minus sign to hide the detail.

The right side of the Explorer in Figure 7.1 is the Link View. Here you see a graphical representation of the Web site, with lines connecting a Web page to any other pages to which it links. This is a most important view of your Web site, because normally the relationships among the pages and files are pretty much hidden from casual observation—you have to dig to find out what links to what.

You can also display a Summary View instead of the Link View. It lists each file in the Web site, along with its size, the date and time it was last modified, the person who modified it, its URL, and any comments that have been attached to it.

You'll learn more about creating and managing a Web with the Explorer in the *Managing Your Web Site* chapter.

As you'll see later in this chapter, you can simply double-click on a page in the Link View window to open that page for editing in the FrontPage Editor. Or you can drag a page's icon into a document in the Editor to create a link to that page.

The FrontPage Editor

As you read in earlier chapters, HTML (Hypertext Markup Language) is a set of textual tags with which you define the structure of a Web page. When someone views that page with a Web browser, the browser displays the contents of the page in accordance with the HTML tags you used.

Creating simple HTML Web pages with any text editor is relatively easy, but as a page grows in size and complexity, you'd have to be a devoted HTML cruncher to succeed. The FrontPage solution for creating Web pages is the FrontPage Editor.

The Editor is essentially an easy-to-use WYSIWYG word processor that has two important virtues:

- It is designed to work specifically with HTML pages and offers you just about all the page-layout options that are available in the most recent version of HTML (plus some features from the next proposed version).

- When you create a page in the Editor, you are assured that the HTML tags in that page will be compliant with the HTML standard and can therefore be viewed by any Web browser (assuming the browser supports the version of the HTML tags you included in the page).

Figure 7.2 shows the Editor containing a Web page. The Editor has many of the tools and features you have come to expect in a Windows word processor, such as a menu bar, toolbars, and a status bar at the bottom of the window. You can open multiple documents in the Editor and copy and paste data among them in all the usual ways.

FIGURE 7.2:

The FrontPage Editor is essentially a Windows word processor for editing HTML files.

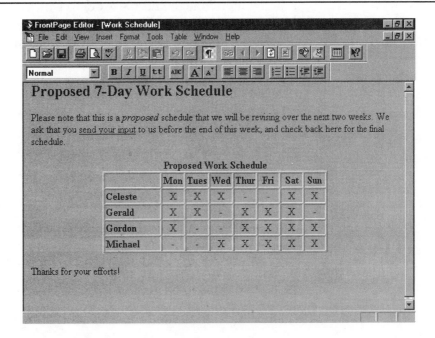

The FrontPage To Do List

Creating and maintaining a Web site is no small feat, at least not if you want to do the job well. You will need to attend to countless Web-related tasks, large and small. To help you track these tasks, FrontPage offers the To Do List, which is shown in Figure 7.3.

FIGURE 7.3:

The FrontPage To Do List helps you manage Web-related tasks.

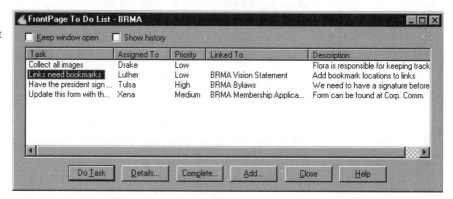

When you invoke the Edit ➤ Add To Do Task command in either the Explorer or the Editor, the task you create is automatically linked to the page or file that was active in the Editor or selected in the Explorer.

Anyone working on the Web site can create a new task in the list and include the following items:

- **Task.** The name you want to call the task

- **Assigned To.** The person responsible for completing the task

- **Priority.** The order of the task's importance: Low, Medium, or High

- **Linked To.** The page or file to which this task applies

- **Description.** Your comments about the task

You can sort the items in the To Do List by clicking on a column-title button at the top of any of the columns.

When you select a linked task in the To Do List and click on the Do Task button, the page or file to which the task is linked opens, ready for you to complete the task.

When you actually finish the task in question, you can mark it as completed by selecting the task in the To Do List and clicking on the Complete button. You can also choose to delete a completed task from the list or to retain the task as history.

Editing Documents in the FrontPage Editor

In this section and the ones that follow it, you'll read about many of the HTML constructs you can create in the FrontPage Editor. You'll see that you don't have to be an HTML expert to create well-designed Web pages that any standard Web browser can view. You need not be deeply intimate with the HTML tags that are used to create headings, bulleted lists, emphasized text, tables, forms, and on and on.

Remember that to take full advantage of FrontPage, you should use the Editor in concert with the Explorer and a FrontPage-aware server, such as IIS. And when you're ready to end your Web-working session, exit the Editor before you exit the Explorer. When you do so, the Explorer can track any changes you made to pages in the Editor.

Creating a New Page

You can create a new Web page in the Editor by starting with a new blank page—simply click on the New button on the toolbar. But when you use the Editor's File ➤ New command, you can create a new page based on a FrontPage template or a Wizard. Figure 7.4 shows the New Page dialog box.

FIGURE 7.4:

You use the New Page dialog box to create a new page from a template or with the help of a Wizard.

A template is simply a ready-made page that you can use as a starting point. For example, FrontPage has Employee Directory, Feedback Form, and Press Release templates. The first template in the New Page dialog box, called Normal Page, simply creates a new blank page, as though you had clicked on the New button on the toolbar.

A Wizard helps you create a new page by asking you a series of questions about the content or layout of the page. It then builds the page based on your responses, and you can get to work on the result.

For example, when you choose the Frames Wizard, you are asked about the number of frames you want on the page, their size and position, and the Web pages that you want to fill each frame. In this case, you never even see the frame page—the Wizard creates it for you and then saves it. When a browser later retrieves that page, the frames are filled with the pages you specified. Using Wizards simplifies what can otherwise be a complicated bit of HTML coding.

Opening an Existing Page

When you have a Web site open in the FrontPage Explorer, you can use the Editor's File ➤ Open from Web command to open a page from that Web site. A Web page is listed both by its URL and its page title, which greatly simplifies the process.

You can instead use the File ➤ Open command, which lets you open files outside the current Web site. You can open HTML files, Rich Text Format (RTF) files, or plain text files. For example, you might save a document from your word processor in the RTF format and then open it in the Editor.

Finally, you can open a file by specifying its URL if you use the File ➤ Open Location command.

Saving a Web Page

You save your work in the Editor as you do in most other programs—on a regular and timely basis! You can save a page in 3 ways:

- For a new, as yet unnamed page, you are prompted to enter its page title and URL. This is an easy way to save the page into the current Web site.

- You can choose instead to save the page as a file in a location outside the current Web.

- If you want to use the page as a starting point for more Web pages in the future, save the page as a template. You are prompted to enter a name, a title, and a description for it, which will be added to the list in the New Page dialog box.

When you save an existing page back to disk, it is saved in its original location and with its original name.

Just Pretend You're Using a Word Processor

When you're working in a page in the Editor, you can pretty much go about your job as though you were creating a document in a Windows word processor.

Figure 7.5 shows a Web page from the FrontPage tutorial. Doesn't it look like something you could dash out in a word processor in no time? In fact, that's how long it takes to create this page in FrontPage—no time at all.

You perform many operations just as you would in a word processor:

- You simply type text, pressing Enter only at the end of a paragraph (the HTML code is <P>) or using the Insert ➤ Line Break command (or press Shift+↵) to break a line without creating a new paragraph (the code is <BR>).

- You can select text or graphic images in the usual ways, with the mouse or keyboard.

- You can invoke a command to act on the selected data (either from the menu bar or by right-clicking on the items in question), such as to make text bold (<STRONG>) or emphasized (<EM>) or to turn selected paragraphs into a bulleted list (<UL>).

- You can move, copy, and delete data in the usual ways.

- You can insert data from another file by using the Insert ➤ File command.

One big difference between the FrontPage Editor and a word processor, and it's an important one, is that the options the Editor offers you on its menus and toolbars are all HTML-related. In other words, everything you can do in the Editor will result in HTML tags that can any browser can view.

Using the FrontPage Editor is as simple as using a Windows word processor.

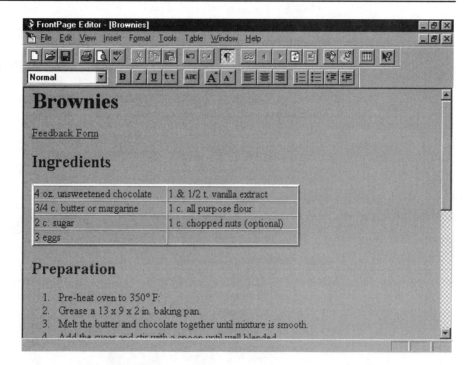

Well, that's the theory at least. The pace of the HTML standards race is so fast and furious that there is a leapfrog relationship between Web browsers and HTML editors. You will find that the latest release of any editor supports a few features that are not yet included in the HTML standard—and probably skips a few of them as well.

For example, the first version of Microsoft FrontPage supported frames but didn't support scrolling marquees. But Microsoft's Web browser of that day, the Internet Explorer 2.0, did *not* support frames but *did* support marquees! But version 3 of the Internet Explorer did handle frames, and presumably the next release of FrontPage will handle marquees, and things will be back in synch...at least for a while. Some of this feature confusion was produced by Microsoft buying FrontPage as a completed product from Vermeer Technologies while adding new features to the Explorer.

That's why I recommended earlier in this book (and quite sternly too) that you test your Web pages with several popular browsers. With that warning issued again, you can otherwise assume that any of the popular browsers can view what you create in the FrontPage Editor.

A great way to learn the ins and outs of HTML programming is the Editor's View ➤ HTML command. It opens a window that displays your page in its raw HTML code. Figure 7.6 shows the View HTML window with the code that underlies the page in Figure 7.5.

FIGURE 7.6:

The View HTML window shows you the HTML code that underlies your Web page.

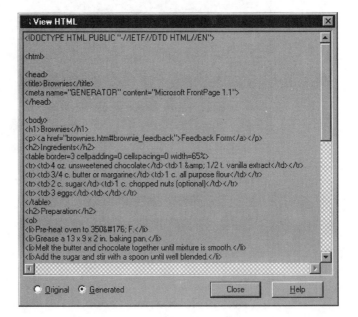

Other Tools in the Editor

Let's take a quick look at some of the editing tools you'll find for creating Web pages:

- Use the Insert ➤ Special Character command to create characters that don't reside on standard keyboards, such as $\frac{1}{2}$ or the copyright symbol, ©. FrontPage will automatically assign the correct HTML code for any nonstandard characters, such as ½ for $\frac{1}{2}$ and © for ©.

- Use the Tools ➤ Spelling command to check the spelling in your Web page.

- Use the Find or Replace commands on the Edit menu to find text within the current page or replace that text with other text. If you want to find or replace specific HTML tags within a page, such as <STRONG>, you can use a text editor such as Windows Notepad. Remember, the HTML file you create in the Editor is just plain text, like any other HTML file.

Printing Your Page

You can print your pages in the Editor just as you do in a word processor, although you will probably need to do so only rarely. After all, the whole point of an HTML Web page is that it can be viewed by anyone with a Web browser and a network connection to the file.

Before you print, you can use the File ➤ Page Setup command to set the page margins and specify a header and footer. And don't forget that you can use the File ➤ Print Preview command to see how your page will look when printed. It can save you a lot of time and timber.

Adding Structure to Pages

As I described in the last chapter, HTML was designed to allow an author to define the structure of a Web page that otherwise consists only of plain text. This allows any Web browser to read the page, interpret the structure, and display it accordingly.

The FrontPage Editor gives you easy access to the various structural elements of HTML. As always, it's up to you to use them in a clear and logical fashion.

Separating Data with a Horizontal Line

Perhaps the simplest way to affect the structure of a Web page is by inserting a horizontal line (<HR>, often referred to as a horizontal rule) that spans from one side of the page to the other. It's a simple but very effective way to delineate one section from another.

Your page might have a banner across the top with a horizontal line beneath it, separating the banner from a table of contents of links. Beneath that would be another line, followed by the main body of the page. At the bottom of the page you could have another line, and beneath it would be the important page identifiers, such as the page's URL, the date the page was last modified, a link back to a home page, and so on.

To modify the look of a horizontal line, right-click on the line and choose Properties to display the Horizontal Line Properties dialog box, which is shown in Figure 7.7.

FIGURE 7.7:

You can change the properties of a horizontal line by selecting options in the Horizontal Line Properties dialog box.

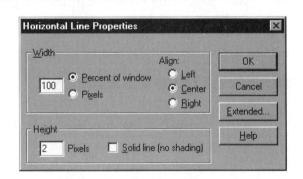

For example, if you set the Width option to 50 and choose Percent of Window, a browser displays the line at half the width of the browser's window.

Creating a Hierarchy with Headings

A common and effective way to add structure to a Web page is through the use of headings. Take a look at the table of contents of this book to see headings in action: A chapter is divided into several main headings, each of which may contain several subheadings, and those subheadings may contain yet other sub-subheadings. It's essentially the structure of an outline, only with lots of text and graphics in between the headings.

A Web page can have a maximum of 6 levels of headings, whose HTML codes are conveniently named <H1>, <H2>, <H3>, and so on. As with all HTML codes, there is no inherent style to the headings—various Web browsers might interpret the look of a heading differently. In general, a level 1 heading will be in a larger, bolder font than a lower-level heading. The way headings appear in the FrontPage Editor just happens to be the same way they look in Microsoft Internet Explorer. What a nice coincidence!

You are free to use the headings in any goofy order you prefer, but it makes very good sense to use them as you would in an outline. In the case of HTML, the level 1 heading is the first, or highest, level, and level 6 is the lowest, or most subordinate.

When you are going to structure a page with headings, the first heading you use should be the highest level, although it doesn't have to be level 1. You might start with level 2 because you know that most browsers display that heading in a smaller font than level 1. In this case, you would never use a level 1 heading since you began by establishing level 2 as the highest level.

Organizing Data within Lists

Another common structural tool is the list. Examples of bulleted lists and numbered lists can be found in this book, and both those styles are available in HTML pages in the Editor. In the world of HTML, the numbered list is often called an ordered list (<OL>), and a bulleted list is called an unordered list (<UL>).

To begin a list, you can click either on the Numbered List or Bulleted List button on the toolbar. Or choose a list with the Insert ➤ List command. For a numbered list, the Editor will insert a number at the left of the current line; it will insert a bullet for a bulleted list.

Simply type the text you want for this item in the list. The text is indented from the bullet or number and wraps to a new, indented line as needed. Press Enter to start a new item in the list. When you want to end the list, you can press Ctrl+⏎ once, press Enter twice, or click elsewhere on the page.

You can also place a list within a list; the subordinate list is indented farther to the right. You will also find the Directory and Menu lists on the Insert ➤ List menu, but you might want to avoid using them because not all browsers support them.

Formatting Pages

Using the FrontPage Editor, you can change the look of the characters on the page, as well as the page itself. The results of these types of enhancements are a bit more ephemeral than the structural changes that I just discussed.

This is because many formatting enhancements are either very new to HTML or are still to be adopted and are therefore not supported by all Web browsers. At the inception of HTML, the formatting of documents for appearances was avoided, in the hope of keeping the language as portable as possible. Instead of specifying boldfaced type in a page for example, there is an HTML tag called <STRONG>. The idea was to let the browser decide how to make text stand out.

Setting Character Properties

You can change the appearance of text on a page with the Format ➤ Characters command. The Character Styles dialog box offers several groups of enhancements, but only the group called Regular Styles offers standard HTML conventions. The others are all extensions to HTML (as of this writing), although they will most likely be included in the language in the near future.

- **Regular Styles.** These include styles such as bold <STRONG> and underline <U> and typewriter font <TT>, which a browser displays as a monospaced font.

- **Font Size.** You can change the font size of text by choosing one of 7 relative sizes <FONT SIZE=6>. Sizes 1 and 2 are smaller than the size called Normal, and the others are larger.

- **Set Color.** Choose a color for the text.

- **Vertical Position.** Choose Subscript or Superscript (Normal is the default), and specify the level to which you want to raise or lower the text. A higher number increases the distance above or below the baseline.

- **Special Styles.** The styles in this group are also nonstandard; so use them with caution. You will find that FrontPage may not display them as you expect, and many browsers may ignore them completely.

Finally, you should generally avoid using underlined text in your pages, since most Web browsers interpret underlined text as a hypertext link. It is a bit of a hurdle for a reader to have to look twice at a page to see if underlined text is actually a link.

Setting Page Properties

You can change a variety of properties for the Web page you're editing by choosing File ➤ Page Properties. Or right-click anywhere on the page and choose Page Properties.

The most important option in the Page Properties dialog box is the one named Title, which is where you change the title for the current page. As suggested in the previous chapter, you want to ensure that the title is informative for a reader who jumps directly to this page, such as via one of the Internet search engines, and bypasses your home page.

The group of options called Customize Appearance offer several ways to enhance the look of a Web page:

- **Get Background and Colors from Page.** If you specify a Web page for this option, all the page-color and background options in that page will be used in the current page. This is a great tool for applying the same style to multiple pages in a Web site.

- **Background Image.** If you're not using the background and colors from another page, you can choose a graphic file to serve as the background image for the current page. A browser tiles the image as necessary to fill the window.

- **Use Custom Background Color.** Choose a color to fill the background of the page. Be careful when you use this, because you may need to set the color of the text on the page as well. There's nothing like black letters on a dark purple background to make a reader decide it's time to jump to a new page.

- **Use Custom Text Color.** Choose a color for text on the page; most browsers otherwise display text in black.

- **Link Colors.** You can change the colors of hypertext links on the page with 3 options: regular links, links you've clicked on (visited), and the active link.

Remember that the character and page properties can make dazzling changes to your Web pages—for better or worse! It's always best to be conservative until your pages have been tested by others using a variety of browsers and who don't mind being honest with you.

Linking Pages to the World

At the heart of every Web page are the links you create to allow the reader to jump to a new page. A link might take the reader to a page on your Web site or to any site on the planet. You'll find that it's easy to create links in the FrontPage Editor. And the FrontPage Explorer has several tools that help track, modify, and validate the links on your Web pages.

Creating a Link

When you create a hypertext link, you select the text or image that will serve as the link in the Web page and then specify the target of the link, which is the page or other Web resource that will be accessed when the link is clicked on or activated.

You can create a link in the Editor in several ways, but the one you'll probably use most often is simply this: Select the text or image that will serve as the link, and then click on the Link button on the toolbar.

Doing so displays the Create Link dialog box. It contains 4 tabs in which you specify the target for the link:

- **Open Pages.** Choose one of the pages currently open in the Editor. You can also choose a bookmark in the selected page to serve as the target (bookmarks are discussed in the next section), or you can choose a frame (frames are discussed at the end of this chapter).

- **Current Web.** In this tab you can choose a target from the current Web site (the Web site that is open in the Explorer).

- **Word Wide Web.** Here you specify a target by its URL on the World Wide Web and the protocol required to access it. For example, you can choose HTTP for standard Web pages or MAILTO to allow a reader to send mail to the target address you specify.

- **New Page.** Enter a page title and a URL to create a new Web page in the Editor that will serve as the target for the link.

When you've specified the target for the link and clicked on the OK button, the text you selected in the Web page is now underlined and in the color blue (or the color you have specified for links in the Page Properties dialog box).

As you pass the mouse pointer over a link, the name of its target appears on the status bar. If a link points to a target in the current Web site, you can hold down the Ctrl key and click on the link to have the Editor open the target page for editing.

Creating a Bookmark

A bookmark is simply a named location within a page to which you can create a link. For example, you can create a table of contents at the top of a page that contains links to various locations (bookmarks) within the page. When a reader clicks on one of those links, the target bookmark location is displayed immediately in the Web browser.

Before you can create a link to a bookmark, you must first define the bookmark. To do so, select text or an image, choose Edit ➤ Bookmark, enter a name for the bookmark, and click on the OK button. Now you can create a link to that bookmark as described in the previous section.

You can also jump to a bookmark in the current Web page by choosing Edit ➤ Bookmark, selecting the name of the bookmark from the list, and clicking on the Goto button.

Modifying a Link

To change the target of a link, click on the text or image that forms the link and then click on the Link button on the toolbar. FrontPage displays the Edit Link dialog box, in which you can modify the target of the link. To change the underlined text that serves as the link, simply edit the text in the usual way.

Letting FrontPage Track Your Links

One of *the* most frustrating aspects of building a Web site is trying to track all the links your pages contain. For example, you might decide to move a page to a new folder on the Web. That's simple enough, but then you must find all the other pages in the Web that contain links to the moved page and then edit the links to reflect the new address of the target page.

That's a lot of work that could create ongoing chaos in the design and maintenance of your Web site. Fortunately, FrontPage Explorer comes to the rescue.

Fixing Links Automatically

If you look back at the Explorer in Figure 7.1, you can see how it presents your Web site in a maplike view. A link in a page is represented by an arrow drawn from that page to the target. With just a glance, you can see which pages contain links and the resources to which they link.

If you want to rename or move a Web page or other resource in the current Web site, you can do so in the Explorer, and Explorer will automatically update all links to that resource.

Simply click on the icon of the resource whose URL you want to change, choose Edit ➤ Properties (or right-click on the icon and choose Properties), and enter the new name in the field labeled Page URL. When you click on OK or Apply, the Explorer updates every link to this resource in all the other pages in the current Web.

If you specify a folder in the new URL that does not yet exist, the Explorer will create that folder within the Web site.

Verifying Links

Your Web site might have many internal links that refer to resources within the current Web site, and it might have many external links that refer to resources outside the current Web site. You can use the Explorer's Verify Links command on the Edit menu to check each link to see if it is still valid.

If an internal link is found to be broken (the target cannot be found), you can choose to edit the link and let the Explorer update all links to the new target URL you specify.

You can also choose to have the Explorer verify all the external links in the Web site, although this could take a long time if there are many of them.

Displaying Images in Pages

You can really make your Web sites sparkle when you include photographs, drawings, icons, logos, and other graphical inline images within your Web pages.

But don't forget the message that was emphasized in the previous chapter: If you include too many images in your Web pages, you can make the pages crowded, confusing, and very slow to transmit across the Internet.

Inserting an Image

To place a graphical image in one of your Web pages in the Editor, first position the insertion point at the location where you want the image to appear. Then choose Insert ➤ Image. In the Insert Image dialog box, you can do the following:

- Select an image from the list of images that already resides in the current Web.

- Click on the From File button to choose an image from outside your Web site.

- Click on the From URL button and specify the URL of an image.

FrontPage can import a wide variety of graphic file formats, including GIF, JPEG, BMP, TIFF, WMF, PCX, and EPS.

When you save the Web page that contains the image, FrontPage will ask if you want to save the image to the current Web, which you generally want to do. When the image is saved, FrontPage converts it either to the GIF or or to the JPEG format, which are the 2 most widely supported formats among Web browsers. When you save a JPEG image, you can choose the level of compression for the file.

Setting Image Properties

You can modify the properties of an image in the Editor by either right-clicking on the image and choosing Properties or by selecting the image and choosing Edit ➤ Properties. The Image Properties dialog box is shown in Figure 7.8.

FIGURE 7.8:

The Image Properties
dialog box

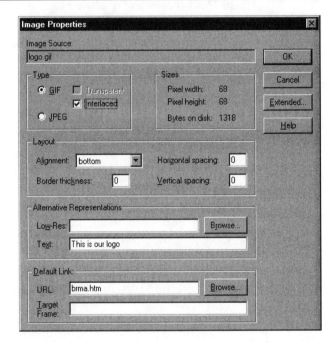

Let's take a look at the options you will find in the Image
Properties dialog box.

- **Type.** The Editor will choose an appropriate graphic type for
  the image: GIF if it has fewer than 256 colors, or JPEG if it has
  more. But you are free to change the image type. When you
  import an image that is converted to the JPEG format, you can
  choose the level of compression for the file, from 1 to 99, where
  99 preserves the best image quality with the least compression.
  If you choose the GIF format for an image, you can also choose
  the Interlaced option so that when the image is sent to a Web
  browser, the picture will "come into focus" within its picture
  frame, instead of appearing line by line. If you have specified a
  transparent color for a GIF image (discussed later), you can
  choose the Transparent option in the dialog box to make that
  color transparent.

- **Sizes.** Displays the size of the image in pixels and the file size.

- **Layout.** In this group of options, you specify how the image will align with the surrounding text. You can set the thickness of the border that will be displayed around the image; setting it to zero, the default, displays no border. You can also set the amount of space, in pixels, between the image and the surrounding text.

- **Alternative Representations.** If the image is rather large and will take some time to appear within a browser, you can specify a secondary, much smaller image that some browsers will display while the main image is loading. You can also specify the text that will be displayed in a Web browser if the image is not available or if the browser does not support images.

- **Default Link.** If the image contains clickable hotspot links (discussed in the next section), you can specify which target should be fetched when the reader clicks on the image outside any of the valid hotspots.

You can choose to make one color in a GIF image transparent so that the underlying Web page will show through any part of the image that contains that color. To do so, click on the image to select it, click on the Make Transparent button on the Image toolbar, and then select the color in the image that you want to make transparent.

Once you have defined a transparent color in an image, you can enable or disable the color via the Transparent option in the Image Properties dialog box, as discussed earlier.

Creating Hotspot Image Links

Within images in the FrontPage editor, you can create hotspots, which are clickable links hidden within the image. An image that contains hotspot links is often called an imagemap.

You may have browsed a Web page that contained an image of a map of the United States. Clicking on a state in the map took you to a Web page relevant to that state.

You create hotspots in an image by using the tools on the Image toolbar, which appears whenever you click on an image in the Editor to select it. The Image toolbar has 3 buttons with which you can define hotspots of different shapes: a rectangle, a circle, and a polygon.

To create a hotspot, you select the image (click on it), click on one of the 3 buttons on the toolbar, and then drag within the image to define the perimeter of the hotspot. When you release the mouse button, the hotspot is outlined in the image, and FrontPage displays the Create Link dialog box. You define the link in the same way that was described earlier in this chapter in "Creating a Link."

When you have defined the link and deselected the image, the hotspot outline disappears. But if you pass the mouse pointer over the hotspot, you will see the name of the link's target in the status bar.

If you find it difficult to see the outline of a hotspot in a selected image, click on the Highlight Hotspots button on the Image toolbar. Doing so hides the image beneath a single color so that the hotspots stand out.

To change the size or position of a hotspot, select the image and click on the hotspot to select it. Then drag its corners to change its size, or drag its center to move it. To delete a selected hotspot, simply press Delete.

Choosing How Your Hotspots Will Be Processed

When a visitor clicks on a hotspot on an image, some processing must occur to determine which part of the image was clicked on and then what target is associated with the hotspot that covers that part of the image.

You can choose between two methods of processing hotspots in your imagemaps:

- **Server-side.** The Web server interprets the mouse click on the imagemap and sends the appropriate target back to the browser.

- **Client-side.** The imagemap in the Web page contains all the necessary hotspot and link information so that the browser can interpret the mouse click on the imagemap and request the appropriate target resource.

The second method frees the server from any extra work—it all happens within the browser. The only caveat is that earlier versions of browsers do not support these client-side imagemaps, although by now almost all the available browsers should.

You choose the type of imagemap handling for your entire Web site via the Advanced tab in the dialog box of the FrontPage Explorer's Tools ➤ Web Settings command.

If you select the Generate Client-side Imagemaps checkbox, all imagemaps in this Web site will have the information needed by a Web browser to follow the hotspot links, without the help of the server.

To specify server-side imagemap handling, choose a server type from the drop-down list. For example, you would choose the FrontPage server if you're using Windows NT 4 with IIS.

If you choose a server and also enable the client-side imagemap, almost any browser can use your imagemaps. You can also choose None for the server type so that the server will never have to process a click on a hotspot.

Automating a Web with FrontPage WebBots

FrontPage has a built-in tool, called the WebBot, that automates some common tasks in a Web page. To take advantage of every WebBot, the server must have the FrontPage Extensions installed. This means that WebBots will run fine under Windows NT 4 with IIS and, of course, under the FrontPage Personal Web Server.

What's a Bot?

A FrontPage WebBot (or just plain Bot as they are often called) is a user-friendly automation tool that you insert into a Web page with the Insert ➤ Bot command (a few other Bots are inserted automatically when you create a form). FrontPage comes with a variety of Bots, and you may find many others from third-party developers.

A Bot within a Web page performs its job either locally, when you save your Web page in the Editor, or on the server, when a Web browser activates the page. The local Bots, therefore, will do their job without your server needing the FrontPage Server Extensions.

The FrontPage WebBots

When you choose Insert ➤ Bot in the Editor, you are presented with a list of all the available Bots in FrontPage:

- **Annotation Bot.** Lets you enter comments into your Web page that will not be displayed by a browser.

- **Confirmation Field Bot.** Displays the results of a form field, such as that displayed for reader-input confirmation.

- **HTML Markup Bot.** Offers you a way to add HTML code to a Web page, even though FrontPage doesn't support that code.

- **Include Bot.** Let's you choose another Web page to include within the current page; see the example later in this section.

- **Scheduled Image Bot.** Within a time period you specify, an image file will replace this Bot; this happens only when you are modifying the Web page.

- **Scheduled Include Bot.** Substitutes a Web page for this Bot, as discussed in the Scheduled Image Bot.

- **Search Bot.** Creates a Web page search form with which a reader can perform a search of your Web site.

- **Substitution Bot.** Chooses a Web configuration variable whose value will be substituted for the Bot and then displayed on the Web page.

- **Table of Contents Bot.** Creates a table of contents of links to all pages in the current Web.

- **Timestamp Bot.** Enters the date and/or time of the most recent revision of the Web page.

When you insert some of the Bots into a Web page, you will see the complete result of each Bot, such as with the Include, Table of Contents, and Timestamp Bots. Other Bots simply leave a placeholder to indicate their presence, such as the Scheduled Include Bot when the current date is out of range.

Now we'll take a quick look at a couple of Bots to illustrate how you use them.

Including Another Page

As discussed in the previous chapter, it's important to give your Web site a consistent look and feel. For example, many pages might share the same banner so that a reader will recognize the pages from your site at a glance.

When you want multiple pages to include the same material, you can let the Include Bot handle the work for you. Use the Insert ➤ Bot command and choose the Include Bot. You are prompted to enter the URL of the page you want to include in the current Web page.

As soon as you click on OK, the page you specified is imported into the current page, as though you had created it yourself. When you save your work in the Editor, the page contains the included page, and that's exactly what a browser will see, as well.

If you ever want to change the look of your Web page banner, the Include Bot can save you hours and hours of work. Instead of your having to edit every page that has the banner in it, simply make the changes you want to the included file. FrontPage will update every page in the Web that includes that file via the Include Bot.

Stamping Your Page with the Date and Time

It's important to let a visitor know how current the information is on your Web pages. Instead of your having to remember to update the date every time you edit a page, you can let the Timestamp Bot do it for you.

When you insert the Timestamp Bot, you'll see the dialog box in Figure 7.9. Here you choose the style in which the date and time will be displayed in the page; choose None to turn off either the date or the time. You also choose whether the date and the time will be updated on the page only when you actually edit the page or whenever the page is updated by FrontPage, such as when you change an included Web page.

FIGURE 7.9:

The Timestamp Bot Properties dialog box

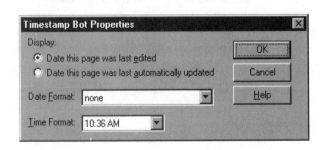

Advanced Features with Tables, Forms, and Frames

With FrontPage, you can develop Web pages that contain just about every popular HTML feature, including the more complex features: tables, forms, and frames. In this section, we'll take a quick look at these powerful design and feedback tools for your Web pages.

Arranging Data within Tables

An HTML table is very much like the tables you can create in many Windows word processors. It contains rows, columns, and cells that make it easy to align data within a page, just as you can in a spreadsheet such as Microsoft Excel.

You've probably seen countless examples of tables while you were browsing Web sites. In some cases, you may not have realized you were seeing a table because it displayed no borders around its cells.

Figure 7.10 shows the Web page from Figure 7.2 that contains a simple table. It illustrates many of the properties you can assign to a table.

To create this table, place the insertion point where you want the table to appear, and either choose Table ➤ Insert Table or click on the Table button on the toolbar.

In the Insert Table dialog box, you specify the number of rows and columns you want in the table (Figure 7.10 has 5 rows and 8 columns), the thickness of the border (1 pixel in the figure), and the width of the table (60 percent of the editor's or browser's window in the figure).

Once the table is in the Web page, you can enter any text or graphics into a cell as you normally would. In fact, a cell in a table can contain just about any HTML feature, including another table.

FIGURE 7.10:

A table consists of rows, columns, and cells, as well as an optional border, a caption, and header cells.

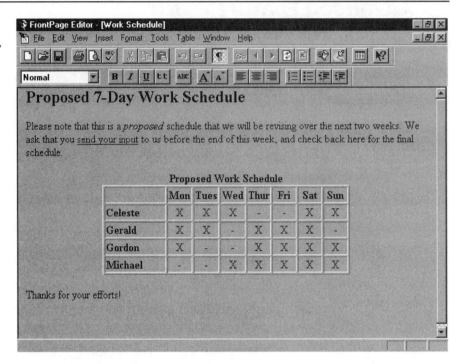

You can change the properties associated with the entire table or with cells within the table. Before you do, you must first display the Properties dialog box for the portion you want to modify.

One way to do so is to select a cell and then choose one of the selection commands on the Table menu: Select Cell, Select Row, Select Column, or Select Table. Once the area is selected, you can choose Edit ➤ Properties. You can also use the following:

- **Table.** Right-click anywhere within the table and choose Table Properties.

- **Single Cell.** Right-click anywhere within the cell and choose Cell Properties.

- **Column of Cells.** Point to the top of the column so that the mouse pointer changes to a downward-pointing arrow; then right-click and choose Cell Properties.

- **Row of Cells.** Point to the left of the row so that the pointer changes to a rightward-pointing arrow; then right-click and choose Cell Properties.

- **Multiple Cells.** Hold down the Alt key and click to select one cell; then hold down Alt+Shift and click to select others.

Here are some of the other features illustrated in Figure 7.10:

- **Caption.** You can create a caption for a table with the Table ➤ Insert Caption command and format the text as you would any other text. The advantage of using a caption is that it always stays with the table, directly above it.

- **Header Cell.** The first row in the table has been defined as a header row. Most browsers display the contents of header cells in boldfaced type.

- **Cell Properties.** The caption and the names in the first column have been formatted as bold. The days-of-the-week columns have their contents' horizontal alignment property set to Center; the column width of those columns has been set to 5 percent.

- **Table Properties.** The entire table has been centered within the window.

Finally, you can adapt a table to just about any configuration of rows, columns, and cells by using the Split Cells, Merge Cells, Insert Cell, and Insert Rows or Columns commands on the Table menu.

Letting the Visitor Interact with Forms

You can build forms in FrontPage that allow visitors to your Web site to send information back to the server. Forms are a very powerful

HTML tool that open countless possibilities for your Web pages—including getting a customer's name, address, and credit card number! Figure 7.11 shows a small customer information form.

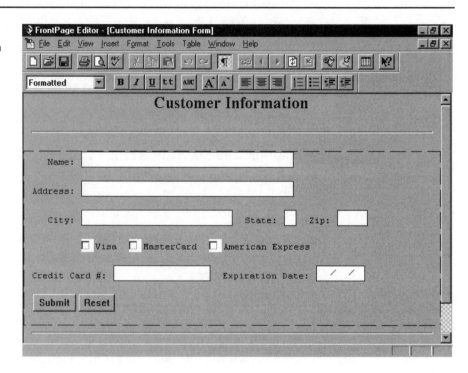

The WYSIWYG environment of FrontPage makes it easy to assemble a form on a Web page. Plus, you can use the Form Page Wizard to get some expert help in the form-building process. In fact, using the Wizard is a good way to see the kinds of decisions that go into creating a form page. Here are the main steps to follow when you are creating a form:

- First, have a plan for what you will do with the data once it is received on your server. For example, will it be appended to a database or perhaps added to an HTML form and displayed to the reader?

- Insert the form fields you will need on a Web page, such as text boxes, radio buttons, and checkboxes, as well as any descriptive text or images you want as part of the form.

- Insert the Submit and Reset buttons into the form, which allow readers to send the data they have entered into the form to your server or to reset the form so that they can start over.

- Define the properties of the form, which will determine how the data that visitors enter will be handled when it is sent back to the server.

You can place more than one form on a Web page. The Editor delineates a form with a dashed line above and below it. You can define the properties of each form independently of the others on the page.

To create a form, use the Insert ➤ Form Field command, whose menu lists the various form fields you can include in a form. Better still, since most forms will have several or many fields, display the Forms toolbar by choosing it from the View menu.

After you insert a form field, you will see the relevant properties dialog box appear, such as the one in Figure 7.12 for a text box field. In this case, you enter a name for the field, specify the field's initial value, the field width, the maximum number of characters that will be allowed in the field, and whether the field should be password-protected.

Each field in a form must have a name, for that is how the content of the field is identified when it is sent to the server. But you will find a variety of other properties for the different types of form fields.

As soon as you insert the first form field outside of any other existing form on a page, a new form is created for that field. Now you can continue to add more elements to that form, including other form fields, descriptive text, images, and pretty much any other HTML features you want to include.

FIGURE 7.12:

The Properties dialog box for a text box form field

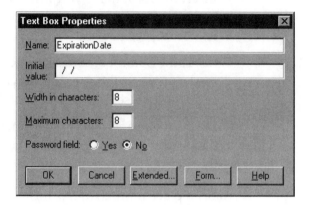

Before a form is complete, you must include a way for the reader to send the data to the server—a push-button field. You can define a push button to be either a Submit button, which will send the data to the server, or a Reset button, which resets all the fields in the form to their initial values.

The final step is to set the form properties—right-click anywhere within the form and choose Form Properties. In the dialog box, you specify the form handler that you want the server to use as it accepts the incoming data from the form.

For example, you can choose Custom CGI Script and specify the program on the server that should handle the data. Or choose one of FrontPage's form-handling Bots, such as the Save Results Bot. In that case, you specify the name of the file to which you want the data saved, the data format of the file (HTML, text, and so on), and any additional information you want saved with the data, such as the date, time, and username.

Be sure to test your forms on your Web server to ensure that both the forms and the server perform as you want. And never make assumptions about information received from a visitor. Even though the form asked for a Zip code, don't assume you will only get numbers in that field; someone will enter the letter O rather than the number 0, and your program might break.

Getting Fancier with Frames

One of the newer features in HTML is frames. A frame is a separate area of a Web page in which another Web page is displayed. You can have multiple frames on a page, which is called a frame set, each displaying a Web page. A frame can display a different page at any time without affecting the other frames.

Creating a frame set can be just the ticket when you want to do tricks such as the following:

- Display a table of contents in one frame on a page. When a reader clicks on one of the links in it, the target of the link is displayed in an adjacent frame, while the table of contents remains as it was.

- Display a menu of choices in a frame across the top of the page, with the target of a menu item appearing in a lower frame.

- Display an article or a story in one frame. When the reader clicks on a link in the story, the target Web page appears in another frame while the story remains in its frame.

- Display a search form in one frame and the results of the search in another.

To create a frame set in FrontPage, choose File ➤ New and then select the Frames Wizard. The Frames Wizard walks you through the choices needed to define the frame set and then saves the resulting Web page to your Web site—you never really see the frame set until you access it from a browser. If you open a frame set Web page for editing, the Editor will automatically bring up the Forms Wizard.

When you choose File ➤ New and the Frames Wizard, you are offered two ways to define the frame set:

- **Pick a Template.** FrontPage has several predefined frame sets from which you can choose; a sample of each is displayed in the dialog box.

- **Make a Custom Grid.** You can define the grid of the frame set from scratch; a sample of the page you create is displayed so that you can see exactly how the frame set will look.

When you create a custom frame set, you first choose the number of frames it will contain; you are free to juggle the number of frames and their sizes.

You then assign a name to each frame, which you will reference when you create a link to a frame in that page. In other words, a link to a frame-set page should always include a frame name.

Finally, you must specify the URL of a Web page for each frame in the frame set. That page will serve as the contents of the frame when the frame-set page is viewed by a browser. For either design method, template or custom grid, you can also specify another Web page to display when a Web browser cannot handle frames.

CHAPTER

EIGHT

8

Checking the Fine Print
of Legal Issues

- Protecting yourself

- Avoiding legal problems

- Documenting security incidents

This chapter deals with several legal aspects of working with material on the Web and describes some things that you can and can't do. I should say at the outset that I am not a legal specialist; I don't even play one on TV. And having said that, the courts have not made many judicial decisions about what is and what is not legal on the Internet.

But if any issues raised in this chapter have the hair on the back of your neck standing up in recognition of something that is happening on your site, seek legal counsel immediately. Although legal advice is expensive, it is nowhere near as expensive as legal actions. Disseminating information from a Web site is considered publishing from most legal viewpoints, and much of what follows relates Web publishing to publishing the printed word.

The basic tenet is that if something is illegal in real life, it is probably illegal on the Web too. If you are in doubt about whether you need permission to use something on the Web, don't hesitate: Get permission.

We'll look at several important copyright issues as they relate to text and to images, both line art and photographs, and to the use of trademarks, and we'll take a look at trade secrets and several important international issues.

Protecting Yourself

Shakespeare asked, "What's in a name?" and we can update that question by asking, What's in a domain name? The answer: Quite a lot. As corporations move onto the Web in larger and larger numbers, the pressure on the existing domain names continues to grow. By January 1996, 237,000 domain names were registered with InterNIC, the organization charged with issuing domain names.

InterNIC is under pressure to provide names in addition to the `.com` name that implies a business organization within the United States. Suggestions have included `.biz`, `.inc`, and `.corp`. It is the task of the Internet Assigned Numbers Authority (IANA) to decide if expansion is needed, and if it is, how it will be accomplished.

One reason for this growth is that there are only so many names. For example, if you run a small cabinet-making business and you want to establish a Web presence but your company name happens to be McDonald's, you can begin to appreciate the size and scope of the problem. As you learned in the *Making All the Right Connections* chapter, the fast-food chain has already reserved that slot. What can you do? Not much, except try to get there first. In most cases, a company can easily obtain the domain name it wants simply by paying the InterNIC registration fee.

The Name Is Everything

Several unscrupulous organizations and individuals have tried to register big corporate domain names to reserve them and then sell them back to the highest bidder. Several states are looking to introduce legislation that will make it illegal to use a company's trademarked name in an e-mail address or a domain name without the permission of that company. Such legislation is likely to have a distinctly limited effect, as it is very easy to move content to a server in another state (or even to a server in another country), one that is outside the jurisdiction of the new laws.

In the real world, trademarks are usually defined according to geographical area; so it is quite possible to have an Allens's Restaurant in Texas and another completely unrelated Allen's Restaurant in

Washington without any conflict. But on the Internet, there is only room for one `allen.com` domain name worldwide.

In one high-profile but essentially light-hearted case, a writer from *Wired* magazine, Joshua Quittner, registered the name `mcdonalds.com` to make some sort of point about how the fast-food company was being left behind in the race to the Web. After an exchange of letters, Quittner finally ceded the name back to McDonald's, in return for McDonald's wiring an inner-city school for Internet access.

In another case involving Sacramento-based Raley's supermarkets, a private individual established a domain name using the Raley's name, with the apparent intent of selling it back to the supermarket chain at a profit. Raley's lawyers approached the ISP involved and explained that the individual had no right to represent the supermarket chain, and the ISP canceled the individual's Internet access account, which was a good first step. Canceling an Internet account does not free up the domain name. Raley's had to pursue the matter with InterNIC to get it back.

New InterNIC Policies

Since these well-publicized events, InterNIC has adopted several new policies aimed at minimizing this sort of conflict. Although names were originally established on a first-come first-served basis, InterNIC now says that companies with a valid trademark have the exclusive right to use it as their domain name. If it is demonstrated that a person or an organization is infringing on that trademark, InterNIC managers will stop its use. InterNIC simply requires that a trademark registration predate the domain name registration. The problem with all this is that the Web is truly worldwide, and this is a worldwide problem.

Mark Newton, who runs a bulletin board in Detroit and who registered the name `newton.com`, refused to give up the name when challenged by Apple Computer Corporation, maker of the Newton hand-held computer system, who wanted to use the same name.

Newton registered the name in 1994 and, because it is his last name, feels that he has the right to use it. Apple, who registered the name as a trademark, also feels that it has a right to use it. Apple complained to InterNIC, and its solution was to suspend all use of the domain name, preventing anyone from using it until the issue of ownership is resolved. InterNIC has indicated that use of the name will remain suspended until such time as the two parties reach an agreement or until a court order or an arbitration panel renders other judgment.

And if your company name is still McDonald's and you still want to establish a Web presence, the best thing to do is to register a name based on the nature of your business rather than on your name.

You should also be sure to pay your registration fee, as some 9000 sites discovered in late June 1996. In one of its weekly house-cleaning efforts, InterNIC suspended them for not paying their domain name registrations. InterNIC, in cooperation with the National Science Foundation, maintains a hierarchy of Internet addresses and controls the root-name server. Although these sites remain on their own servers, search engines and other Internet directories cannot find the sites if they are deleted from the InterNIC root-name server. In what was apparently a mistake, one of the sites that was suspended but quickly restored was MSNBC, the 24-hour news, talk, and information service from Microsoft and NBC.

The Web and Copyright

Both national and international copyright laws protect the intellectual property rights of writers, photographers, and others. You cannot copy and distribute any copyrighted work without the express permission of the copyright holder, and the laws prohibit plagiarism and the creation of unauthorized derivative works. You cannot copyright an idea, such as $2 + 2 = 4$, but you can copyright a written expression of that idea, such as a page in a book that contains the text, "Igor muttered through his thick black beard, '2 + 2 = 4 even in this crazy mixed-up world of ours.'" A basic knowledge of the rights afforded by copyright protection is important in the world of the Web, where making a copy of a document and then distributing that copy all over the world is so easy it is trivial.

Protecting Your Own Copyright

As soon as you create a new work, you own the copyright to that work; you don't have to add a copyright symbol or register the work with the U.S. Copyright Office, although there are several very good reasons for pursuing registration, as you'll see shortly. This applies equally to a photograph, an HTML page, a graphic, a sound, an animation clip, or a video.

Under certain circumstances, the copyright can belong to the organization that you work for, for example, if you created the work when in its employment or under the terms of a contract that grants all rights to the employing party, usually known as a work for hire agreement. In these cases, you do not own the copyright; the organization does.

Copyright laws generally give you the right to sue anyone you find making and distributing unauthorized copies of your work. To protect your copyright, however, you will have to do three things:

- Prove that the work is original

- Prove that you wrote it and own the copyright or that your organization owns the copyright

- Indicate that you gave fair warning to others that the work is copyrighted and has not been placed in the public domain

To protect yourself, add a copyright statement to your Web documents, and indicate to your visitors that they may not copy or distribute the document without your written permission. The statement should also contain the word *Copyright*, the date, the © symbol, the name of the copyright holder or holders if there are several authors, and the text *All Rights Reserved*. The whole statement might look like this:

Copyright © 1997 Peter Dyson. All Rights Reserved.

If you can't find the © symbol, you can simply use (c) in its place. In HTML, you can create a © symbol using the &#169 sequence.

To register your copyright with the U.S. Copyright Office, you complete the appropriate registration forms and mail them (along with 2 copies of the work and a small registration fee), within 3 months of publication, to:

Copyright Office
Information and Publications Section
Library of Congress
Washington, DC 20559

This helps to establish you as the creator of the work and makes it easier to file for damages if someone abuses your copyright. The Copyright Office has specific forms and procedures for registering photographs, text, software, multimedia, and other types of intellectual property; the earlier you begin the process, the better. Registering your copyright before the material is published proves beyond any doubt that you are the copyright holder.

A copyright stays in effect for 50 years after the death of the author or for 50 years after the death of the last surviving author if the document was created by more than one writer. For companies, a copyright stays in effect for 100 years after its creation date or for 75 years after its publication date, whichever comes first.

After your material is registered, you can sue for statutory damages and legal fees if someone violates your copyright. If you wait until after your copyright is infringed to register, you can only sue for actual damages, which can be difficult to prove in borderline cases.

Respecting Other People's Copyright

Even if a Web page does not contain the copyright protection statement described above, it is still protected unless the originators of the page expressly grant you permission to make or distribute copies.

But isn't there a copy of the Web page in your browser when you access a Web site? Yes, there is, and that is perfectly legal because that is why the Web page is there in the first place. The owners of most Web sites will not object if you download, save, and print the page, as long as it is for your own personal use and will not be distributed further or used to generate profit. They will definitely object if you post the material on your own Web page and then give free access to that document to all comers, as you will see in the next section "Abusing Copyrighted Text and Photographs."

There are some important exceptions to watch out for in the copyright law, and one is the fair use provision, which allows you to quote small sections of a document for the purposes of a review and which allows teachers to copy certain documents for educational purposes. Fair use does not normally apply to the commercial use of copyrighted material.

An author can decide to retain copyright of a work, but allow unrestricted access and distribution; much of the shareware software you encounter is distributed under this sort of protection. Or an author can decide to place the work in the public domain and relinquish all copyright.

Abusing Copyrighted Text and Photographs

So what happens if you decide to use material already copyrighted by others? Will anyone come after you? In certain cases, the answer to that question is an emphatic yes.

Copyright owners used to pay little mind to online use of their material by nonprofit organizations, but that is definitely changing. Some copyright holders have become downright vigilant. For example, Dutton Children's Books owns the copyright to Winnie-the-Pooh, and it is concerned about how Pooh is depicted, on the Web as well as in print. When pursuing copyright violations, Dutton applies the same rules to Web and print publishers. It is so easy to alter a scanned image and re-post it as original work that many lawyers are concerned about derivative works too.

Companies such as Playboy Enterprises, Elvis Presley Enterprises, and Tyco Toys all fiercely protect their copyrights, and Web site managers have been asked to remove copyrighted sound clips of "Blue Suede Shoes" and "Hound Dog" from their sites, as well as images scanned in from postcards bought at Graceland.

More and more sites are using photographs to help get their message across. Sprint uses a picture of a phone, and Holiday Inn uses images of business people talking on the phone, sitting at a computer in a hotel room, and aboard a jet in flight. Most of these images are strong and simple, yet they can portray a message even when displayed at a relatively small size. Even black-and-white photographs are popular because they also display well at a reduced size.

If you used a photograph from a photographer or from a stock agency in one of your printed brochures, in an annual report, or in a magazine advertising campaign, can you use that image on your Web site without paying additional fees? The answer is, it all depends. When you use a photograph from one of these sources (but not if the photograph was part of a work for hire agreement) in an advertisement, you really only "rent" the photograph for certain uses; you don't actually buy the image itself. You may have purchased "All North American Rights" or "All North American English-speaking Rights"; so it all depends on the rights specified in the agreement with the photographer. Normally, Web use of a photograph is considered an additional use and requires an additional fee.

Electronic rights clauses are starting to appear in photographer and stock agency contracts, and the fees charged for an image are often related to the size of the image and the number of hits the site receives in a given period. Expect to pay $2,500 and up for 3 months' use of a single image if you have a large and busy site. Some agencies base their charges on length of contract (3, 6, and 12 months), number of images, size of images, and image placement.

The Web is full of sites that include photographs. Can you use one of these images on your Web site? You can if you pay the appropriate fee to the photographer or if the image is released into the public domain. If you go ahead and use it without permission and you are caught, you can be sued in a couple of highly creative ways:

- The photographer can sue you for breach of copyright and loss of income as well as statutory damages if the copyright was registered.

- The subject of the photograph may sue you if the photographer did not obtain a model release and the image contains recognizable people (not celebrities) or identifiable private property.

In the end, it's just not worth the risk; legal fees can be astronomical, and the bad publicity can be extremely hard to shake. If you see an image in a magazine or a book that you want to use on your Web site and you see the photographer's name beside the image, you can use one of the databases on the Web to track down and contact the photographer and then negotiate the appropriate terms for the use you have in mind.

Two other areas of the law concern the right to publicity (a celebrity's right to control the use of his or her image, online or otherwise) and the right to privacy (a person's right to control intrusion on his or her privacy by preventing disclosure of embarrassing private facts, even if true).

Who Owns What on Your Web Site?

One issue you should deal with immediately if you have used any outside help to create or maintain your site is to resolve who owns what. Who created the HTML pages? Who provided the graphics? And who wrote the CGI scripts?

If you hire one designer and then decide to use the services of another designer to develop and maintain your site, can you hand over everything, or are you locked in to your original agreement? Be sure that any work for hire agreements are explicit about these aspects of the work and about the rights of the designer. Can a designer take the scripts you paid to develop and sell them to another company, possibly one of your competitors? Find out.

You should also be concerned about the content on your site. A recent case involved *Atlantic Monthly*. A freelance writer's work was made available electronically after it had appeared in the magazine, but without additional payment. This case was resolved out of court. Atlantic Monthly now negotiates specific rights with freelancers, including the rights to reproduce and distribute rights on CD-ROM, online networks, and online databases and by other means. Check your contract: Is any reuse of a work in electronic format without the author's permission a copyright violation, or do you own the copyright to the work in all formats, print and electronic?

Many prominent authors, including Norman Mailer, Erica Jong, and Gore Vidal, have protested the decision made recently by the New York Times not to publish the work of anyone unless that person cedes electronic rights.

Using Trademarks

A trademark can take several forms, including a company name, a logo, and product names owned by an organization or by an individual. A trademark is what prevents other people from capitalizing on your good name, and trademarks are jealously guarded by people who specialize in trademark law and in making trademark searches. It is definitely to your advantage to use trademarks on your Web site whenever possible to leverage the recognition that the name evokes, but be sure to register your trademarks before you use them.

Keeping Trade Secrets a Secret

A trade secret is a confidential idea or confidential information about a product owned by your company that gives you some sort of technical or business advantage and represents something that you probably don't want to put on your Web site if you are connected to the Internet.

The confidential idea or information must be marked as such, or it must be obvious to the recipient that it is confidential in order for trade secret protection to apply. Generally, it is advisable to have the recipient sign a nondisclosure or trade secrecy agreement before disclosing the confidential information to him or her. Trade secrecy protection varies a great deal from country to country. Some countries do not recognize the concept at all; so a nondisclosure agreement is all the more important in these places.

On an Intranet, however, the situation changes. If you are concerned with training a sales staff or even with putting up something of a technical nature, you may want to incorporate trade secrets in the material on your Web site.

You must also ensure that your site does not compromise the trade secrets of another company, either directly or indirectly. If you get verbal permission to use a trade secret on your site, always follow up and confirm that permission in writing as soon as possible.

A patent, on the other hand, is a very different animal from a trade secret. Because the details of a patent are made public by the U.S. government after you register your patent, you can certainly publish a document describing the details on your Web site. What you can't do, however, is create a product based on that patent without paying the appropriate license fees to the owner of the patent.

Avoiding Legal Problems

In this part of the chapter, we'll look at some of the problem areas on the Web, and I'll talk about some ways that you can avoid these problems. This list is by no means exhaustive, and you should keep your eyes open to new developments that might affect your site or its content.

Asking for Permission

In the past, the Internet had a long tradition of offering everything for free, information as well as access, and in some cases this philosophy is in sharp contrast to the way Internet commerce is developing, with its need for security and encryption of certain information.

As you saw in the discussion of copyright earlier in this chapter, all material on the Web is actually protected, and before you copy or distribute material, you must make certain that you have the appropriate permissions. These permissions should be in writing and should not be in the form of e-mail, which can be altered easily by a knowledgeable person.

You may encounter several versions and implementation of encryption technology on the Internet, but you can't use it in a commercial enterprise just because it is available. If you want to use such software in connection with a for-profit organization, be sure to read and follow any licensing agreements.

Considering International Issues

Several legalities especially apply when you look at the Internet as a whole, in its real global sense. The government of China and several other countries in the Far East have taken a novel approach to Web access. They have restricted general access to only a few "government approved" networks within their own countries and then have limited any connections made from these networks to the outside world to only a few rigorously controlled sites. In this way, the government thinks that it can control both access and content. But this approach is not limited to the Far East.

The German authorities asked one of the major online services to limit access to several of the sexually explicit Usenet newsgroups that the service provides to all its users all over the world. The request was the result of a certain amount of confusion on the part of the authorities about the difference between Internet content and the services sold by the provider. In the short term, the online service withdrew access to these newsgroups for all users, all over the world, not just in Germany. Eventually, service was restored. This raises the specter of one country trying to control content over an area much wider than its own physical boundaries.

Some countries specifically regulate the content of information published over the Internet, and it can be a crime to provide access to prohibited information. A webmaster residing in one of these countries is well advised to check the rules before publishing a Web page or even providing links to other sites containing sensitive information.

Export Controls on Encryption

The U.S. government considers certain types of encryption schemes as munitions and therefore prohibits their export or sale overseas without a special license. Even though the Data Encryption Standard (DES) algorithm has been distributed by the U.S. government itself in a freely available government publication, it is still illegal to export an implementation of the DES code. I can hear you talking about horses and stable doors all the way from here.

You can legally export encryption schemes that use a relatively modest number of bits in a key, but once you go over that limit, export is controlled or even prohibited. This has some odd implications for U.S. software companies who want to expand into overseas markets.

Software businesses in the United States must now offer 2 levels of encryption service: one, very secure, for use only within the United States, and another, distinctly less secure, for use everywhere else. The creator of the PGP (Pretty Good Privacy) encryption package, Phil Zimmermann, had the possibility of prosecution by federal authorities hanging over his head for a long time; they ultimately decided not to prosecute the case.

Avoiding Libel

When you create content for your Web page, you are protected by the First Amendment to the U.S. Constitution, which establishes the right to free speech. The First Amendment allows you to say a great deal, but it does not allow you to defame anyone's character or knowingly publish false information about a person. Libel can be defined as defamation in writing, but it is one area that is constantly shifting as new cases continue to redefine the legal landscape.

And then there are the areas of personal behavior—sex and drugs, religious and political topics, and hot-button topics such as abortion—that you should also stay away from, unless you are a nonprofit organization specializing in these issues.

The 1996 U.S. Communications Decency Act

On Thursday, February 8, 1996, President Clinton signed the Communications Decency Act (CDA) into law as a part of the sprawling 1996 telecommunications legislation. Under the new law, anybody who makes "indecent" or "patently offensive" material available to a minor through what it calls an "interactive computer service" will be subject to a $250,000 fine and 2 years in jail.

The U.S. government maintains that the law is designed to protect children and that it will not affect legitimate online use or Web publishing; it claims that the Web is just like TV or radio (but it does not claim that the Web is like the printed word), which are both currently regulated by the government (although that might be hard to believe sometimes). This means that you can publish a picture or write something in a book or magazine quite legally, but if that same picture or text appears on the Web, you can be prosecuted and, if found guilty, sent to jail. The inevitable conclusion to this is that all online communications would be limited to what children could be permitted to hear, irrespective of all the online warnings and parental blocking devices currently available.

A broad coalition of free speech and industry groups immediately filed a lawsuit, challenging the bill as unconstitutional. Three federal district and appellate court judges in June 1996 blocked the bill calling the restrictions a "profound and repugnant" violation of First Amendment rights and arguing that the Internet must have the broadest possible protection against government intrusion. There is little doubt that the losing side will take the challenge to the U.S. Supreme Court and that a final decision will be made some time in the future.

Poorly worded bills have often suffered badly at the hands of the Court, whose members tend to be conservative. Although they may not understand all the details of Web site operation, they do understand what has happened in several important cases concerning both the written and the spoken word. In cases involving freedom of speech, they tend to rule against further restrictions. In the meantime, the U.S. government has agreed not to enforce the CDA until this series of court cases is resolved.

Avoiding Bootlegged Software

Although pirated software is freely available on many sites on the Internet, be sure that your site is not one of them. We hear a great deal about software piracy in countries such as China, where intellectual property law is less precise than it is in the West, but it is a little known fact that losses in the United States are about five times those suffered in China every year—$2,900 million losses in the United States last year compared with losses of $527 million in China. Penalties for piracy in the United States run up to $100,000 for each copyright violation and can include imprisonment; in other nations, penalties are limited to actual losses sustained through loss of the sale of the product.

Avoiding Pornography

Sexually explicit material of a kind that some people might regard as pornography is illegal in some states and in some countries, but not in others, and any material involving minors or people who appear to be minors will get you into trouble almost everywhere.

If you sell this kind of material as a business, you should at a minimum require user identification on your site as well as authentication of the user's location and age. Although you can buy a magazine that contains pictures of a certain kind at a store, some individuals want access to the same material removed from the Web. More on this in a moment.

If you run an FTP service and let visitors upload files to your server, be especially careful. Pirates don't want to keep bootlegged software or pornography on their server; they would much rather keep it on yours. You must check and recheck the material on your server, and watch out for the following:

- An unusually high number of FTP sessions on your server

- An unusually large amount of hard-disk space consumed by one single user

- A large number of zipped files, graphics files, or binary files stored as uuencode files

- Any mention of the name of your server in the Usenet news-groups that deal with security or that are known to be used by potential intruders

These are all signs that some unusual activity is taking place on your server; so be very careful. In the next section, we'll look at what you should do if you do detect unusual activity on your server.

Documenting Security Incidents

If you detect any unusual activity on your server, it is important to document what you think is going on before you take any action. Here are the rules to remember:

- Don't panic (yet)

- Take good notes

The first step in responding to a breach in security is to decide what you have to do right now. And that depends on the answers to a couple of questions:

- Has the intruder gained access to your system?

- Is the intruder active on your system now? If the answer is yes, you must react immediately; if the answer is no, you have some time to make a considered response.

If the intruder is indeed attacking your system right now, strong measures are called for. Consider severing your connection to the Internet or even shutting down the server until you can decide how best to proceed.

Shutting down the server has several drawbacks, unfortunately, including:

- Destroying information you may need to confirm the attack and the methods used in the attack to gain access to your system

- Disrupting the work of others attached to the server

Shutting down the server also protects only one computer, while several may be under attack. Here are some other suggestions for how to react to an intruder:

- Tell the other people in your organization that need to know, including legal, security, and public relations departments.

- Contact your ISP about what is going on.

- Contact other sites within your organization and alert them to the possibility of an attack; it may have already happened to them and they just haven't noticed yet.

- Make a backup to act as a snapshot of the compromised system. This can be useful in reconstructing what happened later.

- Document the incident. From a legal standpoint, the best records are those made at the time of the incident, preferably in a carbon-copy notebook with numbered pages. If you use single pieces of paper, be sure to label, sign, and date each one individually and have someone witness your signature. Don't use any online methods such as sending e-mail to yourself; almost anything online can be changed and tampered with after the fact.

Once the incident is over, you must figure out exactly what happened and what measures to put in place to ensure that it does not happen again. You should also take the time to analyze your company response to the incident and make proposals to improve the response for any future incidents. Finally, let everyone know that the incident is over, and that they can stand down.

In the movies, the next step is to go after the bad guys and make a stunningly clever arrest after a thrilling but nerve-wracking chase. But this ain't the movies, and your chances of tracing the intruder, much less of identifying him or her and effecting a capture, are just about nil.

To find out what is involved in hunting down an intruder, you might read *The Cuckoo's Egg* by Cliff Stoll. In the 1980s, Stoll was working on a system at Lawrence Berkeley Labs, trying to track down a tiny discrepancy in an accounting program that was used to bill computer time to the various departments. During this process, he discovered that the computer system had been broken into over the Internet. He then became obsessed with finding out who the intruder was and spent months on the chase, using his own time and several novel techniques to record the break-ins.

Stoll actually succeeded in tracking down the intruder and wrote a very popular, useful, and entertaining book in the process. Few of us are likely to be able to emulate his story, but reading the book should give all of us the occasion to reflect on the security of the systems for which we are responsible.

CHAPTER

NINE

9

Announcing Your Web Site to the World

- Spreading the word

- How to mirror another Web site

- Adding a search engine to your Web site

In the *Making All the Right Connections* chapter, we looked at the steps to follow when registering your company's domain name, and in the *Planning Your Web Site* and *Designing and Constructing Your Web Site* chapters, we looked at planning, designing, and then implementing your Web site. In this chapter, we'll look at the next logical step along the road, and that is how best to get the word out that your Web site is up and running. We'll also look at some of the facilities offered by lists, directories, online Yellow Pages, and search engines on the Web, and because IIS supports both FTP and Gopher, we'll look at archive sites for them too. We'll even look at what is involved in adding a search engine to your own Web site. But first, how best to get the word out about your new Web site.

Spreading the Word

The first step in spreading the word is to compose a document rather like a press release. Keep it short and to the point, but be sure to provide enough information to interest potential visitors and tell them how they will benefit from a visit to your site.

The release should include the Web site's URL; and to make the URL very obvious in the body of the release, put the URL on a line by itself, and add a blank line before and after. This makes the URL easy to grab for those users with online access and a windowing environment, who can cut and paste your URL into their browser, and it also makes the hard-to-read and cryptic URL easy to see for novice Web users. This approach also removes any potential confusion over hyphens and other punctuation in a long complicated URL with surrounding text. (Am I supposed to type that last comma, or is that simply punctuation? Is that a hyphen breaking the URL into two parts across a line break, or am I supposed to type it as part of the URL?) Visitors can simply type what they see.

Add the name and e-mail address of the person to contact if the reader has any questions, a voice phone number, and a fax number, and you are all done. Have someone else proofread your announcement, and have that person pay special attention to the spelling of the URL; you don't want any typos here. Once that is done, you are ready to send the announcement to others on the Web. You can send it to several kinds of sites, including:

- One-stop submission sites
- What's New sites
- Web Yellow Pages, indexes, and lists
- Search engine sites
- Metasearch sites
- "Best of" and other award sites
- Commercial indexes and mall sites
- Government indexes
- International directories
- Regional sites
- Mailing lists and newsgroups
- Online publications
- Gopher archives
- FTP sites

In the next few sections in this chapter, we'll look at examples of all these types of sites, and I'll tell you how to get the best of them, and we'll look at a couple of other techniques you should know about such as negotiating sponsorship agreements and mirroring sites. But before we get started on this list, let's look at some more traditional methods.

Traditional Media and Trade Papers

Once your Web site is registered with InterNIC and is up and running, be sure that the site's URL is liberally splashed about everywhere you can think of, including:

- The company stationary, including everyone's business cards
- All print, radio, and TV advertising materials
- All point-of-purchase displays
- The company voice mail and answering machine messages
- The product packaging
- All press kits and newsletters
- All give-aways such as pens and tee shirts
- Yellow Page listings and printed business directories

If you plan to offer customer or technical support via your Web site, be sure the URL appears in manuals and brochures and on all support and training materials.

Send out news releases to magazines and trade periodicals that specialize in your field, and try to slant the material in such a way as to demonstrate how the readers of each publication you target will benefit from a visit to your Web site. For example, *Internet World* magazine, one of the most respected and widely read publications on Web and Internet matters, accepts new Web site announcements addressed to Andrew Kantor at this e-mail address:

ak@iw.com

Send him a copy of your press release. A review, an interview, or other mention in a newspaper or a magazine is a good way to boost the number of hits your site receives. Check all the trade publications that your company subscribes to or advertises in for an e-mail address or a URL for forwarding announcements and press releases.

You can also include the URL of your site in your online signature, placed at the end of all the e-mail messages you send. Limit your signature to a two- or three-line message, and don't add any clever ASCII art, such as an outline of the state of Texas made up of question marks; such antics just annoy people, especially if the signature takes up more space than the message.

One-Stop Submission Sites

Several all-in-one submission sites are on the Web. You announce your new URL to these sites, and they pass the information to other important sites on the Web. Using one of these services certainly gets the word out fast, with a couple of minor drawbacks.

Because of the blanket way your announcement is passed to other sites, you cannot tailor your announcement for an individual audience, and there may be little to separate your announcement from one of the other hundreds of announcements these sites make every month. Also, you may not know who gets your message, and that makes it impossible to track its impact.

Submit It!

The first place to start is at Submit It! (see Figure 9.1), where you fill out only one form, which is then automatically posted to the following directory sites: Apollo, EINet Galaxy, JumpStation, Harvest, Infoseek, Lycos, Open Text Web Index, New Rider's WWW Yellow Pages, Netcenter, Nikos, Pronet, Starting Point's New, Web Crawler, What's New Too, Whole Internet Catalog, World Wide Web Worm, Yahoo, and YellowPages.

You can find Submit It! at:

http://www.submit-it.com

Expect a 2- to 4-week delay between the time you submit your announcement and the time visitors can use one of these sites to find your Web site.

PostMaster

Another popular all-in-one submission site is PostMaster, where you complete one form, and your announcement is sent to 17 directory sites for free, or you can post to a rather larger group of 300 print, radio, and TV sites for a fee of $500. You can find PostMaster at:

http://www.netcreations.com/postmaster/

A1 Index

The A1 Index of Free WWW Promotion Sites, at:

```
http://www.vir.com/~wyatt/index.html
```

provides a listing of several hundred sites to which you can submit your URL.

Making the Most of Search Engines

Once your announcement has gone out to the one-stop sites mentioned in the last section, you can use one of the very popular Web search engines to ensure that your site is listed where you think it should be. A search engine is a special Web site that a visitor can use to search for Web sites based on specific keywords. (See a later section in this chapter, "Adding a Search Engine to Your Web Site," for much more detailed information about search engines.) Access to most search engines is entirely free, as the companies that support them make their money by selling advertising space on their Web pages.

Many of the newer search engines actively go out and search the Web, checking that existing links still work and adding material to their giant databases from new sites. The programs that perform this function are called *spiders*, *Web crawlers*, or *bots* (short for robot). You must manually tell some older search engines about any new sites. Some search engines store only the title and address of the sites that they include; others index every word of a site's content.

When you access one of these search engines, check that it has found your home page, but also check that it has found all the pages on your site that you want people to access. Because you will be looking at the same information that visitors will see when they think about accessing your site, redesign your site if you don't like what you see, presenting information in a more appropriate or effective light.

AltaVista

The immensely popular AltaVista (see Figure 9.2) search engine is sponsored by the Digital Equipment Corporation. It processes more than 2.5 million search requests every day, and to date has cataloged more than 15 billion words on 30 million Web pages. You can also search through all 13,000 Usenet newsgroups. Check out AltaVista at:

```
http://www.altavista.digital.com/
```

FIGURE 9.2:

The opening AltaVista screen

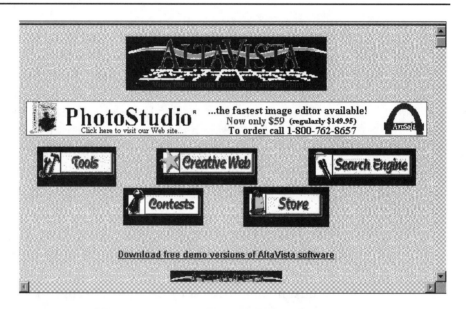

The default simple search is easy to use and surprisingly accurate; the advanced search options are harder to use, and you may have to look at the Help page to get started. Once you have the hang of how to use them, you'll find that they are extremely powerful.

Chances are that AltaVista found your site already, by itself, but if not, you can complete an online form to make sure that it does. The spider that updates the AltaVista database runs on a DEC 3000 with a 30GB hard disk and 1GB of memory; it is so fast (the fastest of all the spiders out there, according to DEC) that it collects Web pages at the rate of 2.5 million a day, and that means that the entire database can be updated every few days. The main AltaVista search engine also runs on some pretty powerful hardware: a 10-processor AlphaStation with a 210GB RAID hard disk system and 6GB of memory. How'd you like that lot sitting on your desk.

AltaVista checks every word of every page on your site (as well as those on all the other sites that it can find on the Web, which is quite a task); so think about the kinds of searches people looking for information are likely to make and about how well (or badly) these keywords or phrases match the information on your pages. If the match is poor, go back and redesign the affected pages. Literally thousands of people start their search for Web information with this very popular search engine site; so it is well worth your while to make sure that your material is presented in the right way here.

AltaVista's search language contains keywords that you can use to restrict your search to specific parts of a Web page, including document titles and embedded links to other Web sites. You can find out how many other Web sites contain links to your own site by entering the following on the Simple Query page:

```
+link:http://company.com -url:http://company.com
```

Just be sure that you substitute your site's URL for *company.com*

in the line above. This search excludes links from your site to your site and so will give an accurate indication of the number of external links to your Web page.

Excite

The Excite database of 1.5 million Web pages lets you search by keyword or by concept. A concept search will find a Web page related to the word or words you search on, even if your chosen keywords are not actually present on that Web page. You will find Excite at:

```
http://www.excite.com/
```

Excite also offers a searchable, browsable directory of more than 50,000 reviewed Web sites, a Usenet database of more than 1 million articles, and a search of the Usenet classifieds from the last 2 weeks. Although Excite may not be the largest of the Web search engines, it is certainly one of the most useful.

HotBot

HotBot is a joint venture between Inktomi and HotWired Ventures, a subsidiary of Wired Ventures, publisher of *Wired* magazine. HotBot features a menu-driven search engine at:

```
http://www.hotbot.com/
```

and has HTML code optimized for each of the browsers that it recognizes. Using the search window, you can customize your search by file type, date, geographic location and domain, or Web site. And advertisers like that banners can be attached to relevant searches.

InfoSeek

InfoSeek is a full-text search system with which you can search Web pages, Usenet newsgroups, and FAQs. Search results are displayed in order of relevance, and you can use a match from a search to locate similar pages. A normal, free search is limited to the first 100 matches, which should be enough for most people. InfoSeek Professional, which costs $4.95 a month for a maximum of 50 transactions, offers more powerful options—including searches of computer, medical, and business news, press releases, and even technical-support databases. Find InfoSeek at:

```
http://www2.infoseek.com/
```

You can submit your URL by e-mail to this address:

```
www.request@infoseek.com
```

Lycos

Named after a family of spiders that hunts down its prey, the Lycos search engine at Carnegie Mellon University is used by more than 500,000 people every week and catalogs almost 20 million Web pages, FTP sites, and Gopher sites. The site is at:

```
http://www.lycos.com
```

Links to matching sites are presented 10 at a time, along with the size of the page and a proprietary rating system that shows how well the pages listed match the search string you entered. Documents with the highest rating are listed first, and you can adjust this to screen out documents that have no application to your search. Lycos also has many binary files in its database, including files in GIF, JPEG, WAV, and MPEG formats.

You can submit your URL to the Lycos search engine at this address:

```
http://www.lycos.com/register.html
```

Open Text Index

The Open Text Index, a powerful, multilingual search engine, is at:

```
http://www.opentext.com:8080/
```

Advanced search options use pop-up menus to specify Boolean or proximity operators and to specify which part of the site you want to search. You can also specify a weighted search that ranks the results based on the weighting factor that you assigned to each search item, on the number of times that the keyword appears on the Web page, or on both. The Open Text Corporation is the creator of the search engine used on the very popular Yahoo directory site and accepts URL submissions at this address:

```
http://www.opentext.com:8080/omw/xsubmit_c.html
```

WebCrawler

The WebCrawler, a free service from America Online, gives you fast access to a 200MB database of 2 million indexed World Wide Web documents. You will find it at this URL:

```
http://webcrawler.com/
```

You can submit your URL to this address:

```
http://webcrawler.com/WebCrawler/SubmitURLS.html
```

World Wide Web Worm

The World Wide Web Worm won the Best of the Web Award in 1994, and it lets you search URLs, titles, or hypertext entries of indexed documents. Find it at:

```
http://www.cs.colorado.edu/home/mcbryan/WWWW.html
```

You can submit your URL to this address:

```
http://guano.cs.colorado.edu/home/mcbryan/WWWadd.html
```

Making a Metasearch

A new kind of search engine has started to appear on the Web recently, a search engine that is capable of applying a single query to several databases—sometimes one at a time, sometimes simultaneously, depending on the search engine. Some of these search engines are described below.

SavvySearch

SavvySearch (see Figure 9.3) can make parallel searches on as many as 5 databases simultaneously and combines and displays the results on a single page, with all duplicates removed. Find SavvySearch at:

```
http://www.cs.colostate.edu/~dreiling/smartform.html
```

FIGURE 9.3:

The SavvySearch opening page

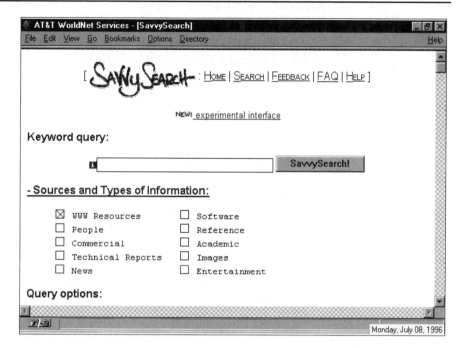

You can also create a Search Plan using your search keywords, SavvySearch's own information, and information gleaned from past searches to rank and group as many as 21 other search engines according to their potential application to your original search. Simply select one of the groups to perform additional parallel searches.

Internet Sleuth

The Internet Sleuth has what is probably the largest, most comprehensive collection of searchable databases on the Web, well over 900 at the present time, including some specialized databases for topics as diverse as carnivorous plants, abstracts from American Medical Association journals, and a database of travel books. You will find Internet Sleuth at:

```
http://www.intbc.com/sleuth
```

All-in-One Search Page

The All-in-One Search Page has more than 200 basic search forms on its Web site, but you must enter your search keywords into each form separately. Searches are performed in sequence. Find the All-in-One Search Page at:

```
http://www.albany.net/allinone/
```

Other Metasearch Sites

Several other metasearch sites are up and coming, and some of them are listed in Table 9.1. This is a category of Web site that we will see grow in size, scope, and ease of use during the next few months as these sites get better and better and more come online.

TABLE 9.1:   Some metasearch sites and their URLs

Site	URL
All4one	`http://all4one.com`
CUSI	`http://www-cetc.ucsd.edu/cusi.html`
Metasearch	`http://metasearch.com/`
Searchers	`http://gagme.wwa.com/oba/search.html`
Starting Point Metasearch	`http://www.stpt.com/search.html`
W3 Search Engines	`http://cuiwww.unige.ch/meta-index.html`
Web-Search	`http://www.biddeford.com/~soaring/`
W3Catalog	`http://cuiwww.unige.ch/w3catalog/`

What's New Sites

Several sites on the Web are known as What's New sites. Every week, or sometimes even more frequently, they compile listings of new and notable Web sites. And because lots of people start Web searches at one of these sites, get your URL mentioned on as many as possible. New URLs are often listed at What's New sites much faster than they are listed on the search engines we looked at in the last section; so if timing is important to your company, inform these sites first.

Starting Point's New

Starting Point's New will list your new URL within a few hours after you submit your announcement, but this site includes a mixture of what the owners consider the best and the worst of the new Web sites. Find it at:

```
http://stpt.com/new.html
```

NCSA What's New

The NCSA (National Center for Supercomputing Applications) What's New is somewhat choosy about which new sites it promotes, and it is biased toward promoting particularly content-rich sites and sites that are being updated frequently. Because the editors actually review your site according to their criteria, it may be a couple of weeks before your site appears here. Find NCSA What's New at:

```
http://www.ncsa.uiuc.edu/SDG/Software/Mosaic/Docs/
whats-new.html
```

And you can send your submission to this URL:

```
http://www.ncsa.uiuc.edu/SDG/Software/Mosaic/Docs/
whats-new-form.html
```

What's New Too

Manifest Information Services What's New Too claims to post several hundred new announcements within 36 hours of submission. Find this site at:

```
http://newtoo.manifest.com/
```

You can enter your submission at this URL:

```
http://newtoo.manifest.com/WhatsNewToo/submit.html
```

Netscape's What's New

Netscape's What's New site is at:

```
http://home.netscape.com/home/whats-new.html
```

This site is updated weekly and is accessible directly from the Netscape Navigator browser, which makes it extremely important. Send your submission to:

```
http://home.netscape.com/escapes/whats_new.html
```

Finding Other What's New Sites

Several other What's New sites are available on the Web, and Table 9.2 lists some of the more popular ones.

TABLE 9.2: Some What's New sites and their URLs

Site	URL
New on Yahoo	`http://www.yahoo.com/new/`
Net-Happenings	`http://www.midinet.net/`
New Items	`http://www.lsu.edu/~poli/newexcit.html`

Using Web Yellow Pages, Indexes, and Lists

People who use Yellow Pages, listings, and Web indexes are among some of the most serious and qualified people who will ever visit your site. They are not idly surfing the Web; they are actively looking for information.

Yahoo

The Yahoo site (see Figure 9.4), started by Jerry Yang and David Filo, graduate students who dropped out of Stanford in 1994 to index the Web, has become the index of all indexes on the Web. Find this busy site at:

```
http://www.yahoo.com/
```

FIGURE 9.4:

The Yahoo index opening page

Yahoo lists more than 200,000 Web sites in more then 20,000 categories, but the indexing of new sites is done by hand. If you don't make a point of telling Yahoo about your new Web site, you may not be listed at all. Regional sites are cross-referenced to their main subject entry and so should appear twice in Yahoo's structure.

Yahoo also includes a very competent search engine; so you can find things quickly in this database. A utility lets you extend your search to other search engines such as AltaVista, Lycos, or WebCrawler.

Galaxy

TradeWave provides the Galaxy business directory at:

```
http://www.einet.net/
```

This site is one of the best-organized business directories on the Web. Categories include Business Administration, General Resources, and Products and Services; select any link to go directly to a list of servers. You'll find lists of business dictionaries and glossaries, statistics, and information on overseas and international business. Galaxy also has links to comics, gardening, cigars, and leather products sites; so it is not all work and no play.

If you want your company listed on one of the commercial directories that follow, send a message to the e-mail address at the bottom of the first Web page asking for information on rates. Prices vary widely from site to site.

The Whole Internet Catalog

The Whole Internet Catalog, at:

```
http://nearnet.gnn.com/wic/
```

may not be the biggest listing on the Web, but it certainly gives you access to some excellent material, including government and non-profit sites, Internet commerce sites, and listings on personal finance, real estate, and taxes.

CommerceNet Directories

The CommerceNet Directories supply an interesting cross-section of business resources. Find this site at:

```
http://www.commerce.net/directories/
```

You can link to many CommerceNet participants, including American Express, FedEx, Hitachi, IBM, Lockheed, and Silicon Graphics. One of the most useful and popular resources is the News and Information Directory, with its links to the CNN daily headlines.

IOMA Business Page

The Institute of Management and Administration offers this well-organized business directory site at:

```
http://www.ioma.com/ioma/
```

Under Departments, you will find extensive categories, including Administration, Finance, and Sales and Marketing. Subcategories include Corporate Profiles, Accounting and Taxation, and so on.

McKinley's Magellan Internet Directory

You will find McKinley's Magellan Internet Directory at:

```
http://magellan.mckinley.com/
```

This site rates Web sites using one to four stars, and you can use this star rating to narrow any searches; you can also search Magellan's database of still-to-be-reviewed sites.

Locating Other Directories

As with the other categories we have already looked at, there are plenty more good quality directories on the Web, and Table 9.3 lists some of them.

TABLE 9.3: Some directory sites and their URLs

Site	URL
Apollo	`http://apollo.co.uk`
BigYellow	`http://www.bigyellow.com/`
ClearingHouse	`http://lib.umich.edu/chhome.html`
Excite NetDirectory	`http://excite.com/Subject/`
LinkStar	`http://www.linkstar.com/`
New Rider's WWW Yellow Pages	`http://mcp.com/newriders/wwwyp/`
Nynex Interactive Yellow Pages	`http://niyp.com/`
StartingPoint	`http://www.stpt.com/`
Tribal Voice	`www.tribal.com/search.htm`
Virtual Yellow Pages	`http://www.vyp.com/`
World Wide Yellow Pages	`http://www.yellow.com/`
WWW Virtual Library	`http://www.w3.org/hypertext/DataSources/bySubject/Overview.html`
Yellow Pages	`http://theyellowpages.com/`

"Best of" and Other Award Sites

Several Web sites post Web-site reviews, recognize worthy Web sites, propose sites that others might like to vote on, or recommend sites you might like to visit.

Point Top 5 Percent Reviews

Point Communications provides reviews and ratings of Web sites at:

http://www.point.com/

Web sites are reviewed daily and rated on a scale of 1 to 50 according to several categories, including content, presentation, and experience. Your award-winning site can display a Top 5 Percent badge.

Interactive Age's 100 Best List

This site (see Figure 9.5) lists 100 absolutely top-class commercial Web sites that have been judged by *Interactive Age* as the best at presenting Web resources to visitors. Find it at:

http://techweb.cmp.com/techweb/ia/features/hot100.html

Some of the chosen sites might be easy to access and navigate, and others offer unusual or eye-catching design or unusual content.

FIGURE 9.5:

The *Interactive Age* 100 Best List

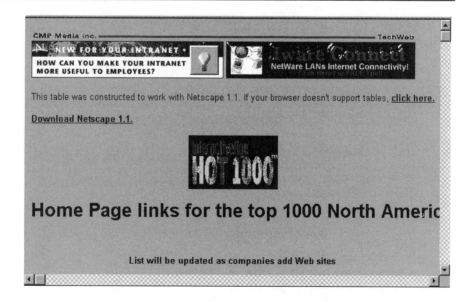

This site is a good place to get examples of business Web design at its very best; the list of sites reads like a Who's Who of Corporate America and includes Apple Computer, AT&T, Compaq, DEC, Eastman Kodak, Goodyear, and Hewlett-Packard, as well as many, many others.

You can also look at *Interactive Age*'s list of the top 1000 U.S. corporations, ranked by size, with a link to those companies that have a Web site. Find this list at:

```
http://techweb.cmp.com/techweb/ia/hot1000/hot1.html
```

Locating Other "Best Of" Web Sites

As with the other categories we have already looked at, there are more "Best Of" sites on the Web, and Table 9.4 lists some of them.

TABLE 9.4: "Best Of" sites and their URLs

Site	URL
Cool Site of the Day	`http://cool.infi.net`
Dynamite Site of the Nite	`http://www.vpm.com/tti/dsotn.html`
Funky Site of the Day	`http://www.reality.com/cybstars/index.html`
Hot Site of the Night	`http://www.euro.net/5thworld/hotnite/hotnite.html`
NetGuide Hot Spots	`http://www.winmag.com/flanga/hotspots.htm`
USA Today's Net Site of Note	`http://www.usatoday.com/life/cyber/cyber1.htm`
Wave of the Day	`http://www.marketsquare.com/wave/`

Commercial Indexes

A fast-growing area on the Web is that of market-specific directories, or vertical market listings, services that focus on a single industry or market segment.

IndustryNet Online Marketplace

The IndustryNet Online Marketplace is a national database of suppliers; find it at:

```
http://www.industry.net/
```

When you select a supplier, you link to that company's home page, where you can send the company e-mail, request a catalog, or look at the company's latest products and services. First-time users can take a guided tour of this well-organized site, but you must register to get complete access to this free service.

The Ultimate Industry Connection

This site is a complete list of companies involved in the computer industry, and you can find it at:

```
http://www.hardware.com/complist.html
```

You will find links to almost every hardware and software company in the United States, as well as to magazines, newsgroups, and many of the most important FTP archives.

Computer and Communications Companies

The Computer and Communications Companies site at:

```
http://www-atp-llnl.gov/atp/companies.html
```

is a list of software companies that maintain a Web presence, arranged alphabetically by company name, with product type and headquarters location listed alongside.

Government Indexes

The directories in this section give you an exhaustive listing of national, regional, and local government agencies. These sites do not provide detailed content, but they do provide links to the sites that do. If you work in one of these government sectors, be sure that your Web site is listed and that the link to it is up to date and valid.

U.S. Federal Government Agencies

The WWW Virtual Library: U.S. Federal Government Agencies site at Louisiana State University, located at:

```
http://www.lib.lsu.edu/gov/fedgov.html
```

lists U.S. government agency sites in all their awe-inspiring detail. This is a very long list and contains links to about 80 percent of the departments on it.

The Federal Web Locator

This site at Villanova University is even bigger that the last one, and the last one was big. Check out:

```
http://www.law.vill.edu/fed-agency/fedwebloc.html
```

You will probably not be too surprised to find that the number of government Internet sites is just astonishing. Did you know that a complete listing of all NASA Internet sites would fill more than 25 screens?

Infosearch

You can use the Mr. Smith E-mails Washington site provided by Infosearch at:

```
http://www.searcher.com
```

to send e-mail to members of the executive branch of the U.S. government and to senators and representatives of all 50 states.

International Directories

The World Wide Web is a global phenomenon, and the number of quality resources listing international opportunities is constantly growing. Here are some of the best overseas sites; in the next section, we'll look at specifically regional sites.

Asia Business and Leisure Directory

The Asia Business and Leisure Directory Web site (see Figure 9.6), at:

```
http://www.asiadir.com/
```

is a treasure trove of links to companies in Southeast Asia, including Hong Kong, Indonesia, Malaysia, Taiwan, and Thailand. If you do business in these countries, you need to check into this site. If you are thinking of expanding your operations into this area, this site will give you a good idea of the type of competition you are likely to encounter.

The Nihongo Yellow Pages

This site is designed for international suppliers who want to reach the Japanese market and is at:

```
http://www.nyp.com/HTML/directory.html
```

The site contains information in both Japanese and English, but you will need a special browser to look at the pages in Japanese.

FIGURE 9.6:

The opening page of the Asia Business and Leisure Directory

Canadian Business Directory

This site contains information on businesses, government agencies, universities, and other organizations all across Canada that have a Web presence:

```
http://cibd.com/cibd/
```

If you do business in Canada, check into adding links at your site to the Canadian Business Directory.

Canadian Internet Business Directory

The Canadian Internet Business Directory site lists tens of thousands of Canadian companies at:

```
http://www.net-mark.mb.ca/netmark/search.html
```

and includes a built-in search engine that you can use to locate a company name, location, industry, or product.

Europages World Wide Web

If you plan on doing business in Europe, check out the Europages World Wide Web site, which lists well over 150,000 businesses in more than 25 countries and lets you search in 5 languages, including English, French, German, Italian, and Spanish, at:

```
http://www.europages.com
```

UK Business Directory

This site is designed to help you find suppliers in the United Kingdom:

```
http://www.milfac.co.uk/milfac/
```

If you do business in the UK, you need to be listed in this extensive directory.

Regional Sites

Many Web sites list companies and other resources by geographic location, including by city or by state. Don't count out this kind of site; you need to get the word out to as many lists and directories as you possibly can.

The Virtual Tourist

The Virtual Tourist actually has two Web sites. One at:

```
http://wings.buffalo.edu/world/
```

gives you access to local servers anywhere in the world based on CERN's master list of databases. The second site at:

```
http://wings.buffalo.edu/world/vt2/
```

is an imagemap interface into the City.Net database.

City.Net

The City.Net Web site lists well over a thousand cities, organized by country and state:

```
http://www.city.net/
```

Start by finding the country you are interested in, then the city; if there is a directory of the businesses in your local area, the chances are excellent that it is listed here. You can also simply run a search on your city name.

Using Mailing Lists and Newsgroups

A mention of your site in an appropriate Usenet newsgroup or on a mailing list can add traffic to your site, but only if you go about this in a suitably subtle way. Some newsgroups are extremely sensitive to commercial organizations using their bandwidth, and the moderators of such newsgroups may come down hard on what they consider behavior or information outside the normal scope of the newsgroup.

The general rule is: Do not post a commercial message or an announcement to what is clearly a noncommercial mailing list or newsgroup. If you do, your reward will be lots of hostile flames from the other subscribers. In the past, people have done things such as sending a message to every single newsgroup; and instead of bringing in new business, the overwhelming response has been to ridicule the people and companies involved.

The case of Lawrence Canter and Martha Seagle is an example. They sent a message advertising their services to almost every newsgroup in existence. This almost guaranteed that everyone using the Internet and reading Usenet newsgroups would see their message, and, of course, many thousands of people saw the message twice or three times because they read more than one newsgroup. The response from the Internet community was immediate; Canter and Seagle's mailbox was flooded with junk mail, exceeding the capacity of their ISP to handle the traffic. One man in Australia set up an automatic script to send Canter and Seagle a thousand phony requests for information every day; in the end, their ISP pulled the plug on their account. So don't even think about doing it; Usenet newsgroups are not the same as the Web, and they exist for entirely different purposes.

Mailing Lists

A mailing list tends to cover a specific subject, usually of fairly limited general interest. To subscribe to a mailing list, you must first send a subscribe message to the listserver that manages the mailing list. Once you are on the list, you will begin to receive e-mail from the mailing list members. This subscription process is free, and so it is not like starting a magazine subscription. You can leave the mailing list at any time by sending an unsubscribe message to the listserver.

One of the many sites on the Internet that contain lists of mailing lists is :

```
http://tile.net/listserv
```

Newsgroups

Unlike mailing lists, the thousands of Usenet newsgroups are open to everyone. To subscribe to a newsgroup is much easier than subscribing to a mailing list; all you have to do is read the postings in the newsgroup, and anyone (yes, anyone) can post an article. You can view a list of newsgroups at:

```
http://www.w3.org/hypertext/DataSources/News/Groups/
Overview.html
```

Before posting to a newsgroup, read the articles posted by others for a week or so to get a feel for the volume and scope of the newsgroup.

After warning you about posting to noncommercial mailing lists and newsgroups, I can tell you about several newsgroups to which such announcements are appropriate, including:

- `comp.infosystem.announce` contains general announcements of new Web sites, Gopher sites, and so on. This is the best place to start.

- `comp.infosystem.www.announce` contains announcements of new Web sites.

- `comp.internet.net-happenings` is based on a mailing list of the same name.

- `biz.comp.services` is for announcements of new commercial services.

- `alt.internet.services` is for announcements of new noncommercial services.

The scope of the Usenet newsgroups is just astonishing; there are newsgroups on almost every imaginable subject. For example, if you run a nonprofit Web page aimed at the educational needs of children, you might check out the K-12 educational newsgroups, including:

- `k12.chat.teachers` a teachers discussion forum

- `k12.ed.soc-studies` a social studies discussion forum

- `k12.library` a librarians' discussion forum

- `alt.education.alernative` for alternative educational methods

If you want to find something in a Usenet newsgroup, remember that the major search engines not only let you search Web pages, but also let you search the contents of all newsgroups. AltaVista's advanced Usenet search can also search through the "from" and "subject" article headers, as well as keywords, summaries, and specific newsgroups. Excite and InfoSeek also have excellent Usenet searches.

Using Online Publications

New and better online publications seem to appear every week. Table 9.5 lists some of the better ones and includes contact information. Read a publication for a while before sending it any messages or announcements.

Negotiating Sponsorship

Another way of getting the word out about your site is to enter into mutually beneficial agreements with other companies that have Web sites—a sort of "you advertise my Web site, and I'll advertise yours" agreement. You can even consider purchasing space on another Web site, particularly one that generates lots of traffic.

Another method is to create a sort of "road-rally" competition, in which players have to visit many Web sites, find clues to a puzzle, answer questions, collect tokens, and go on to the next site. If you have a marketing technique that applies particularly well to your market segment or industry, see if there is a way that you can do the same thing on the Web.

TABLE 9.5: Online publications information

Publication name	Editor's name	E-mail address	URL
Computergram International	Maya Anaokar	maya@power.globalnews.com	http://power.globalnews.com/apt/cgi.html
Cybertalk	Terry Taylor	ttaylor@wimsey.com	http://www.cybertalk.wis.net/
EduPage	John Gehl	gehl@educom.edu	http://www.educom.edu/web/edupage.html
HiTech Bulletin	Doug Willoughby	dougw@pinc.com	http://vvv.com/hi_tech/flashes.html
Info Highway	Paul Lavin	plavin@caversham.win-uk.net	http://www.infohighway.co.uk/infohighway/
Internet Business Journal	Michael Stragelove	michael@strangelove.com	http://www.phoenix.ca/sie/ibj-home.html
Internet Week	Minda Morgan Ceasar	mceasar@phillips.com	http://www.phillips.com/iw/
Matrix Mews	John Quartermain	mids@mids.org	http://www.tic.com/mids/mn.html
Net Day	Tristan Louis	news@iworld.com	http://www.iworld.com/netday/
Web Digest for Marketers	Larry Chase	chase@advert.com	http://www.advert.com/wdfm/wdfm.html

Gopher Archives

Because Microsoft's Internet Information Server also supports a Gopher server, we'll take a look at some of the ways you can use what is called Gopherspace, the whole set of Internet resources accessible using Gopher, and then in the next section, we'll look at FTP.

In many ways, Gopher appears to have been a cruder text-based precursor to the World Wide Web. Gopher presents Internet resources as a series of menus and so shields you from the underlying mechanical details of IP addresses and the resource access methods.

Gopher menus may contain documents that you can download, searches you can perform, or additional menu selections. When you choose an item from one of these menus, Gopher does whatever is necessary to obtain the resource you selected, either by downloading the document or by jumping to the selected Gopher server and opening the top-level menu.

You can search Gopherspace from many of the search engines discussed earlier in this chapter, but other tools are available, including Veronica, that those without access to the Web can use.

When you use Veronica to search a series of Gopher menus (files, directories, and other items), the results are presented as another Gopher menu, which you can use to access the resources located by your search. Veronica supposedly stands for Very Easy Rodent-Oriented Net-wide Index to Computer Archives, although there are those who might dispute that.

To look at one of the largest Gopher archives, try:

```
http://galaxy.einet.net/gopher/gopher.html
```

and if you want to use Veronica, you must first gopher to:

```
gopher.unr.edu
```

and then select:

```
/search
```

Your Gopher client will present the results of your search as another Gopher menu. Remember that when you are using a Gopher search, only directory names and filenames are indexed, not the contents of every page as is the case with some of the more complex Web search engines.

And if you use one of the search engines described earlier in this chapter to locate Gopher or FTP archive sites, be careful, because the search engine is likely to find literally tens of thousands of sites if you simply search for "Gopher archives" or "FTP archives." Try it; you'll see. Choose the keywords to search on as carefully as you can to narrow the search to a small number of relevant sites. Even in these Web-oriented days, much of the traffic on the Internet is still generated by FTP file transfers rather than Web pages.

FTP Sites

The FTP program began life as a Unix utility, but has been ported to almost every computing environment. It uses the File Transfer Protocol described in the *TCP/IP in a Nutshell* chapter to move files from an FTP site or archive to a client program that is running on your system.

Anonymous FTP is a way to access an FTP site if you don't have an account on that system. You simply log in to the FTP server with the username *anonymous* and use your e-mail address as your password. You cannot use this method to log in to every computer on the Internet, only to those set up this way by their administrators. The system administrator decides which files and directories will be open to public access, and the rest of the system is considered off limits and cannot be accessed by anonymous FTP users.

As an extra security measure, many anonymous FTP sites will only let you download files from them; you cannot upload files to them. All this aside, the world open to anonymous FTP is simply enormous; there are tens of thousands of anonymous FTP servers on the Internet, and hundreds of thousands of files you can download.

In the same way that you can use Veronica to locate Gopher resources, you can use a utility called Archie to find FTP resources. Archie was written by students and volunteers at McGill University's School of Computer Science in Montreal, Canada, and is available all over the world.

Once a week, special programs connect to all the known anonymous FTP sites on the Internet and collect a complete listing of all the publicly available files from each site. This information is kept in the Internet Archive Database, and when you ask Archie to find a file, only this database is searched rather than the whole Internet. You can then use anonymous FTP to retrieve the file.

Several Web sites also perform this search function, including FTPSearch, which is easy to use, has lots of search options, and covers more than 3,000 FTP archive sites. Find it at:

```
http://129.241.190.13/ftpsearch/
```

Snoopy offers a very fast search of more than 5.6 million files, but with very few options, and the results list only the filename and size. Snoopy is at:

```
http://www.snoopy.com/
```

Shareware.com, originally known as the Virtual Software Library, offers great search options into more than 175,000 files of shareware, freeware, demos, upgrades, and the like. Find it at:

```
http://www.shareware.com/
```

Jumbo lets you browse your way through several categories of software and provides a full program description to read before you download a file. Jumbo is at:

```
http://www.jumbo.com/Home_Page.html
```

How to Mirror Another Web Site

Mirroring another Web site is the act of duplicating the contents of one site on another Web site and is usually done to provide visitors with alternative methods for accessing the same data. Many large companies who expect very high traffic on their sites use mirroring.

If a company's Web site is at:

```
http://www.company.com
```

it may call its mirror site:

```
http://www.company2.com
```

The company hopes to lighten the load on its `www.company.com` site by providing the mirror at `www.company2.com`, which might be in a different country to allow international users to connect more easily.

Mirroring is usually done when a larger than normal load is anticipated for a particular Web site, for example, when a NASA space probe is about to enter the atmosphere of a hostile planet. Mirroring is not used all that often, but several large software companies (mentioning no names) should consider it as an alternative to making people wait for a connection to their main server.

Adding a Search Engine to Your Web Site

Earlier in this chapter, we looked at just how useful a search engine can be when searching the Web; imagine that capability on your own Web site. A search engine is definitely one of the features you should think about adding sooner rather than later if you have a large Web site or if your site contains a great deal of technical or product information. Internet sites can offer a sophisticated search facility, and Intranet sites, such as sales support or human resources sites, instantly become much more effective with an integrated search facility. Several solutions are available for NT users, ranging from full-featured commercial products to free offerings from the makers of other types of software.

How Search Engines Work

All the popular search engines work in the same general way, often based on the Z39.50 protocol, a standard for database format and search utilities devised well over 10 years ago. They usually perform two distinct functions: indexing and searching.

The indexing program looks at the data—HTML, ASCII, or other files—on your Web site and creates a file called a *source* that acts as an index into your data. This file includes a list of every word in the original material, where it is located, and how many times each word occurs. When you want to find a specific keyword, the searching program accesses the source file rather than the original data, which is much more efficient.

When you install a search engine on your Web site, the first task is to run the indexer, telling it where to find the data files and what to call the source file it creates. This source file is likely to be about half the size of your original data files; so be prepared with the appropriate amount of hard-disk space. Once the initial indexing is done, and it is usually done quickly, you can run updates to reflect any changes in the content on your Web site. On some sites this will be a daily task; on others, weekly or even monthly.

Search Engines for Windows NT

The 3 search engines described below are among the most popular that you can install under Windows NT. Some offer advanced search options, but others are easier to administer. The developers of all three have Web sites that you can visit to find out more about each product, and at least one site will offer you a demonstration of the product. Try them, and then think carefully about installing one on your Web site; your visitors will thank you.

CompassWare's CompassSearch

CompassSearch offers what CompassWare calls *conceptual querying*: A visitor enters a simple phrase or keyword, and the search engine (called MagnetSearch) locates the appropriate words, phrases, and concepts. MagnetSearch can assign various weightings to concepts, ideas, definitions, keywords, and phrases, and results are presented in a ranked order. For more information, visit:

```
http://www.compassware.com/products/web_server.html
```

Architext Software's Excite

If you have visited the Excite site described earlier in this chapter, you have already used this search engine. In exchange for giving this product away (yes, it is free), Excite wants to monitor the content on your site so that its central engine can update its database quickly and easily.

The Excite engine is small, compact, and easy to install. It requires 32MB of memory and about half again as much disk space as your data currently occupies. You can get more information at:

```
http://atext.com
```

or visit Excite at:

```
http://excite.com
```

Verity's TopicSearch

Verity has been in the intelligent text-retrieval business for a long time and is now offering TopicSearch for free. TopicSearch allows searching by keyword and by Boolean expressions. It is easy to install and configure, supports both HTML and text documents, and adds both CGI and ISAPI interfaces for superior performance, scalabilty, and administration.

Visit Verity's site at:

```
http://www.verity.com
```

for details of this and other Verity products and also to run your own demonstration of TopicSearch.

More Search Engines for NT

You will find a list of more search engines that will run under Windows NT in Table 9.6.

More on Search Engines

Here are some Web sites you can visit to collect more information on search engines. Visit Yahoo for a list of links to search engines at:

```
http://www.yahoo.com/Computers_and_Internet/
World_Wide_Web/Databases_and_Searching
```

For information on search engines and CGI scripts, visit the Programmer's Page at:

`http://www.ifu/%7Ejifgriff/progp.html`

and the Strange Visual Basic Homepage at:

`http://www.infinet.com/~mstrange/.`

TABLE 9.6:   Search engines that run under Windows NT and their URLs

Company	Product	URL
EMWAC	WAIS Server	`http://www.emwac.ed.ac.uk`
Fulcrum Technologies	Surfboard	`http://www.fulcrum.com/`
InTEXT Systems Inc	InTEXT Retrieval Engine	`http://www./intext.com/`
Open Text Corp	.Livelink Search	`http://www.opentext.com/`
Pacific Coast Software	WebCatalog	`http://www.pacific-coast.com/`
Personal Library Software	PLWeb	`http://www.pls.com/`
Tippecanoe Systems	Tecumshe	`http://tippecanue.com/`
ZyLAB International	ZyIndex	`http://www.zylab.com/`

PART III

Administering and Maintaining Your Web Site

CHAPTER

TEN

10

Windows NT Server
Operating System Security

This chapter covers the internal security features of the Windows NT operating system. You'll learn how to add users and groups, how to set user permissions and resource-sharing permissions, as well as how to establish security audit trails and how to review the Windows NT event logs. Implementing and maintaining the account and other security elements are some of the most overlooked aspects in managing a network computing system. Begin with the premise that any user of your Web site is a potential intruder, and design your checks and balances accordingly.

A Little Historical Background

Maintaining the security of a computer system has long been a priority. Initially, that control was required for inter-department billing for computer services in a company. Today, security from intruders requires serious attention, especially if you are connecting to the Internet.

System security on Microsoft networks has evolved proportionately, and Microsoft has had the advantage of being a relatively new player to the operating system market. There were literally hundreds of proposals, trials, errors, modifications, and enhancements over the years that Microsoft developers could analyze carefully as they designed the foundations for the security systems built into Windows NT Server. As a result, Windows NT is one of the most secure and robust operating system platforms on the market today.

Microsoft's first major operating system, MS-DOS, contained absolutely no security features. In fact, no version of MS-DOS has ever had any significant security features. The first security mechanisms for Microsoft Windows were actually not provided by Microsoft but by the manufacturers that made network operating systems to connect computers running Microsoft Windows.

Not until the development of Windows for Workgroups did Microsoft begin to include even the slightest security, and it was implemented when you installed Microsoft's NetBEUI networking software. In this situation, a user received a logon name and password combination and a workgroup name, and those in the same workgroup could share disk drives and printers—really not much security at all compared with the security features found on other network operating systems.

Real security was, however, a feature of Windows NT version 3.1. A crucial part of Windows NT design is the focus on security. Windows NT version 4 has even more security features than were in Windows NT version 3.51. In this chapter, we'll look at the security features of Windows NT in detail. If you are installing Windows NT and IIS, read this chapter carefully and take the necessary steps to secure your Web site and server. Without security, your server can become a playground for malicious intruders.

An Overview of Windows NT Security

Although the Windows NT security model involves several components, it is an integral subsystem that affects the entire operating system and makes it easy to control security on a number of servers. The security subsystem controls access to resources, known as *objects*. Within this subsystem is the Windows NT version of a domain. An

NT domain is a collection or association of servers and has nothing to do with the Internet domains we looked at in earlier chapters.

A domain is a workgroup with centralized security control; a server is designated as the *primary domain controller* or, in some cases, as a *secondary domain controller*, and these servers act as security administrators for all the objects within the domain. Using domains has several important advantages, including the following:

- A domain has a single password, and that password grants access to all the resources in the domain that you have authorization to use.

- This password is user-specific and can be administered by an individual user. Thus, network administrators can assign particular file or printer access permissions to individual users.

This idea of the domain is the fundamental building block upon which Windows NT networks are constructed, and we will look at domains in more detail in a moment.

Security in NT also extends to the user and the file level; you can say that user A can only read file B, whereas user C can both read and write file B. The users belong to user groups. Each user or group of users can have varying rights to objects and to the operation of the network. Windows NT security provides event auditing and detailed logging and allows you to monitor the access and use of objects on your network. Actually, Windows NT security structures are not that different from other types of network security. They are, however, much more reliable.

The Windows NT security model consists of these components: Logon Processes, Local Security Authority, the Security Account Manager, and the Security Reference Monitor. Each component is an integral part of the overall security model, and here is what each one does.

- **Logon Processes** (LP) accept the actual logon requests from users via the initial logon dialog boxes and through remote logon processes for remote users.

- **Local Security Authority** (LSA) ensures that users requesting access to resources do in fact have the correct permissions.

- **Security Account Manager**, commonly referred to as SAM, maintains the actual user account database, which contains all the permissions and rights for users and groups belonging to a domain. SAM provides user validation services to the Local Security Authority.

- **Security Reference Monitor** (SRM) ensures that a user or a process has permission to access an object and determines that whatever action the user is attempting to perform is actually allowed in that user's security profile. The Security Reference Monitor enforces access validation and any audit generation policies that the Local Security Authority has defined.

Windows NT Domains Explained

As I mentioned above, a Windows NT domain is a group of one or more controllers, servers, and workstations, along with the associated users and objects. A domain is a purely logical grouping of computers and has nothing to do with their physical arrangement; members of a domain can be connected on the same local area network or can be scattered to the four corners of the earth, connected by high-speed communication links. An *object* is any information made available for use on the network. You can also think of an object as a resource. When you share an object, it becomes a shared resource.

A domain is controlled by a Windows NT server that is installed and configured as a primary or a secondary domain controller. You must designate a Windows NT server as a domain controller when you install and configure Windows NT Server. If you install Windows NT as a server, and not as a domain controller, you must reinstall Windows NT if you change your mind later and want that server to be a domain controller.

Domain controllers provide security for access to objects, including objects in other Windows NT domains. Domain controllers in the same domain share security policies information and user account databases and can be configured to allow access to other Windows NT domains and their resources through trust relationships. Other Windows NT servers on the network can join the domain and share their objects with the domain. Within a domain, the network administrator creates one user account for each user; this account specifies user information, group memberships, and security policy information. The user can then log on to the domain once, using one password, rather than logging on to each server in the domain in turn.

Several Windows NT domain models are available when you design your network. Selecting the right model for your network depends on your requirements and how you need to secure access; so plan carefully. The Windows NT Resource Kit has a nice little tool called the Domain Planner that can assist you.

When you load TCP/IP on Windows NT, you define a TCP/IP domain name, also called an Internet domain name. Do not confuse this domain name with the Windows NT domain name. They are two separate names; one is for TCP/IP, and one is for Window NT. This also holds true for the host name and the server name. The Windows NT server name is completely different from the TCP/IP host name.

Overall, the Windows NT domain structure allows a network to be designed so that users and resource objects can be created, grouped, and controlled in a reasonable fashion.

To complete this discussion of NT domains, we need to introduce another Microsoft concept: the *workgroup*. A workgroup is a collection of computers (not a collection of users) that do not belong to a domain. Within a workgroup, each computer tracks its own user and group account information and does not share this information with other workgroup computers, which is in sharp contrast to domain controllers.

Looking at User Security

The Windows NT domain—including users, groups, and resources—is administered by a user who has the authority to do so, usually the system administrator. Generally, the first step after setting up a Windows NT server should be to add an additional user for yourself, or the network administrator. After you add the basic user account, add the user ID to the NT Administrators group.

Adding an Administrator

Adding a user to the Administrators group gives the user the authority of the Administrator—the user can configure all aspects of Windows NT security. An important reason for adding a user to the Administrators group is that it creates an audit trail, a mechanism for tracking all the security settings the user changes. If you simply use the Administrator logon ID and share the password with numerous users, you have no way of telling who actually made changes.

Guest User Accounts

Now that you understand the importance and use of the Administrator account and the Administrators group, I'll mention one other important aspect of security—the Guest user account. When Windows NT Server is initially installed, it adds two user accounts by default. One is the Administrator account, and the other is the Guest account. You cannot delete, disable, or remove the Administrator account; thus, it is impossible to lock yourself out of the network by accidentally deleting or disabling all the administrative accounts.

During the installation procedures, you are asked to define a password for the Administrator account; however, you are not asked to define a password for the Guest account. The installation process establishes this account with a predefined password, and the account is disabled by default. Thus, no one can logon with this user account. It is usually best to leave this account disabled until you have a genuine need to enable it. Be sure to verify that it is in fact disabled.

User security is important when installing IIS because anonymous access to the services actually uses the authority of a user account, which by default is called IUSR_*MACHINE_NAME*, where *MACHINE_NAME* is the computer's name. For example, if the computer name is MARKETING, the anonymous user account is IUSR_MARKETING. We'll cover configuring user permissions under Windows NT in detail in this section of the chapter.

User security is managed by a network administrator, who creates an account for each user of the domain that needs network resources. Windows NT generates a unique security ID for each user account, and that unique ID is stored with the user's permissions and rights as part of that user's profile. When a user attempts to log on, SAM checks the logon information against the user information in the user accounts database and attempts to authenticate the logon.

Global and Local User Accounts

The Windows NT security model has two types of user accounts: global and local. This arrangement is similar to that of global and local user groups; however, the parameters of user groups are somewhat different from the parameters of user accounts.

On computers running Windows NT Server, user accounts that are not domain controllers are global user accounts. Global users are authenticated by the primary or secondary (backup) domain controllers or through the trust relationships established with other Windows NT domains.

Local user accounts fully participate in a domain through a remote logon. Don't be confused here by the phrase "remote logon." Remote doesn't always mean logging on through a dial-up or other distant communications link. In this instance, a user with a remote logon is "remote" from the domain. In other words, the workstation and user do not belong to any domain other than the domain to which the user account is being added. Thus, any user that is a local user and not a global user must be authenticated by the Windows NT server on which that the account is being created. Such a user cannot be authenticated through a trust relationship with another domain. For example, in a network composed of one or more Windows NT domains, one or more Windows workgroups, perhaps a Unix system, and maybe even a Novell NetWare network, member users are considered local users and are subject to local user limitations.

Adding a New User

In Windows NT Server, the User Manager for Domains is the administrative tool used to control user accounts, groups, and security policies for domains and computers on the network. The network administrator uses it to do the following:

- Create, modify, or delete user accounts in the domain
- Define a user's desktop environment and network connection
- Manage the domain's security policies
- Manage the relationships among domains on the network
- Add logon scripts to user accounts

In NT Server, a user account contains a variety of information, such as username, password, and group membership, as detailed in Table 10.1.

The process of creating a new user requires that you specify much of the information listed in Table 10.1; other important information is added automatically by NT behind the scenes. For example, every newly created account is assigned a security identifier (SID), a unique number that identifies the account to NT's security systems. When an account is deleted, the SID is also deleted; SIDs are never reused. Every new account is assigned a new SID, even if all the user information is the same as an old account. Thus, the new account cannot assume any of the rights and permissions accorded to the old account, and security is preserved. NT's internal processes refer to the account's SID rather than to the user or group name.

TABLE 10.1:   Information in a user account

Account element	Description
Username	The unique name that the user types when logging on; often a combination of first and last names
Full name	The user's full name
Description	Any text describing the user or the account
Password	The user's secret password
Logon hours	The hours during which the user is allowed to log on and use network resources
Logon workstations	The computer names of the NT workstations that the user is allowed to work from
Expiration date	The future date when the user's account is automatically disabled
Home directory	The name of the user's private directory on the server
Logon script	A batch file or script that runs automatically every time the user logs on
Profile	A file containing details of the user's desktop environment
Account type	The type of account, either local or global

To add a new user to the Windows NT domain, follow these steps:

1. Click on the Start button, choose Programs, select Administrative Tools, and then select User Manager for Domains. Windows NT displays the User Manager dialog box, as shown in Figure 10.1. This dialog box lists all the accounts in the domain, followed by a list of all the groups defined in the domain.

FIGURE 10.1:

The User Manager dialog box

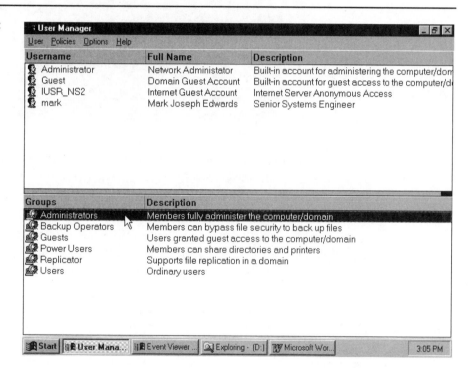

2. From the User drop-down menu, select New User. Windows NT displays the New User dialog box, as shown in Figure 10.2.

FIGURE 10.2:

The New User
dialog box

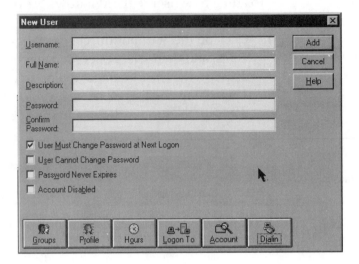

3. Fill in the Username, Full Name, Description, Password, and
   Confirm Password text boxes. The options in the lower half of
   the dialog box are detailed in Table 10.2. At the bottom of the
   New User dialog box you will see 6 buttons: Groups, Profile,
   Hours, Logon To, Account, and Dialin. You use these buttons to
   define the other properties of a new account. We'll go through
   the details of setting up all these options.

TABLE 10.2: Password and account options for a new account

Option	Description
User Must Change Password at Next Logon	Establishes a temporary password for this user. The next time this user logs on to NT with this password, he or she must select a new password immediately.
User Cannot Change Password	Prevents this user from changing his or her password. This is useful for shared accounts, but does not apply to administrators.
Password Never Expires	Gives this user a permanent password. Selecting this option is usually a bad idea.
Account Disabled	Creates a disabled account that cannot be used until it is enabled.

To specify which groups the new account will belong to, click on the Groups button at the bottom of the dialog box. Windows NT displays the Group Memberships dialog box, as shown in Figure 10.3. NT Server includes several predefined groups as you will see in a moment. In this example, I'll assume you're adding a user to the Administrators group.

This dialog box displays which groups the user is and isn't a member of and uses two types of icons next to the group names. An icon displaying a globe behind two faces indicates a global group; an icon displaying a terminal behind two faces indicates a local group. I'll define the differences between these two kinds of groups a little later in this chapter.

FIGURE 10.3:

The Group Memberships dialog box

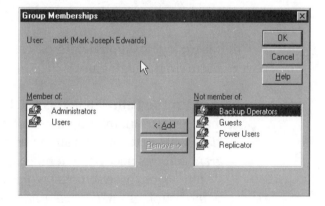

In the Member Of list box, click on Administrators and then click on the Add button. Click on the Close button to establish the group. Windows NT displays the New User dialog box again.

A user account must be a member of at least one group, called the *primary group*, which by definition is a global group and one that cannot be removed.

You use the other buttons in the New User dialog box to establish the user environment for the account; let's start with the Profile button.

In the New User dialog box, click on the Profile button. Windows NT displays the User Environment Profile dialog box, as shown in Figure 10.4.

FIGURE 10.4:

The User Environment Profile dialog box

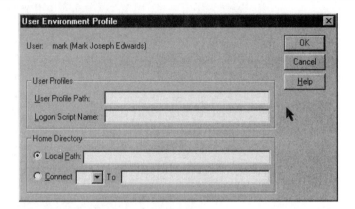

In this dialog box, you define the following settings that can be very useful in managing users:

- **User Profile Path.** Fill in this text box to define a user profile for the user account by typing its full path and filename. A *user profile* is a file that contains all the user-specific desktop and program settings needed to define a user's environment. The system loads these settings, which are identified by username, as the user logs on. *Local user profiles* are created the first time that a user logs on and are always available for that user in the future. *Roaming user profiles,* specified here by a complete path and filename, are downloaded each time the user logs on and are updated with changes when the user logs off. *Mandatory user profiles* are created by the administrator and cannot be changed by the user. When the user logs off, the user profile is not saved, and the local profile is not copied to the server.

- **Logon Script Name.** Fill in this text box with the name of a command file or a batch file that runs on the client machine when this user logs on.

- **Local Path.** Click on this radio button, and then in the text box, to define a modified path for the files and programs for this user. This path to the user's home directory becomes the default for File Open and Save As dialog boxes.

- **Connect To.** Click on this radio button to select a network drive and path from the drop-down list box as the local path instead of using the Local Path setting. When you are done, click on the Close button, and Windows NT displays the New User dialog box once again.

Now let's look at the Logon Hours dialog box, used to specify the days and hours during which this user can access the network.

In the New User dialog box, click on the Hours button. Windows NT displays the Logon Hours dialog box, as shown in Figure 10.5. By default, users can connect to the network all day every day, but at times, you might want to be a little more restrictive. For example, if a user doesn't need to use an account outside normal business hours, adjusting the logon hours might prevent an intruder from using that account outside the specified times.

FIGURE 10.5:

The Logon Hours dialog box

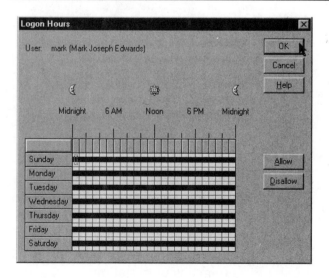

In the Logon Hours dialog box, you specify the hours a user can log on to the network by dragging the cursor over a specific set of hours. Or, you can select all the hours in a specific day by clicking on that day's button on the left side of the dialog box. Then choose the Allow or the Disallow button to permit or deny network access during the selected hours. The logon hours are set to the same time zone as that used by the primary domain controller, which is not always the same time zone as that used by the local server or the workstation. Click on the Close button to return to the New Users dialog box once again.

When you select the Logon To button in the New Users dialog box, Windows NT displays the Logon Workstations dialog box shown in Figure 10.6. You use the options in this dialog box to specify the workstations from which a user can log on to the network. As with the logon times, the default is no restrictions; the user can log on from any workstation on the network.

FIGURE 10.6:

The Logon Workstations dialog box

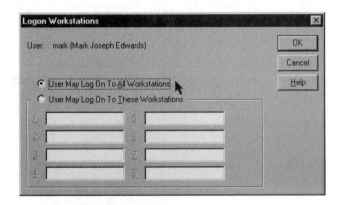

In the Logon Workstation dialog box, you use two selections to control the user's choice of workstation:

- **User May Log on to All Workstations.** If you select this radio button, which is the default, the user can log on to the system from any workstation.

- **User May Log on to These Workstations.** Select this radio button to restrict the workstations that a user can log on from, and enter the names of those workstations in the text boxes (without the preceding backslashes). You can specify a maximum of 8 workstations.

When you are happy with your choices, click on the Close button to return to the New Users dialog box.

Now let's take a look at the Account Information for this user. In the New User dialog box, click on the Account button. Windows NT displays the Account Information dialog box, as shown in Figure 10.7. You can use the settings in this dialog box to force an account to expire after a certain period of time.

FIGURE 10.7:

The Account Information dialog box

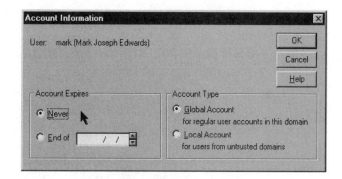

The options in this dialog box are as follows:

- **Account Expires.** You can click on the Never radio button to create an account that will never expire, but it is a much better and secure practice to specify a date upon which the account will cease to function. (When an account expires, the account is not deleted, but the user can no longer log on to the network unless the account is reset. To specify when the account will expire, click on the End Of radio button, and enter a date in the text box or select one from the drop-down list.

- **Account Type.** Since we assume we are adding a user to the Administrators group in this example, click on the Global Account radio button. By default, a new user account is a global account; to make the account local, select the Local Account radio button.

Click on the Close button to return to the New User dialog box again.

Windows NT Server provides domain-based security for RAS users. To allow mobile users to connect from a remote system, use the Dialin button in the New Users dialog box. When you click on this button, Windows NT displays the Dialin Information dialog box, as shown in Figure 10.8.

FIGURE 10.8:

The Dialin Information dialog box

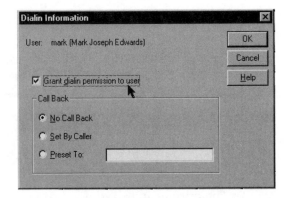

In this dialog box, you specify whether and how a user can dial in to the network. The options are as follows:

- **Grant Dialin Permission to User.** Check this checkbox to give the user access to the network via a dial-in connection.

- **Call Back.** Use the three selections in this part of the dialog box to specify how a user can connect to the server. Click on the No Call Back radio button to ensure that the user is connected immediately with no call back. This option offers no added security and so is a poor choice for most installations. Click on the Set by Caller radio button, and the dialin server calls the user back at a number the user has defined once the user's account has been validated. This option also offers little in the way of security, but it is one way for mobile users to avoid running up large telephone bills. Click on the Preset To radio button, and enter a phone number in the text box. This is the only secure option of the three available. It is useful for mobile users that always call in from the same number. After the user calls in and the account is validated, the RAS server breaks the connection and then calls the user back at the preset number. If a user tries to call in from a different number, he or she won't be able to make the connection.

Click on the OK button when you are done, and in the New User dialog box, choose the Add button to complete the creation of this new user.

Those are the basic steps and parameters for adding users to the Windows NT Server and domain. There are many other aspects to user security policies; however, they are beyond the scope of this book since it focuses on establishing a Web server, not on the details of Windows NT security administration. Let's move on and take a look at Windows NT group security.

Understanding Group Security

Windows NT User Groups categorize users according to privileges and rights; a *user group* is a set of users who all have identical network rights. Windows NT predefines several groups, a feature you will find beneficial. The most important group is the Administrators Group. Users in this group have complete control over the domain security and certain hosts on the network; so be careful which users you assign to it.

You can also define your own groups and assign them the privileges and rights you choose. In a nutshell, using groups eases the management of assigning access to the various resources on the network.

For example, you have installed some accounting software on your server, and you want only certain users to have access to that shared directory. You can create an Accounting group and then add the users you want to it. Now, instead of manually giving each user permission to access the share, you simply give the group permission.

Global and Local Groups Defined

The two types of Windows NT user groups are global and local. *Global groups* can contain only individual user accounts from the domain in which the group was created, collected together under one group account name, and cannot contain other global or local groups. Global groups are useful in granting permissions and rights to groups of users, either for local resource access or for resource access in another trusted Windows NT domain. When you install Windows NT, there are 3 predefined global groups: Domain Admins, Domain Users, and Domain Guests. None of these groups can be deleted.

Local groups can contain individual user accounts and global group accounts, grouped together under one group account name. Local groups allow the export of users and groups from other domains to the local domain. A local group can have only the permissions and rights assigned to it inside the domain in which it was created.

When you install Windows NT as a server, there are 6 predefined local groups:

- Administrators
- Users

- Guests

- Backup Operators

- Replicator

- Power Users

When you install Windows NT Server as a primary or secondary domain controller, 3 additional local groups are established:

- Account Operators

- Print Operators

- Server Operators

Adding Users to Groups

Adding users to groups is a fairly simple process. First, you must be logged on with administrator privileges, and the users must already have been added to the user database. Once this is done, simply follow the steps below. In this example, we assume we are adding a user to the Administrators group.

1. Click on the Start button, choose Programs, select Administrative Tools, and then select User Manager for Domains. Windows NT displays the User Manager dialog box once again.

2. In the Groups area (in the lower part of the dialog box), double-click on Administrators. Windows NT displays the Local Group Properties dialog box, as shown in Figure 10.9.

FIGURE 10.9:

The Local Group
Properties dialog box

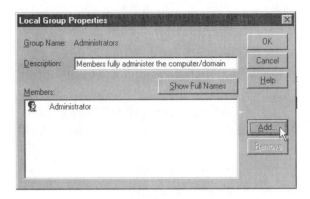

3. Click on the Add button. Windows NT displays the Add Users
   and Groups dialog box, as shown in Figure 10.10, which lists all
   the users and groups on your system. Click on a name in the
   Names list and then click on Add; in this example, I chose Mark
   from the Names list.

FIGURE 10.10:

The Add Users and
Groups dialog box

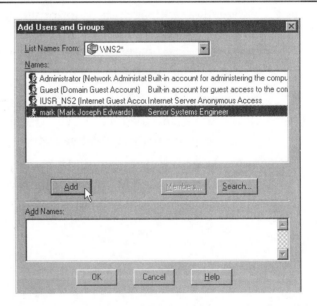

4. Click on OK. Windows NT displays the Local Group Properties
   dialog box (see Figure 10.11), which shows the user Mark added

to the group in the Members list box. Click on OK to close the dialog box and return to the User Manager dialog box.

FIGURE 10.11:

The Local Group Properties dialog box with a member added to the Administrators group

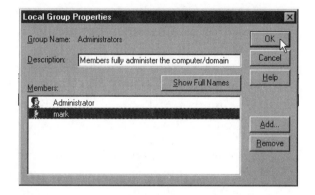

User groups can be a powerful tool in administering user security and control over your Windows NT domains.

Windows NT File System Security

In this section, I'll review the file system types and features and discuss managing file system security and shared directories.

Two basic types of file systems are supported under Windows NT Server 4: the FAT file system and the NTFS file system. Windows NT version 3.51 supported an additional file system called HPFS (High Performance File System); however, that file system is no longer supported by Microsoft. HPFS was developed for use on OS/2 version 1.2, which was released in 1989. It has been phased out of Windows NT in favor of Microsoft's own NTFS.

FAT versus NTFS

FAT stands for File Allocation Table and was originally developed by Microsoft for use under MS-DOS. The FAT file system has no real security features other than the ability to set the attributes of a file to "system" or "read only," which simply makes it harder to accidentally delete a file. The only real advantage of the FAT file system today is that it is supported by MS-DOS. For a secure network connected to the Internet, FAT is a very poor choice. I don't recommend using it at all on Windows NT servers; you should use NTFS instead.

NTFS stands for NT file system and is certainly the correct choice for your Intranet or your Internet connection. NTFS offers a robust mechanism to control access to the hard drives and their contents. It also offers performance features over MS-DOS file systems. Some of the main features of NTFS include the following:

- It allows permissions to be set on files and directories.

- It gives faster access to larger sequential access files.

- It gives faster access to random access files.

- File and directory names can be a maximum of 254 characters.

- It automatically converts long filenames to the MS-DOS standard of 8.3 when accessed by MS-DOS workstations on the network. (The 8.3 standard dictates an 8-character filename with a 3-character extension.)

- It allow file- and directory-sharing with Macintosh systems.

- It uses drive space more efficiently.

- It automatically sorts directories.

- It supports upper- and lowercase letters in filenames and supports Unicode characters.

Converting File Systems

A few words of caution are in order here. When you convert your file system to NTFS, you can no longer boot your server up to MS-DOS using a floppy disk and access the NTFS partition. MS-DOS doesn't understand NTFS and simply cannot read it. Additionally, if you are converting a Novell NetWare server to Windows NT Server, as so many administrators are, you cannot simply convert the file system to NTFS; doing so would destroy all the data on the NetWare volume. First, back up your NetWare server. Now, install Windows NT Server, and then restore your data to the hard drive after it is converted to NTFS. After you have finished the conversion, make a complete backup of your entire system *immediately* so that you have an up-to-date backup in the new format.

Now that we have reviewed the file systems themselves, let's talk about file system security. Most servers on a network act as repositories for data files of various types and for software programs that network users can access and run. Before users can access files and programs across the network, they must be *shared.* Sharing a directory allows users to connect to the share and use it as if it were a local drive on the user's workstation. Once a directory is shared, all its contents (files, subdirectories, and files in those subdirectories) are accessible to the users that have permissions to access the share. Some restrictions can be applied to the contents of a directory, which allows a bit more control over access to its contents. I'll go over that later in this section.

Sharing Directories

File system security under Windows NT has four basic parts: share permissions, directory permissions, file access, and ownership. I'll cover each of these in this section.

Sharing directories is really straightforward. Under Windows NT Server 4, you begin this process by opening the Explorer (see Figure 10.12); select Start, choose Programs, and then select Windows NT Explorer. Explorer is a very welcome replacement for the old File Manager found in all previous versions of the Windows NT operating system.

FIGURE 10.12:

Windows NT Explorer

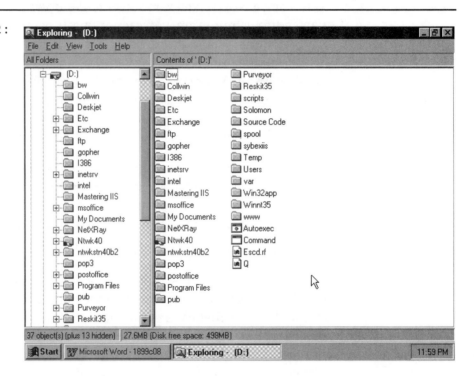

On the left side of the Explorer dialog box, you will see a directory tree listing all the directories (also called folders sometimes) on the chosen hard disk, and on the right side of the dialog box, you will see a list of all the files and folders that the selected directory contains.

Follow these steps to create a shared directory:

1. On the left of the Explorer, locate the name of the directory you want and right-click on it.

2. In the pop-up menu that Explorer displays, select the Sharing option. Windows NT displays the Properties dialog box, with the Sharing tab selected by default (see Figure 10.13).

FIGURE 10.13:

The Properties dialog box, with the Sharing tab selected by default

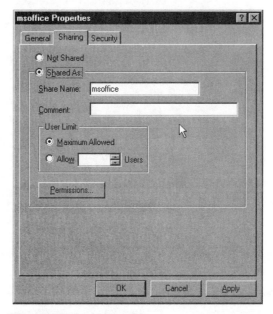

3. Click on the Shared As radio button. The name of the directory appears in the Share Name text box, and the other fields in the dialog box are now enabled. The name in the Share Name text box is the one that users will see across the network when they access a shared resource.

In some cases, using a descriptive Share Name such as MSOffice may be beneficial; in others, you may want to disguise the share's true contents by giving it a nondescriptive share name. The Comment field also appears to users accessing shares across the network, and you can use this field for information that you want users to read. The Comment text box need not be filled in; however, you must fill in the Share Name text box to share a resource such as a directory.

You can use the other options in this dialog box to help control server loads as follows:

- **Maximum Allowed.** Click on the Maximum Allowed radio button, which is selected by default, if you want the maximum number of users that the server can handle to connect to the share.

- **Allow.** To manually limit the number of simultaneous connections to the share, click on the Allow radio button and select or enter the number in the drop-down list box. You might want to do this to ensure that the server doesn't get overloaded or to prevent more than the prescribed number of users from accessing a licensed software package that is installed in a shared directory. Normally, you can leave the default of Maximum Allowed.

- **Permissions.** Click on this button to establish the permissions for the share. Windows NT displays the Access Through Share Permissions dialog box, as shown in Figure 10.14.

FIGURE 10.14:

The Access Through Share Permissions dialog box

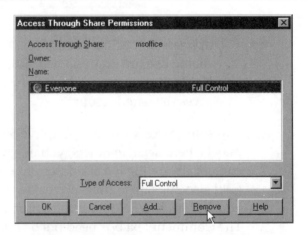

4. NT Server gives global access to a new share as the default, and because that is not usually what you want, be sure to remove it. The Everyone group on Windows NT encompasses every user

in the domain. Since in this case we don't want everyone to have access, select Everyone and click on the Remove button.

5. To add permission for a group of users to access the share, click on the Add button. Windows NT displays the Add Users and Groups dialog box, as shown in Figure 10.15.

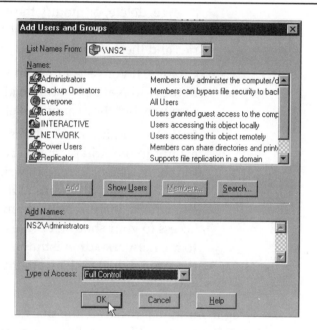

6. The upper part of this dialog box lists all the defined groups in your domain. To see a list of the users in each group, click on the Show Users button. In this example, we want to give permission to access the share to a user group called Administrators; so select Administrators in the list and click on the Add button. The name of the Administrators group appears in the Add Names list. To define the group's type of shared access, select the Type of Access drop-down list. Click on the downward-pointing arrow, and you'll see the four basic types of access that can be assigned:

- **No Access.** If you select this access type, users in the groups in the Add Names list do not have access to the shared directory, its subdirectories, or any files in these subdirectories.

- **Read.** If you select this access type, users in the groups in the Add Names list have read-only access. They cannot change, delete, or modify the contents of the share in any way; they can change to the shared directory's subdirectories and then run application programs stored there.

- **Change.** If you select this type of access, users in the groups in the Add Names list can read and write to the shared resource, but they cannot delete it.

- **Full Control.** If you select this type of access, users in the groups in the Add Names list can do as they please with the share. They can read it, write to it, execute programs in it, add files and programs to it, change permissions, and even delete it entirely. Be careful about who has this type of access to your shares; it makes sense to restrict Full Control to the network administrator. Full Control can be self-defeating when you are attempting to secure your network server's resources.

Keep in mind that these are the share access types and not the directory access types. More on directory access types in a moment.

7. Because we want the Administrators to have full control over the share to do with it what they may, select the Full Control access type. Now, click on the OK button to establish the permissions and close the dialog box. Click on OK again to close the Access Through Share Permissions dialog box.

8. In the Properties dialog box, click on the Security tab. Windows NT displays the Security section, as shown in Figure 10.16.

FIGURE 10.16:

The Properties dialog box, with the Security tab selected

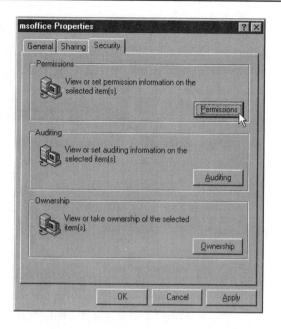

This dialog has three areas of interest: Permissions, Auditing, and Ownership. We'll cover each of these in a fair amount of detail in the following sections.

By placing permissions on a directory, you can specify the type of access that a group or an individual has to that directory and the files it contains, but this doesn't necessarily grant the same permissions to the subdirectories that it contains.

9. To look at or change the permissions on a directory, click on the Permissions button. Windows NT displays the Directory Permissions dialog box, as shown in Figure 10.17.

FIGURE 10.17:

The Directory
Permissions dialog box

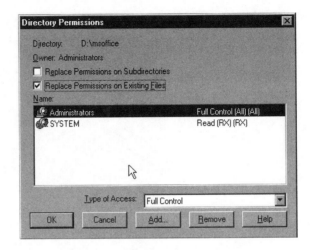

To select an access type for the Administrators group, click on the downward-pointing arrow in the Type of Access drop-down list box. You'll see the following options:

- **No Access.** Select this access type to prohibit any type of access by any user in the group, even if he or she belongs to another group that has access to this directory.

- **List.** Select this access type to allow users in this group to view this directory, its subdirectories, and its files.

- **Read.** Select this access type to allow users in this group to view this directory, its subdirectories, and its files and to run programs in this directory and its subdirectories.

- **Add.** Select this access type to allow users in this group to add files to this directory and its subdirectories but not allow access to the files in the directory unless allowed by other directory or file permission settings.

- **Add & Read.** Select this access type to give users in this group all the permissions of the Add access type as well as permission to run programs from the directory and its subdirectories.

- **Change.** Select this access type to give users in this group all the permissions of the Add & Read access type as well as permission to delete the directory, its subdirectories, and its files.

- **Full Control.** Select this access type to give users in this group all the permissions of the Change access type as well as the permission to change permissions on the directory, its subdirectories, and its files and to take ownership of the directory and its files. (More on ownership later in this section.) Assign this type of access with care; you don't want to compromise the security of your network server resources.

- **Special Directory Access.** Select this access type if you want to customize the permission settings for this directory. When you select Special Directory Access, Windows NT displays the Special Directory Access dialog box, as shown in Figure 10.18.

- **Special File Access.** Select this access type if you want to customize the permission settings for files. When you choose this option, Windows NT displays the Special File Access dialog box shown in Figure 10.19.

FIGURE 10.18:

The Special Directory Access dialog box with Read and Execute permissions selected

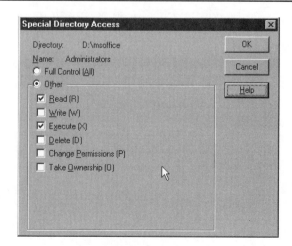

The options in this dialog box are listed in Table 10.3.

TABLE 10.3:   NT Server individual permissions

Permission	Description
Read (R)	Allows users in this group to view the names of files and subdirectories in this directory
Write (W)	Allows users in this group to add files and subdirectories to this directory
Execute (X)	Allows users in this group to change to subdirectories in this directory
Delete (D)	Allows users in this group to delete this directory
Change Permissions (P)	Allows users in this group to change the permissions for this directory
Take Ownership (O)	Allows users in this group to change ownership of this directory

By default, all files in a directory inherit the permissions of the directory in which they reside. If a user has Access Not Specified permission, he or she can prevent this inheritance and can customize the permissions on a per file basis. When you select Access Not Specified, Windows NT displays the Special File Access dialog box (shown in Figure 10.19) with which you specify permissions for an individual file. These permissions are the same as those listed in Table 10.3.

10. When you have completed your settings, click on OK. Windows NT displays the Directory Permissions dialog box, which has the following options:

- **Replace Permissions on Subdirectories.** Check this checkbox to set the same permissions on all files and subdirectories of this share.

- **Replace Permissions on Existing Files.** Check this checkbox, which is the default, to apply permission settings to files in the directory and to the directory itself. Clear this checkbox to apply your permission settings to the directory only. If the Replace Permissions on Subdirectories box is checked, permissions are also set on all subdirectories.

The Special File Access
dialog box, with which
you specify permissions
for an individual file

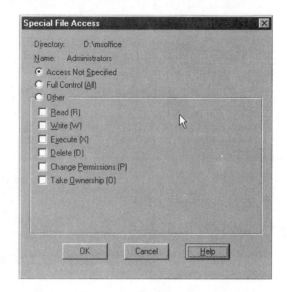

Click on the OK button to close the Directory Permissions dialog
box. Windows NT displays the Properties dialog box once again.

Directory Auditing

At times you will want to monitor different kinds of user activity, both
to assess network performance and for security reasons. Windows NT
Server gives the network administrator several important tools to
audit network events and stores this information in one of three logs:
the Applications Log, the Systems Log, and the Security Log.

In NT Server, you can specify which groups or users, as well as
which network actions, should be audited for any file or directory.
You set audit policy using the User Manager for Domains. To do this,
in the User Manager dialog box, select the Policies menu, and then
choose Audit to open the Audit Policy dialog box. We'll return to this
dialog box and cover all its options in detail in a moment.

One of the options in this dialog box is File and Object Access; be
sure to check this box, and notice that you can audit both successful

and unsuccessful accesses. Once this is done, the next step is to return to the NT Explorer and choose the files and/or directories and groups of users that you want to audit. Continuing with the example we started earlier, here are the steps to follow:

1. In the Properties dialog box, be sure that the Security tab is selected and then click on the Auditing button. Explorer displays the Directory Auditing dialog box, as shown in Figure 10.20.

FIGURE 10.20:

The Directory Auditing dialog box, with the Administrators group selected

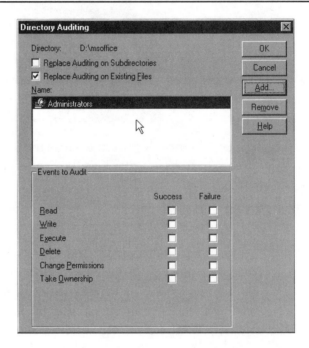

2. In the Name list box, select the Administrators group (since that is the group for which we are establishing permission) and click on the Add button. In the bottom half of this dialog box, select the events to audit. (All audit trails are written to the Event Log, which is covered later in this chapter.) The options are as follows:

   • **Read.** Audits the display of filenames, attributes, permissions, and owners.

- **Write.** Audits the creation of subdirectories and files, the changes to attributes, and the display of permissions and owners.
- **Execute.** Audits the display of attributes, permissions, and owners and the changes to subdirectories.
- **Delete.** Audits the deletion of the directory.
- **Change Permissions.** Audits the changes to directory permissions.
- **Take Ownership.** Audits the changes to directory ownership

3. Above the Name list box are the following checkboxes:

- **Replace Auditing on Subdirectories.** This option applies auditing to the directory and subdirectory only, but not to existing files in either.
- **Replace Auditing on Existing Files.** This is the default setting. When you select it, you allow the auditing to apply to the directory and to the files within that directory only, not to any subdirectories.

Check both boxes to apply auditing to the directory and its files as well as to any existing subdirectories and files it contains.

Clear both boxes to apply auditing to the directory only, and not to any of the files or directories it contains. It is worth remembering that the more items you audit, the larger the audit file will become.

Click on OK to set the audit trails and close the Directory Auditing dialog box. Explorer returns to the Properties dialog box.

Ownership Properties

Every file and directory on an NTFS hard disk under Windows NT has an owner. When you create a file or a directory, you become its owner. Owners can grant permissions, controlling how the file or directory is used. The owner of a file or a directory and members of the Administrators group can grant permission to other users to take ownership of a file or directory.

Although any administrator can take ownership of a directory or a file, an administrator cannot transfer ownership to others. This preserves the security mechanism. For example, only an administrator who takes ownership and changes permissions can gain access to a file on which you have set the No Access permission. By checking the ownership of a file, you see that the ownership has changed and find out who violated the permission you set on the file.

To ensure that your files are secure, check their ownership regularly. Furthermore, always establish a degree of auditing, and routinely check the Event Log for security-related events. We'll cover both auditing and the Event Log in a fair amount of detail later in this chapter.

To check ownership, follow these steps:

1. In the Properties dialog box, be sure that the Security tab is selected and click on the Ownership button. Windows NT displays the Owner dialog box, as shown in Figure 10.21. This dialog box shows the directory name and the current owner of the directory.

FIGURE 10.21:

The Owner dialog box, showing the directory name and owner

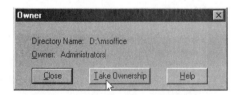

2. If you are logged on as an administrator and you don't have permission to view the owner, you will be given the option of taking ownership of the file. Taking ownership lets you look at all the security information for the file. Once transferred, ownership cannot be transferred back to the file's original owner. Windows NT displays the Properties dialog box once again

If you have to take control of a directory, to delete it, for example, don't be surprised if you can't seem to access it for a few minutes. The change in ownership may not be immediately reflected across the domain in all the security databases.

Finally, let's take a look at the information contained in the General tab of the Properties dialog box. Click on the General tab, and Windows NT displays the General section of the Properties dialog box, as shown in Figure 10.22.

FIGURE 10.22:

The General section of the Properties dialog box

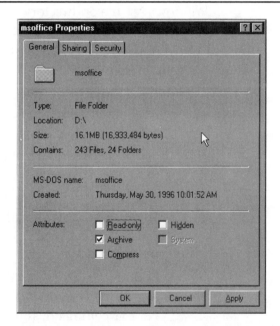

The first part of the General section shows you the name of the file or directory for which you are establishing parameters and its associated icon; in this case, MSOFFICE. It also contains the following information:

- **Type.** MSOFFICE is a file folder, or directory.

- **Location.** The hard disk on which the file or directory is located.

- **Size.** The number of bytes.

- **Contents.** If the file type is file folder (or directory), the number of files and folders it contains.

- **MS-DOS Name.** The MS-DOS filename, the 8.3 form of the file-name, which is used by MS-DOS operating systems that have access to the directory. In this case, the file type is directory and so has no filename extension.

- **Created.** The day, date, and time the file or directory was created. At the bottom of the General section of the Properties dialog box are 5 checkboxes that correspond to the 5 attributes that any Windows NT file or directory can have. File attributes allow low-level control over the directory. They are established by Windows NT when the file or directory is initially created and are defined as follows:

  - **Read Only.** Ensures that the file or directory can't be accidentally rewritten or deleted.

  - **Archive.** Indicates that this file has changed since it was last backed up, and so the archive copy of this file is now out of date. Some software programs use this setting to determine whether to back up a file or a directory.

  - **Compress.** Shows whether this file or directory is compressed. Windows NT can compress files and directories on the fly, saving precious hard disk space.

  - **Hidden.** Indicates that this file or directory is hidden and not normally visible in Explorer or when you issue the NT `dir` command. You cannot use a hidden directory or a hidden file unless you know its name and location. Hiding a file can sometimes be useful, following the basic principle that "if you can't see it, you can't fool around with it." Be aware, however, that there are ways of seeking and finding all hidden files on a hard disk.

  - **System.** Indicates that the file or directory is typically part of the operating system and is required for the operating system to run properly. By default, system files appear in the Explorer folder listings. Do not delete files with this attribute unless you know exactly what the file is for and you are absolutely certain that you can do without it.

In review, you can see that establishing file system security consists of setting two types of parameters: file system and shared resource. You can think of the file system security parameters as being underneath the shared resource security parameters. The two are complementary and provide a great deal of control over who has permission to access the file systems.

Setting Up Printer Security

Establishing printer security is not that different from establishing shared file and directory resources. You do, however, need to configure the parameters carefully so that when a user logs on to the printer server itself at the server's local console or attempts to connect to a shared printer resource across the network, nothing goes awry.

In this section, I'll assume that you have already installed an HP DeskJet 660C printer driver and that you want to establish sharing for the device. I'll also be somewhat brief on the security establishment of printer shares since they are not directly related to running a Web server.

To establish printer sharing, follow these steps:

1. From the Windows NT Desktop, click on the Start button, select Settings, and then select Printers. Windows NT displays the Printers folder.

2. Right-click on the icon for the HP DeskJet 660C. In the pop-up menu, select Properties. Windows NT displays the HP DeskJet 660C Properties dialog box, as shown in Figure 10.23. By default, the General tab is selected.

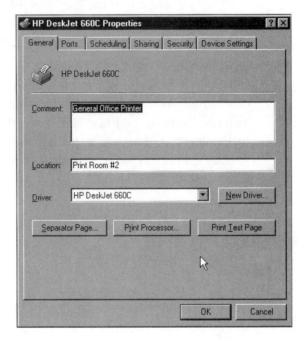

Because we are focusing on printer security in this section, I won't go into all the options in this dialog box, only those that pertain to security.

3. Fill in the Comment and Location boxes as necessary, and be sure the correct printer driver is selected in the Driver list.

4. Now, click on the Scheduling tab. Windows NT displays the Scheduling section of the HP DeskJet 660C properties dialog box, as shown in Figure 10.24.

5. In the Available area, you define when the printer is available to produce output. Click on the From radio button to enable the From and To list boxes. Enter a time in each box, or click on the downward-pointing arrow and select a time.

6. In the Priority area, you establish the printing order of documents. Higher priority documents print before those of lower priority. In this example, we'll leave the priority set to Lowest, or Priority 1, which is the default.

FIGURE 10.24:

The Scheduling section
of the HP DeskJet 660C
Properties dialog box

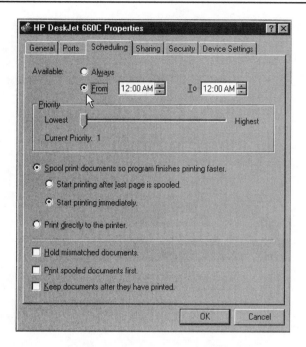

7. Now, click on the Sharing tab. Windows NT displays the
   Sharing section of the HP DeskJet 660C Properties dialog box, as
   shown in Figure 10.25. We'll use this part of the dialog box to
   establish the printer share and assign permissions for users and
   groups who will access it across the network

8. Click on the Shared radio button, and enter the name of your
   printer in the Share Name text box. In the Alternate Drivers list
   box at the bottom of this dialog box are the names of drivers for
   other operating systems that may need to use the printer share.
   This particular setting has no impact on security, but go ahead
   and select any additional drivers you may need. Bear in mind
   that you will need the driver disk or installation disk for each
   operating system's print driver that you select to install; so have
   them handy or come back and add them later when you do have
   them.

FIGURE 10.25:

The Sharing section of the HP DeskJet 660C Properties dialog box

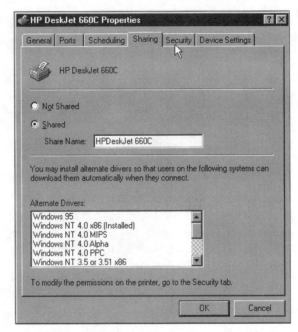

9. Now, click on the Security tab. Windows NT displays the Security section of the HP DeskJet 660C Properties dialog box, as shown in Figure 10.26.

10. Click on the Permissions button. Windows NT displays the Printer Permissions dialog box.

11. Now click on the downward-pointing arrow in the Type of Access drop-down list box. The types of printer access are as follows:

- **No Access.** Select this access type to prevent use of the shared printer. This access type is useful for including the Everyone group and then simply excluding the users and groups that you do not want to have access.

FIGURE 10.26:

The Security section of
the HP DeskJet 660C
Properties dialog box

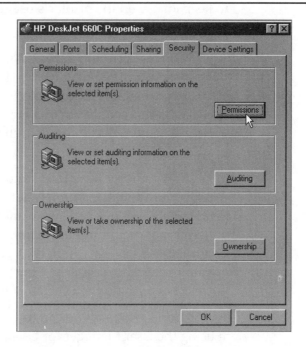

- **Print.** Select this access type to allow a user or a group to send documents to the shared printer.

- **Manage Documents.** Select this access type to allow a user or a group to manipulate the documents in the print queue. A user or group with this access can reprioritize documents, place them on hold for printing at a later time, or delete them altogether.

- **Full Control.** Select this access type to gives users and groups Manage Documents access and allow them to delete the printer share or change its ownership.

Make the appropriate selection, usually Print, and then click on OK when you are done. Windows NT displays the Security section of the HP DeskJet 660C Properties dialog box.

To keep an eye on the printer's usage, we'll enable printer auditing in the following steps:

1. Click on the Auditing button. Windows NT displays the Directory Auditing dialog box. This dialog box will look familiar; it is very similar to the Directory Auditing figure we looked at earlier in this chapter. In this example, we'll establish auditing for everyone. Select Everyone, click on the Add button, and then click on OK. This enables the Events to Audit checkboxes.

2. You can audit for the success and failure of the following occurrences: Print, Full Control, Delete, Change Permissions, and Ownership. In this case, we want to audit for the changing of permissions and for the deletion of the share in a successful or unsuccessful event. Check the Success checkboxes and the Failure checkboxes for the Change Permissions event and for the Delete event, and then click on OK.

Bear in mind also that you can turn on auditing for the entire system using the User Manager for Domains dialog box. Doing so implements individual auditing for some aspects of Windows NT, but not all; and in these cases, the audit switches are simply On/Off.

You have successfully established the sharing of this printer for users and groups on your network.

Using the Administrative Wizards

If you are using Windows NT Server version 4, you could use one of the Administrative Wizards located in the Administrative Tools menu to create a new user account, to manage aspects of file and folder access, and to set up a printer.

The following wizards are available to make some aspects of system administration easier and faster:

- Add User Accounts
- Group Management
- Managing File and Folder Access
- Add Printer
- Add/Remove Programs
- Install New Modem
- Network Client Administrator
- License Compliance

Each wizard is designed to take you through a specific process, step by step, prompting you with possible choices at each decision point.

These wizards are not available in Windows NT Server 3.5 or 3.51; so if you are using one of these systems, you have no choice but to use the User Manager for Domains to accomplish these tasks.

Windows NT Logging and Auditing

The three types of logging in Windows NT are System, Security, and Application. Each type keeps its own log records, and each is viewed with the Event Log, which is in the Administrative Tools folder.

Each log tracks the same basic parameters in and around an event: the date and time of a log entry, the source of the event, the event subcategory, the event ID, the user-related event entry if any, and the machine name of the system on which the event occurred.

The Event Log

The Event Log uses a few standard icons to represent the urgency of a log entry. The most common are: the typical information icon represented by a blue circle with the letter "i" in the center; the warning icon, represented by a yellow circle with an exclamation point inside; and the error icon, represented by a red stop sign shape with the word "stop' in the center. (You can see these icons in Figure 10.28, later in this chapter.) Informational entries are usually just FYI (for your information) and normally require no immediate action on your part. Warning log entries are items that Windows NT wants you to know about and that may require some action. Error log entries are serious, and you should handle them as soon as possible.

Basic logging is always enabled on Windows NT. You can, however, enhance the logging levels of a Windows NT server by turning on the audit trails in the User Manager for Domains. To do so, follow these steps:

1. Click on the Start button, choose Programs, select Administrative Tools, and then select User Manager for Domains.

2. In the User Manager dialog box, select the Policies menu, and then select Audit. Windows NT displays the Audit Policy dialog box, as shown in Figure 10.27.

FIGURE 10.27:

The Audit Policy
dialog box

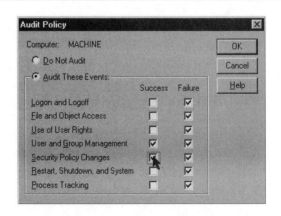

The default is Do Not Audit; when this option is selected, all the Audit These Events checkboxes are grayed out and unavailable. When you activate auditing, information about the selected event type is stored in NT's Security Log when the event takes place. You can look at the contents of the Security Log, along with the Application and Systems logs, with the Event Viewer, as you'll see in a moment.

Check the appropriate checkboxes to audit the following events for either success or failure:

- **Logon and Logoff.** Tracks each logon and logoff event that occurs and tracks all connections to the network.

- **File and Object Access.** Tracks the use of files and resource objects in the domain if they are set for auditing; also tracks print spooling if the printer resource is set for auditing.

- **Use of User Rights.** Tracks any exercise of a user's rights, except for logon and logoff events, which are tracked by Logon and Logoff.

- **User and Group Management**. Tracks when a user account or group is created, changed, or deleted; when a user account is renamed, enabled, or disabled; and when a password is changed.

- **Security Policy Changes.** Tracks changes to user rights, audit policies, and trust relationships of the domain.

- **Restart, Shutdown, and System.** Tracks startup and shutdown of the server and events that affect the entire security system or Event Log.

- **Process Tracking.** Tracks events such as program activation, indirect object access, and process exits.

You should make system auditing a normal part of day-to-day operations on your network, and you should review the logs regularly; if you suspect an intruder is attempting to gain access to your system, you and your staff should review these logs on a daily basis.

To change the size of the logs on your system, use the Log Settings option from the Log menu in the Event Viewer. You can adjust the size of your individual logs simply by using the Log Settings option in the Log drop-down menu of the Event Viewer.

The System Log

Let's take a look at some log entries that you may encounter. First, let's look at a System event. To do so, choose Start, Programs, Administrative Tools, and then Event Viewer. Once the Event Viewer opens, select Log from the menu bar and choose System. You'll see a list of logged events; to view any of them, simply double-click on its entry.

The System Log tracks all system level events, including successful and failed events that take place during system startup, such as services starting, drivers being loaded, disk capacity checks, and many other items that may be of interest or concern to the administrator. Take a look at Figure 10.28 for an idea of what a System Log entry might look like when displayed in the Event Detail dialog box. This particular event was logged because an Ethernet driver failed to load properly, and you can see information such as the time and date the event occurred, the name of the computer the event occurred on, the event ID number, and the Windows NT Server element that created the event. In this case, the event was created by the NT Service Control Manager.

The Event Detail dialog
box, displaying a System
event

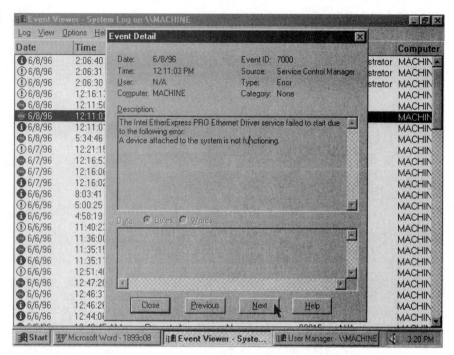

The Security Log

Now let's take a look at a Security event log entry (see Figure 10.29).
The Security Log tracks all security-related events, including changes
in security policy, attempts to log on to the system, and attempts to
access a file or directory based on the policy you established when
using the Audit Policy dialog box in the User Manager for Domains,
described in an earlier section in this chapter. This example entry
shows that someone attempted to log on with the Administrator
account at 3:36 PM on June 8, 1996, and failed. The entry also tells us
that the machine used to attempt the logon was called MACHINE
and that the reason for the event being logged is an unknown username or a bad password.

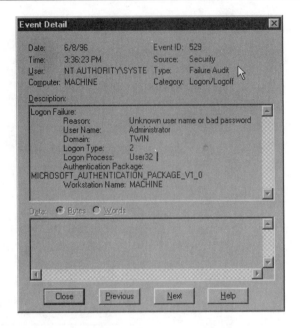

FIGURE 10.29:

The Event Detail dialog box, displaying a Security event

Application Logs

Application Logs are generated by application programs that execute on the network. Technically, an application is software other than the Windows NT operating system. The log entry in Figure 10.30 shows that NT chkdsk command ran and displays the results. In this instance, chkdsk found 527138816 bytes of total disk space, 2203648 bytes in 58 hidden files, 2383872 bytes in 281 directories, 443916288 bytes in 5325 user files, and 78635008 total bytes available on drive D.

Auditing and the Event Logs are very necessary and useful tools in the administration of your network and its related services. Logs can help you find out why certain aspects of the system or network are not functioning properly, and they can give you distinct information that may assist you in identifying and preventing intrusion. Learn to use them accurately, and make a habit of checking them thoroughly and routinely.

The Event Detail dialog box, displaying an event in the Application Log

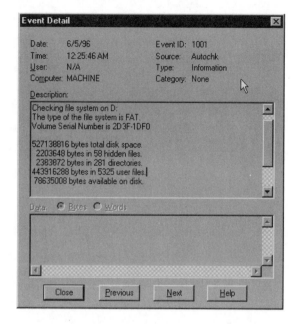

Microsoft TCP/IP Security

With the release of Windows NT 4, Microsoft has added the ability to filter out packets from certain types of protocols destined for the TCP/IP network. This feature is commonplace in the world of TCP/IP and is commonly referred to as *packet filtering*.

The three types of network traffic that you can limit with the new TCP/IP configuration are TCP, UDP, and IP. The process for limiting these traffic types is based on a port address for which the traffic is destined. Thus, if you want to stop any traffic from arriving at your DNS port, which is a UDP port, you do so by configuring the security aspects of the Microsoft TCP/IP protocol settings as well as those of UDP and IP. This is a very powerful way of securing your TCP/IP network; traffic that can't get to a TCP/IP port on your server can't break in. To learn which types of services and protocols use which ports, take a look at the file called SERVICES located in the

\%SYSTEM_ROOT%\SYSTEM32\DRIVERS\ETC directory. Replace the %SYSTEM_ROOT% parameter with the name of the directory in which you installed Windows NT, such as NT40. This file lists most of the common protocols and their associated ports, but certainly not all of them.

Let's take a quick look at the TCP/IP security settings in the new TCP/IP protocol version, as shown in Figure 10.31. To open the TCP/IP Security dialog box, follow these steps:

1. Click on the Start button, choose Settings, choose Control Panel, and then click on Network.

2. In the Network dialog box, select the Protocols tab.

3. In the Protocols section, double-click on TCP/IP Protocol.

4. In the Microsoft TCP/IP Properties dialog box, click on the Advanced button.

5. In the Advanced IP Addressing dialog box, check the Enable Security checkbox, and click on the Configure button. Windows NT displays the TCP/IP Security dialog box.

FIGURE 10.31:

The TCP/IP Security dialog box, showing TCP Port access restricted to Port 80

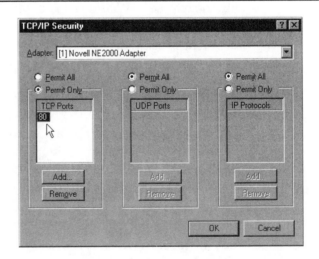

In this dialog box there are three groups of settings: TCP, UDP, and IP. Each has a Permit All radio button to allow access on all ports and has a Permit Only radio button to restrict access to certain specific ports. Let's assume that we want to allow access only to the Web server port, which is normally port 80 and uses the TCP protocol.

With Microsoft IIS, you cannot configure the Web server port address manually; thus, you must run your IIS Web server on port 80, which is the standard default port for any Web server.

To restrict access to all TCP ports except port 80 for the Web server, follow these steps:

1. In the TCP Ports section, click on the Permit Only radio button.

2. Now, click on the Add button, and enter **80** for the port number.

3. Click on OK

That's it. You've just eliminated all TCP traffic other than Web traffic from your server!

You can permit access to any ports you wish; you simply need to know the protocol type and its actual port number. Packet filtering is a basic and powerful way to control access to your server; so don't be afraid to use it.

Windows NT Installation Considerations

This section reviews some considerations you may want to take into account when installing Windows NT Server or Windows NT Workstation.

First, when installing Windows NT Server or Windows NT Workstation, be sure that all other Windows NT domain controllers and backup domain controllers are turned on and live on the network before you begin. For Windows NT machines to be able to join a domain, a domain controller must be available on the network during installation. This avoids the possibility of accidentally installing two primary domain controllers in the same domain and also ensures that the machine is authorized to join the domain.

You will want to use the NTFS file system over the FAT file system, since when using the FAT, a large portion of the security features built into Windows NT are simply unavailable.

Think carefully about how your domain should be structured, about who will administer it, and about how users will be allowed to access it. When installing Windows NT, be careful to record the Administrator's password and keep it in a safe place. Once the server is up and running, immediately add at least one user account to the Administrators group. If you lose your Administrator password and no one is a member of the Administrators group except the Administrator, you'll be forced to re-install Windows NT. There is no way to recover lost passwords. You can only reset them; and without access privileges to do so, you're out of luck.

Microsoft IIS Installation Considerations

Before we get into this brief section, I'll remind you that the Internet Information Server relies almost entirely on Windows NT for most of its security functionality. Windows NT provides IIS the tools it needs to work: features for user and file system security. The actual step-by-step installation processes and configurations are covered in the *TCP/IP in a Nutshell* and *Installing Microsoft Internet Information Server* chapters of this book.

When planning your IIS installation, you don't have many considerations; IIS takes care of most settings for you by default. Do pay attention, though, to the username that IIS sets up for anonymous logons and to the starting directory for your Web site files, which is commonly referred to as the home directory.

Your home directory can actually reside on any server available to the IIS server itself across the network. When choosing the location of your Web site's files, consider that locating them on another server could, in some cases, degrade performance. Be sure that the host for your files isn't already overburdened. As a rule, you'll find that locating them and the IIS server on the same machine provides the best overall performance. This may not be possible if you plan to use databases or information that resides on other systems, but keep it in mind.

As I mentioned, IIS uses a normal Windows NT user account to facilitate anonymous logons to your Web server. Are anonymous logons important? The answer is: absolutely. In general, most public Web sites use only anonymous logons—the user is not required to enter a username and password. If you're establishing a Web site for the general public, leave anonymous logons enabled.

When the IIS installation is complete, open the User Manager for Domains dialog box and review the security settings for the IIS user account. This account has a name that is easy to locate: IUSER_MACHINENAME, where MACHINENAME is the NetBIOS name of your computer. Be sure that all the security settings are in line with the policies for your site.

You should know the purpose of your Web site before it's installed. Granted, the purpose may change over time, but you should at least know the initial purpose. If it involves delivering Web pages that contain sensitive information, you'll have to establish a security policy for the directories that will contain the sensitive information. Doing so is a direct function of who you want to access the information. You can establish usernames and passwords to control access to certain parts of your Web site, and IIS provides three methods of user authentication: anonymous, clear text, and Windows NT challenge/response.

Internet Information Server, in conjunction with the Internet Service Manager, allows you to do two things that I find rather powerful for a Web server: control the amount of total bandwidth, and restrict or grant access by IP address. You actually control the amount of total bandwidth that your Microsoft Internet services use as a whole—the FTP, Gopher, and Web servers combined—using the Internet Service Manager. Initially you may not think of this as a security feature, but consider an intruder practicing a form of "denial of service"— for some reason, users are not getting through to your server. An intruder could be bombarding your server with unnecessary requests, thereby effectively shutting down the use of the server and creating a lot of unnecessary traffic on your network.

The second neat feature of the Web server, restricting or granting access by IP address, comes in handy if you want only local users or a select group of users to access the server. You configure these settings by using the Internet Service Manager and opening the Web Server Properties dialog box. Look for more on the Internet Service Manager in the *Advanced Web Site Administration* chapter.

Microsoft FTP and Gopher Security

Users can upload files to and download files from your system using FTP (File Transfer Protocol). Gopher is a service you can use to make documents and information available for access across the network; you can search these files by keywords. FTP and Gopher security is very important, since both allow remote access to the server. You establish security for both in essentially the same way; so I'll cover them in this section and explain the subtle differences. Look for detailed coverage of the Internet Service Manager in the chapter *Advanced Web Site Administration.*

One way to control access to FTP and Gopher services is by limiting access to certain IP addresses. In this example, we'll look at how to do this for the Gopher service; the steps are the same for FTP. Here are the steps:

1. Select Start, Programs, Microsoft Internet Server, and then Internet Service Manager.

2. In the main Internet Service Manager window, select the Gopher icon, or use the Properties menu to open the Gopher properties sheet. A properties sheet is much like the tabs we used to set various permissions earlier in the chapter and is used to display or change Internet service configuration information.

3. In the properties sheet, click on the Advanced tab and use the settings on this page to configure the access you want to allow to your server.

4. Click on either the Granted Access radio button or the Denied Access radio button, and then specify which computer or group of computers (by their IP address) will be granted or denied access. Click on the Add button.

5. Choose Single Computer and provide the IP address to include or exclude a single computer from access, or choose Group of Computers and provide an IP address and subnet mask to exclude a group of computers from access.

If you choose to grant access to all computers by default, you can then specify the computers to be denied access. And conversely, if you choose to deny access to all users by default, you can then specify which computers are allowed access. Either way works wonderfully, with your choice depending on which is easier to manage based on the volume of addresses to which you are restricting or granting access.

You can enable anonymous FTP logons by selecting the Allow Anonymous option on the FTP Service property sheet in the Internet Service Manager. When using anonymous logon, a user does not need an active account on your NT server. The user logs on with the username of anonymous and any password, but typically this password is the user's e-mail address. This logon ID and password are recorded in the system Event Log and viewed using the Event Viewer. Anonymous access can add lots of users, but should be set up carefully. Anonymous logons run under the IUSR_MACHINENAME account; so be sure that you double-check the permissions of that account.

Additionally, for a user to be able to FTP into a Windows NT server, the file system security must be set up to allow that use. In the case of anonymous logons, the IUSR_MACHINENAME account must be allowed access to whatever files and directories you are making available through FTP. If it is not, anonymous users cannot access the file system and will be rejected when attempting to log on. This is one of the most overlooked aspects when setting up FTP or Gopher services.

At this time, the only to access Gopher is with anonymous logon. You establish Gopher access in the same way that you establish FTP access. The only difference is that with FTP you can allow anonymous access or require a valid user ID and password.

Under Windows NT, FTP is entirely controlled by file permissions. For users to be able to FTP to your server, they must have access permissions to the FTP service's home directory. Without these permissions, even users with valid IDs and passwords will be denied logon access. This is one of the most frustrating aspects when you are first learning about FTP on Windows NT. Therefore, if a valid user cannot log on successfully, double-check the file permissions for the FTP service's home directory. They should at least allow read and execute access for the directory, and they should allow read access for the files. If they do not, logons will fail every time.

Unix versus Windows NT

In designing Windows NT, Microsoft has taken advantage of the successes and failures of various Unix system security developments.

On a Unix system, potential intruders will approach several "sweet spots." The most common are the mail server, the FTP server, the Web server, and several of the commands that allow remote logons. You can fully expect intruders to seek similar holes in your Windows NT system.

Windows NT can also support Windows NT connections across the Internet, mapping shared resources on remote systems using the TCP/IP protocol.

A Note about Passwords

Choosing or specifying a password is a subject I have touched on several times in this chapter, and now it is time to suggest some guidelines you can follow to make your password choices as effective as possible:

- Passwords should be a mixture of upper- and lowercase letters and numbers.

- Passwords should be a minimum of 6 characters.

- Keep passwords secret and change them frequently. The worst passwords are the obvious ones: your name, your initials, your telephone number, the name of your city, names of your pets or you children, names of TV characters or anyone associated with *Star Trek*, birth dates, groups of the same letter or sequences such as *qwerty*, or complete English words. The English language has a finite number of words, and a computer can run through them quickly.

- Change all passwords at least every 90 days, and change those associated with high-security privileges more often.

- Be sure that all default passwords are removed from the system. If a service company set up your server, be on the lookout for passwords such as GUEST, MANAGER, SERVICE, and the like. Remove these passwords immediately.

- Do not allow more than 2 invalid password attempts before disconnecting.

- Promptly remove the accounts of transferred or terminated employees, as well as all unused accounts.

And you should also remember to review the log files covered earlier in this chapter on a regular basis.

Testing Your Security

Administrators in the Unix world have been using a set of programs collectively known as SATAN to test the effectiveness of the security established at their site. Users of NT Server can now use Kane Security Analyst (KSA) from Intrusion Detection Inc for this same purpose.

SATAN, or Security Administrator Tool for Analyzing Networks, is available free on the Internet, and for this reason, many critics have argued that SATAN lets potential intruders take advantage of the information it contains on how to infiltrate systems. So far, at least, the program seems to have acted as a wake-up call to network administrators.

Kane Security Analyst is a complete commercial package, and is also available for Novell's NetWare versions 3.x and 4.x. Future versions will be available for Unix systems and networks using Lotus Notes. Check out the Web site at http://www.intrusion.com for more details.

Kane Security Analyst examines your NT Server system and then presents 3-dimensional bar charts of the following 6 major categories:

- Account Restrictions assesses password controls, use of logon scripts, and password expiration dates.

- Password Strength rates your password policies. A future version will include a password-cracking dictionary to show you how easily your passwords can be guessed.

- Access Control checks user rights and removable drive allocations.

- System Monitoring collects together a miscellaneous set of security-related concerns.

- Data Integrity checks the UPS installation and configuration.

- Data Confidentiality tests to see if passwords are stored in clear text or in encrypted form.

The KSA Report Manager is easy to use and offers almost 30 reports; data can be exported in the usual database formats. KSA creates no accounts or services. To use it, you must be logged in as the administrator, although once the analysis is complete, the results can be shared with all users with access to the system. KSA takes an instant snapshot of the state of your system; as you follow its recommendations and make improvements in your security policies, you will have to rerun the program to see how you are doing.

KSA can do little to actually catch intruders; that's up to you. What it can do is present the security weaknesses in your system to you in a very powerful form that is just about impossible to ignore.

Taking the Intruder's Point of View

Like it or not, your network and its systems are an open invitation to intruders. They are a motivational challenge to the would-be intruder, and you should always keeps this in mind. If you do not guard the access to your network and its resources carefully, they can be compromised.

The best information I can give a network administrator is this: Intruders love simple passwords and old passwords that never change. Make passwords difficult, unrelated to an individual, and cryptic, and change them often. Remember, intruders may use a dictionary and a robot program in attempting to guess your passwords!

External Security and Firewalls

- Counting the cost of security breaches

- The Internet and security

- Defining security threats

- Establishing a security policy for your Web site

- Secure Web site configurations

- Protecting your Web server with a firewall

- What is a proxy server?

- Using IIS with a proxy server

- Breaking in to your own system

- How intruders break in to your system

Building on the basis we established in the previous chapter on internal NT security, this chapter covers system security outside Windows NT Server and includes general security concepts, firewalls, Internet security, methods that intruders may use to gain unauthorized access to a system, and how to deal with intrusions and attempts to intrude.

Additionally, we'll take a look at some of the reasonable steps you can take to stop intruders. I use the word *reasonable* because it is very, very difficult to both service your normal users without inconveniencing them and keep out intruders. And never assume that your system is bullet proof. As soon as you do, you've let your guard down, and someone will surely break in, which could cost you your entire network, your sensitive data, or even your business. Read this section carefully before finalizing and implementing your security methods, policies, and procedures.

Counting the Cost of Security Breaches

Let's take a quick look at how much poor security costs both business and the U.S. government each year. The size of the figures involved should help you concentrate on implementing the appropriate security measures at your own site.

According to information released recently by the U.S. Senate's Permanent Investigations Subcommittee, intruders cost big business more than $800 million last year. In most cases, the attacks on their systems and the resulting losses were not reported to law-enforcement agencies for fear that an extended investigation with its attendant publicity would harm the corporation.

The report indicates that the problem is worse in private industry than in government computer systems, with intruders concentrating on banks (always a popular target) and hospitals, in which cases of record-altering are on the rise. Of the $800 million losses, about half, or $400 million, were incurred by U.S. companies; the rest, by companies operating in other countries.

According to this same report, there were an estimated 250,000 attacks on the U.S. Department of Defense computers last year, and the rate of attack is doubling every year. And these are the attacks that were detected. Who knows how many were either undetected or went unreported for other reasons? Recent attacks on unclassified U. S. Department of Defense computers are reportedly successful 65 percent of the time.

Some of these attacks were considered of nuisance value only, but some were a serious threat to national security. One of the best-documented took place during spring 1994 at an Air Force laboratory in Rome, N.Y. Two intruders made more than 150 trips into the lab's computer systems, collecting passwords from outside users and then using these passwords to invade more than 100 other computers attached to the Internet. An investigation led to the arrest of one of the intruders, a 16-year-old boy living in London, England. The other intruder was never identified and never apprehended.

The problem is certainly considered serious because more than 90 percent of the Pentagon's daily traffic is carried by unclassified computer systems connected to the Internet, and anyone tampering with logistical information or shipping information could cause chaos to military operations.

A recent report in the *Times* of London claimed that U.S. and British agencies are currently investigating more than 40 attacks on financial computer systems made since 1993. The methods used, according to the article, ranged from planting logic bombs—new code added to an application that can cause it to perform in a destructive or compromising way—to sniffers and password crackers, even high-emission radio frequency guns that can wipe out computer systems. In the United States, there has been only one publicly reported case of a major attack on a bank: Citibank lost $400,000 to a group of intruders in St Petersburg, Russia, who had the assistance of a mole working inside the bank.

When intruders gain access to your Web site, they may do one of several things. They may deface your Web pages with a message such as "The system has been Cracked!" or they may erase your Web site pages and replace them with their own. Sites as diverse as the British government, the American Psychoanalytic Association, and the Nation of Islam have suffered from such attacks in the recent past.

Although most attacks on Web sites so far seem to have been malicious in intent, weak system security could lead to much larger forms of industrial sabotage, such as changing pricing structures, altering the text of technical, medical, or legal documents, or creating financial losses on an unprecedented scale.

The Internet and Security

A few years ago, security wasn't a major concern for most sites connected to the Internet. As far as the universities participating in the Internet were concerned, the basic premise was to provide free access to everything, and if a few people took advantage, that was the price you had to pay. Many universities on the Internet still follow this philosophy and impose few restrictions of any kind. Most control access with only a user ID and a password, and many still allow anonymous use of their systems—anyone can log on without a valid user ID and a password.

The huge potential for commerce on the Internet has changed much of this thinking, and many system and network administrators now feel that any user of their site is a potential for intrusion. This is actually true. Therefore, they usually begin with the premise of "don't trust anyone." Today, this is definitely the best policy.

Orange Book Security Classes

Even with this attitude of openness, security has still been a big concern of the non-university types participating in the Internet. As mentioned in earlier chapters of this book, the Internet started out as the ARPAnet and was driven mainly by the U.S. Department of Defense. As such, it should be apparent that the Department of Defense would be very concerned about security, and they are. The Department of Defense has published several documents relating to security and security specifications.

One of the better known is commonly called the Orange Book, which is a nickname for Department of Defense specifications called Department of Defense Trusted Computer System Evaluation Criteria, which has a standard number of 5200.28. The purpose is to provide technical hardware, firmware, and software security criteria and associated technical evaluation methodologies in support of the overall automatic data-processing system security policy model.

The Orange Book breaks security levels into four basic parts: A, B, C, and D. These classes are defined as follows in increasing order of security:

- **Division D.** Minimal protection; operating systems such as DOS and System 7 for the Macintosh that have no system security fall into this category.

- **Division C.** Discretionary protection; most of the commercially used operating systems claim to meet Division C security, usually C2. There is a big difference between being C2 certified by the

National Computer Security Center (NCSC) and claiming your operating system adheres to the published C2 guidelines.

- **Class (C1).** Discretionary security protection—features include the use of passwords or other authentication methods; the ability to restrict access to files, directories, and other resources; and the ability to prevent the accidental destruction of system-level programs. Many versions of Unix and certain network operating systems fall into this category.

- **Class (C2).** Controlled access protection—features include those found in C1 plus the ability to audit or track all user activity, to restrict operations for specific users, and to ensure that data left in memory cannot be accessed by other users or applications.

- **Division B.** Mandatory protection; must be able to provide mathematical documentation of security and be able to maintain system security even during a system failure. Division B is divided into three classes:

  - **Class (B1).** Labeled Security Protection
  - **Class (B2).** Structured Protection
  - **Class (B3).** Security Domains

- **Division A.** Verified protection; must be able to prove that the security system and policy match the security design specification. Division A is divided into two classes:

  - **Class (A1).** Verified Design
  - **Beyond Class (A1)**

An operating system that allows anyone complete access to all system resources falls into Class D. C1 and C2 security can be reasonably implemented in a commercial environment. After B1, however, the computing environment rapidly changes, and many of the mandatory access-control mechanisms become impractical for normal commercial operations, although they have their place in ultra-secure systems run by government agencies.

If you want to take an in-depth look at the contents of the Orange Book, check into this URL:

```
http://tecnet1.jcte.jcs.mil:8000/htdocs/teinfo/directives/
soft/stan.html
```

Red Book Security

Some aspects of C2 apply directly to computers in a networked environment, and so the National Computer Security Center released a separate publication, known as the Red Book, to address security implementation in a networked environment. The official title of this publication is *Trusted Network Interpretation of the Trusted Computer System Evaluation Criteria, NCSC-TG-005*.

The Red Book is really a guide to interpreting the Orange Book; each of the C2 criteria are described in the context of a network. The single most important distinction made in the Red Book is in defining the role of what it calls the network sponsor. Older mainframe systems have an easily defined owner in the mainframe itself, but networks make it more difficult to establish ownership.

A second set of security principles is being developed by the Information Systems Security Association (ISSA); called the Generally Accepted System Security Principles, it is usually known as GSSP. Fifteen principles have been defined and published in a draft form, and these principles relate more to the individuals managing the security of the system than to the actual system itself. We will be hearing more about GSSP in the future.

C2 and Your Security Requirements

The major features of the C2 standard are that a system must:

- enforce the security policy.

- maintain an audit log and take steps to protect the audit log from tampering.

- maintain a domain for itself and must protect that domain against tampering.

- force identification and authentication of all users.

- protect the identification and authentication mechanism against tampering.

- maintain a security kernel and protect it from tampering.

- require strict identification and authentication for any access to any security systems such as audit logs, password files, and the security kernel itself.

Windows NT falls into the C2 security division, complying with all its guidelines, provided the server is constantly kept behind a locked door. This major advantage of Windows NT security was not present in the first release, but now that it is, Microsoft can bid on government contracts for operating systems that require certain levels of security. This has become a major boon for Microsoft's Windows NT Server sales. It also means that when you purchase Windows NT Server or Workstation, you're purchasing a very secure network operating system indeed.

Netscape's Secure Socket Layers

Many of the large companies flocking to the Internet are attempting to set standards for various ways of securing systems and data transmissions, and as a result, many new products are being released.

Microsoft and Netscape are two of the key players. Netscape proposed and implemented Secure Socket Layers (SSL), which is a way of allowing Web browsers to connect to Web servers and transmit data back and forth on a secure level using data encryption methods.

VISA, Mastercard, and other merchant service companies are also developing security standards, and you can fully expect this trend to continue. Of course, you can implement secure data transmission in many ways, and this chapter covers some of them.

While establishing your network security policies, you should keep in mind the checklists below.

Internet Connection Checklist

Here are some of the basic problems facing administrators connecting their networks to the Internet:

- Millions of people are connected to the Internet now, and more connect every day. Some will invariably behave unethically.

- Proper security configuration and administration can become very complicated. Don't be afraid to get some training.

- Many host systems are run by administrators with little or no experience. Don't be one of them. As I said, don't be afraid to get some training.

- Most administrators connect their sites to the Internet and then think about security. Later in this chapter, you'll see a great example of why you shouldn't make this mistake.

- Many computers run software systems that have unpatched security holes. Even when you buy new software off the shelf, contact the publisher to see if any patches have been released or are planned.

- Internet traffic, and network traffic in general for that matter, are very vulnerable to sniffers and other forms of electronic eavesdropping. Encrypt sensitive network traffic, even if it's not destined for the Internet; you may have potential internal intruders.

Network Security Checklist

Here are some suggestions that you can use as you formulate network security policy for your own site:

- Ensure that your file servers, routers, and gateway equipment are in a locked, secure location with a minimum number of people having access. This is part of the C2 security requirement.

- Create and enforce a password assignment and use policy.

- Inform users about your security policies and about their responsibilities.

- Frequently back up your data and store it in a certified off-site facility.

- Add expiration dates to user accounts to force password changes and the termination of short-term user accounts, such as those assigned to vendors and contractors.

- Activate intruder detection and lockout features as provided in your operating system.

- If you use dial-in access servers, implement the strongest authentication methods allowed by your software. Use callback capabilities whenever possible.

- Periodically, security sweep your network to detect potential problems. Third-party security-sweeping programs are available for most platforms.

- Provide virus protection for all users, and scan all file servers and workstations daily. Use real-time virus scanners that stay loaded and run all the time.

- Ensure that all operating system patches are installed immediately when they are distributed. Don't expect the manufacturer to track you down and tell you about them!

- Use the maximum level of auditing and logging capabilities to detect unauthorized activity before it creates damage.

Internet Security Checklist

If you plan to connect your Web server to the Internet, here are some tips to remember about Internet security and its impact in your computing environment:

- Treat the Internet as the potentially hostile environment that it is.

- Don't allow the reuse of passwords. Use "smart cards" or "card keys" for user authentication to sensitive systems whenever possible.

- If you must allow passwords that are valid for more than one logon, choose strong password policies that mandate frequent changes, and don't allow the reuse of old passwords.

- Install a firewall or a proxy server to protect your network. More on this later.

- Do not send confidential information in clear text across the network. Instead, encrypt all sensitive messages and files before transmitting them across any network, including the Internet.

- Limit the services that are offered on your network to those that are necessary. Never run software just for the sake of saying that you have it installed.

- Provide security training for your network administrators.

- Establish your network security properly. Install software patches, don't use guest accounts, activate intruder detection schemes, and establish lock-out mechanisms for too many bad password attempts.

- Do not run your own Internet e-mail, FTP, Web, or other information servers unless you have the in-house experts to configure and manage them safely and securely.

E-Mail Security Checklist

Consider these tips on e-mail security as part of your policies and procedures:

- Assume that any unencrypted message you send via e-mail can be intercepted and read by prying eyes. Use an encryption tool such as PGP to encrypt all sensitive e-mail. Over time, your e-mail could fit together like the pieces of a puzzle, eventually revealing vital information and facts you may not want known. The rule of thumb here is: Never send any unencrypted information in e-mail that you wouldn't want broadcast on national television.

- E-mail addresses can be "spoofed," or faked, so that someone can make a message appear that it came from someone else.

- You may want to use a separate file for highly sensitive information: Encrypt it, attach the encrypted file to the e-mail message, and then encrypt that message and file attachment again as a whole.

- Your e-mail passwords should always be different from any of your other network passwords. Never use the same password for two different things, and never reuse an old password.

Defining Security Threats

The many common security threats range from complete network infiltration to simple virus contamination. Some threats are accidental, and others are malicious; some affect hardware, and others affect software. We'll look at them all in this next section.

Internal Threats

Internal security problems are probably the most common. Users entrusted with certain levels of access to systems and hardware can be a major threat if not controlled and monitored carefully. Put simply, you never know what someone is going to do. Even the most loyal employees or workers can change their tune and get into a malicious mode, wreaking havoc on your computing environment. Check your workers' backgrounds, references, and previous employers carefully, and routinely change and audit your security methods.

External Threats

External security threats are the most problematic. You never know when an outsider will attempt to breach your systems or who the perpetrator may be. Some people go to great extremes to gain access to your systems and information. There are many documented cases of outsiders easily gaining access to systems that were assumed to be protected. Even the Department of Defense admits that its computer systems were attacked more than 250,000 times in 1995. That statistic alone should stop you in your tracks and make you think a bit. It has been recently theorized that a well-funded group of computer hackers could bring the entire country to a screeching halt within 90 days with almost no trouble at all!

Intruders Are People

Intruders may use your own policies and routines against you. Any intruder could pose as a person from one of your departments or come in as a worker representing another firm that would normally be considered non-intrusive. Someone posing as part of the cleaning crew, as a utility worker, as a building inspector, as an insurance official, and so on could have only one purpose: gaining the knowledge needed to infiltrate your network. You can even assume that people are digging through your trash looking for keys to assist them in breaching your systems. You may do well to get yourself a paper shredder and implement a mandatory "shredding policy." The basic thing to understand here is that anything is possible and that people will do anything to get what they want.

Beware of strangers asking questions about how the system works, and never give anyone your password. The notorious Kevin Mitnik used very subtle persuasion techniques that came to be known as social engineering to first gain people's confidence and then their passwords.

Securing Hardware

The most obvious manifestation of your computer system is the hardware you use. Let's take a look at some of the more common threats to your hardware:

- Theft of a computer, printer, or other resource.

- Tampering by a disgruntled employee who interferes with dip switches or cuts a cable.

- Destruction of resources by fire, flood, or electrical power surges. And don't forget that those sprinklers in the ceiling can put out hundreds of gallons of water a minute; most of the damage to computer systems comes not from fire, but from the water used to put out the fire.

- Ordinary wear and tear. A normal preventive maintenance program should inhibit wear and tear.

Securing Software

The second component of your system is software. Threats to software include the following:

- Deletion of a program, either by accident or by malicious intent.

- Theft of a program by one of your users.

- Corruption of a program, caused either by a hardware failure or by a virus. More on virus attacks in a moment.

- Bugs in the software; yes, they do happen, and their effect may be immediate and catastrophic or very subtle and not come to light for years.

Securing Information

The third component of your system is the data and data files used by the corporation. Threats to information can include:

- Deletion of a file or files. Again, make and test your backups regularly.

- Corruption, caused either by hardware problems or by a bug in the software.

- Theft of company data files.

The Threat from Viruses

One of the most common threats to computer security comes from a computer virus. There are literally thousands of strains of computer viruses, ranging from harmless ones that simply put a message on the screen, all the way to vicious ones that destroy all data they can reach on the local machine and the network. Most viruses can reproduce themselves over and over on every system they touch. Virus eradication can be a most painful experience indeed.

Today, with the vastness and power of the Internet, malicious intruders can gain access to any number of viruses in a matter of seconds by doing a simple search on one of the popular search engines. For example, I used my Web browser to access Excite's search engine at `http://www.excite.com` and then entered the key phrase "hacking into computer systems." Within a few seconds, I had a list of various sites on the Internet where I could find information and programs that assist in intrusion attempts. Within 10 minutes of that initial search, I had located dozens of viruses and could download them right away. I even found a program that generates viruses for you. It's really that simple, and, subsequently, it's really that dangerous.

How Do You Catch a Virus?

How does a virus find its way on to your computer systems? Quite easily in fact, and through any number of methods. A customer can give you an infected floppy disk or program file. Someone can even give you a seemingly harmless Microsoft Word document that contains a Word macro that had a destructive purpose! A user can also download a software package from an online system that contains a virus. Your computers and networks can contract a virus in any number of ways. The single best way to prevent viruses is to implement a policy that mandates a virus scanner be used all the time on all your computer systems and to practice safe computing.

Finding Antivirus Software

Some of the better-known virus-prevention software packages can easily be found and downloaded from the Internet. Some leaders in the field of virus prevention are listed in Table 11.1, along with the addresses of their Web sites where you can find the software you need.

TABLE 11.1:   Suppliers of antivirus software

Company	Software	URL
McAfee	Virushield	`http://www.mcafee.com`
McAfee	AntiVirus NT	`http://www.mcafee.com`
Cheyenne	NetShield	`http://www.cheyenne.com`
Symantec	AntiVirus	`http://www.symantec.com/avcenter`
CT Software	SafetyNet Pro	`http://members.aol.com/ron2222/snpro.htm`
TCT	Thunderbyte Anti Virus	`http://www.thunderbyte.com`

Of course, many other antivirus software packages are available today. Locating them using the Internet is a simple process and absolutely worth your time.

Establishing a Security Policy for Your Web Site

Today's computing world is radically different from the computing environments of yesteryear. These days, many systems are in private offices and labs, often managed by individuals or persons employed outside the traditional computer data center or IS department. And more important, many systems are connected to the Internet, exposing them to the entire world and giving users of networks connected to the Internet the avenues they need to reach internal networks! Keep all that in mind as you read this section and establish your own policies.

Defining Security Goals

When you are defining security procedures against potential threats, consider the following:

- Look at exactly what you are trying to protect.
- Look at who you need to protect it from.
- Look at what you need to protect it from.
- Determine the likelihood of potential threats.
- Implement measures that will protect your assets in a manner that is cost-effective for you or your firm.
- Review your processes and procedures continuously, and improve them every time a weakness is found or a new security mechanism becomes available.

The goals of your security policy should be to minimize all types of threat and ensure that threats are as infrequent as possible. A secondary goal is to minimize the effect of any security breach once it occurs.

Aim your network security policy toward the following goals:

- Preventing malicious damage to files and systems
- Preventing accidental damage to files and systems
- Limiting the results of any deletions or damage to files that does occur
- Protecting the integrity and confidentiality of data
- Preventing unauthorized access to the system
- Providing appropriate disaster-recovery systems so that the server can be restored and be back online again quickly

Establishing Security Measures

Once your security goals are in place, you can decide which of the many available security techniques make sense for your installation. Here are some suggestions:

- Be sure the server is physically secure.

- Use power-conditioning devices such as line conditioners or a UPS (uninterruptible power supply).

- Implement fault-tolerant services on the server. Take advantage of RAID (redundant array of inexpensive disks). Windows NT supports several levels of RAID; so choose the level that makes most sense for your operation.

- Make regular and frequent backups and test them to ensure that they contain what you think they do.

- Install callback modems to prevent unauthorized logon attempts from remote locations.

- Use all the audit trail features of Windows NT.

- Control access to certain files and directories.

- Control uploading privileges on your FTP server to minimize the possibility of someone infecting you with a virus.

- Consider using traffic padding, a technique that equalizes network traffic and thus makes it more difficult for an eavesdropper to infer what is happening on your network.

- Implement packet filtering, which makes eavesdropping almost impossible.

- Prepare a plan that you can execute when you detect that your network is under attack. Decide what you will do and the sequence in which you will do it. Define when you will shut down the service, the connection to the Internet, or your own internal network.

Know Thy Server

The reason you are establishing your Web site should directly dictate a portion of your security policies. For example, if your Web site is designed to deliver information internally, don't put it on a place on your network where it is exposed to the entire Internet. Put it behind a firewall, or put it on an isolated part of your network where there is no Internet access.

If your Web site is designed to deliver information and content to people on the Internet and if you want to control who has access to that information, establish a portion of your security policy to dictate guidelines for access. Decide how you will control access. The most common way is with user IDs and passwords. You must establish the procedures used for verifying a user. Don't assume that anyone will be truthful when filling in your online survey form, and verify as much of the information as you can.

Some of the policies that you establish for preventing external intrusion of your Web server are the same as those for preventing internal threats. You can, however, use other mechanisms, such as firewalls and proxy servers, to diminish external security threats. I'll discuss them at length later in this chapter.

Secure Web Site Configurations

You can configure your Web server securely in two ways; one involves the physical isolation of the server, and the other isolates the server based on the networking protocol in use. Let's take a look.

Physical Isolation

Placing your Web server on a section of your network where it cannot be accessed by unknown users of the Internet is always a great policy. This, in effect, eliminates most of the possibilities for intrusion from an outsider. A potential intruder would have to physically gain access to your premises in order to violate security and gain access to the Web server. Physical access to your premises is something you can control, and it goes a long way in securing your Web site. Consider the physical location of the server itself. It should probably be behind a door with lock and key, even during normal business hours. You can install mechanisms that require the use of card keys on the server for access before someone can actually sign on to the server using the server's keyboard.

Protocol Isolation

Protocol isolation techniques involve Web servers that do not use TCP/IP as the primary means of network communication. Microsoft's Internet Information Server is, or will be, capable of using other network protocols to communicate with Web clients needing access. For instance, you can opt to use Microsoft's NetBEUI protocol, or perhaps you can use IPX/SPX, which is more performance oriented than NetBEUI. If your Web server has no way of talking to the rest of the Internet, logic dictates that a potential intruder would have no means of reaching your Web server from across the Internet.

Another way to use protocol isolation internally is to design your network so that part runs on one protocol and another part uses TCP/IP. With this design, only those users that need access to the Web server run TCP/IP on their workstations.

Protecting Your Web Server with a Firewall

Firewalls are becoming a very popular way of controlling access to network systems; in fact, well over one-third of all Web sites on the Internet are protected by some form of firewall. According to a recent survey, 10,000 firewall units were shipped during the whole of 1995; this is expected to expand to 1.5 million by the year 2000.

A firewall is either a hardware device (such as a router) or a software package running on a specially configured computer that sits between a secured network (your internal network) and an unsecured network (the Internet). The firewall performs several important tasks, including preventing unauthorized access to your network, limiting incoming and outgoing traffic, authenticating users, logging traffic information, and producing reports.

The fundamental role of a firewall is to monitor all the traffic that flows between the two networks, but to block certain kinds of traffic completely; if the firewall does its job properly, an intruder will never reach your internal protected network.

Some firewalls permit only certain types of network traffic through them; others firewalls are less restrictive and block network services that are known to be problems, such as FTP. Firewalls based on routers rather than on complete computer systems tend to have fewer reporting functions available.

Configuring Your Firewall

Where you locate your firewall depends on the design of your network and exactly what you want to protect. Figure 11.1 shows a simple configuration in which the firewall sits between your internal network and the Internet. The firewall blocks access from the Internet for everything except incoming e-mail.

FIGURE 11.1:

Simple firewall
configuration

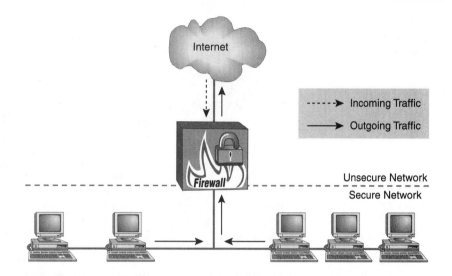

Figure 11.2 illustrates a slightly more complex example of a dual-homed firewall, a common configuration that is often used these days by companies that have Web servers. The firewall has two network connections: (1) to the secure internal network, and (2) to the Internet. Network traffic originating in the secure network can pass out to the Internet or to the bastion host; incoming traffic from the Internet can only access the bastion host and the services that it offers.

The bastion host (the name comes from the highly fortified projections on the outside walls of medieval castles in Europe) is your public presence on the Internet and is exposed to possibly hostile elements. But even if the bastion host is compromised (and you should plan for that), your internal network is isolated and is still secure.

Don't allow user accounts on the bastion host if you can avoid it; they make the host more susceptible to attack while at the same time making it more difficult to detect those attacks when they do occur.

FIGURE 11.2:

Dual-homed firewall configuration

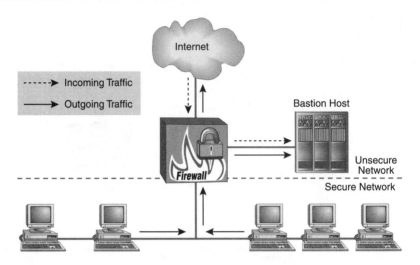

A variation on this configuration is shown in Figure 11.3. Here the firewall has three network interface cards: (1) the external connection to the Internet; (2) a connection to the secure internal network; and (3) a connection for the bastion host. This arrangement brings the bastion host inside the secure area, but it is still isolated from the secure internal network.

FIGURE 11.3:

Extending the firewall configuration

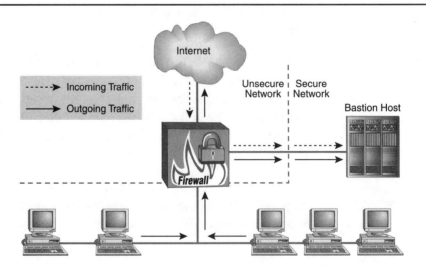

Firewalls and Your Security Policy

It is certainly a truism, but a firewall can't protect your network against an attack that doesn't come through the firewall. Many companies that connect to the Internet are very concerned about proprietary data leaking out through their Internet link, but have no coherent policy about how dial-in access via modems should be protected or how backup tapes are to be handled and secured. For a firewall to be useful in protecting your network systems, it must be one element of a consistent overall security policy.

When implementing a firewall, ask these questions:

- What do you want the firewall to do?

- What level of control do you want?

- How much can you spend to get it done right?

- What will maintaining it cost?

You can install firewalls at the network level and at the application level.

Network Firewalls

Network-level firewalls route traffic according to the source address, the destination address, and ports in individual IP packets. Network-level firewalls are becoming increasingly sophisticated; they can even maintain internal information about the state of connections passing through them and the contents of various data streams. Network-level firewalls tend to be very fast and invisible to users.

Application Firewalls

Application-level firewalls are hosts that run proxy servers which permit no direct traffic between networks. They can also perform detailed logging and auditing of traffic passing through them. Proxies are explained in detail in the next section of this chapter, but I'll cover a little bit about them here.

You can use application-level firewalls as network address translators. Network traffic goes in one side and out the other, after passing through an application that effectively masks the identity of the originating connection. Having an application in between you and your data source can in some cases impact performance, making a proxy style firewall less desirable.

Early versions of application-level firewalls were not particularly invisible to end users, who needed some training to use them correctly. Current application-level firewalls are often fully invisible to the end user, eliminating the need for training. Application-level firewalls tend to enforce more conservative security models than network-level firewalls, primarily because they are more limited in what they can achieve.

Benefits of Using a Firewall

Let's take a look at some of the major benefits you might expect from adding a firewall to your armory of security tools:

- Controlled access to sensitive systems
- Protection for vulnerable Internet services
- Centralized security administration
- Logging and statistics on network utilization
- Sophisticated packet-filtering schemes

- Configuration from standalone hardware systems, not dependent on other hardware and software systems

A firewall can act as a very efficient choke mechanism, giving you a great deal of control over the point at which your network connects to the Internet. You can use it as the focus your security policies.

Reasons for Not Using a Firewall

Benefits aside, there are also drawbacks to using a firewall, including the following:

- Access to desirable services can be more restricted than you would like or can become more complex than normal.

- The potential for backdoor access increases if not prevented against.

- Additional administration and training are required.

- The cost can be prohibitive.

- The configuration can be too complex to implement correctly.

And then there are the threats that no firewall, no matter how capable, can protect you against, including viruses, malicious staff with access to the secure portion of your network, and new and undefined threats from outside your system.

Finding Firewall Products

The National Computer Security Association (NCSA) recently announced the results of its tests on firewalls. Products were subjected to a veritable barrage of attacks from outside the firewall, while a set of fairly typical business applications, including e-mail and FTP and Web servers, ran on the secure side of the firewall.

The 15 vendors whose products passed these tests can label these products NCSA certified. When you are looking for firewall software, therefore, try a product from one of these companies:

- Atlantic Systems Group
- Border Network Technologies Inc
- Digital Equipment Corporation
- CheckPoint Software Technologies Inc
- Global Technology Associates Inc
- Harris Computer Systems Inc
- IBM
- Livermore Software Laboratories International
- Milkyway Networks Inc
- On Technology Inc
- Technologic Inc
- Trusted Information Systems Inc
- Radguard Ltd
- Raptor Systems Inc
- Sun Microsystems

What Is a Proxy Server?

A proxy server can run on a dual-homed server or on a bastion server; the only requirement is that it be a host that your users can reach, which in turn can talk to the outside world of the Internet. A user's Web browser talks to the proxy server rather than to a real server out on the Internet, and the proxy decides which requests to pass on to the real server and which to ignore. If a request is approved, the proxy server communicates with the real server on the Internet on behalf of the Web browser. The proxy sends requests from the browser to the Internet server and then sends the replies back to the browser. The browser never contacts the Internet server directly by itself. Figure 11.4 illustrates this concept.

FIGURE 11.4:

How proxy servers work

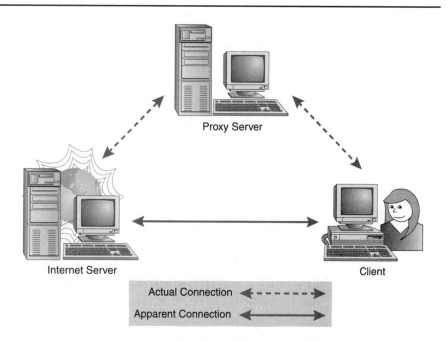

Proxy Server

Internet Server

Client

| Actual Connection | ◄ - - - - - ► |
| Apparent Connection | ◄————► |

The user perceives no difference between talking to the Internet server and talking to the proxy server, and the Internet server does not know that the requests are coming from the proxy rather than from the Web browser. Proxy servers are usually paired with some mechanism that can be used to restrict IP-level traffic between the Web browsers running on your network and the real Internet servers. With IP-level connectivity between the browser and the real servers on the Internet, users can bypass the proxy server.

Proxies can be configured with what are commonly referred to as "bad addresses." A bad address is not routable through the Internet.

Several sets of IP addresses are set aside for testing, and they cannot be routed to any specific location using the Internet. These addresses are commonly used to configure networks behind a proxy firewall server. One common set of bad addresses that I like to use is the 10.0.0.0 Class A network. InterNIC has set aside this entire block of addresses for testing purposes, which could most certainly include use behind a proxy server. Here is example of how to do this.

First, set up your proxy server hardware with two network cards. One network card has a real, routable Internet address of something like 204.176.47.2, and the other uses a bad address of 10.0.0.1. Plug the 204.176.47.2 network card into your Internet router connection, such as an ISDN router, and plug the 10.0.0.1 network card into your local network. This creates an isolated barrier between the Internet and your network.

Now, configure each workstation with a unique address on the 10.0.0.0 network, using a gateway address of 10.0.0.1, or the server's bad address. Next, configure each application that understands and uses a proxy server with a proxy server address of the server, 10.0.0.1. That's it. Now, when the client software needs to access the Internet, the requests are sent to the network card in the server that has the address 10.0.0.1, at which point the proxy server actually forwards the request to the destination after including its own valid address of 204.176.47.2. When the request is returned to the server, the server returns it to the originating workstation. Simple enough right? Well, it's sounds that way and actually is fairly simple to set up. For a workstation to use a proxy server, however, it must have software that knows how to talk to a proxy server. Netscape Navigator and Microsoft Internet Explorer Web browsers can both use a proxy server, as can many other e-mail, news, FTP, Web, and Telnet software packages.

Using a proxy server can be a very cost-effective way to establish a secure barrier between you and the Internet. Microsoft has its own proxy server code named Catapult, which is in beta testing right now, and appears to be more inclusive than others I've seen.

Benefits of Using a Proxy Server

As always, there are arguments for and against using proxy server technology. Here are some benefits of using a proxy server:

- It blocks access to services you don't want users using.
- It protects vulnerable Internet services.
- It hides the real identity of the user.
- It provides logging and statistics on network utilization.
- It is inexpensive compared with hardware-based firewalls.
- It is easy to configure and manage.
- It doesn't require the use of valid Internet IP addresses.
- It is often distributed as part of a Web server package.
- It completely blocks access to systems "behind" the proxy server.

Reasons for Not Using a Proxy Server

And to present the other side of the argument, here are some drawbacks to using a proxy server on your network:

- It requires client software that can "talk" to a proxy server.
- It provides no protection from inside intruder attacks.
- It requires additional administration and training.
- It requires some end-user training.
- It can somewhat degrade application performance.
- It doesn't provide packet filtering.
- It doesn't support all TCP/IP application protocols yet.

Using IIS with a Proxy Server

You can use IIS with a proxy server; in fact you can even make a couple of configuration changes to IIS to make it easier to work with one. Open the Control Panel, and double-click on the Internet icon to open the Internet Properties dialog box. The settings in this dialog box govern which NT Server system will be used for access to the proxy server.

Check the Use Proxy Server checkbox; then in the Settings portion of this dialog box, enter the IP address and port number of the proxy server you want to use. In the Bypass Proxy On field, enter the computer name and domain or port number of computers on the Internet that you want to access without going through the proxy server. Separate each entry from the next with a comma. For example, if you enter:

```
dyson.com,:80
```

you can gain access to computers inside the dyson.com domain and also to computers on port 80 (the normal port used for Web access) without going through the proxy server. These options can be useful if you want to gain access to Internet servers that are actually connected to your own local area network, but be sure you are not opening any unanticipated holes in your system security.

Click on the Apply button to put these configuration changes into effect, or choose the Cancel button to return to the Control Panel.

Breaking In to Your Own System

The best way to test your network security is to simply try to break in yourself. And not just once, but routinely. Better that you find the holes before a would-be intruder does, right?

One subject worth emphasizing again is the process you use to manage passwords on your system. Surveys indicate that more than 80 percent of all security violations are a direct result of someone exploiting a poorly chosen password. Thus, one can conclude that that 80 percent of all intrusions can be prevented by choosing good passwords. The *Windows NT Server Operating System Security* chapter goes into detail about how (and how not) to choose passwords.

You might do well to download a password-cracking program from the Internet and use it on your own systems! It's far better that you find bad or easily guessed passwords before a would-be intruder does.

A Cautionary Tale

The following is a true story. An intruder broke in to a site by using another company's network. This technique is common; an intruder breaks into one system and then uses that system as a base to break into another. Once the intruder has access to password information on the first system, other downstream systems cannot separate the intruder from a real user; after all, as far as the computer system is concerned, they are the same person.

The company was notified of the break-ins and, with a little effort, discovered that the intruder was working from a list of .com domain names. The intruder was looking for hosts with easy-to-steal password files. In this case, easy-to-steal referred to sites that had an easily guessed NIS (Network Information Service) domain name and an accessible NIS server.

Unix systems commonly use an NIS to manage passwords, host address information, and access permissions. Using NIS, you can configure information consistently across all systems; you locate a master database on one system and then make it available to all the other computers on the network. You can thus avoid the problem of inconsistent updating of information on the different systems; but on poorly secured systems, you can introduce other problems.

Not knowing how far the intruder had got, the company thought it should warn the sites it considered vulnerable. Of the 656 hosts in the intruder's .com list, 24 had password files that were easy to steal. One-third of these files contained at least one account that had no password assigned to it, yet had an interactive shell that was activated upon logon—an easy access point.

One system on the intruder's list provided a password file that was attacked with a password-cracking program. The file had a grand total of 1594 password entries. Running Crack, a publicly available password cracker, for 10 minutes revealed more than 50 passwords. Within another 20 minutes, Crack found another 40 passwords, and within an hour it found one of the root passwords. The root password on a Unix system is like the master key to all locks; once you have the root password, you can gain complete control of the system with no trouble at all. After a few days, Crack had found 5 root passwords and had identified 259 of 1594 passwords. That's a terrifying 1 in 6 ratio!

Checking Your FTP Server

You should also take a close look at your FTP server. Log on anonymously if your site allows it. And even if your site does not allow anonymous logons, try it anyway to see how the system responds to your attempt. Then log on as a normal user and see how far you can navigate the directory trees. Chances are good that you will find something wrong. A practice I always follow is that whenever I establish a new FTP account for a user, I always test its access abilities myself by logging on with that user's ID. You can't go wrong doing this; so think about adopting this practice as one of your policies.

Another Cautionary Tale

One more word of caution: Get your security in place *before* you connect your network to the Internet. I learned why this is so important the hard way. I was in the process of opening up shop as an Internet Service Provider and was really excited about getting online as fast as I could. My System Design Engineer cautioned me that we should get all the security in place and checked out first. I agreed, but was still in a hurry. Fortunately, the engineer took his time and was as thorough as he was trained to be.

The day our T1 link to the Internet was installed, we plugged in our computer systems to the link about 5 PM. The next morning at 7 AM, I walked in to the office and looked at the server's monitoring screen, and there it was plain as day! During the night, 7 attempts had been made to break in to our system, and it had not been online to the Internet for even 24 hours! And what was even worse, the attempts to break in continued as I watched.

To avoid being traced, the would-be intruder was trying to break in from more than 10 locations simultaneously. This was happening so fast that we knew robotic software was at work. The good news is that the attempts were futile and all failed.

Using the Internet to Your Advantage

Intruders use the Internet to their advantage in many ways, including information gathering, and so should you. You can use the Internet to do several things that can greatly minimize your chances of intrusion. First, read the newsgroups that deal directly with security and breaking in to computer systems. If you find people talking about your networks, monitor the postings closely and take detailed notes, saving copies of the messages. This could help you identify and catch an intruder.

You can also use your favorite search engine to search for cracking and hacking software; use it on your own networks to search for documents that may contain information about your systems. You may very well discover some security risks that you've missed. Try keywords and phrases such as the following: security, breaking in to computers, hacking, cracking, scanners, sniffers, and worms.

How Intruders Break In to Your System

Intruders break in to your systems in any number of ways. With the advent of the Internet, lots of Unix software is being ported to Windows NT, and so are a lot of the security holes in that Unix software. This means that your seemingly harmless and brand new software may in fact be a new generation of an age-old problem.

Sendmail

Intruders have traditionally used services that run on computers to gain access to them. One of the most widely used holes is in Sendmail and its many derivatives. Sendmail can actually assist a potential intruder in creating files, altering files, and even mailing sensitive files to the intruder. Go over your mail server software carefully, and find out its origins. If it turns out to be a Sendmail port from Unix, use the Unix hacking techniques against it.

A Security Hole Closed in an Early IIS Release

An early release of IIS contained a bug that was potentially dangerous to all Web sites. It was fixed as soon as it was found, and new releases of IIS were placed on Microsoft's Web server in March 1996 and June 1996. Here's what happened.

Microsoft initially shipped IIS with a huge gaping hole in the CGI interface that essentially allowed any knowing user to send any command to a Web server for execution.

For example, if a user sends this URL to your Web server:

```
http://www.yoursite.com/scripts/baloney.bat?dir
```

it returns a directory listing, and you have a gaping hole in your Web server! Take the Web server down and get it patched or replaced immediately.

This works because of the way in which Windows NT handles script execution. Windows NT spawns a command shell in which to run a script, and all the arguments passed to the script are sent as command line arguments. If the script does not exist, the shell is still spawned, and the arguments are still passed to the command line.

Here's what happens. The URL above is supposed to run a batch file called `baloney.bat`, which we know doesn't exist. Windows NT opens a command shell anyway and sends the argument `dir` to the command shell as its first argument. Windows NT interprets the first argument of any command as the name of the program to execute. The Windows NT `dir` command runs because a separate executable program called `dir` does not exist and returns the results of the command as a directory listing. I don't need to tell you that the `dir` command could just as easily have been a `format C:` command, which wipes out your hard drive.

Today, this security hole in Windows NT Web server software is widely known, as is the fact that it has been very firmly closed.

Checking CGI Scripts

Web servers by themselves pose only moderate security risks, particularly when protected by a firewall or a proxy server. But the one concern is how your system uses CGI scripts. You Web server may be configured to create HTML pages on the fly using a script written in Perl or in some other scripting language.

When considering these external programs, ask these questions:

- Can a knowledgeable attacker trick the external program into doing something that you don't want it to do?

- Can a knowledgeable attacker upload an external program and have that program execute on your system?

You can minimize the threat from both these sources by using some of the techniques outlined earlier in this chapter and by ensuring that your Web server does not contain anything that you don't want revealed to the outside world.

Do not to take it for granted that someone's really nifty Web enhancement software is completely safe and harmless. Writing CGI scripts is not particularly easy, and writing secure scripts can be a job for the experts. You can completely assume that some programmer is writing a nice little CGI script to complement your Web site, one that you won't be able to resist trying out and that will invariably put the holes in place that others need to infiltrate your systems and networks.

Lots of programmers hide backdoors, tricks, and traps in their seemingly harmless software for their own convenience in testing and debugging and then forget to remove those elements when they release the package. You may think you have just downloaded and installed the world's greatest page counter, whereas in reality you have just installed an open door on your system. Always test shareware and freeware thoroughly on a standalone system, and ask others for their reviews on the software before you place it on one of your production servers. Otherwise, you may lose everything.

Spoofing Your System

Some intruders may attempt to use "spoofing" to gain access to your systems. Spoofing is the process of replacing parts of the TCP/IP header with bogus information in an effort to fool your firewall or proxy into thinking that the network traffic came from an allowed and trusted origin. Be sure your firewall can prevent this sort of trickery, and implement its prevention fiercely.

Password Attacks

Intruders use programs called password crackers more than any other tool to gain unauthorized access to systems, and poorly chosen passwords increase your risk of intrusion tremendously. Download at least one or more password crackers, and use it on your own systems to test the kinds of passwords that you routinely provide your users.

And when you do crack a password, adjust your policies to disallow similar password schemes in the future, and obviously change that cracked password immediately. I found more than 15 password crackers in just a few minutes of searching the Internet.

As mentioned earlier, the Computer Emergency Response Team/ Coordination Center (CERT/CC) at Carnegie-Mellon University (CMU), a group that monitors security threats and preventive measures, estimates that 80 percent or more of the intrusion problems they see have to do with poorly chosen passwords. If you don't remember anything else in this chapter, remember this! And tell your friends.

You should also have a procedure in place to manage expiring passwords so that users actually do change their passwords routinely. Old passwords are increasingly vulnerable to attack; the longer a password stays unchanged, the more time a potential intruder has to crack it. As I mentioned earlier in this book, intruders routinely use dictionaries in conjunction with password-cracking programs to automatically attempt various user ID and password combinations. These robotic software programs can run through thousands of combinations in a day, making an old and poorly chosen password a literal walk in the park to discover.

You should also caution your uses against using the same passwords in different places, such as using their network logon to access their screen saver.

Keystroke Grabbers

Another way intruders gain access is to implement a keystroke grabber. These programs actually monitor and record every keystroke on a given computer. Typically, a keystroke grabber records keystrokes on the machine on which the program is running. Thus, the intruder must have internal access or gain access externally through the network connections. If you want to take a look at some keystroke grabbers, use one of the popular search engines on the Internet, and enter the keywords *keycopy* or *playback*. You will find several without much effort.

One of the best ways I can think of on a Windows NT network to guard against unauthorized software installation is by using Microsoft's Systems Management Server (SMS), part of the BackOffice suite of programs. SMS performs numerous tasks to help you manage the PCs on your network, and one of its more interesting features is the ability to monitor the software on one of your workstations.

SMS will actually let you know when new software is installed and when software has been removed. This may tip you off to a potential problem before it gets to serious proportions. You will find information on SMS at Microsoft's Web site.

Sniffers

Intruders don't have to steal keystrokes to find out what is happening on your network; sometimes they use a sniffer to access information that you want kept secret. A sniffer watches the network packets as they go to and from your site and a remote site; it can see the information being transferred.

Hardware and software sniffers are readily available and are used to monitor network traffic. If that traffic happens to contain a user ID or a password, your network security is at risk. Hardware sniffers normally have to be used on the physical cable of your network, which reduces the threat from internal users somewhat. Software sniffers can run from a workstation attached to your network and even over a dial-up link.

Intruders may use a sniffer to look at your passwords or your data. Protecting your passwords is easy; change them often. Protecting your data is more difficult and may involve end-to-end encryption techniques.

FTP Problems

FTP can be a real problem, and you should take great care when configuring your FTP server. Double- and triple-check your file permissions for every FTP user account. Log on as that user, and ensure that the access is restricted in the way you want it. Additionally, many intruders use anonymous FTP servers to upload and stash pirated software, cracking tools, and other illegal material that you do not want on your FTP server. One easy way to protect your site is not to allow users to upload files to your FTP site; just let them download the material you originally established the FTP server to manage and distribute. If it is important that you allow uploads, set the directory permissions so that you have to explicitly specify who can upload files.

Closing a Back Door on Your System

When an intruder successfully breaks in to your system, he or she usually creates a back door for easy return. If you have detected and obstructed an intruder, scour your systems for back doors. One of the easiest, although sometimes painful, ways to wipe out back doors is to simply reformat your server's hard disk and reinstall the operating system. This wipes out anything out of the ordinary.

Tools for Intruders

Some great sites on the Internet are packed full of tools and information for intruders. Use your favorite search engine to search for any of the intruder terms used in this section.

Alternatively, point your Web browser to:

`http://www.ecnet.net/users/mumbv/pages/crack/text.html`

Intruders may use this site to learn more and find tools of the trade, and so should you and your staff.

CHAPTER

TWELVE

12

Managing Your Web Site

- Managing day-to-day operations

- Duties of the webmaster

- Managing your Web site with FrontPage Explorer

- Administering Webs with FrontPage Explorer

- Dealing with e-mail

- Installing scripts on IIS

- Configuring MIME types

- Using Web-to-database connectivity tools

- Coping with disasters

- Troubleshooting your server

In this chapter we'll take a look at the day-to-day operations on your Web site and at some of the tasks you will be performing. We'll look at how to use Microsoft FrontPage to manage your Web site and how best to add and control new HTML content, how and when to back up your Web site, how to deal with e-mail from visitors, and where to find Web server-to-database connectivity tools you can use to link legacy databases to your Web server. We'll also look at disaster planning and then close with a section on troubleshooting your Web server. Let's start by looking at day-to-day operations on your Web server.

Managing Day-to-Day Operations

If you thought that you were done when you finally went online to the Internet, I have a surprise for you: The real work is just beginning. You will want to add new material to your Web site to keep it looking fresh and to keep those visitors coming back time after time, you will have to design a backup strategy so that you can reload and restore your Web site after a catastrophic accident, and you will have to deal with inquiries, suggestions, and complaints from your visitors in the form of e-mail. But first, lets look at the duties and responsibilities of the Web site administrator or webmaster.

Duties of the Webmaster

Your site may be small enough that one person can perform all the duties needed to keep it in tip-top condition, but if you run a large corporate Intranet, you may find that you need a department of people to keep everything ticking nicely. But no matter how many people it takes to do the job, the duties are essentially the same and include the following:

- Preparing and adding new HTML content
- Inspecting system logs
- Testing active links and locating new links
- Testing CGI scripts
- Responding to feedback from users
- Keeping up with the latest developments in Web technology
- Backing up the server
- Installing software upgrades and system patches
- Troubleshooting server problems
- Upgrading system hardware

We'll look at some of these duties in this chapter and the rest of them in the next chapter, *Advanced Web Site Administration*.

Managing Your Web Site with FrontPage Explorer

In the *Creating Your Web Site with FrontPage* chapter, you read about the Web-publishing tool included with Windows NT 4. You'll take the best advantage of the power of FrontPage if you use it from Day 1 in the building of your Web site. When you use it in concert with NT Server and IIS, FrontPage simplifies much of your Web building and maintenance. Remember that in FrontPage, a Web is considered anything from a single page of HTML to an entire Web site.

Creating or Opening a Web Site

When you create a new Web site in the FrontPage Explorer, the Explorer creates a new folder for the Web site off the root Web (within the folder FrontPage Webs\Content by default) and installs the files it needs for managing your Web.

In the Explorer, choose File ➤ New Web or click on the New Web button on the toolbar to display the New Web dialog box, as shown in Figure 12.1. You can create the new Web with either a template or a Wizard, just as you can when creating a new page in the FrontPage Editor.

FIGURE 12.1:

You choose a template or a Wizard in the New Web dialog box.

Each template contains a set of pages that can serve as the basis for the Web you build. For example, the template named Project Web contains a home page with a What's New section, a send mail link, Include Bots for a header and a footer, and links to other pages in the Web site called Members, Schedule, Status, Search, and Discussion. You use the template called Learning FrontPage in conjunction with the FrontPage tutorial—choose Learning FrontPage in the help system's table of contents.

A New Web Wizard will ask you a series of questions about the new Web, such as what type of pages you want in it, the contents of the home page, and the contents of a feedback form page. It then builds the pages accordingly.

If you want to start a new, empty Web, choose either the Normal Web or the Empty Web option. The first contains a single blank Web page; the latter is completely empty of pages.

When you create a new Web, you must choose the server on which it will reside (if you have multiple servers) and give the Web a name, which will also name the Web's folder or directory on disk. When you have a Web site open in the Explorer, the dialog box for the File ➤ New Web command lets you add the new Web to the current Web. All the pages associated with the new Web will be imported into the current Web.

Unlike the pages you work on in the FrontPage Editor, there are no data that you must save in the Explorer, since all changes are saved automatically. Note, however, that you should always exit the Explorer *after* you exit the FrontPage Editor. When you do so, the Explorer is aware of any changes you make to Web pages in the Editor.

To open an existing Web site in the Explorer, choose File ➤ Open Web, or click on the Open Web button on the toolbar. You choose a server from the Open Web dialog box and then choose a FrontPage Web site from that server.

Note that you cannot work with multiple Web sites in the Explorer; opening a site closes any other open site.

Changing Explorer's View of the Web

The layout of the FrontPage Explorer was discussed earlier in the *Creating a Web Site with FrontPage* chapter. It described the Explorer window as being divided into an Outline View pane and a Link View pane. You can change from the Link View to the Summary View to see page-related details on every file in the Web, such as the date and time each was last modified. Use either the relevant commands on the View menu or their buttons on the toolbar.

You can sort the list of items in the Summary View pane in the usual way: Click on a column title to sort by that column; click on it again to sort by that column in reverse order. You can change the size of the panes by dragging the center divider to the left or right.

When the Link View is displayed, you can choose to expand the view with three commands on the View menu (or their buttons on the toolbar):

- **Links to Images.** Displays links to any image files; you can turn this off to reduce the number of icons in the Link View pane.

- **Repeated Links.** If a page links to a target multiple times, this option displays every link to that target; turn this off to reduce the number of icons in the Link View pane.

- **Links Inside Pages.** Displays a link to the same page that contains the link, such as a link that refers to a bookmark on the same page. Again, you can turn this off if the View Links pane is too crowded.

Importing Web Pages and Resources

You can import individual pages or other resources into the FrontPage Explorer, where they will be incorporated into the current Web site. To do so, choose File ➤ Import, click on the Add File button in the Import

File to Web dialog box, and go to the folder that contains the file or files you want to import.

Select the files you want to import; you can use the Shift+Click and Ctrl+Click methods for making multiple selections. Click on the Open button to add them to the list of files to import. You can click on the Add File button again to select files from another location.

In the Import File to Web dialog box, you can change the URL of any of the files you've selected before you import them, or you can remove files from the list. You can even close the dialog box for now and return to it later.

You can select only those files you are ready to import and then click on the Import Now button. As the files are brought in, those that contain links to existing files in the current Web will show the appropriate arrows to those files in the Link View pane. Any graphical image files are placed in a default folder named Images within the Web site; so you may have to change the URL for graphic images in the incoming pages.

Importing an Entire Web

If you already have an existing Web site that was not created under FrontPage, you can still import all the files from that site into the FrontPage Explorer, where you can build and manage the site with all the FrontPage tools.

The method includes all the steps discussed in the previous section. The only difference is the target location for the incoming files—before you import the files, first create a new, empty Web site.

One small but important point to keep in mind is that FrontPage recognizes only the name `index.htm` as the home page of a Web site. You should consider giving that name to the home page of the Web site you will be importing. If you do, you'll see the home page where you expect it to be—at the top of the Outline View in the Explorer.

To import the Web site into the Explorer, first choose File ➤ New Web, choose the Empty Web template, and name the new Web. Now you can use the Import File command to bring all the files from the existing Web site into the new one.

Managing Links in a Web

There is one routine but time-consuming job that the Explorer turns into a quick and easy task—tracking links within the Web pages. For example, to change an existing link in multiple pages in the Web site, simply right-click on the target file of those links in the Link View or Summary View pane. In the Page URL text field, enter the new name. The Explorer automatically updates the link reference to that URL in all pages in the Web site.

You can also take advantage of the Explorer while you are working in the Editor. To create a link in a page, you can drag the target's icon from the Explorer's Link View or Summary View pane into the Web page in the Editor. The resulting link's text will be the target page's title (or URL for other resources), but you can edit the text as needed.

Administering Webs with FrontPage Explorer

The FrontPage Explorer offers a variety of tools that help you administer a Web site. In the next few sections, we'll look at how you can get the most out of them.

Assigning Rights to a Web

When you install FrontPage, you give access rights to the root Web to an administrator with a password (the root Web in FrontPage is normally the folder FrontPage Webs\Content). You can later add other administrators, authors, and users to the root Web or to individual Webs within the root Web.

To change the access rights to a Web site, first open the Web in the Explorer. If you want to change the highest level rights, open the one called the Root Web. Otherwise, open any other Web site to assign rights to that Web only.

Now choose Tools ➤ Permissions, which displays the Web Permissions dialog box shown in Figure 12.2.

FIGURE 12.2:

In the Web Permissions dialog box, you assign access rights to administrators, authors, and users.

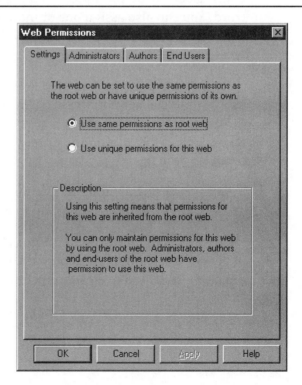

The Web Permissions dialog box has the following tabs:

- **Settings.** For all Webs beneath the root Web, you can choose either to assign the same permissions as the root Web or to assign unique rights.

- **Administrators.** Add or remove administrators to this Web, who have rights to all aspects of the Web, including the rights to change the permissions and delete, copy, or rename the Web.

- **Authors.** Add or remove authors who can create new pages or delete pages.

- **End Users.** You can choose to let anyone browse the Web site or to restrict access to registered users only.

When you add a new name to the Administrators, Authors, or End Users lists, you are prompted for a password and to verify the password. You can also assign one or more IP address masks to each administrator, author, or end user. By default, the mask *.*.*.* allows access to any IP address.

Security in IIS is implemented largely using NTFS permissions; a user is first checked for access permissions in IIS, and if granted, the user account is screened for access by the NTFS file system. Let's take a look at the minimum permissions required to use FrontPage on an IIS system.

Table 12.1 lists the minimum permissions that are needed by IUSR_*computername* or a group to which it belongs.

If a directory name in Table 12.1 has an asterisk beside it, that level of permission should be applied to all files in the directory, to the directory itself, and to all subdirectories within that directory.

TABLE 12.1: FrontPage and IIS permissions

Directory name	NTFS (rwxd)	WWW (rxn)
_vti_bin	rwx	x
_vti_bin/_vti_aut	no access	x
_vti_bin/_vti_adm	no access	x
_vti_log	r	n
_vti_txt*	r	n
_vti_shm	r	n
images	r	no access
_vti_pvt*	rwxd	n
_private	rwx	no access
_vti_cnf	r	n

FrontPage Author groups and FrontPage Administrator groups also require the additional permissions listed in Table 12.2.

By default, all NT Administrators are FrontPage Administrators, and administrative rights are needed only to create or delete entire Webs.

As FrontPage Administrators create new Webs, the IUSR _computername will receive read or full control over those Webs, depending on whether this account has write permissions in the copy of shtml.exe in the _vti_bin directory of the root Web. If rx access is granted, any other Webs created by FrontPage within that root will grant only read rights to the IUSR_computername account. However, if rwx or greater rights are given, any other Webs created by FrontPage will grant full control to the IUSR_computername account. This can have important repercussions in a Discussion Web. In a Discussion Web, this account will need to be able to delete the current table of contents when it makes new posts to the group; it will also need the rights to create the posts themselves and their indexes.

TABLE 12.2: Additional permissions required by FrontPage Author and Administrator groups

Directory Name	NTFS (rwxdn,)
FrontPage Author Groups	
`_vti_bin/_vti_aut`	`rx`
`winnt/system32`	`rx`
`winnt/system`	`rx`
`winnt`	`rx`
`FrontPage/servsupp`	`rx`
`content directories`	`rwxd`
FrontPage Administrator Groups	
`_bti_bin/_bti_adm`	`rx`

When you use FrontPage and the IIS, you can use the built-in Interactive account to ensure appropriate access for the account `IUSR_computername`, as well as for all FrontPage authors and administrators. To add or remove a user from this account, use the User Manager for Domains.

Renaming or Deleting a Web

To remove a Web site completely, you must have administrator permissions to the root Web. In the Explorer, open the Web you want to delete and choose File ➤ Delete Web. Because this command actually deletes all the files and folders associated with the Web, you will be asked to confirm the deletion.

You can rename the current Web site in the Explorer by choosing Tools ➤ Web Settings and selecting the Configuration tab. There you will find two edit fields:

- **Web Name.** Because this is the actual name of the Web site and its folder on disk, the name must conform to the server's file-naming conventions.

- **Web Title.** Both administrators and authors can change the Web title, which is a descriptive name that you see in the Open Web dialog box and in the Explorer's title bar.

Putting a Web onto the Server

When you have been building a Web site "off site" (not on its ultimate server), you can let the Explorer handle the job of getting the Web up to the server. Only an administrator has the access rights to do so.

In the Explorer, open the Web site and choose File ➤ Copy Web. In the Copy Web dialog box, select the destination server from the drop-down list of available servers. Then enter a name for the Web site, which will also name the new folder or directory for the site on the server.

When the job is done, you'll have a new Web site under the name you specified that is a duplicate of the source Web. Note that permission settings are not copied to the new Web; so only the administrator will have access to it at this point.

Planning Your Content Directories

If your Web pages are all contained under a single directory tree, all you have to do to install them on the IIS server is to copy them into the default World Wide Web directory called `\wwwroot`.

But if your content files are in several directories or even on several computers, you will have to create virtual directories to make those files available. If your Web site is very complex, use the Directories property sheet in Internet Service Manager to specify the directories from which you want to publish. We'll look at the Internet Service Manager in detail in the next chapter, *Advanced Web Site Administration*.

Note that Web, FTP, and Gopher services cannot publish content from redirected network drives, or, in other words, from drive letters assigned to network shares. To use network drives, you must specify the server and UNC name (as in *computername**sharename*\wwwfiles). If you specify a username and a password to connect to a network drive, all remote users requesting access to that drive must use the appropriate username and password, rather than the anonymous ISUR_*computername* account or any other account you may have specified. Once again, I want to remind you that remote users could make changes to the network drive when accessing your server in this way; so be sure that the appropriate security checks are in place and that you have tested them.

FrontPage expects a home page name of index.htm, but you can change this if you edit the following line in the srm.cnf file in \frontpage\webs\server\conf:

```
#DirectoryIndex index.html
```

Remove the # symbol that makes this a comment line, and change index.html to the name of the file you want to use as your home page.

Planning Virtual Servers

Each domain name, such as www.dyson.com is a *primary server* that usually relates to a single computer, but you can use IIS to create what are called *virtual servers* so that a computer can appear to support several servers, perhaps one for each of the major departments within your company. These servers might appear to the outside world as `marketing.dyson.com` or `technical.dyson.com`.

To do this, you will need IP addresses for the primary server and for each of the virtual servers that you want to create. This makes your installation look like several computers when viewed from the Internet, when in reality only one copy of IIS is running. Use the Network object in the NT Server Control Panel to specify the additional IP addresses for your network adapter card.

Adding HTML Material

Keeping your Web site up to date is one of the primary duties of the webmaster. Your content should be as fresh as possible and should also be as free of errors as possible.

You need not halt or restart IIS when it is time to update the HTML documents; you can simply write the new documents over the top of the existing tree of files. Some webmasters like to develop content files offline from the Web server machine and only transfer them when they are complete and have been thoroughly tested. Others edit files while the server is online to the Internet by keeping two parallel Web structures—one for online Internet access and the other for offline editing and content preparation. I prefer to use the first approach and develop material offline; there is less potential for damage to the running server by accidentally deleting files or copying the wrong file on top of a good working copy.

From time to time you may have to move large sections of your Web site's content, perhaps when your site undergoes a major reorganization or to deal with disk-space constraints. Many things can go wrong during this sort of operation; so plan the steps carefully, and be sure you have a recent backup.

Testing Your Web Site

You have heard this from me before, but I can't emphasize it enough: When you make changes to the content on your site, particularly if you add or change links, be sure you test and test again. If you start to use an addition or extension to the standard HTML you have used in the past, test and test again. Use one of the HTML syntax checkers or validators that are becoming more popular. If you are running an Internet, test the effects of your changes by looking at them with various browsers so that you will see them as visitors to your site will see them. If you are running an Intranet, you can, of course, simply use the company's browser of choice.

Dial in to your site over the Internet to gauge the speed of downloads and the effects that a full load of visitors have on the response time of your site. We'll look at how to use the NT Performance Monitor and other NT monitoring tools in the next chapter, *Advanced Web Site Administration*.

Checking for Expired Links

Few things are more annoying than visiting a Web site only to get error messages telling you that some of the links have expired and that the document you requested could not be found on the server. It is one of the webmaster's jobs to check all the links on the site, and as we saw earlier in this chapter, this is easy to do with FrontPage. One thing to watch for is that new Web site content might be provided to you in two different forms:

- As an update to an existing HTML file

- As a new HTML file

In the first case, all you have to do is lay the new version of the file over the top of the old version, but the second case is more complex. You may have to support both the original file as well as the new file, and so you may have to retrace your steps and create links to the new file; otherwise, visitors to your site will never find it.

You should also verify links to other sites on the Internet, those that point to sites external to your own. If you are following the guidelines I gave earlier in this book on how to keep visitors focused on your site, you will have only a small number of these links to check. These links are not easy to test automatically, and you have to look for two things:

- That the URL still works and that the site is still in use

- That the original content you wanted to include in your site is still there and is still timely and appropriate

The Web is constantly changing with thousands of pages appearing and disappearing each day; the more links you have to other sites, the more chances that links will expire. If you must use links to other sites, be sure you check them often.

Dealing with E-mail

Another of the webmaster's important duties is responding to visitors' questions, comments, and complaints, many of which will arrive as e-mail. On small sites, the webmaster may be able to respond to the e-mail each day, as well as perform all the other day-to-day chores, but on larger sites, one or more people will be dedicated solely to answering e-mail.

E-mail will range from a few compliments on your Web site, to comments, right through to down-right complaints and bug reports; some visitors will even go so far as to report expired links that are still available on your site.

As with many business tasks, when responding to e-mail, you must remember to be professional and polite (even if you consider the complaint unjustified), and you must reply to each e-mail within 24 hours unless it is received just before a weekend or a holiday. Visitors to your Web sites are all possible customers, and you must treat them that way. You can use two techniques to help make your e-mail manageable: (1) You can use a special Web page as an e-mail form, and (2) you can collect a set of questions and answers together into an FAQ.

Creating a Web Mail Form

With just a little programming you can create a special Web page on your site to act as an e-mail template. The form needs input fields for the following:

- The visitor's e-mail address so that you know where to send your reply

- The e-mail subject

- The e-mail body text

You can also add help information as you see fit to remind visitors of the normal form of an e-mail address, what this e-mail template is for and what it does, and so on. You may well be able to find such a form at one of the CGI script or Perl sites listed in the appendices at the end of this book.

This e-mail can be sent directly to an account or to an *alias* that represents the account. One advantage to using an alias is that it can point to the e-mail address of each staff member responsible for replying to e-mail as they all take turns. In this way, one e-mail address can represent several members of the support staff, and you don't have to change the e-mail address on your Web site each time a new staff person takes over e-mail duties.

Setting Up an FAQ

Many of the newsgroups on the Internet use FAQs (Frequently Asked Questions) to collect together common questions and the appropriate answers to avoid having to answer the same questions over and over, and that is a technique that you can use too. Visitors can look at the FAQ page on your site and see that their question has been asked by someone in the past, and they can read the answer you provided.

Put a short table of contents at the top of the page so that users can quickly find answers to questions about specific products or services that your company offers. Also be sure that your customer service 800 number is displayed in a prominent position on this page so that people can call a service representative if they wish. In addition, be sure that your customer service voice-mail system gives out the URL of your Web site.

Installing Scripts on IIS

You can create scripts to run on IIS using several programming languages. Once you have crated a script, you should place it in the \scripts directory, a virtual directory for applications that has execute access. This directory is designated an application directory, and only an administrator can add programs to such a directory. Thus, an intruder cannot copy a malicious application into this directory and then execute it—at least not without securing administrator privileges first.

You must also ensure that every process that your script starts uses an account with the appropriate permissions; and if your application uses other files, the account you use with the program must have the right permissions to use those files. The default anonymous account is the IUSR_*computername* account, and this account cannot change or delete files in the NTFS without specific permission from an administrator. Even if an intruder *were* able to copy a malicious application onto your system, he or she would not be able to do any damage from within the IUSR_*computername* account with its limited permissions.

If your application does not ask a visitor to enter information, you can create a link to your application in an HTML file. If it does require data from a visitor, you will probably use an HTML form to collect that information. You can also use a URL, containing data variables, to invoke a program.

Because you can use one of many programming languages to prepare your scripts, IIS uses filename extensions to decide which command interpreter to invoke to process the script. The default interpreter associations are shown in Table 12.3.

TABLE 12.3:   Default script interpreter associations

Filename extension	Default interpreter
BAT, CMD, COM, EXE	CMD.EXE
IDC	HTTPODBC.DLL\

You can use the NT Server Registry Editor to create additional associations as you'll see in the next section.

Configuring MIME Types

If you plan to publish files in multiple formats, you must be sure that NT Server has a MIME (Multipurpose Internet Mail Extension) mapping for each file type. If you don't set up MIME mapping on the server, visitors may not be able to retrieve a file with their browsers. You must set up this mapping in the NT Server Registry using a program called regedt32.

The NT Server Registry is a hierarchical database of settings used by NT, including information on users, system hardware configuration, and application programs. Knowing how to work with the Registry is an important factor in NT Server tuning and system configuration and is a topic well beyond the scope of this book. We'll take a very quick look at one aspect of the Registry, however, that of MIME file types. For much more information on the NT Server Registry and how you can tune some of its other operating parameters, see *Mastering Windows NT Server 4* by Mark Minasi, available from Sybex.

Run the program `regedt32` from a command prompt, and you will see the Registry Editor main window open as Figure 12.3 shows.

FIGURE 12.3:

The main Registry Editor window

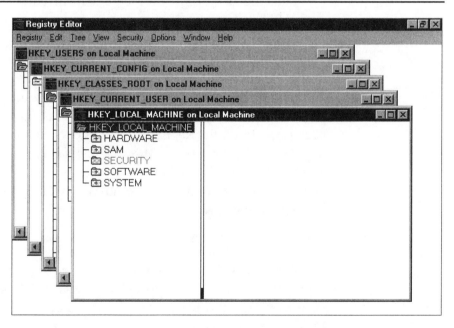

The Registry stores all the settings in structures known as *subtrees*, and in Figure 12.3, each subtree has its own separate window. These subtrees divide Registry information into like groups of settings and consist of the following:

- **HKEY_LOCAL_MACHINE.** Contains configuration information, including hardware and applications that are running on the system.

- **HKEY_CLASSES_ROOT.** A subkey of HKEY_LOCAL_MACHINE\SOFTWARE that contains the information used to open the appropriate application when the NT Explorer opens a file.

- **HKEY_USERS.** Contains user profiles

- **HKEY_CURRENT_USER.** A subkey of HKEY_USERS that contains the user profile for the person currently logged on to the NT Server computer.

- **HKEY_CURRENT_CONFIG.** Contains hardware information used by NT Server when the system first starts running

If Figure 12.3 showed the NT Explorer, you would expect the elements in the windows to be directories containing subdirectories, but because it shows the Registry, the windows contain settings grouped together as *keys*, and below them as *subkeys*, and then as *sub-subkeys*, and so on. In fact, in the NT Server help system, you will see these keys and subkeys written as though they were directory names; something like this:

```
HKEY_LOCAL_MACHINE\SYSTEM\CurrentControlSet
```

And that is exactly how you locate an item such as `CurrentControlSet`; you start at `HKEY_LOCAL_MACHINE`, then `SYSTEM`, and then `CurrentControlSet`, just as though they were directories.

To add the value for the MIME mapping, you must use this syntax:

```
mime_type,filename_extension,unused,Gopher_type:data_type
```

and each element must be separated from the next by a comma, except for *data_type*, which is separated from the rest of the entry by a colon. Here's what it all means:

- **mime_type.** This element specifies the kind of information and is often divided into the MIME type and the Subtype. For example, you might see `application/zip` representing a zip file created by PKZIP, or you might see `image/gif`, representing a GIF file. There are hundreds of these MIME identifiers

- **filename_extension.** Next, the filename extension associated with this file type appears. To continue the examples above, you might see `ZIP` and `GIF` associated with the appropriate mime_type. You may see several lines in the Registry all identifying slight variations of the same filename extension; for example, you might see `JPEG`, `JPG`, and `JPE` all specified as the same mime_type.

- **unused.** In most cases, the *unused* element is simply left out, and you will see only the two commas next to each other.

- **Gopher_type.** This is an ID number used by both Gopher and Web services to categorize the data type even further. Table 12.4 lists the most common Gopher ID codes.

- **data_type**. The final element in an entry specifies the kind of data to expect. In other entries in the Registry, you may see yes/no values; in this area you will find that they are all string values. Table 12.5 lists the most common Registry data types, their descriptions, and the name of the editing dialog box in the Edit menu used to change their value.

TABLE 12.4:   Gopher ID codes

Type	Description
0	Text file
1	Gopher directory
2	CSO name/phone book server
3	An error message from the server
4	Macintosh binary (HQX) file
5	PC binary file
6	Unix uuencoded file
7	Full-text index search
8	Text-based Telnet session
9	Binary file
c	Calendar of events
g	GIF graphic file
h	HTML file
I	Image file
I	Inline text
m	BSD-format box file
P	An Adobe PDF (Portable Document File)
s	Sound file
T	A tn3270 mainframe session
: (colon)	A bitmap image

TABLE 12.5:   Registry data types

Data type	Description	Editor
REG_BINARY	Raw binary data presented in hex	Binary
REG_DWORD	Binary data stored as 4-byte words	DWORD
REG_SZ	Simple string	String
REG_EXPAND_SZ	Variable length string	String
REG_MULTI_SZ	Multiple string	Multi String

An example MIME Registry entry might look like this:

```
text/html,htm,,h
image/jpeg,jpeg,,5
```

Let's bring these two separate threads together now with an example. Here are the steps to follow to edit a MIME type in the NT Registry:

1. Open the NT Registry using the `regedt32` program.

2. Select the HKEY_LOCAL_MACHINE window.

3. In the left side of this window, select each of these Registry keys in sequence:

    - `CurrentControlSet`

    - `Services`

    - `InetInfo`

    - `Parameters`

    - `MimeMap`

You may see this written like this:

```
HKEY_LOCAL_MACHINE\CurrentControlSet\Services\InetInfo\
Parameters\MimeMap
```

Figure 12.4 shows what you will see when you get to the correct destination: the Registry entries for MIME file types.

FIGURE 12.4:

Registry entries for
MIME file types

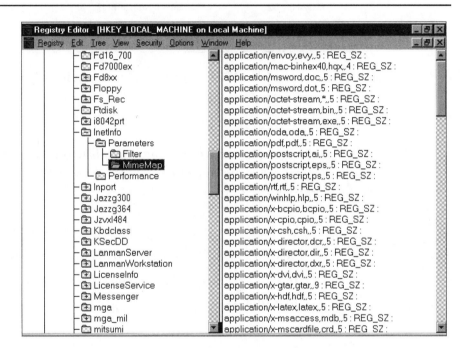

On the right side of Figure 12.4, you will see the entries that define the current MIME file-type mappings. The entry with the filename extension shown as an asterisk (*) is the default MIME type that is used when MIME mapping has not been specified.

4. You can edit an entry in two ways. You can either double-click on an entry in the right window, which will automatically open the correct editing dialog box based on the `data_type` in question, or you can select the entry and then use a selection from the Edit menu to open the appropriate editing dialog box.

5. Enter the new information, and click on OK when you are done. You will have to restart NT Server to put your new setting into action.

To create a new entry use Add Key or Add Value from the Edit menu, depending on what you want to add.

You can also use the Windows Explorer to look at and change some Registry information. Open the Explorer and then choose Options from the View menu. Select the File Types tab, and then click on the New Type button to add a new file type, or click on the Edit button to change an existing registered file type. You can also click on the Remove button to delete a registered file type.

How do you find out what all the other keys and subkeys in the Registry do? Simple. In the *NT Server Resource Kit* from Microsoft—if you haven't got one, order your copy now—you will find a couple of hundred pages describing all of them.

Using Web-to-Database Connectivity Tools

In line with software developers in other fields, the database vendors are all hurrying to develop usable and convenient connections to the Internet and the corporate Intranet. If in the past you have struggled with the front-end development tools that some of these vendors provide, no doubt the idea of using a Web browser as your user interface has put a gleam into your eye.

No matter which commercial database you use, the fundamental mechanisms are the same, and reduce to three essential processes:

- Using data-entry statements to build the database

- Forming and submitting a Structured Query Language (SQL, pronounced "sequel") query to the database

- Receiving and processing the results of the query

SQL contains about 60 commands used to create, modify, query, and access data in a database. Originally developed by IBM, SQL has been implemented by all the major database vendors. SQL is implemented in one of two ways:

- **Static SQL** statements are coded into application programs, and as a result, they do not change. These statements are usually processed by a precompiler before being bound into the application.

- **Dynamic SQL** statements are much more interactive, and they can be changed as necessary. If you normally access SQL from a command-line environment, you are using the dynamic version, which may be slower than static SQL, but is obviously much more flexible.

Whether you use an on-screen query or enter the SQL by hand is not important; the objective is the same—to pass the query to the database in a form it can understand. And when the database answers the query, the data must be formatted into a report or a screen so that it can be read by the users. Figure 12.5 summarizes the transactions that take place when accessing database content using a Web browser.

When you use a Web browser to access the database, there are some important differences:

- Your users (or customers if you are connected to the Internet) perform queries by completing HTML data-entry forms with fill-in-the-blanks fields.

- CGI scripts or ISAPI programs take the information entered into the form, process it into a SQL query, and then pass it to the database.

- The same set of scripts receive the data back from the database, format the results using dynamic HTML pages, and send the results off for display by the customer's Web browser.

FIGURE 12.5:

Accessing a database using a Web browser and SQL

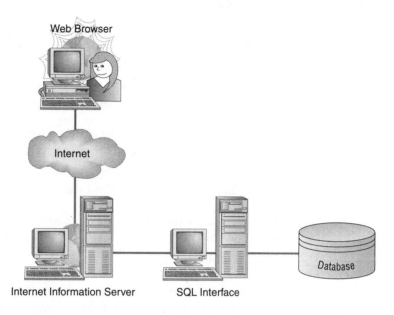

The HTML data-entry screens take the place of the user interface provided by the database vendor, and the scripts replace the custom programming done using the software development tools also provided by the vendor.

Each piece of data entered by the user into the HTML screen can be passed back to the database for processing, but much more data is available in any typical session, including the customer's Web browser type, the TCP/IP address and hostname of the user's computer, the visitor's user ID and access authentication, and the MIME types and subtypes supported by the browser. All this information can be passed back to the database if it is of interest to your company; for example, you can tailor your HTML pages based on the type of browser your visitor is using today.

Looking at ODBC

ODBC (Open Database Connectivity) is a Microsoft API that allows a single application to access many types of database and file formats. Before ODBC was defined, applications programmers had to write specific code to access every database to which they wanted to connect.

ODBC frees programmers from this restriction and uses the same set of function calls to talk to any database from any vendor. Drivers are available for almost all the popular database systems, and you can even access simple text files or Microsoft Excel spreadsheets.

NT Server uses the Registry information to decide which ODBC drivers are needed to talk to a specific data source, and these drivers are loaded automatically.

The only disadvantage to using ODBC that programmers have voiced is that using ODBC is a little slower than accessing the database directly; this is the price we have to pay for the convenience of writing code for a single interface, and most people agree that it is a small price to pay.

Using the Internet Database Connector

Windows NT Server 4 includes the Internet Database Connector (IDC), an ISAPI application that lets the Internet Information Server access ODBC-compliant databases (such as Microsoft's own SQL Server) directly.

The Internet Database Connector is an ISAPI DLL called `httpodbd.dll` that uses ODBC to give access to a database. Figure 12.6 shows how this works.

Components connecting
IIS to an ODBC database

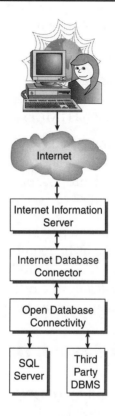

The process is much as I described in the section above but with some subtle differences:

1. A user makes a request using a Web browser.

2. This request is passed through IIS to the ISAPI DLL, which turns the request into a form that ODBC can understand.

3. ODBC passes the processed results to the appropriate driver, which in turn passes the query to the database.

4. The data extracted from the database travels in the reverse direction, going from the database to ODBC to the ISAPI DLL to the IIS and eventually back to the user's Web browser.

The IDC used two types of files to manage database access and Web page construction:

- IDC files (with the filename extension of IDC) contain the information needed to connect to the right ODBC source and execute the SQL statement. This file also contains the name and location of the HTML extension file.

- An HTML extension file (with the filename extension of HTX) is the template for the HTML document that will be returned to the Web browser once all the database information has been filled in by IDC.

When you first installed IIS, version 2.5 ODBC components were installed as IIS requires. Version 2.5 supports System Data Source Names (DSN), introduced so that Windows NT can use ODBC. See the *Installing Microsoft Internet Information Server* chapter for more information on installing ODBC.

Creating System Data Sources

You configure ODBC on Windows NT Server using the ODBC icon in the Control Panel. Here are the steps to follow:

1. Open the Control Panel using the Start menu, and then select the ODBC icon.

2. When the Data Sources dialog box opens, you may see several data sources displayed in the list box if you have already installed ODBC drivers.

3. Click on the System DSN button to open the System Data Sources dialog box. Be sure that you use the System DSN button; this is an IDC requirement.

4. Click on the Add button.

5. In the Add Data Sources dialog box, select SQL Server from the list box and click on OK.

6. In the ODBC SQL Server Setup dialog box, as shown in Figure 12.7, enter a description of the data source in the Data Source Name field. For example, for a customer service database, you might enter **Customer Data**.

7. Enter a description of the data in the data source in the Description field.

8. In the Server field, enter the name of the SQL Server on your network; you can select a server from the list or type the name yourself. To use a local copy of SQL Server, enter **"(local)"**, including the quotes and the parentheses.

9. Enter the address of the SQL Server from which the ODBC will retrieve data. For Microsoft SQL Server, you can usually leave this set to the default.

10. Enter the name of the SQL Server Net Library DLL that the SQL Server uses to communicate with the network software in the Network Library field. Again, you can usually leave this set to the default.

FIGURE 12.7:

The ODBC SQL Server Setup dialog box

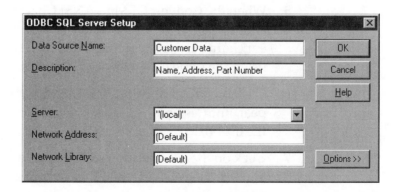

The server name, network address, and network library are all specific to your NT Server installation. To access the remaining fields in the ODBC SQL Server Setup dialog box, click on the Options button, and follow these steps:

1. In the Database Name field, enter the name of the SQL Server database.

2. Choose the national language you want to use with SQL Server from the Language Name list box.

3. When the Generate Stored Procedures for Prepared Statements option checkbox is checked (the default setting), the SQL Server driver prepares a statement by placing it in a procedure and compiling it. When this checkbox is cleared, stored procedures for prepared statements are not created.

4. If a translator has been selected, you will see its name in the Translator box; if this box is blank, a translator has not been chosen. A translator is a DLL that converts the data passing between an application and a data source. The most common use of a translator is to convert data from one character set to another, but a translator can also encrypt and decrypt data or apply and remove data compression. To add or change a translator, click on the Select button and make your choice from the Select Translator dialog box.

5. When the Convert OEM to ANSI Characters checkbox is clear and the SQL Server client and server machines are using different characters sets, you must specify a translator. If both are using the same character set, check this box.

6. Click on OK, and the System Data Sources dialog box will reappear, but this time with the name of the data source displayed in the list box.

7. Click on the Close button to close the System Data Sources dialog box; then click on the Close button again to close the Data Sources dialog box.

Using Other Database Connectivity Tools

New products designed to access corporate databases using Web tools and technology are appearing all the time. As you might expect, each vendor's product provides access to its own databases, and they all work in much the same way.

A user with a Web browser enters static or dynamic SQL statements using HTML forms. Through CGI or ISAPI calls, the Web server submits the data from the form to a database agent, which in turn converts these statements into SQL that the database can understand. The results from the database are then formatted into HTML and returned through the CGI or ISAPI gateway to the customer and the Web browser. I cannot cover all the products currently available, but we can take a quick look at some of them.

Oracle Corporation's WebServer

Oracle is one of the giants of the database world, and it provides a whole suite of applications, including an integrated HTTP server that gives you live access to Oracle 7 databases. The package includes Oracle Web Agent and Oracle Web Listener for converting HTML forms to database queries and sending the results to the Web browser. HTML pages created by this package can also contain SQL procedures, giving application developers access to existing libraries of procedures.

Oracle Developer/2000

Oracle also offers Developer/2000, a package of Web-development tools designed for use with its InterOffice workflow and multimedia suite of applications. Developer/2000 lets you create Web applications that can tap into InterOffice data and applications.

Computer Associates OpenIngres/ICE

OpenIngres/ICE (Internet Commerce Enabled) from Computer Associates is aimed at commercial Internet and corporate Intranet sites. OpenIngres/ICE lets developers create dynamic HTML forms with SQL queries and includes an interesting feature that lets an application notify a user when a specific condition has been met.

Allaire Corporation's Cold Fusion

Allaire Corporation's Cold Fusion Professional is a different kind of product from the last two and is actually middleware—a layer of software that sits between the user's data-entry screens and the database. Cold Fusion lets developers create complex Web-based applications that can send generic SQL commands to almost any database system. You might check out Cold Fusion if the supplier of the database you use does not provide the kind of access you need or if it is behind schedule in providing the features you want to use.

Microsoft's SQL Server

Microsoft's own entry to this field is known as Microsoft SQL Server Internet Connector license. Available at a fixed price per server, it allows unlimited numbers of Web users to access a SQL Server database. The price does not include any software.

At the time of writing, the next release of Microsoft's SQL Server was still in beta testing, but Microsoft has planned a feature that will automatically convert database information into HTML, making integration with the Internet and Intranet even easier in the future.

Coping with Disasters

In just the same way that you need a security plan for your Web server, you also need a contingency plan to help you cope with catastrophic events such as major hardware failures. In this section we'll look at some things that you can and should plan for and at some things that are outside your control, but for which you still have to be prepared.

Preparing the Plan

The first step in preparing your contingency plan is to decide what is an appropriate definition of a *disaster* for you and your company; the second step is to develop a plan you will put into place to recover.

Permanent loss of all the HTML files on the server would certainly be a disaster in the minds of most people, but how long can your company tolerate being without access to the Internet through the ISP or tolerate the server hardware being out of commission? A day? A week? Longer? When writing a contingency plan, you must consider everything that might cause your Web site to be out of commission and prepare accordingly.

Is It a Hardware Problem?

If you have a hardware problem, one of the easiest ways out is to reserve another, hopefully identical, computer all prepared and ready to go. Such as system is known as a *hot backup* or a *hot start* server. All you have to do is take the old system offline and bring the replacement online.

Hard disk failures certainly happen, but NT Server has several hard-disk management features you can take advantage of, including disk duplexing and disk mirroring, as well as several levels of RAID. Disk duplexing and disk mirroring are two approaches to hard disk fault tolerance in which the same information is written to two hard disks at the same time.

In disk mirroring, both hard disks uses the same disk controller; in disk duplexing, each hard disk uses a different disk controller. Figure 12.8 shows you how this works.

FIGURE 12.8:

Disk mirroring and disk
duplexing

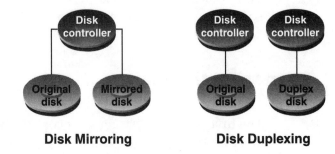

Disk Mirroring   **Disk Duplexing**

If one disk fails, information from the other can be used to continue operations. But, and this is a *but* that most people forget or choose to ignore, both disk mirroring and disk duplexing are designed to protect the system against a single disk failure, not against multiple, long-term disk problems. Neither technique is a substitute for a well-planned series of hard-disk backups.

If the server is running but no visitors are on your Web site, suspect the communications link to your ISP. Check the hardware to be sure the link is still up.

And if the server is running and the link to your ISP is fine, the next obvious suspect is the network cabling itself. A connector may have worked loose, or you may have a short or even a real break in the cable.

No, It's a Software Problem

And if the problem is not hardware but software, start looking for the last thing that was changed. Suspect the last system upgrade or the last revision of the server software. Find your most recent backup, the one you made *before* you installed the new software, and reload it so that you can at least recover to the point you were before the new stuff was installed. More on backups in just a moment.

If the server will reboot, but NT Server will not function as you expect, use the system diagnostics and your Emergency Boot Disk to recover as much as you can; then reload the latest backup.

Backing Up Your Server

A backup is an up-to-date copy of all your files that you can use to reload your Web server in case of an accident. It is an insurance policy against anything happening to the hundreds or thousands of files you might have on your server.

If the unthinkable were to occur—losing all your files due to a major hard-disk problem and not having any backup copies—it could take you months to rebuild all those HTML files. And for all those months, your Web site would be offline and unavailable to users. It is crucial that you make (and test) regular, consistent back-ups; no one else will do it for you, and it is a sad fact of life that hard disks do fail occasionally, usually at the most inconvenient moment.

Why Should You Make a Backup?

I'm sure you've heard them all before, but here once again are the reasons that making a backup is so important:

- Protection against hard-disk failure is the most important reason to make a regular backup of your hard disk. A hard disk can fail at almost any time, but when it does, it is always at the most inconvenient moment. You can reload an up-to-date backup of your Web site files very quickly and be back online in minutes.

- Protection against accidental deletion is another prime reason for making a backup. If you run an active site with lots of content changes, your chances of accidentally deleting a file are higher than if you never change your content.

- Protection against an intruder defacing or erasing your Web pages is another excellent reason for taking security precautions; a current backup can help you restore the site in minutes rather than hours or days.

- Moving files or large sets of files and directories is a convenient way to move content from one computer to the Web server.

- You should also make a precautionary backup before performing any maintenance work on your Web server.

When Should You Make a Backup?

One of the most neglected topics in discussing backups is the emphasis on a consistent backup plan. Plan your strategy—and most important—stick to it. With no plan, you'll simply accumulate backup tapes haphazardly, you will waste tapes, and you will waste time looking for the right file when it is time to restore a missing file.

So how often should you make a backup? For an answer that fits the Web site you run, ask yourself the following questions:

- How frequently do your content files change? Every day, every week, every month?

- How important to your day-to-day operations are these files? Can you work without them, and how long would it take to recreate them?

- How much will it cost to replace them in terms of time spent and business lost?

In our computerized world, it takes hours to create an HTML page with just the right look, but it can be lost or destroyed in milliseconds. A hard-disk failure, a mistaken delete command, overwriting a file with an earlier version with the same name—these can destroy a file just as completely as fire or flood. You just have to lose one important file to become a convert for life to a program of regular, planned backups.

What Kind of Backup Should You Make?

A common backup strategy is to make a complete backup once a week, say on Friday, and then make partial backups each day or twice each day of all the files that have changed since that backup. This ensures that you have all your files on tape somewhere. If your Web server crashes, you can reload the Friday tape and then reload all the intermediate partial backups to rebuild the system.

Some webmasters back up of their servers immediately before and then immediately after making substantive changes to the content files. In this way, if something goes wrong with the upgrade, they have an immediate fall-back position and can reload the files from just before they made the changes.

It is a good idea to keep one full backup of your system in storage somewhere (and I'll tell you where that should be in the next section) for at least six months; a year is even better. The file that you most want to recover may be a file you deleted three months ago, and your most recent backup won't show a trace of it.

And finally, don't use cheap tapes in an attempt to save money; this will turn out to be a false economy. Always use the best quality tapes you can get; in the long run, those tapes translate directly into your time. Replace your backup tapes on a regular basis, and if you start to see read or write errors on a tape as you create the backup, throw the tape away immediately.

Timing the Backup

The World Wide Web is active all day every day, but after your Web site has been up for a while, a usage picture will start to emerge showing you the times when the largest number of visitors access your site. You can use this information, along with your estimate of how long the backup will take, to plan when to start the backup.

You should have the backup process run at the time of day when you expect the smallest number of visitors. Running the backup during off-peak hours will cause the least noticeable system slowdown, and the minimum number of visitors will be inconvenienced. In a moment, we'll look at the different ways that NT Server lets you automate the backup process.

Choosing Between On-Site and Off-Site Storage

You should rotate your backup tapes to a secure off-site storage facility, just as you would for other important business documents such as financial records, photographs, drawings, and patent or trademark applications. Many people take the first step and back up their systems and then leave the tapes sitting right next to the computer. If the computer is damaged by an accident—be it fire, flood, earthquake, or vandalism—there is a good chance that the backups will be destroyed too.

Be sure the facility specializes in handling and storing magnetic media and has the appropriate temperature, humidity, and fire protection systems in place, as well as procedures for controlling human access to the tapes. Most services will pick up and deliver tapes to your company location on a regular basis, but be sure that they can also deliver a tape to you at very short notice at midnight in the middle of a three-day national holiday. Look in the Yellow Pages under Computer Data Storage or Business Records Storage.

The usual way to rotate your backups through an off-site storage is to label all the tapes from week one as Backup Set 1 and send them off to the storage company. Then during week two make Backup Set 2 and send it out for storage. Then start making Backup Set 3, and ask the storage company to return the tapes that make up Backup Set 1 so that you can reuse them during week four. In this way as you are creating a new backup set, one set is always in secure storage, and another, older backup set is in the process of being returned to you for reuse. Keep multiple copies of backups; redundancy should be a part of your backup plan.

If you do decide to keep your backup tapes on company property, remember that most fire-proof safes are rated for paper. Your backup tapes will melt at much lower temperatures than 415 degrees F, the temperature required to ignite paper. You should also protect your tapes against extremes of temperature and against the presence of magnetic fields and contaminants, such as dirt, dust, moisture, smoke, and chemicals. And don't take backups home as an alternative to off-site storage. The company will not look kindly on your reporting that the tapes were lost during a residential burglary.

Making the Backup

You will find the Backup program in the Administrative Tools menu, and when you open the Backup program, you will see a window like the one shown in Figure 12.9.

FIGURE 12.9:

The Backup opening
screen

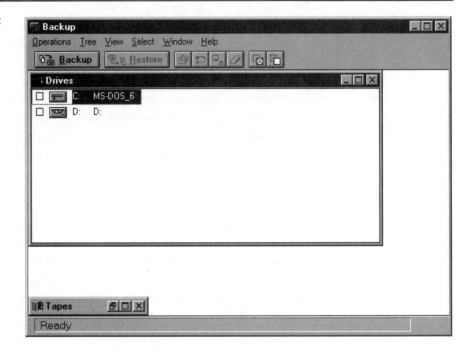

To back up a drive, you need to select it first even if you have only
one drive on your Web server; click in the checkbox next to the drive
to put an X in it. Now select the Backup button at the top left of the
window, or select the Backup option from the Operations drop-down
menu. The Backup Information Dialog box opens next and shows
you information about the tape loaded in the tape drive and lets you
decide how you want to perform this backup.

If you click on the arrow next to the Backup Type list box, you can
select from the following options:

- **Normal.** The default option that creates a full backup of everything on the disk and resets the archive bit on each file to indicate that it has been backed up. Use this option for your first
  backup and then for each weekly backup you make thereafter.

- **Copy.** Creates a full backup of the selected files without resetting the archive bit.

- **Differential.** Backs up only those files with the archive bit set and doesn't reset it when the backup is complete.

- **Incremental.** Backs up only those files with the archive bit set and resets it when the backup is complete. A good option to choose for your daily backups.

- **Daily.** Backs up only those files that have been modified today and does not reset the archive bit.

Once the information on the Backup Information dialog box is complete, click on OK to start the backup. The Backup Status window opens, listing the names and sizes of the files being backed up, as well as any errors encountered during the backup.

Label the tape clearly (this will help you avoid erasing the tape by accident in the future), and be sure it is ready for the courier to take to the secure storage facility.

Testing the Backup

A very important aspect of your whole backup strategy should be to test the backups that you make. Only by doing this can you be certain that your backup tapes actually do contain what you think they contain. Be sure that you and your staff are all familiar with running through the complete backup and restore procedure.

You should also make sure that the tape drive used to make backups is cleaned and maintained properly; run a cleaning tape through the tape machine at least once a week.

Backing Up from the Command Line

You can also make a backup using the `ntbackup` program from the command line. A set of command-line arguments give you almost as much flexibility as the graphical Backup program, but they are a little more difficult to use.

To run `ntbackup`, use this general form:

```
ntbackup backup path options
```

where *path* is the drive and directory that you want to back up and *options* is one of the arguments in Table 12.6. You can specify more than one drive if you like; simply type the drive letters with colons after them.

TABLE 12.6:   Command-line arguments used with `ntbackup`

Argument	Description
/a	Appends this backup to the end of an existing backup. If you omit this argument, the backup will overwrite anything already on the tape.
/v	Verifies the operation by comparing the data on the tape with the original data on the drive when the backup is complete. This adds to the time that the backup takes, but verifies that the data was written to tape correctly.
/r	Restricts access to the tape's owner and the system administrator.
/d "text"	Lets you write a description of the backup contained in "*text*" on the tape.
/b	Backs up the local registry.
/hc:	Specifies hardware compression. To turn it on, use /hc:on, and to turn it off, use /hc:off.
/t option	Specifies the backup type where *option* is either normal, copy, incremental, differential, or daily. These are the same options as those available in the Backup program.
/l "filename"	Creates the backup log file specified by *filename*.
/e	Specifies that the backup log include only exceptions.
/tape n	Specifies the tape to use by number, where *n* is a number between 0 and 9 that corresponds to a tape drive number listed in the registry.

Let's look at a couple of examples of how to use `ntbackup`. To back-up all the document files in the /winword directory on drive C, use:

```
ntbackup backup c:\winword\*.doc
```

To make a differential backup of all the files on drives C and D, verify the backup, and label the tape "All files on C and D" while restricting access to the owner and the network administrator, use:

```
ntbackup backup c: d: /v/r/d"All files on C and D"
```

Using `at` and WINAT

Now that you can use the command-line version of the backup program, you can automate the whole process and perform scheduled backups using the NT scheduler. Start the scheduler by typing:

```
net start schedule
```

and then use the `at` command to set up your automatic backup. The `start schedule` command starts the NT scheduler, which you can use to run commands on a certain computer at a certain time. You can also start the scheduler using the Services icon in the Control Panel.

By default, the scheduling service is configured to log on under the system account, but if it logs on under that account, the `at` command can only be used for programs to which the Guest account has access. To run a restricted program such as `ntbackup`, you must configure the scheduling service to run under an account with rights to the `ntbackup` program and any other programs you want to run.

To start the backup program, you must specify the following:

- The `ntbackup` command along with any arguments you want to use, all contained within quotation marks.

- The time and date to run the command. You can specify that an operation take place regularly by entering `every:` *day*, where *day* specifies the day of the week. You can also abbreviate the names as in every:M,W,F for Monday, Wednesday, and Friday, or use dates as in every:7,14,21. Be sure there are no spaces between the colon and the numbers or letters.

- The computer on which you want to run the program; the default is the computer where you specified the at command.

So, to back up the contents of drive C at 10:00 every Friday, you enter:

```
at 10:00 every: Friday "ntbackup c:"
```

The command is entered into the NT scheduler job list, which you can see by typing the at command at a command prompt.

The *Windows NT Resource Kit* includes a program called WINAT, which is a much simpler interface to the scheduler than using the at command. WINAT lets you do exactly the same setup operations as the at command; it's just a bit easier to use. And, yes, the scheduler must also be running for WINAT to work. If you start WINAT and the scheduler is not running, a message box opens to tell you that it is not running and to ask if you want to start it. When you select Yes, the scheduler starts running.

For much more on using the scheduler, on making backups, and on NT in general, see *Mastering Windows NT Server 4* by Mark Minasi, available from Sybex.

Restoring Files

Making the backup is only the first part of the story; you must also know how to restore the backup. Open the Backup item in Administrative Tools, and when the Backup window (see Figure 12.9 earlier in this chapter) opens, select the Restore button at the top of the window. Select the tape you want to restore, and then click on the Restore button.

The Restore Information dialog box is much simpler than the Backup Information dialog box, and to restore the entire tape, all you have to do is choose whether to verify the information as it is loaded onto disk (always a good idea) and where you want to write the log file. Select OK, and the restore will start; you can watch its progress in the Restore Status window if you like.

If your entire system is wiped out and you are rebuilding everything, be sure that NT is loaded along with all the associated system files, including service patches, before you try to reload data and Web server content files. Doing so ensures that all the services needed by each layer of software are present before you try to load the next layer on top.

Preventing Electrical Problems

Power conditioning is the use of protective and conditioning hardware to filter out power spikes and surges from the main power provided to you by the utility company. Many influences act on that power after it leaves the power-generation plant and before it reaches the wall socket that your server is plugged in to. Atmospheric changes such as wind, rain, and lightning all affect the quality of the power you receive as can very common office equipment such as large laser printers, copying machines, and elevators. Power conditioning helps to iron out these electrical disturbances.

The three main kinds of power-conditioning devices are the following:

- **Suppression devices.** These devices protect equipment against sudden destructive transient voltages.

- **Regulation devices.** These devices modify the power waveform back toward a clean sine wave. A UPS (uninterruptible power supply) is a common form of voltage regulator and is of two types. An online UPS actively modifies the power fed into it, providing a smoothed output; an offline UPS kicks in only after the main power dips below a preset low level.

- **Isolation devices.** These devices protect against noise on the power signal and can get to be very expensive.

Because power-conditioning equipment can get so expensive so quickly, it is invariably used only for the server and its monitor; other devices are usually protected by surge suppressors.

Connecting Your Web Server to a UPS

NT Server is designed to control a UPS and to act on information received from a UPS; this is done by means of a serial cable connecting the UPS to the server. This cable is supplied by the manufacturer of the UPS. NT can send one signal to the UPS and can receive two signals from the UPS:

- **Remote UPS Shutdown.** NT can instruct the UPS to temporarily disconnect the battery if it detects erratic signals from the next two sources.

- **Power Failed.** This signal goes from the UPS to the server and means that the input power to the UPS has failed and that the server is now running on battery power alone.

- **Battery Low.** Some UPS systems leave NT to guess how much battery power is left once the main power goes down; others can send a signal to NT indicating that approximately two minutes of battery power remain.

Once you have plugged the correct serial cable into the server and the UPS system, open the Control Panel and choose the UPS icon. The dialog box shown in Figure 12.10 opens.

FIGURE 12.10:

The UPS configuration
dialog box

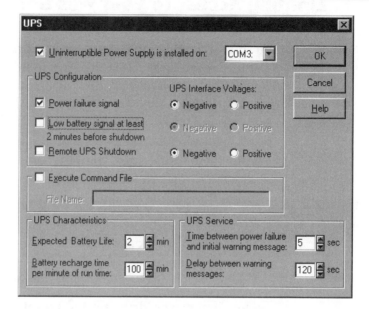

Because there are no real standards for the signals on the serial line between the server and the UPS system, this screen lets you configure the UPS interface voltages as either positive or negative. You will have to locate information on exactly how to configure this screen from the UPS manual; it is impossible to generalize on the settings.

You can include a command file to execute during the system shutdown, but you can expect some constraints on what this file can do:

- It must complete everything it is supposed to do inside 30 seconds (test it to be sure that it does).

- It cannot open any dialog boxes asking for user input, because that could extend its execution time.

- It must have a filename extension of EXE, CMD, COM, or BAT.

Prepare the file and place it in the *systemroot*\\SYSTEM32 directory; then choose the Execute Command File option in the UPS dialog box, enter the name of the command file, and click on the OK button.

Limiting Access to Your Web Server

You should locate your Web server in a secure area, preferably behind a locked door. After all, why would anyone but the webmaster have any reason to work directly on the server? Here are some more suggestions:

- Disconnect the server's reset button and on/off switch, and relocate them in a secure part of the server cabinet. When you do so, the only way to reset the server is by using the Shutdown option from the Start menu. And that is just how the system should be shut down.

- Disconnect any floppy disks connected to the server. When you do so, it is impossible to reboot the server from the floppy drive using NT, DOS, or any other floppy-based operating systems.

- Implement a no-drinking and no-eating policy in the server room; the last thing you need is to find out just how difficult it is to clean someone's Coke out of the server.

- Never allow smoking in the server room. Cigarette smoke and disk drives do not go together well at all.

- Locate the Web server out of direct sunlight, and be sure that the building's air-conditioner is providing enough cool air. The normal air-conditioner may not be powerful enough to cool a locked room full of computer and communications equipment all working and pumping out heat 24 hours a day. In certain northern climes or in Europe where offices are not normally air-conditioned, you may have to install extra cooling.

Troubleshooting Your Server

One of the main duties of the webmaster is to troubleshoot server problems. Trained staff should be available on a 24-hour basis to keep your Web site running smoothly, and your ISP should also have staff available at all hours.

Server problems, other than the hardware and software problems covered in the last section, invariably fall into one of two areas: configuration problems or access problems. Let's look at configuration problems first.

Fixing Configuration Problems

Finding and fixing configuration problems can be a real challenge. Configuration problems can be subtle and hard to pin down, but there is one thing going for the webmaster: A configuration problem is most likely to occur immediately *after* someone has made some sort of change on the Web server. "It was working OK yesterday" and "I didn't change anything" are two frequently heard cries in Web serverland. Here are some things that can and do go wrong.

Errors in Filenames

Many configuration problems you are likely to encounter will be wrong or misspelled filenames. When HTML files are prepared on a system not connected to the Web server, a simple typo in a filename can prevent all sorts of operations from working properly. Image-maps that once performed flawlessly now refuse to work at all, and links that once led to other files on other systems now generate error messages. Nothing is more frustrating than clicking on a link and then seeing the message "ERROR: The requested document is not available." Always double-check your typing.

Finding HTML Errors

If you are preparing your HTML content files without the benefit of an HTML publishing application, check your HTML syntax very carefully. Check for missing quotation marks in your HTML code; certain browsers can produce some very funny looking output if you forget to close a set of quotation marks.

Look for nesting errors in your HTML code. Almost all HTML elements can be nested, but the rules concerning which element can be nested inside another can be complex. And remember that elements can never overlap; you must always end one element before you start the next one. Certain browsers will apparently let you get away with nesting errors, making them very difficult to spot, which emphasizes the need to test your HTML code with several browsers.

The HTML specification states that when a browser encounters HTML code that it does not understand, the browser should ignore the tag or the attribute. This in itself may lead to unexpected results that have nothing to do with your coding but with the capabilities programmed into the browser.

If you encounter problems with your imagemaps, be sure that the HTML code contains `ISMAP` in the `<IMG>` tag and that the configuration files that map the portions of the imagemap are still correctly named.

CGI Script Problems

Errors connected to CGI scripts can be very obvious and easy to see but very difficult to troubleshoot and fix because several elements are at work—the IIS itself, the script, and the file or databases with which the script interacts. It might be as simple as a missing file, or it might be a complex programming problem. If you have a previous version to fall back to, do so as you trace the problem.

Be sure that the permissions are all set appropriately and that the directories containing any executables are all accessible. And don't forget to check the NT Server error logs to see if there is another reason for the script not executing properly. One of the most obvious causes of script failure is that something is wrong with one of the files on which the script itself operates.

Because the main tool used to access the results of a CGI script is the Web browser itself, troubleshooting scripts can be a tedious job indeed. And the browsers can even mask problems with its inconsistent error-message reporting.

If your script manages information that a visitor has entered into a form, don't make assumptions about any data you receive. Even though you have asked a visitor to enter his or her Zip code in the form, don't assume that the field will actually contain numbers—you never can tell what a visitor will enter.

Isolating Access Problems

The second common kind of error you will encounter is that a visitor can get only limited access to your Web site or, in some cases, no access at all.

Assuming that the visitor has the basic components in place to access any Web site on the Internet, including a browser, a fairly fast modem, and an Internet account, what might prevent someone from accessing your Web site? Let's take a look at what can go wrong on your Web server.

Server Access Problems

If your visitors cannot get through to your Web site, there may be a problem with the communications link between your Web server and your ISP or between your ISP and the rest of the Internet. When you first contact the ISP with a view to using its services, ask about the monitoring equipment it uses and its service guarantees. You can also ask to see its performance statistics.

If the problem is in the communications link between your site and that of your ISP, it is probably time to call the phone company. This kind of problem, unfortunately, can lead to a great deal of fingerpointing as each player blames the problem on someone else.

You can help isolate the problem yourself by using your favorite browser, first on the server itself and then, if that works, by moving farther and farther from your server until the connection ceases to work. This does not have to be physical distance. You might try first to access the server from a computer on your local area network; if that works, try dialing out to the Internet using another computer, and then try connecting to your site as any visitor would.

Errors on Connection

If you can connect to the server, the problem is not in the various communications links between your server and the Internet; it is probably on the server itself.

A visitor may be trying to access a password-protected area of the server using the wrong password, or a visitor may be trying to access the server from a new and unusual location with an IP address that you have decided to screen out.

If the visitor can actually access your site but his or her browser displays an error message when attempting an operation, the error number associated with the message should give some clue as to the nature of the problem. Table 12.7 lists some of the most common HTTP error codes along with the reasons they might occur.

TABLE 12.7:   HTTP error numbers and descriptions

Error number	Description
400	The request syntax was wrong.
401	The request requires an `Authorization:` field, but none was provided.
402	The requested operation costs money, but the browser did not specify a valid `Chargeto` field in the request header.
403	You have requested a resource that you do not have the permissions to request.
404	The server cannot find the URL you requested.
500	The server has encountered an internal error of some unspecified kind and cannot continue with your request.
501	The request you made is a legal request, but is not supported by this server.

If you are using the latest additions and extensions to HTML, a certain number of visitors to your Web site will not have browsers that support these new features, and they will not be able to see some or all of your content.

And if you have loaded your site with imagemaps and other complicated graphics, users with slow modems will either go to another site rather than wait for the image to load or will access your site in text mode to avoid the problem altogether and speed their access. Either way, they will not see what you intended them to see.

CHAPTER

THIRTEEN

13

Advanced Web Site Administration

- Using the Internet Service Manager

- Using services

- Reviewing IIS security

- Setting up your Gopher service

- Setting up your FTP service

- Monitoring your Web server performance

- System diagnostics and recovery

- Managing IIS log files

- When should you upgrade your server hardware?

In this chapter, we'll look at how to keep your Web site running smoothly from the point of view of the administration tasks you or the site administrator will perform. We'll look at how to control and configure the IIS using Microsoft's Internet Service Manager, and we'll also look at other NT Server system tools, including the Performance Monitor, the Network Monitor, and NT Diagnostics.

We'll look at setting up and configuring both Gopher and FTP services on your Web server, and we'll examine some of the benefits and the drawbacks of using these services. We will also quickly revisit several system security topics relating to Web, Gopher, and FTP services. Let's start by taking a look at the Internet Service Manager.

Using the Internet Service Manager

Once you have completed the installation and basic configuration of IIS, you adjust the advanced configuration options with the Internet Service Manager, or ISM for short. In this section, we'll look at how you can review your IIS services using the ISM Report View, the Servers View, and the Services View. We'll also look at all the options you can use to tailor IIS services to your needs with the four properties sheets: the Service property sheet, the Directories property sheet, the Logging property sheet, and the Advanced property sheet. We'll begin with the default ISM display, the Report View.

The Report View

The Internet Service Manager Report View, shown in Figure 13.1, is the default ISM display and is the most useful for sites with one or two Web servers.

FIGURE 13.1:

The Internet Service
Manager Report View

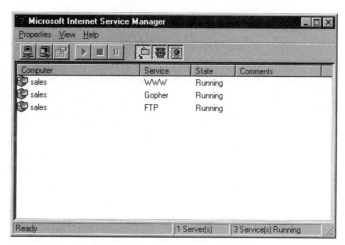

Each of the three ISM Views has the same line of icons on the toolbar; you can also use the selections in the Properties and View menus to perform many of these functions. These icons are grouped in three groups of three. You use the first group of three icons on the left of the window, in order from left to right, to:

- Connect to a specific IIS server

- Locate all the IIS servers on a network

- Display a property sheet to configure a service

You use the next three VCR-like icons to perform a function on whichever IIS service you select. Also in order from left to right, click on these icons to:

- Start the specified service

- Stop the specified service

- Pause the selected service

And you use the last three icons on the right to display information relating to the three IIS services in the main window:

- FTP service information

- Gopher service information

- Web service information

If you are using Microsoft's Internet Access Server (previously known by its code name Catapult), you will see two additional icons here: the Remote Windows Sockets and the Proxy.

In the main part of the window, you will see the names of the computers running IIS services on the left side, the name and current status of the service in the center, and any comments on the right side of the window.

If you click on the heading of a column in this main window, ISM sorts the listing. If you double-click on a service in the window, the appropriate property sheet opens; you can also use the selections in the Properties menu to do the same thing. At the bottom of the window you will see server and service status information.

The Servers View

The Servers View, shown in Figure 13.2, is most useful for those sites that have many IIS services on the same NT Server.

This view displays the services running on each server listed by the name of the server. You can click on the plus symbol next to a server name to see a list of the services running on that server, or you can double-click on a service name to open the property sheet.

FIGURE 13.2:

The Internet Service
Manager Servers View

FIGURE 13.2:

The Internet Service
Manager Servers View

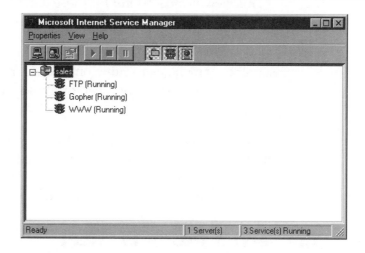

The Services View

The Services View presents information by service type, grouping all the FTP servers together, followed by all the Gopher servers, followed by all the Web servers. Figure 13.3 shows this view.

FIGURE 13.3:

The Internet Service
Manager Services View

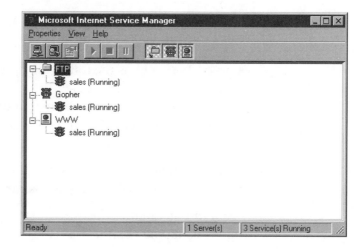

This view is most useful for those networks on which the IIS services are distributed among several NT Server computer systems.

Click on the plus sign next to a service name to see the name of the server on which it is running on, and double-click on a computer name to see the property sheet for the service that is running on that computer.

The ISM views present information about which IIS service is running on which server, but if you want to look at or change the configuration information that these services use, you must use the ISM property sheets. We'll look at them next.

The Service Property Sheet

In the ISM window, double-click on a computer name or on a service name to open the appropriate property sheet. You will see the four tabs across the top of the sheet indicating the categories of settings you can configure, and they all work much as you would expect. Once you have confirmed the settings for each of the services, select the OK button to return to the main ISM window once again.

The Service property sheet, shown in Figure 13.4, controls who can use your server and specifies the account used by anonymous users.

This property sheet has the following options:

- **Connection Timeout.** Sets the maximum length of the timeout for each connection before the server automatically disconnects an inactive visitor.

- **Maximum Connections.** Specifies the number of simultaneous connects you will allow on your server at one time.

- **Anonymous Logon.** Most sites on the Web allow anonymous logons using the IUSR_computername account. If you want to use your current security settings to control access to your site, change the name in the Username field to an existing account on your server, and then enter the appropriate password.

FIGURE 13.4:

The Service property sheet

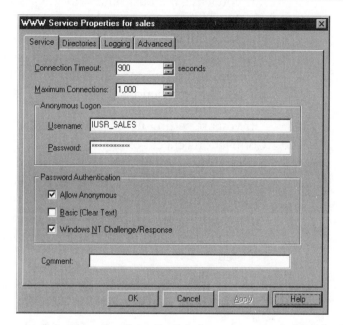

- **Password Authentication.** In this box, you can select the level of password authentication that you want to use on your IIS server. IIS supports three levels:

  - **Allow Anonymous.** When this box is checked, anonymous connections are processed, and the anonymous username and password are used. If this box is left unchecked, all anonymous requests are rejected, and one of the two following authentication types must be selected.

  - **Basic.** When this box is checked, basic authentication is used. Remember, this level of authentication sends NT unencrypted usernames and passwords over the network.

  - **Windows NT Challenge/Response.** When this box is checked, a proprietary system is used. Windows NT

Challenge/Response authentication is currently available only with the Internet Explorer Web browser.

If you leave the Basic and Windows NT Challenge/Response checkboxes unchecked and if you check the Allow Anonymous checkbox, all client requests are processed as anonymous requests. If a client does provide a username and password, he or she will be ignored, and the anonymous account will be used instead, with all the security restrictions that may apply to this account.

If you are setting up an FTP service and the Allow Anonymous Connections checkbox is checked, all logons in which the user enters a username of anonymous will be processed. If you leave the box unchecked, your users must enter a valid NT Server username and password to be able to use your FTP service. And if the Allow only Anonymous Connections box is checked, any user who tries to log on with a username of anything other than anonymous will be rejected.

The Directories Property Sheet

The Directories property sheet, shown in Figure 13.5, lists the directories available to IIS visitors in the Directory window. At the bottom of the Directories property sheet you will see these two checkboxes:

- **Enable Default Document.** Check this box to enable the file whose name appears in the Default Document field to be displayed to visitors who do not request a specific file when accessing your site. You can place a default document in each directory; if users do not make a specific request, they always see something.

- **Directory Browsing Allowed.** When turned on, directory browsing lets visitors to your site look at a hypertext listing of the directories and files on your system and thus know how to navigate your system.

Most administrators do not allow directory browsing because it exposes more of the underlying site structure than they want to show to a casual visitor.

A hypertext directory listing is sent to the browser if directory browsing is enabled and no default document is available.

If you are using FrontPage, remember that it uses the default file-name of index.htm and IIS uses a default filename of default.htm. The *Managing Your Web Site* chapter tells you how to change the FrontPage default filename.

Adding a directory to this property sheet allows the selected service (Web, FTP, or Gopher) to make information contained in the directory, and in its subdirectories, available to clients visiting your site. Directories not listed here are not available to clients. Every service must have a home directory that is the root directory for that service.

IIS provides a default home directory for each of the three services—\wwwroot, \gophroot, and \ftproot—and you can also add other directories outside the home directory that appear to a Web browser as through they are a subdirectory of the home directory. Such directories are known as *virtual directories* and are most helpful when used with the Web service. Because FTP is an older protocol, any virtual servers you create remain invisible. They are present, and any visitor who knows the alias can access them, but they will not appear in directory listings.

To configure a home or a virtual directory, follow these steps:

1. Select the appropriate service in the main Internet Service Manager window.

2. Open the Directories property sheet and then click on the Add button.

3. When the Directory Properties dialog box opens, check either the Home Directory or the Virtual Directory checkbox, and then enter the name of the directory in the Alias text field.

4. Select the appropriate permissions.

5. Click on the OK button, and then click on Apply and OK.

Some FTP clients require that FTP information be presented in Unix format rather than in NT Server format. Set the Directory Listing Style to Unix rather than MS-DOS for the maximum level of compatibility.

The Logging Property Sheet

You use the Logging property sheet, shown in Figure 13.6, to specify when and how IIS service logging is performed. In this section, we'll look at how to set up the logging function on your server. For more information on what is contained inside an IIS log file, see the "Managing IIS Log Files" section later in this chapter.

FIGURE 13.6:

The Logging
property sheet

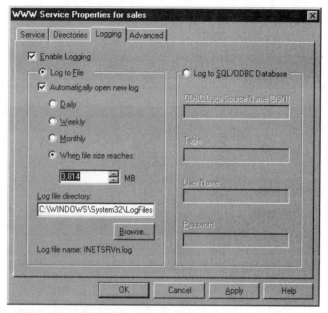

The Logging
property sheet

After you select the Enable Logging checkbox to turn on IIS logging, you have two choices:

- **Log to File.** Check this box to create a normal IIS log file, and then choose the interval to use when creating a new log file: daily, weekly, monthly, or when the file reaches a specific size. If you do not choose one of these options, the log file will continue to grow indefinitely.

- **Log to SQL/ODBC Database.** Check this box to send the IIS log information to a SQL or ODBC database. You must also specify the Data Source Name (DSN), Table, and a username and password to the database. Using this option you can direct logging of all IIS services to a single location and then use an ODBC-compliant application to look at your log data.

When logging to a file, the maximum total log line is 1200 bytes, and each field is limited to 150 bytes. When logging to a SQL or ODBC database, each field is limited to 200 bytes.

The Advanced Property Sheet

By using the Advanced property sheet, shown in Figure 13.7, you can control access to your server very precisely indeed.

FIGURE 13.7:

The Advanced property sheet

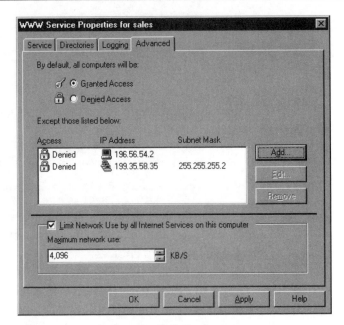

Two checkboxes control overall default access:

- **Granted Access.** Check this box to allow all computers access to your server except those specified by IP address in the box below.

- **Denied Access.** Check this box to deny all computers access to your server except those specified by IP address in the box below.

You can then use the list box to enter exceptions to the default access policy. You can block access to specific individuals or to whole networks based on their IP addresses.

You can also limit the amount of network bandwidth allowed for all services on your IIS server. Check the box marked Limit Network

Use by All Internet Services on This Computer, and then select the maximum bandwidth you will allow in the Maximum Network Use field. This value is in KB/S, or kilobits per second.

This option is something of a two-edged sword, and you should use it with care. You can certainly control the amount of network bandwidth your server makes available to visitors, but at the same time, by doing so, you may reduce the perceived response time of your server. Remember that you can also specify the maximum number of simultaneous connections to your Web server in the Service Property sheet (shown in Figure 13.4). By carefully tuning the maximum number of connections and the maximum bandwidth, you can control access to your Web server very precisely indeed.

The Messages Property Sheet

If you double-click on the FTP service in the main ISM window, you will notice an additional tab labeled Messages. You can use the text boxes on this tab to specify various messages specifically for users of your FTP service, including:

- **Welcome Message.** This long message is displayed to FTP clients when they connect to your FTP server and can be used to display the rules of your FTP site.

- **Exit Message.** This short message is displayed as clients disconnect from your FTP server.

- **Maximum Connections Message.** This text is displayed if a client attempts to connect to your FTP service when the maximum number of connections allowed are already in use; you can use it to display a message saying that your FTP server is at its maximum of *nnn* connections and that visitors should try again later.

These messages are not available to users of your Gopher or Web services.

Using Services

To round out this section on controlling IIS and related services, I want to remind you that the NT Server Control Panel has several applets that you can use with IIS, including the Network applet, which is used to set up and configure the TCP/IP networking protocol, the ODBC applet, which is used to establish ODBC connectivity, and the Services applet. You use the Services applet to start, pause, or stop any NT Server service, including Web, Gopher, or FTP. Select the Services icon in the Control Panel, and you will see the Services dialog box shown in Figure 13.8.

The three columns in the list box in this dialog box are Service, Status, and Startup. On the left side in the Services column, you will see a list of all the Windows NT Server services listed in alphabetic order. In the Status column, you can see whether a specific service is started or is waiting to start, and in the Startup column, you can see an indication of whether the selected service is run automatically when NT Server starts or is started manually.

FIGURE 13.8:

The Services dialog box

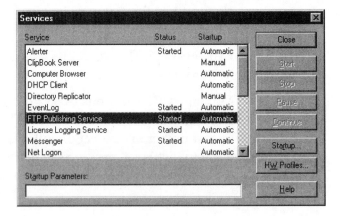

Select a service and then click on the Startup button (or double-click on the service you want to work with in the list box) to open the Service dialog box. Here you can select the Startup Type from Automatic, Manual, or Disabled, as well as set other logon parameters for the service.

Changing the status of the Web server service in this dialog box will override any settings in the Service property sheet in ISM.

Reviewing IIS Security

In the *Windows NT Server Operating System Security* chapter, we looked at the security elements an administrator uses to control user accounts, particularly the IUSR_*computername* account, and we also looked at the various important elements that control security and permissions in the NTFS. I will not repeat that information here, but I will take a moment to review security with specific reference to IIS configuration. It is worth pointing out that if your security selections differ between NT Server and IIS, the stricter settings are always used automatically.

Administrative Checklist

Here are some other administrative points you should consider:

- Turn on auditing of NTFS files and directories and review the log files daily so that you can detect any attempts at unauthorized access.

- Run only the Server services that you need; if you do not offer FTP or Gopher services, turn them off.

- Unbind any unused network protocols from network interface cards connected to the Internet.

- Double-check permissions on network shares to ensure that you have set them correctly. Check file permissions too.

The Elements of IIS Security

Internet Information Server uses all the security elements provided by the underlying NT Server operating system and those built into the NTFS. Internet Information Server also adds additional security by using IP address security and directory access settings. A simplified path through each part of the security system follows these steps:

1. Internet Information Server receives a request.

2. Is the IP address permitted?

3. If the IP address is permitted, is the user permitted?

4. If the user is permitted, do the IIS permissions allow the access in the request?

5. If the IIS permissions allow the access in the request, do the NTFS permissions allow the access?

6. If the NTFS permissions allow the access, access is granted.

If any one of these tests fail, access is denied. Let's look closer at some of these steps.

IP Address Security

The IP address of every data packet that IIS receives is checked against the settings in the ISM property sheets we looked at earlier in this chapter. You can configure these settings in two ways: to allow access by all systems except those specifically excluded, or to deny access to all users except those specifically included. IP address security can exclude specific individuals or entire networks.

Username Authentication

All anonymous access requests use the IUSR_*computername* account created when IIS is installed, and username authentication is most useful if you want to control access to your server by a particular user or group.

IIS and NTFS Permissions

The Web server in IIS allows you to set three kinds of permissions to files and directories:

- **Read.** Allows users to read the files in a directory.

- **Execute.** Allows users to change directories and to start applications or scripts stored in these directories. By default, all ISAPI and CGI scripts should be placed in the directory \scripts. Execute permission must be enabled in both IIS and NT Server for scripts and applications installed on an NTFS drive.

- **Secure SSL Channel.** Allows users to send information to the Web server in encrypted form. More on this in a moment.

The FTP service supports Read and Write permissions only; the Gopher service supports only Read permission.

Configuring a Secure Web Service

To be able to use your Web service, a user must log on to the system with a username and a password. Before you allow anonymous logon using the IUSR_*computername* account, be sure that the system-wide User Rights (in the User Manager for Domains Policies menu) do not allow the IUSR_*computername* account, the Guests group, or the Everyone group any rights other than to Log on Locally. And then double-check that the directory and file permissions are set on your IIS content directories.

You should also review the Advanced properties page in the ISM and check that the Granted Access and Denied Access radio buttons are appropriately set and that IP addresses have either been granted or refused access to your service correctly.

Finally, review the Directories properties sheet, and be sure that the Directory Browsing Allowed checkbox is cleared. Directory browsing can expose the whole file system; so be sure that you do not allow it on your server.

If changes that you make to NT's security elements (adding or removing users from a group or changing NTFS permissions) don't take effect quickly enough for you, you can stop and then restart the IIS services. Under normal circumstances, changes to use configurations will not appear until the security-token cache has been cleared and new tokens are initiated, and that happens by default every 15 minutes. Stopping and restarting the IIS services will force the new security settings to be used.

Using Secure Sockets Layer (SSL)

Internet Information Server gives users access to a secure communications channel based on support for Secure Sockets Layer (SSL) and RSA encryption. Internet Information Server can send and receive communications across the Internet from the Microsoft Internet Explorer or from one of the other SSL-enabled Web browsers.

Secure Sockets Layer provides server authentication, encryption and decryption, and data integrity services:

- **Authentication.** Assures the Web client that the data is actually being sent to the right server and that the server is secure.

- **Encryption/decryption.** Transforms the data so that it cannot be read by anyone other than the secure target server.

- **Data integrity.** Ensures that the data stream has not been altered or tampered with in any way.

Instead of replacing HTTP, SSL creates an intermediate layer between the high-level HTTP protocol and the low-level TCP/IP. Rather than calling TCP/IP library routines to open and close connections and to send and receive data, Web browsers and servers make calls to SSL routines, which manage the task of setting up a secure communications channel. Secure Sockets Layer uses public key encryption to encrypt inbound and outbound messages, as well as to create verifiable digital signatures for user authentication. You'll find the SSL specification at:

```
http://home.netscape.com/newsref/std/ssl.html
```

Secure Sockets Layer Digital Certificates

Enabling SSL on IIS involves several steps:

- Generating a key pair file and a request file
- Requesting a digital certificate from a Certification Authority
- Installing the digital certificate on your server
- Activating the SSL security on your server

A *digital signature* is a unique value associated with a transaction and is used to verify the identity of the sender as well as the origin of a message. By using a digital signature, you can demonstrate that you wrote a message and that the message has not been tampered with, and you can prevent others from signing your name to messages that you did not write.

A digital signature is short, only a few hundred bytes, and is created by a special algorithm that combines a private key with a message. The recipient then verifies the digital signature using the sender's public key and the message. The digital signature is secure in the sense that it is virtually impossible to find another message (other than the message transmitted) that will produce an identical signature.

Acquiring an SSL digital certificate requires several steps, including contacting a qualified certifying organization such as the Internet security company VeriSign. See VeriSign's own Web site at:

```
http://www.verisign.com
```

for more information on applying for a digital certificate. It makes most sense to complete all these steps long before you want or need to implement SSL security on your Web site.

Once the SSL security is in place and enabled with ISM, you must remember several points:

- Once enabled and configured, only SSL-enabled Web browsers will be able to access your SSL-protected directories.

- URLs that point to an SSL protected directory must use `https://` instead of `http://`.

- You can enable SSL security on the root directory (`\wwwroot` by default) or on one or more virtual directories.

- If your site offers both secure and public content, set up two sets of directories, one for each kind of content. And do not configure an unsecured directory as a parent for a secure directory.

Using Key Manager

Microsoft's Key Manager helps you with the background information needed to apply for a digital certificate by preparing this information and then creating the files you will need. The first file is a key file containing the key pair, and the second file is a certificate request file.

To create a key pair follow these steps:

1. Open the Key Manager from the Peer Web Services or from the IIS program menu.

2. In the Key menu, select Create New Key.

3. In the Create New Key and Certificate Request dialog box, shown in Figure 13.9, fill in the information for all the fields. Table 13.1 lists this information.

4. When you are done, click on OK.

5. Enter the password once more when you are prompted for it, and then click on OK.

6. Your key will appear in the Key Manager window under the appropriate computer name.

Do not enter commas into any field; if you do, they will be interpreted as field separators and will generate an invalid request without any warning.

FIGURE 13.9:

The Key Manager Create New Key and Certificate Request dialog box

TABLE 13.1: Create New Key and Certificate Request dialog box options

Option	Description
Key Name	Name of the key file you are creating
Password	Password used to encrypt the private key
Bits	Number of bits for the key pair; default is 1024 bits
Organization	Company name
Organizational Unit	Name of your division within the company
Common Name	Domain name of your server
Country	Two-letter country abbreviation—US, UK, and so on
State/Province	Complete name of your state or province; Iowa, for example
Locality	Complete name of your city
Request File	Name of the request file you are creating

The key created by the Key Manager is not valid for use on the Internet until you obtain a valid key certificate for it from a certifying authority. Send the certificate request file to this authority according to its procedures, and it will send you a digitally signed certificate. Once you have that certificate, use Install Key Certificate from the Key menu in the Key Manager to install it on your server. Once installed, you must activate the SSL feature for your Web service using the Directories properties sheet in the Internet Service Manager.

Using Server Side Includes

I have not talked about server side includes for two main reasons: (1) They can degrade Web server performance, and (2) they can compromise server security. They require additional hard disk accesses because they build the HTML file from the component pieces. Server side includes can be a natty programming trick, but they become dangerous when associated with CGI scripts that include code that modifies other HTML or that modifies user input to an HTML document. And because they can quite legally include anything at all, you could be facing a major security breach if someone creates a completely bogus include.

Setting Up Your Gopher Service

Gopher is a popular Internet client/server application that presents Internet resources as a series of menus so that users do not have to be concerned with the underlying details of IP addresses and different access methods.

Gopher menus can contain documents you can look at or download, searches you can perform, or additional menu selections. When you choose one of these items, Gopher does whatever is necessary to obtain the resource you requested, either by downloading the document or by jumping to the selected Gopher server and presenting its top-level menu.

Gopher actually performs many different functions, including logging on to the remote computer, transferring FTP files, conducting searches, and logging off—all without your needing to know a single IP address. Many Gopher clients let you save the details of a favorite Gopher site using a bookmark so that you can access it again quickly and easily without retracing your steps. When you perform a search using Gopher, the results are presented as another Gopher menu; make your selection, and away you go.

Gopher is so good at hiding the mechanical details of the Internet that the term *Gopherspace* was coined as a collective to represent all the resources reachable using Gopher. If some of this sounds familiar, don't be surprised; many people consider Gopher the forerunner of the World Wide Web. And it is also true to say that the popularity and ease of use of the Web has allowed the Web to grow at the expense of Gopher; given the choice, most users will choose to use a Web client rather than a Gopher client.

Both text-based and graphical Gopher clients are available for all the major operating systems, including DOS, Windows 3.1, Windows 95, Windows NT, OS/2, all varieties of Unix, and the Macintosh.

Configuring Your Gopher Server

To set up a Gopher server, you must complete the following configuration tasks:

- Set up the directory or directories that will contain Gopher files.
- Create tag files and decide how they will be stored on the server. We'll look at what a tag file is and how to make one in the next section.
- Specify the maximum number of connections you will allow to your Gopher server at one time, and set a time limit for each connection.
- Set up the activity logs.

Most of these tasks are done using ISM as we saw earlier in this chapter. Creating a tag file was not covered; so we'll look at how to do that next.

Creating Tag Files

Gopher clients read and process two kinds of files that they get from the Gopher server as a result of a Gopher request: (1) the file that builds and displays the Gopher menus, and (2) the files that contain the actual content, image or text, that your site offers.

All the management information sent from your Gopher server to a Gopher client is contained in what is known as a *tag* file, a hidden file that the visitor never sees. You may also hear tag files referred to as *links.* A tag file contains several important pieces of information, including its display name, host name, port number, the file's creation date, as well as details of the administrator's name and e-mail address. When you select an item from a Gopher menu, the Gopher client uses the information stored with the menu name in the tag file to construct the next Gopher request. If the requested item is another menu, another tag file is loaded, and another Gopher menu is loaded and displayed. If the requested item is the last element in the structure, the item itself is located and displayed.

To create a tag file, open a command prompt, and use this syntax:

```
gdset -c  -gn -f "description" -a "name" -e email filename
```

This command creates a hidden tag file. See Table 13.2 for a description of these command-line arguments

TABLE 13.2:   Command-line arguments used to create a Gopher tag file

Argument	Description
-c	Creates or edits a tag file.
-g*n*	Specifies the Gopher ID number, between 0 and 9. (See Table 12.4, Gopher ID Codes, for more information.)
-f *"description"*	Adds the specified text description to the tag file.
-a *"name"*	Adds the specified administrator name to the tag file. If you omit this argument, the value defaults to the service administrator's name in the ISM Service dialog box.
-e *email*	Adds the specified e-mail address. If you omit this argument, the value defaults to the service administrator's e-mail name in the ISM Service dialog box.
filename	The name of the tag file with which you are working.

First, you create the file, and then you move it to the server and place it in the appropriate directory:

1. Use the syntax above to create the tag file.

2. Make the file visible.

3. Move the file to the appropriate directory on the server.

4. Make the file invisible once again.

If much of the material you want to add to a tag file is the same for a range of files in the same directory, you can write a simple batch file to do the job for you.

Gopher Checklist

Here are some items to check as you prepare your Gopher site and get ready to go online:

- Be sure that all the file permissions are appropriately set so that files can be read by visitors to your site and cannot be written to by intruders.

- Make an outline of the structure of your site. Because Gopher uses menus, an outline is a useful design tool for now and a memory jogger for the future.

- Make the difference between links to data on your Gopher server and links to other Gopher servers elsewhere as obvious as possible. If you do so, visitors will know that you are not responsible for everything accessible through your server.

- Don't advertise your FTP access if you plan to provide both Gopher and FTP services. Using Gopher to access FTP files is not a good use of resources; direct use of FTP is far more efficient.

As time goes on and the Web continues to grow, fewer and fewer people will use Gopher-based services; the Web is just more fun.

Setting Up Your FTP Service

FTP is the abbreviation for File Transfer Protocol, the member of the TCP/IP suite of protocols designed to allow a remote logon, to list files and directories, and to move files from one computer to another. FTP supports a range of file types and formats, including ASCII, EBCDIC (Extended Binary Coded Decimal Interchange Code, an 8-bit character code used on certain IBM mainframe systems), and binary files. FTP allows FTP clients to transfer, or *upload,* files to FTP servers, as well as to transfer, or *download,* files from FTP servers.

Using an FTP Client

Just as Gopher clients are available for almost all operating systems, FTP clients are also available. Both NT Server and NT Workstation contain character-based FTP clients. Type FTP at a command prompt, and the FTP interpreter starts; type ? ↵ to see a list of commands you can use in an FTP session. The normal prompt is ftp>. Although a whole range of commands is available for FTP clients, you can become quite an FTP expert with only a few:

open	Establishes a connection to a remote computer
ascii	Sets the file transfer type to ASCII
binary	Sets the file transfer mode to binary
get	Transfers a specified file from the server to the client system
put	Transfers a specified file from the client to the server system

quit   Closes the connection to the remote computer and terminates the FTP session

You can also use the Internet Explorer to access FTP sites; simply remember to preface the URL with `ftp` rather than `http`. For example:

```
ftp://ftp.company.com/
```

Because many files on FTP archive sites were originally created using one of the variations of the Unix operating system, you may encounter files with unusual filename extensions. Table 13.3 lists some of the file types you may come across when using FTP.

Some of the popular Windows utility programs such as WinZip can handle many of these compressed file formats. Also, most of the popular Unix file-compression utilities are also available in DOS or Windows formats.

Populating Your FTP Archive

When you start adding files to your FTP archive, separate them in some meaningful way so that they appear as organized as possible. If your company has ten products, place material for each product in its own directory. If your company is using the FTP site to make new device drivers available, for example, group them by operating system. Create directories named after these operating systems; put the NT files in a directory called \NT4, and put the Macintosh files in a directory called \MACINTOSH. Don't worry if you end up with only a few files in each directory; your users will thank you for making the organization obvious and easy to navigate.

TABLE 13.3: Common Internet file types

Filename extension	Description
tar	A tape archive file created by the Unix `tar` utility.
Z	A file created by the Unix `compress` utility. You must use the `uncompress` utility to restore the file before you can use it.
tar.Z	A compressed tape archive file.
z	A compressed file created using `pack`. You must use `unpack` to restore the file before you can use it.
ZIP	A compressed file created using PKZIP that must be uncompressed with PKUNZIP before you can use it.
gz	A Unix file compressed by the GNU `gzip` utility. This file must be decompressed before you can use it.
HQX	A compressed Macintosh file.
SIT	A Macintosh file compressed by StuffIt.
TIF or TIFF	A graphics file in TIFF format.
GIF	A graphics file in GIF format.
JPG or JPEG	A graphics file in JPEG format.
MPG or MPEG	A video file in MPEG format.
TXT	A text file.
1	An `nroff` source file.
ps	A PostScript file ready for printing on a PostScript printer.
uue	A `uuencoded` file. You must use `uudecode` before you can use the file.
uue.z	Compressed `uuencoded` file.
shar	A Usenet newsgroup archive file created by the `shar` program.
shar.Z	A compressed `shar` file.

Here are some other items you can add to make it easier for visitors to navigate your FTP site:

- Each directory can contain an annotation file that the visitor's browser will automatically display. Create the file with the name ~FTPSVC~.CKM, and make it a hidden file so that it does not appear in directory listings. Keep this file up to date.

- Include an INDEX.TXT file in each directory to tell visitors exactly what they can expect to find. An index usually contains both the name of the file and a short description of its function. Keep this file up to date.

- Add a terms-and-conditions statement. Your legal department may require you to add this material as a reminder to users about copyright and trademark restrictions on the material on the FTP site.

Internet Information Server also adds some additional useful features. You can create directories with the same name as a user, (called a user-name directory); when that user logs on to your FTP server, that directory is used as the root. You can also create a directory called ANONYMOUS. When a visitor logs on using the password *anonymous*, this directory is used as that visitor's home directory. This kind of configuration detail can be very helpful if users are other company employees, but restrict permissions even in a directory such as this so that unauthorized users cannot gain access where you don't want them.

A major benefit of FTP is that almost anyone with an Internet connection can use it; there is no need for fancy graphics here. FTP transfers are fairly fast, and they are very efficient. The two kinds of FTP access are *anonymous FTP* and *user FTP*.

Anonymous FTP

This is the most popular FTP Internet service and is the one you will most probably provide from your IIS server. Anonymous FTP lets anyone access your server, whether that person has an account on the system or not. Visitors can simply log on with the username anonymous and then use their e-mail address as a password. These visitors are restricted to that part of your server known as the "anonymous FTP area." Because this kind of FTP access is relatively safe and can support almost any file type, as Table 13.3 shows, it is a popular way to provide access to large numbers of files of different types; indeed, many large FTP sites are known as FTP archives because of this.

Configuration is a piece of cake with an anonymous FTP service: All you have to do is put the file into the correct directory, and you are done. There is no HTML to worry about, and there are no links to other files or sites. All you have is a directory structure containing the files you want to make available for users to download.

Both Gopher and the Web support links to FTP sites; so your FTP server can perform double duty. It can appear as a standalone FTP server and as a Web server at the same time.

User FTP

This version of FTP is only for users who already have an account on your system, and they must log on with a username and password. They can download any file they would be permitted to read if they logged on locally, and they can upload to any directory for which they have write access.

The FTP service provides for only certain functions such as listing and changing directories and sending and receiving files; so users do not have full and complete access to your system. This version of FTP can present a security risk. When a user logs on to the FTP service from the Internet, his or her password is sent as clear text. Anyone with a sniffer program on an intermediate system somewhere can determine the username and password and use them to log on to your system.

Allowing FTP Uploads

Whether you allow anonymous FTP users to upload files to your site is a decision you will have to make on a server-by-server basis. Uploading a file from a Web browser to a server is one of the few things that a Web client still cannot do; although having said that, I'm sure someone is working on how to do it. Allowing users to upload files poses a definite security risk. In many documented cases, unscrupulous users have exploited FTP archive sites to store their own personal files, including copies of bootlegged software, pornography, and other material of questionable legality. They don't want this stuff on their own systems, but they will quite happily use yours for temporary storage; and many administrators are just too busy to notice. Upper management at your company would not be very impressed to find out that your newly established FTP site is known all over the world as one of the premiere sources of pornographic material or bootlegged software.

If you have to permit anonymous FTP users to upload files, create a special directory called \INCOMING to receive the files. Set the permissions so that users can write and execute only in this directory. This will be slightly inconvenient because users will not be able to look at files uploaded by others, but it will prevent them from altering or deleting those files. You set these permissions using the Internet Service Manger.

Testing Your FTP Site and Going Online

Before you announce your FTP site to the world at large, spend a little time ensuring that your site works as you think it should. Use an FTP client to access the site, list a few files, and change to a few directories. Also download at least one ASCII file and one binary file, and upload a set of test files if you plan to offer uploading services to your users.

You must also ensure that users *can't* do the things that you don't want them to do, such as access files or directories outside the limits you have set or overwrite important files.

Archie is an FTP search utility that maintains a database of FTP servers and the files available on each one. To include your new FTP site in the Archie search indexes, send e-mail to this address:

```
archie-admin@bunyip.com
```

Include the fully qualified domain name of your FTP server and the root directory from which you will be making information available.

Monitoring Your Web Server Performance

Windows NT Server performance is usually excellent, even right out of the box, and NT Server includes several powerful tools you can use to look at your Web server's system performance:

- **Task Manager** gives you a quick overview of how each application or thread running on your system is using system resources as well as total CPU and memory use.

- **Performance Monitor** lets you look how your server is doing and then decide if any tuning steps are needed. You can use the Performance Monitor to:

  - Collect maximum, minimum, and average values for critical system values.

  - Display a view of your server's performance.

  - Dispatch alerts to you (or any other user) when a specific event occurs on the server.

- **Network Monitor** can track and display network frames for troubleshooting and monitoring network applications.

- **Server Manager** tracks session and user activity information, as well as managing server resources.

In the next few sections, we'll look at how to use all these performance-monitoring tools, and we'll look at the sort of evaluation tasks for which each is best suited

Using Task Manager

To start Task Manager, right-click on the NT Server toolbar, and then select Task Manager from the menu. The Task Manager opens, displaying the main Task Manager window. From the menu bar, you can access the File menu to select a new task or close the Task Manager; the Options menu, which contains selections you can use to customize the Task Manager display; and the View menu, which contains selections you can use to change the display update speeds, force the graphics to be refreshed, and display kernel usage times. As you would expect, a Help menu is also available.

The main Task Manager display contains three tabs or pages:

- **Applications.** This tab lists all the tasks running on your server and shows the current status of each.

- **Processes.** This tab lists all the processes running on your system by name, along with process ID (PID) number, CPU times, and memory usage.

- **Performance.** This tab is the most impressive of the three, with its constantly updating displays of current and historical CPU and memory use. This display also includes useful totals for file handles, processes, and threads and for virtual-memory, physical-memory, and kernel-memory usage.

Even if you think that your server is sitting there doing nothing, when you look at the Performance display, you will see that your server is running somewhere between 20 and 30 processes and that you have a CPU utilization of between 3 to 5 percent, with occasional peaks to 100 percent. Figure 13.10 shows the information displayed by the Performance tab.

FIGURE 13.10:

The Task Manager
Performance tab

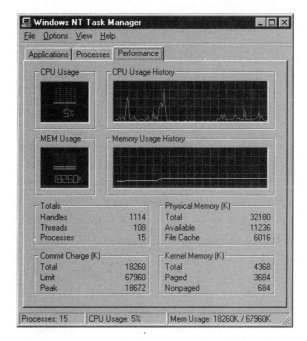

The NT Server Task Manager gives you a very useful snapshot of the current activity on your server, but if you want more detail on specific aspects of server operation, turn to the NT Server Performance Monitor.

Using Performance Monitor

The Performance Monitor offers more extensive capabilities than the Task Manager and lets you look at resource use for specific NT system-level components. You can even use it to troubleshoot performance problems and to assess hardware upgrade requirements.

Select Start, Programs, Administrative Tools, and then Performance Monitor, and you will start the Performance Monitor in chart mode. Time is shown along the horizontal axis of this chart, and the performance item that you are interested in examining is shown on the vertical axis.

Choose Edit and then Add to Chart. In the Add to Chart dialog box, use the Object list box to look at all the system areas you can monitor. The first item, Processor, includes information on several *counters* listed in the Counter box; for example, the variable that reports how many interrupts per second the system processes is called the Interrupts/sec counter. These counters track system data, such as the number of network packets transmitted per second or the number of pages swapped in and out per second, and you can use them to create charts and reports that help you assess and tune system performance. You can even use the Performance Monitor to look at activity on several servers at the same time so that you can make accurate comparisons.

Tracking disk space is always a concern for the network administrator, and you can use the Performance Monitor to show you current hard-disk usage. But what is even more useful is that you can configure the Performance Monitor to tell you when the amount of free disk space drops below a certain level. Here are the steps:

1. In the Performance Monitor, open the View menu and select Alerts.

2. In the Add to Alert dialog box, select Free Megabytes from the list of counters.

3. In the Alert If box, check the Under radio button, and enter the number of megabytes of free disk space you want to use as your minimum threshold.

Now you have to decide what you want the Performance Monitor to do when the amount of free space falls below this threshold value.

4. From the Options menu, choose Alerts. You can choose between adding an entry to the system log or sending a message to a specific computer (such as MARKETING) or to a specific username (such as Mark).

You can also log the counters that you are interested in to a disk file and then read them back into the Performance Monitor for later review and analysis. From the View menu, choose Log to select the counters you want to store, and then use Log in the Options menu to name the file and to set the update rate. To play the log back later, choose Options and Data From.

Windows NT Server is usually shipped with the disk-performance counters turned off. You can turn them on by typing this command at a command prompt:

```
diskperf -y
```

followed by Enter. Now restart your server, and you will be able to monitor disk usage.

When you install IIS on NT Server, a large number of additional counters are added. Table 13.4 lists them. You can use the WWW, HTTP Service, and Internet Services Performance Summary objects for realtime evaluation of your Web server.

You can also load previously saved Performance Monitor charts so that you don't have to re-create your favorite displays each time you want to look at a particular counter or at the relationship between two counters. Performance Monitor chart files are saved with the filename extension .pmc, and you will find a particularly useful set of counters in the file msiis.pmc in the windows\system32\ inetsrv\wwwroot\samples\tour directory.

Looking at the most important Performance Monitor counters can give you a head start on planning your future hardware acquisitions, and Table 13.5 lists the counters you can use to track specific system resources.

TABLE 13.4:   Performance Monitor Counters for IIS evaluation

Bytes Sent/sec	Files Total
Bytes Total/secs	Get Requests
Cache Flushes	Head Requests
Cache Hits	Logon Attempts
Cache Hits %	Maximum Anonymous Users
Cache Size	Maximum ISAPI Requests
Cache Used	Maximum CGI Requests
Cached File Handles	Maximum Connections
CGI Requests	Maximum NonAnonymous Users
Connection Attempts	Measured Async I/O Bandwidth usage
Connections/sec	Not Found Errors
Current Anonymous Users	Objects
Current Blocked Async I/O Requests	Other Request Methods
Current ISAPI Requests	Post Requests
Current CGI Requests	Total Allowed Async Requests
Current Connections	Total Blocked Async Requests
Current NonAnonymous Users	Total Rejected Async Requests
Directory Listings	Total Anonymous Users
Files Received	Total NonAnonymous Users
Files Sent	

TABLE 13.5:   Performance Monitor counters used in resource planning

System resource	Counter
Logical disk	% Free Space
Memory	Pages/sec, Available Bytes
Physical disk	% Disk Time, Avg Disk sec/Transfer
Processor	% Processor Time, Interrupts/sec
Server	Bytes Total/sec
System	File Read/Write operations/sec

Start by logging this information to a log file at 15-minute intervals every day for a week. Once you have identified the peak network usage times, collect this same data at 5-minute intervals. Remember, occasional values of 100 percent on some of these counters are not necessarily bad (unless the processor queue length is too long), but sustained values of 100 percent are unacceptable and certainly call for remedial action.

Using Network Monitor

Network administrators can monitor and troubleshoot network-related problems using the NT Server Network Monitor to capture and display network *frames*, or packets. To make the most of Network Monitor, you have to know a great deal about networking protocols and their data formats, and those topics are well beyond the scope of this book. All I can do is tell you where to find the Network Monitor and what you can use it for; after that, you are on your own.

Network Monitor is not part of the default NT Server installation. To install Network Monitor, follow these steps:

1.   Select the Control Panel and open the Network object.

2. Choose the Services tab, and then click on the Add button.

3. In the Select Network Services dialog box, choose Network Monitor Tools and Agent from the selections in the Network Services list box.

4. Click on OK, and NT Setup copies the appropriate files from your original NT Server CD-ROM onto your hard disk.

Once installation is complete, you can start the Network Monitor by choosing Start, Programs, Network Administration menu.

Network Monitor looks at the data stream on your network, which includes all the data being transmitted at any given time—control information as well as data. Because this can be an inordinate amount of data, Network Monitor lets you design a *capture filter* so that you can select a subset of the data frames on your network. You can design this filter on the basis of source or destination address, for a specific protocol property, or by several other methods. That done, you create a *capture trigger* that takes a specific action when a predefined network event occurs.

Once you capture the data, you can use the Network Monitor to display the results, and, in fact, one of the best features of this program is that it performs much of the data analysis for you by translating the raw data into its logical frame structure automatically.

For reasons of security, Network Monitor captures only frames sent to or from the local computer. Network Monitor also provides password protection and the ability to detect other instances of itself operating on the same network segment.

Using Server Manager

The NT Server Manager plays two roles: It manages server resources, and it displays up-to-the-minute information on shared resources and relationships between servers. In this section, I'll concentrate on its monitoring and reporting functions.

Using Server Manager you can look at and track the following:

- Information on the number of printers in use and the number of open file locks
- The resources open during a session
- How long a resource has been open
- How long a session has been idle
- Information on all users with currently active sessions on the selected computer

Server Manager presents a snapshot of system usage. To see the server's usage statistics since startup, type this command:

```
net statistics server
```

from a command prompt, followed by Enter.

The best place to start looking at your system is by using the Server Manager's Properties dialog box, which you can open in several ways. Select Start, Programs, Administrative Tools, and then choose Server Manager to open the main Server Manager window. Now, do one of the following:

- Select a computer from the list in the main window, and then choose Properties from the Computer menu.
- Select a computer and press Enter.
- Double-click on the computer's name.

You can also open this dialog box by selecting the Server icon in the Control Panel on the computer about which you want to collect statistics.

The Properties dialog box opens, displaying the Usage Summary box and below this a row of five buttons. The Usage Summary box shows the following:

- The total number of user sessions
- The total number of shared resources currently open on the server
- The total number of named pipes currently open on the server
- The total number of file locks held by open resources on the server

The buttons below this box include the following:

- **Users.** Lets you look at all the users connected to the server and the resources opened by each user. You can disconnect one or all of the currently connected users.

- **Shares.** Displays the server's shared resources and which users are connected to which resource. You can also disconnect one or all of the currently connected users here.

- **In Use.** Displays all the open shared resources on the server and lets you close one or all of the resources.

- **Replication.** Allows you to manage directory replication for the server, as well as the path for logon scripts.

- **Alerts.** Lets you look at and manage the list of computers and users that will be notified when an alert occurs on the server.

Before you disconnect any users, you should send them a message to tell them of your intentions. You can use Send Message from the Computer menu for this.

Once you become familiar with the information available in all these NT Server monitoring tools under normal operating conditions, you will be much better equipped to detect abnormal conditions when they do occur.

System Diagnostics and Recovery

In this section, we'll look at some things you can do and the programs you can use to prepare for the inevitable day when a piece of server hardware fails. We'll look at the NT Diagnostics, the System object in the Control Panel, and the Last Known Good Configuration.

Using NT Diagnostics

This program is not a hardware diagnostic, but a program you can use to look at or print system configuration information about your server. You can look at everything from the stepping level of your Intel processor to the version date of the video driver you are using. Select Start, Programs, Administrative Tool, and then NT Diagnostics. When the program starts, you will see these tabs across the top of the main window:

- **Version.** Lists general NT and product registration information.

- **System.** Displays information about computer hardware and about the CPU.

- **Display.** Gives details about your display adapter, BIOS date, chipset type, and device driver information.

- **Drives.** Lists all the floppy, removable, hard, and CD-ROM disk drives on your system. Double-click on a drive icon to see a detailed report on that drive.

- **Memory.** Details the total amount of physical, virtual, and kernel memory available and in use, as well as information on the NT swap file.

- **Services.** Lists all the NT services and whether they are running, stopped, or in some other state. Double-click on a service or use

the Properties button to see a detailed report on the selected
service.

- **Resources.** Lists system hardware and hardware abstraction
layer (HAL) virtual devices. Select the IRQ, I/O Port, DMA,
Memory, or Devices buttons to switch between the detailed
reports.

- **Environment.** Lists the NT Server operating system environment. Use the System and Local User buttons to switch between
the two displays.

- **Network.** Displays a variety of network-related information.
Use the General, Transport, Settings, or Statistics buttons to
switch between the displays.

Once you select the report or reports that you want to look at, use the
selections in the File menu to print or save the reports and to set up
the printer.

System Recovery Configuration

When NT Server encounters a severe error (also known in some circles as a *fatal system error,* a *STOP* error, or a *blue screen*), the operating
system follows a default set of procedures, as follows:

- Writes the event to the System Event log.

- Sends a message to the Administrators.

- Makes a copy of system memory (known as a memory dump)
at the time of the error and writes the dump to a file called
MEMORY.DMP. You can sometimes use the contents of this file to
reconstruct the circumstances leading up to the system crash.
To preserve the contents of this file, copy it to another name as
soon as the system restarts; otherwise, it will be overwritten
when the next STOP error occurs.

- Automatically restarts NT Server. This can be both a blessing and a curse. On the one hand, downtime may be minimized by restarting the operating system immediately, but that makes one very large assumption—that the problem that originally caused the crash has gone away. If it has not, the system comes up again and crashes immediately.

Use the System object in the Control Panel to look at and change these settings. You will find them in the System Properties dialog box under the Startup/Shutdown tab.

Using the Last Known Good Configuration

If you have trouble restarting NT Server after you have made a configuration change or installed a new device driver, don't panic. All is not lost. You can start the server using what is known as the Last Known Good Configuration. Here's how to do it:

1. Start your server. When your screen shows:

   ```
   OS Loader V4.00
   ```

   press the spacebar *immediately*.

2. A Hardware Profile/Configuration Recovery menu appears on the screen. You can do one of the following:

   - Choose a hardware profile that you can use to start the computer
   - Load the Last Known Good Configuration
   - Restart the computer

3. Type **L** to select the Last Known Good Configuration. This option starts NT Server using the configuration from immediately *before* you made those last little changes that caused all the bother. This should boot your computer.

The only drawback to this procedure is a very minor one: The configuration changes that caused all the trouble are lost. They didn't work anyway; so most people consider this a small price to pay to get their server back online quickly.

Making and Using an Emergency Repair Disk

So what do you do if the steps in the last section didn't work? If the NT Server system files or the boot partition are corrupt, you can use an Emergency Repair disk with the Repair process in the Windows NT Server Setup program to get going again.

You can create an Emergency Repair disk as a part of the NT Server installation process, but this disk contains an NT registry based on your initial setup and does not contain information on your users. You can use the rdisk utility from a command prompt to update this disk or to create a new Emergency Repair disk based on your system configuration as it is now.

When you use:

```
rdisk /s
```

the Repair Disk Utility dialog box opens, giving you the choice of updating an existing Emergency Repair disk or of creating one from scratch. The /s command-line argument makes rdisk store information about user accounts and file permissions on the Emergency Repair disk. Choose the appropriate button and follow the instructions on the screen as the disk is made. If you don't have a current Emergency Repair disk, go make one now.

To restore Windows NT Server running on an Intel processor, using the Emergency Repair disk, follow these steps:

1. Insert your original Setup floppy disk in drive A and boot the computer.

2. In the text-based screen where the installation program prompts you to learn about Setup, make an installation, repair a damaged installation, or quit setup, type **R** to repair your system.

3. Setup asks you for the Emergency Repair disk. If you don't have one, Setup shows you a list that NT installation found on your hard disk and asks which one you would like to repair.

4. Follow the instructions on the screen, inserting the Emergency Repair disk and other NT Setup disks as prompted.

5. When the final message appears, remove the Emergency Repair disk from drive A, and reboot your server.

The steps to follow on a RISC-based system are almost identical; you have to start the Windows NT Setup program according to the manufacturer's instructions because the procedure varies from vendor to vendor.

And if the Emergency Repair disk didn't work, what then? Well, in that case it is time to reinstall Windows NT Server from your original distribution CD-ROM. But you should first make absolutely certain that all your hardware is in proper working order, because although installing NT Server is relatively quick and easy, reconfiguring the system is no fun, and you only want to go through that process once.

Managing IIS Log Files

As you saw earlier in this chapter, you establish the criteria for saving log files using the Internet Service Manager. Open the Logging property sheet for the service you are interested in and use the settings to do the following:

- Specify the frequency with which the log information is collected.

- Configure the directory you want to use for the log files.

- Choose the form in which the data will be collected.

Make it part of your routine to archive the log files to prevent them from growing too large and to make log analysis easier; and we all know that the easier you can make any job such as log-file analysis, the more chance there is that you will actually do it. You can even automate the archive process.

Here's a list of the fields you will see in a log file:

- Client's IP address

- Client's username

- Date and time

- Service: WWW, FTP, or Gopher

- Server name

- Server IP address

- Processing time

- Bytes received

- Bytes sent

- Service status code

- NT status code

- Name of operation

- Target of operation, usually a filename

- Parameters for operation

All the fields in the log file terminate with a comma; a hyphen acts as a placeholder in the event that a field is empty and contains no data.

Once the log data has been collected, you can use custom-built statistical programs or even a spreadsheet to look at the number of hits per hour or per day that your site receives.

Windows NT Server 4 contains a utility called `convlog` in the `\inet\admin` directory that can convert the IIS log files into the format used by the European Microsoft Windows NT Academic Centre (EMWAC) Web server or into the Common Log file format used by most other Web server software. Once in one of these alternative formats, you can use other analysis tools to look at the files. To see a help screen and a couple of examples of how to use the utility, type the following at a command prompt:

```
convlog -h
```

When Should You Upgrade Your Server Hardware?

As soon as your Web site goes online, someone will tell you that it is too slow. This is going to happen; so you might as well get ready for it now. A visitor's perception of the performance of your Web site is influenced by the following:

- The speed of the visitor's communications link
- The speed of the visitor's computer and the nature of his or her Web browser
- The speed of the Internet connections between the visitor's access point and your server

- The level of traffic on the Internet when the visitor tries to access your site

- The number of simultaneous visitors your Web site is currently managing

- The number of non-Web-related tasks that your Web server is currently handling

- The speed and capacity of your Web server hardware

Notice that I said a visitor's *perception* of the performance of your Web site; the problem may not be on your server, and it may not be within your control. You should do some checking before you assume that you need more powerful hardware. You should also review the design of your Web pages and look for the common mistakes described in the *Designing and Constructing Your Web Site* chapter. Eliminating these design faults can help your Web site to be more efficient. And don't run a screen saver on the server; they often perform some quite intense calculations to decide what to do next, which can impose a completely unnecessary load on your server.

Having said all that, of course, a time comes when you will need to upgrade your Web server hardware. How will you know when? You can either wait for the complaints to start arriving from visitors, or you can keep your finger on the pulse of your Web site by becoming a frequent visitor to the site yourself.

The main areas that you should monitor when considering system performance are:

- **Processor performance.** You can upgrade to a faster CPU, or you can add another CPU in a multiprocessor system. Think seriously about using SMP systems for large Web servers.

- **Main system memory use.** NT Server and NT applications are memory hungry; NT often uses as much as half your hard-disk space as a disk cache. You can't do much to speed up memory, but you can add a faster hard disk so that virtual memory operations are optimized. You can also improve performance by removing unnecessary NT services; if you don't have a printer on your Web server, you don't need the Spooler service. NT starts a large number of services by default; look at the list carefully, and run only the ones you need.

- **Hard disk space and use.** Remember that hard-disk space can be consumed in two ways: (1) It can be occupied by your Website content—HTML files, CGI scripts, FTP archives, and the like; and (2) it can be used as virtual memory swap space. Buy big disks with fast seek times, and be sure you don't choke performance by using slow disk controllers. Use 32-bit SCSI-II or SCSI-III host adapters.

- **Network interface cards.** Use 32-bit network interface cards if your server hardware can support them; PCI and EISA certainly can. In some high-traffic cases, 16-bit network cards can perform poorly.

- **Network performance.** If you use several protocols on your network, you may find that TCP/IP drops more messages than you might anticipate. This is because the high-traffic IPX protocol can grab more processor time. Limit your network to supporting only the TCP/IP protocol if you can possibly do so.

You can use the NT Server Performance Monitor described earlier in this chapter to track the level of CPU utilization on your server and to look at the number and frequency of pages swapped from memory to your hard disk as part of NT Server's virtual memory management system. Combine this with memory and other system information from the Windows NT Diagnostics displays, and you will quickly build a complete picture of your server's performance. When the server consistently maintains high utilization levels, it is time to upgrade your hardware. NT Server is a scalable operating system, and many hardware platforms are available as potential Web servers.

PART IV

Managing Your Own Intranet Web Site

CHAPTER

FOURTEEN

14

How to Build an Intranet

- Intranets defined

- Looking at the benefits of an Intranet

- Intranets: For your eyes only

- Twelve Intranet case studies

- Making the most of your Intranet

- Groupware and your Intranet

- Finding Intranet products

- Group discussion software on your Intranet

- Workflow software on your Intranet

- Having Webbed suites

- The future of Intranet applications

In the first half of this book we have been concerned with planning, designing, building, and connecting your Web site to the Internet. In this chapter, we'll look at the relatively recent appearance of Intranets, or internal company networks that use TCP/IP and Internet tools and standards.

A small revolution is underway in the corporate world, a revolution that will start to break down the monolithic structures and company turf wars that conspire to block communications and the flow of information. Intranets are built from the same components used on the Internet, but they are used only by company employees, and most are off limits to outsiders.

All the material presented in the two earlier chapters, *Planning Your Web Site* and *Designing and Constructing Your Web Site*, applies also to your Intranet. As you will see in a moment, all the fundamental elements are the same in both the Internet and an Intranet. The major difference is in terms of focus: An Internet site looks outward from the company, and an Intranet site is usually for internal use.

Some corporate Intranets do have connections to the outside world, either to allow remote users to connect to the Intranet or to allow employees to connect to the Internet. Groups ranging from individuals to project teams to entire departments are setting up Web pages and FTP servers, particularly in Fortune 1000 companies; for example, DEC has more than 400 internal Web sites, and Sun Microsystems has more than 1,000. Many of these sites were created outside the normal MIS sphere of influence. They all offer an inexpensive, easy-to-navigate system that employees can access using their PCs and workstations and a TCP/IP network.

To help you get your Intranet off the ground, I'll go through the creation process, step by step. We'll look at a number of case studies from several industries, showing you how different companies are utilizing this technology, and then I'll end the chapter with a review of some products you can use to make your Intranet as effective and efficient as possible.

Intranets Defined

But first, what is an Intranet, and how does it differ from the many kinds of internal networks that have been in place for many years and have been used to great effect by many companies?

Many of the developments that fueled the explosive growth of the Internet helped to spawn the Intranet, including the following:

- The spread of networked computer systems based on PCs

- The availability of TCP/IP on almost every computer platform, large and small

- The wide adoption of open standards such as HTTP and HTML

- The development of cross-platform support for Web browsers

- The availability of low-cost, high-power Web servers such as the Internet Information Server

All these elements, along with the growth of the Internet, have led many companies to use the same technology on their internal Intranets. Many of the problems of connecting older legacy systems with newer networks simply disappear when you use TCP/IP and Internet technology to link them.

Most companies store documents in some kind of electronic form on a computer somewhere, and to access such a document on the older networks, you had to enter a long, cryptic path name to specify the directory and the filename of the document you wanted. Using Internet technology and HTML, specifying a document becomes as simple as clicking on an HTML link, and with links inside other documents, users can navigate their way around and find files much more easily than before.

A recent survey published by Zona Research, a market-research company in Redwood City, California, indicates that 1998 revenues from the sale of Web servers used in Intranets will be four times those for the Internet. Application designers and developers will certainly find more opportunity in sales for Intranets than they will in sales for the Internet.

Looking at the Benefits of an Intranet

We'll start this section by looking at the various advantages and disadvantages of using an Intranet, and then we'll look at some specific ways you can apply Intranet technology to solve real-world problems in your organization.

Here are some advantages of using an Intranet:

- Web technology is scalable and can be applied across wide area networks as well as small- to medium-sized local area networks.

- Intranet technology is an excellent way to publish large numbers of frequently changing documents within your corporation.

- Web servers typically do not need the computational power or hard-disk space that groupware applications such as Lotus Notes require; fewer numbers are crunched.

- Easy-to-use Web browsers are available for virtually all operating system and hardware combinations; all of them are cheap, and many of them are free.

- There is no single-vendor solution to the Intranet marketplace; no single company dominates the scene, but as a result of the open nature of the Internet standards, products from different sources interoperate very well.

- Advances in HTML authoring tools and the addition of new features to desktop application suites make it much easier to create HTML pages for Web servers.

Several disadvantages are associated with using an Intranet; whether these are important in your particular circumstances, only you can decide. They include the following:

- Intranets require the TCP/IP protocol and may not work with your existing protocol choices.

- The collaborative features of groupware applications, such as Lotus Notes or Novell's GroupWise, are much stronger than those in Intranet products. If it is vitally important for your company to have people actively collaborate on projects, groupware is the way to go—at least for the time being.

- Most Intranet applications do not support replication (the process of synchronizing data stored in databases on two or more computers) for remote users, but groupware does support replication.

- HTML is not a development language; you will have to use CGI or Perl scripts, or even C or Java programs, to access legacy database systems. Java standards are currently very fluid as the language evolves, but who knows what the future might bring.

- A limited number of off-the-shelf tools exist for linking Web servers to legacy databases and applications.

For a discussion of the other questions you should ask to help you decide between groupware and an Intranet, see the section "Groupware and Your Intranet" later in this chapter.

Improving Your Internal Communications

In the past, companies have used printed sales material, employee handbooks, price lists, and sales guides, which are expensive to produce and distribute. And how do you make sure that all your offices and manufacturing plants receive this information when they *need* it rather than when you can *send* it to them?

Formerly, Hewlett-Packard published a sales-force newsletter that weighed in at 8.5 pounds per issue. This huge tome was published regularly each month, but between publication dates new information was simply not available. If an industry-shaking event occurred and sales were affected, too bad; the sales force just had to wait for the next issue. Hewlett-Packard decided to publish the information in one central location, on its Intranet (known as InfoNet), and let the sales staff pull out the information they needed when they needed it. The sales staff now has continuous access to absolutely up to date information, and HP has saved a huge amount of money in printing and distribution costs.

Across all sorts of industries, organizations are using Intranet technology to meet departmental, companywide, and international communications needs and to help improve productivity. As you saw in the last section, one of the great strengths of using Intranet technology is the ability to provide access to published documents. The range of applications that can be developed to meet specific industry or corporate needs is huge.

Most of the applications fall into one of the following categories:

- *One-way communications*. A department posts new information rather than updating, printing, and mailing bound paper copies of directories, telephone lists, sales presentations, product lists, and price lists.

- *Two-way communications*. A person needs to download the latest copy of a device driver or a technical drawing.

- *Many-way communications*. Several people contribute to a discussion, and their information is made available to all members of the group.

Lets take a look at some more specific examples.

Sales and Marketing Intranets

One of the main headaches faced by corporate sales staff is the problem of getting timely sales and marketing information out to the sales force in the field. This problem is compounded many times over when the sales force is widely scattered all over the country or all over the world in many time zones. Sales people need information just before making an important presentation or before signing an important deal, and they need information that is up to the minute. Without that, they may not close the deal, and they may end up losing the sale to a competitor.

Some of the types of information you can publish on an Intranet include:

- Sales presentations, including text, slides, and multimedia. You can run a PowerPoint presentation from the Intranet server or download it for later use.

- Product information.

- Price lists.

- Information on sales leads.

- Analysis of the local competition.

- Details of planned sales campaigns, discounts, give-aways.

- Sales training materials.

Sales staff can use remote connections into the Intranet to log sales and complete company paperwork, place orders, and check on the status of orders and deliveries. They can complete competitor analyses, document recent important developments likely to affect future sales, and even report on the tactics used by the competition in their area of the world.

Research and Development Applications

Product managers and team members can use an Intranet for internal reporting and to do the following:

- Update project schedules and important milestones

- Circulate technical drawings

- Post technical specifications

- Circulate design ideas for peer review or structured walk-throughs

- Circulate information on competing products

- Ask technical questions and locate experts that have specific skills

- Collect feedback from sales staff on proposed new product specifications

- Conduct interactive training sessions that incorporate sound and video, in which employees can participate at their own pace without the need for a formal classroom schedule

Access to at least some of this information should be protected so that unauthorized people cannot see important company plans and schedules.

Improving Customer Service and Technical Support

Customer service and technical support, even internal IS departments, can benefit from the Intranet in the following ways:

- Conduct training sessions on customer service, technical support, or even on how best to create an HTML Web page

- Publish the latest fix or work-around for a particular problem

- Determine the status of a specific bug or customer problem

- Locate order-status information quickly

- Publish technical support bulletins to support staff throughout the world

- Locate experts with experience in a particular odd problem or regional variation

Human Resources Applications

One of the major issues in many large corporations is the sheer volume of paperwork involved in updating and distributing corporate policies and procedures manuals. Most people have the three-ring binder containing the original manual that they were given when they first joined the company and a set of large envelopes containing the updates and changed policies that they have failed to file in the binder over the years. Some people update their manuals and others don't; so everyone ends up working with a different set of policies.

And if employees need to find out how a current policy works, they don't look in the binder or sort through the updates in the envelopes; they get on the phone and call someone in the human resources department.

Once the manual is available on the Intranet, not only do all employees have access to the latest version of the policies, but the only time they will have to pick up the phone is to get an interpretation of a tricky aspect of a policy or to check on the number of vacation days they have accumulated. And if you have a secure system, they can find this information on the Intranet also.

Human resources departments can publish information such as the following:

- Corporate policies and procedures
- Company benefits
- 401K plan information
- Current job vacancies
- Expense claim-form information
- Worldwide telephone listings and company directories
- Corporate mission statements
- Company organization charts
- Government regulation information, including minimum wage and nondiscrimination policies
- Listings of unwanted office equipment
- Employee development programs
- Employee meetings
- Cafeteria menus
- In-house newsletters
- Safety rules and disaster-recovery regulations
- Date and location of the company picnic
- Goods for sale by employees

Examples of secure online transactions might include:

- Enrolling in a 401K plan
- Checking vacation accruals
- Checking income tax deductions and other employee information, such as address changes
- Checking stock-purchase options
- Submitting employee change of status forms after a promotion or a change to a new department

If you simply put human resources manuals on an Intranet, you can quantify the savings. If the cost to publish and distribute the manual is $20 and 1,000 people in the company need a copy, the first print run costs $20,000. If 20 percent of that information is out of date three months later and has to be revised, republished, and redistributed, that update will cost $4,000. You don't have to go through many revisions before the numbers really start to add up.

Accounting Applications

Even the finance department can take advantage of the Intranet by posting clear financial objectives for both corporate staff and worldwide sales staff in far-flung offices around the world. Other applications include the following:

- Monitoring the company stock price
- Publishing the current status of an Initial Public Offering
- Publishing the corporate annual report
- Publishing a video of the chairman's remarks to the shareholders' meeting
- Establishing partnerships with suppliers

Intranets: For Your Eyes Only

Creating an Intranet and creating an Internet presence for your company require different focuses. The whole world can access your Internet site, and so it must be seen as a marketing tool, a way to educate people about your products and services. An Intranet, on the other hand, is linked to your company's internal ideas and goals. The Internet site presents the company's external face to the world; the Intranet contains the core of its being. Creating the Internet site has more to do with look and feel; data and the flow of internal information are the dominant forces on the Intranet site.

Really, the differences between an Intranet and the Internet are questions of semantics and of scale. Both use the same techniques and tools, the same networking protocols, and the same server products. Most company data is not intended for outside consumption; indeed, some data, such as sales figures and client and legal correspondence, should be protected very carefully. DEC's Intranet, for example, is protected from unauthorized access by authentication and encryption schemes. And from the point of view of scale, the Internet is global, and an Intranet is contained within a small group, department, or corporate organization.

The Internet is famous, and rightly so, for being a chaotic jumble of useful and irrelevant information; the meteoric rise in popularity of Web sites devoted to indexes and to search engines is a measure of the need for an organized approach. This doesn't mean that your Intranet should be chaotic—quite the contrary; but it does mean that you will have to do some careful planning and organizing and assign duties and responsibilities accordingly.

In the sections that follow, I'll describe the steps you will need to follow to establish your own Intranet. We'll look at some choices you will have to make along the way, and I'll point out how you can avoid some of the pitfalls.

Starting Work

An Intranet is a perfect solution for any organization of about 50 to 100 people who all work at the corporate headquarters or who are scattered over a wide geographical area and will access the system from a remote location. It is an ideal fit for any situation in which a large amount of constantly changing information must be made available to all these users simultaneously and as cost-effectively as possible.

The first step in creating an Intranet is to conduct an audit or an appraisal of existing systems, including hardware, software, and file formats used for data files. You should also explore what the company wants to get out of using Intranet technology and how much of what kind of information the Intranet will hold. Most companies do not want to put documents on their Intranet that are considered sensitive in either a competitive or a legal sense, and most companies avoid putting personal files and payroll information on an Intranet unless an effective security system is in place.

An Intranet is most useful for broadcasting general kinds of information, but company officials must still decide how open the company wants to be with its employees and which documents it is appropriate for all employees to see. Establishing the hardware and software systems for your Intranet is the easy part; deciding on the content is much more difficult.

Who's in Charge Here?

The person or group in charge of a Web site will need all sorts of skills, some technical and some diplomatic. Here's a list of some of those in the cast of characters:

- Web administrator. This person is responsible for the day-to-day running of the Intranet, monitoring the usage logs, adjusting the configuration as needed, and making the backups and system upgrades as needed.

- Content authors. These people create the content used on the Intranet. They are not necessarily technical people, but they must know their subject, be able to prepare an HTML document, and be able to write well. They will also be responsible for submitting new material and updating old material as things change within the organization.

- Script developer. This person develops the scripts needed to do the things that you can't do using HTML. The script developer is essentially a programmer who can develop code to make your Web site do new things.

- Webmaster. This person receives all the e-mail sent to your site. Actually the Webmaster address is usually an e-mail alias set up to forward e-mail to an existing account or set of accounts. The Webmaster is the point of contact with visitors and the world of users and is responsible for replying to complaints and suggestions and for coordinating with other sites.

Some companies will find it easier to assign site maintenance responsibilities to the departments that originate the content for the site, rather than have one person or group manage all the Web sites within the company.

As well as deciding who has access to what kind of information, you must also keep tabs on network usage, check usage statistics, and continue efforts to fine-tune the daily operation of your Intranet.

Managing the Transition

Once the group, department, or corporation has made the decision to implement an Intranet, several important factors will determine whether this transition from a traditional host-based system to an Intranet will be a smooth process or a violent upheaval. Many of these issues are not straightforward technical issues with one correct answer, but are thorny political issues that will take all your diplomatic skills to resolve. Here are a few questions to get you started in this process.

Evaluating Your Internet Experience

The first step in this evaluation process is to look at the resources you already have within the company. Technical people that have experience with open systems, Unix, the Internet, scripting languages such as Perl, TCP/IP, and so on will simplify the switch to an Intranet. If your experience is restricted to the mainframe legacy systems in place, it is time to get some training and upgrade your technical skills.

Taking the Technical Lead

Someone has to take the technical lead, establish the Web servers for the Intranet, and keep up to date on the almost daily advances and developments in areas as diverse as the latest hot Web browser, new networking hardware, and improvements in server and operating-system software. You don't have to implement all these improvements on your Intranet immediately (just think of the training costs), but it is very important that someone in your organization stays current on the latest developments.

As new Web site development tools appear from the software vendors, the skill level needed to set up and then run a Web site will fall and will continue to fall as these tools get better and better. This can shift some of the emphasis from your technical staff to your users, but don't expect your users to be able to evaluate and make technical recommendations on the other important Intranet issues such as hardware upgrades and operating system changes. You or someone on your technical staff will continue to perform that function.

How Will You Use TCP/IP in the Enterprise?

One of the thorniest problems has to do with networking protocols and how any new additions fit into the overall corporate picture. The TCP/IP set of protocols is at the center of the Intranet and must be at the center of yours. In some corporations, several protocols will be in use at the same time, and staff and machine resources will be needed to support each protocol. Many corporations will use Novell NetWare products with IPX/SPX protocols, while others will use older, mainframe-based systems.

The recent releases of IBM's OS/2 and of Microsoft's Windows 95, Windows for Workgroups, Windows NT Workstation, and Windows NT Server all contain TCP/IP; so upgrading to one of these systems can help to make TCP/IP easier to deploy. These operating systems can also easily handle multiple protocols on the desktop and the server. Unfortunately, the cost of adding TCP/IP to a large number of DOS/Windows 3.1 computers could be quite significant.

Another approach is to use a NetWare-to-TCP/IP gateway server. A gateway server allows the PCs on your network to continue to run their Novell IPX/SPX protocols and allows you to run TCP/IP on the server.

Many companies set up their own IP subnet addresses, but if you plan to connect your Intranet to the outside world of the Internet, you must be a part of the formal addressing scheme used by the rest of the Internet. All this and more was detailed in the *TCP/IP in a Nutshell* chapter.

If you run large legacy systems over SNA (IBM's proprietary Systems Network Architecture) 3270 systems, adding TCP/IP may mean utilizing a product such as Attachmate's TCP Server. TCP Server can run IP to each desktop, provide access to the SNA host, and run individual sessions to each desktop.

Setting Up the Web Server

Next, set up the Internet Information Server on your selected hardware, making the choices described in the *Advanced Web Site Administration* chapter. We looked at the hardware requirements for IIS earlier in this book, but to reiterate quickly, you should use a system with at least 32MB of memory, a 1 to 2GB hard disk, and at least VGA graphics.

Maintaining the Content

The process of setting up the Web server is an important first step, but deciding on and then maintaining the content is even more important and is much more difficult. Just tracking the changes needed to keep your site's content up to date can be a full-time job.

Look back to the section "How to Link Pages Successfully" in the *Designing and Constructing Your Web Site* chapter earlier in this book, and review the various ways you can organize and link information. If you are creating a training manual or a tutorial, a simple linear design will work well; each page will link to the one before and the one that follows. Applications that impose a hierarchy on your data, such as a table of contents, require more careful design; lay the information out on paper first, and be sure you understand all the intricate dependencies before you start to code the HTML.

A grid-based design, in which one page links to many and each of these new pages also contains many links, is another difficult design task. It sometimes helps to use a model from the print world as a guide. Does your material resemble a printed catalog, with lots of listings of part numbers? Or is it a technical support bulletin that has separated, self-contained sections? Or does it resemble book in which one chapter leads into the next?

Depending on the sources you are using to process your company data into a form suitable for display on your Web site, you may be able to automate the data-preparation to save time and effort. For example, if you routinely calculate new prices at the end of each month, be sure this data is in a form that you can convert easily to an HTML document.

If you are a parts distributor and you add several hundred new parts to your inventory each month, be sure that your suppliers give you the information that you need in the right form. And if you are presenting training material or policies and procedures materials, buy one of the converters available to process this material into the right form for your Web site. Do you want your employees to have access to a corporate database? If so, what sort of database support is needed—Microsoft's ODBC or SQL? Later in this chapter, we'll look at some applications you might want to use for some of these tasks.

Going Live

Once you assemble all the pieces, it is time to bring up your Intranet and start providing service to your users. Beginning with a small number of test users is the best way to start; you can bring more and more users online after you iron out the startup wrinkles. Feedback is likely to be loud and immediate, and you will find some of it useful. Implement the best suggestions as you broaden the scope of your Intranet and increase the number of users.

As you read through the Intranet case studies later in this chapter, you will see that several of the most successful Intranet sites started as pilot or proof-of-concept projects that later grew into full-fledged Intranets.

If you find that you are providing access to hundreds or thousands of constantly changing documents as part of your system administration duties, consider using one of the document management packages available; several are detailed in the section "Finding Intranet Products" later in this chapter.

Providing User Training

One of the greatest attractions of using an Intranet is that all users need learn and use only one application, the Web browser. Unfortunately, new versions of the two most popular Web browsers seem to appear every few months, and version control, distribution, and user training can be a nightmare.

First, you have to decide if the new version of the browser will actually bring any benefit to your users; perhaps it offers new features your users want or fixes an annoying bug. Once you decide that you need the new version, you have to figure out how to distribute it in a reasonable and cost-effective way, and you have to ascertain if your users will need additional training as a result of the new features.

Managing Browser Support Issues

The last section pointed out the need for user training as browsers change, but what should technical support staff do in the face of constantly changing browsers? Here are a few tips you can use whether you support Internet or Intranet Web sites:

- Be sure that your users know your policy and understand which browsers you support and which ones you do not. Publish this policy on your Intranet.

- Most browser problems appear when you try to use the latest and greatest additions or extensions to HTML. By staying just behind the browser curve, you can minimize these.

- Offer training classes in browser use to new users. Not everyone spends the evening surfing the Web and, therefore, intuitively knows how to use a Web browser.

- Stay current with the problems reported on the browser you choose as your main interface to the Intranet.

- If the company currently uses several browsers and you want to support only one, be sure to set a reasonable deadline for when you will stop supporting those other browsers, and be sure everyone knows about your deadline and understands what it means.

- If you plan to support multiple browsers, you should also provide HTML pages optimized for each of them.

- If you plan to support multiple browsers, be sure that you test your Web pages with each of them to see how colors and graphics are displayed.

- If your site relies on a helper application or a browser add-in, distribute it with the browser so that users do not have to wait for it to load from the Intranet.

Most companies do not support more than one browser, but try to keep costs down by choosing one and then ensuring that everyone has access to and training on it. Supporting two or more browsers can increase costs 30 to 50 percent, which is not a viable option for most companies.

Providing Intranet Access to Third Parties

One of the larger questions that will come up sooner or later in your company is whether to allow third parties access to your Intranet. Giving access to others can raise certain security warning flags; so be sure you have a very good business reason for allowing it.

A recent survey from Forrester Research indicates that of the Fortune 1000 companies polled, 46 percent allowed some kind of third-party access, and 26 percent did not. A substantial number, however, almost 30 percent, were planning to add third-party access in the near future.

The same survey asked companies to describe who had access to the Intranet. All responded that their employees had access, 49 percent allowed access by business partners and members of strategic alliances, and 14 percent allowed their customers to access their Intranet.

Twelve Intranet Case Studies

In this part of the chapter, we'll look at some real case studies of how several major companies are employing Web technology in an Intranet. We'll look at how each designed its Intranet and what it hoped to achieve from using it that couldn't be achieved with more traditional networking technologies. Because by definition an Intranet is a closed system and is not accessible by outsiders, I cannot show you any screens for these corporate Intranets.

Boeing Corporation

At Boeing, the aircraft manufacturer located in the Pacific Northwest, the Intranet has been in place since 1995 and consists of 300 Web servers containing more than 50,000 pages of information. Of the current total of 107,000 employees, approximately 25,000 have access to the Intranet, and that number is growing by about 1,000 employees a week.

The company has issued guidelines on what may and may not be posted on the Intranet and offers technical training and help on how to set up new Web sites. The main impetus to establish the Intranet sites, however, comes from the workgroups and individual divisions within the company.

Cargill International

Cargill International is the world's largest privately held corporation, employing more than 70,000 people engaged in commodities trading in every time zone in the world. A year ago, Cargill launched a proof-of-concept pilot project that was received enthusiastically, and now thousands of people are joining the rush to the Intranet.

The current goal is to distribute all sorts of company materials, from product manuals to Human Resources Department information, to employees around the world and to do it as cost effectively as possible. With only 25 percent of the material now on the Intranet, Cargill estimates it saves tens of thousands of dollars every year by posting electronic updates rather than printing, binding, and distributing them by the more traditional methods.

Harris Corporation

The Harris Corporation of Melbourne, Florida, has long used Web-related technology to assist in the its day-to-day business. The present system has grown out of a collection of 80 company bulletin boards, several internal Usenet-like newsgroups, and a collection of automatic listserver e-mail systems.

The Intranet is used for many tasks, including internal job postings, health and safety information, and access to searchable employee databases. It also plays an important role in the company's Quality First drive, which includes a database of best industry practices derived from internal company sources and outside consultants and experts, training materials, and tutorial documents.

Harris has also placed the contents of its "Red Book" on the Intranet. This publication details the policies and procedures governing all Harris business units. Now that it is available on the Intranet, users don't have to track down a physical volume; they can simply access the information they need using a Web browser right from their desktop.

Levi Strauss & Company

Levi Strauss uses an Intranet system called Eureka! as a way to capture and distribute ideas across the corporation. With 37,500 employees in 60 countries, the company needed a way to capture good ideas and implement them while they were still timely, without regard for an individual's geographical location or time zone.

Eureka! began as a pilot project with 25 users at 6 sites; by the time that all divisions worldwide have the appropriate PC hardware in place, the system will be able to support full-motion video. Instead of videotaping and mailing the quarterly employee meetings, Levi will put the video on the server, making it available to everyone in a few short hours. Levi also plans to use Eureka! for training and for distributing consumer research information and clips from Levi's TV commercials from around the world.

Motorola Inc

Motorola's Cellular Subscriber Division (CSD) uses its Intranet to help develop new software. After developing paper-based procedures for defining user requirements, specifying the design process, defining coding standards, and the other elements of the software development process, it was relatively easy to transfer these paper documents to the Web and publish them on the Intranet. The system also has search capabilities and data-entry features and is designed to fulfill the requirements of the Carnegie Mellon's Software Engineering Institute (a program along the lines of ISO 9000), the Total Quality Management certification program.

Promina Health Systems

Promina Health Systems of Atlanta, Georgia, started with two, apparently unrelated goals: to link 9 hospitals, and to get rid of as much paper as possible. The Human Resources Department wanted to publish the policies and procedures manuals—hundreds of pages of complex material—on a network so that everyone could have access to the same up-to-date material.

The result is an Intranet that ties all 9 hospitals together, that is used to distribute Human Resources information, and that takes advantage of several Microsoft Internet-enabled tools such as Word, PowerPoint, and Excel. Before implementing the Intranet, Promina was evaluating IBM's Lotus Notes. Now that the Intranet is gaining steam, it is unlikely that Notes will ever be installed, and that will save a great deal of money.

Future applications under consideration include a phone book, a calendar of events and important dates, a home page for each physician in the system, training systems, and the electronic distribution of the enormous number of policy manuals that each hospital has to publish.

MTC Telemanagement Corporation

MTC, with 140 people in Petaluma, California, sells international telecommunications services such as cellular phones that work in a large number of countries and such as switching services that allow long-distance calls to be routed in the most cost-effective way. Sales are made by 15,000 sales representatives operating in more than 160 countries.

The sales force was linked to company headquarters by long-distance phone and by fax, but as sales grew, so did the cost of doing business. MTC decided to use an Intranet, linked to the Internet by a

Window NT Server running a firewall to preserve system security, to bring down these costs.

To save time and money, MTC decided to keep its existing databases —housed in Microsoft Access, DBF, and SQL—and to use a Web browser as the front end for the sales force. The firewall isolates the Intranet from the Internet and accepts only a limited number of remote procedure calls (RPC). The sales force requests information, and the firewall queries the appropriate ODBC data-base, collects the information, and then formats it in a way suitable for display on the Web browser. By isolating the two parts of the system with ODBC, MTC can upgrade its SQL databases at any point, and the upgrade will have no effect on the front end used by the sales staff.

For security purposes, each member of the sales force has a password and a user ID, and all international transactions are encrypted in both directions. MTC estimates that this system is not only saving a considerable amount of money previously spent on long-distance phone calls, but also that it can increase its worldwide sales force substantially without any additional support staff in Petaluma.

In the past, MTC flew sales representatives to California for two-day company training sessions. Now all the training materials are available on the Intranet, and training can be completed at a fraction of the previous cost.

Sales representatives can also play PowerPoint sales presentations right from the server or can download them for presentation to a client later. As sales-support material becomes outdated, the slides on the server are replaced with new material, and that new material is immediately available to the worldwide sales force. Previously, updates to sales materials and new slide shows might have taken several days to reach outlying districts.

In those areas of the world where Internet access is not available, is slow, or is very expensive, MTC is considering becoming an ISP in support of its worldwide operations. In the future, it may bill over the Intranet, saving printing and postage costs.

Schlumberger Ltd

Schlumberger Ltd is the leading provider of wire-line services to the oil industry all over the world. With worldwide headquarters in Paris, Schlumberger has 51,000 employees in 450 locations in more than 100 countries. Currently, 20,000 people have access to the Intranet.

During the 1980s, Schlumberger established an internal network based on TCP/IP for file transfers and e-mail, and its Intranet grew from these beginnings. The Intranet was not formally planned; it grew as the influence of the Internet grew and is now administered by a 4-person Web support group. About 200 servers are in place; many of them run from an individual's desktop.

This group set standards for the company and produced the guidelines defining the role and responsibilities of the people running the Web sites. It also provides technical training and HTML stylesheets for others to use as templates when establishing new sites. The Web support group charges other departments in the company by the hour for assistance in setting up and maintaining Web sites. The rate is purposely set to be just below what an outside consulting company would charge, making it more cost effective to use the in-house services.

Schlumberger field engineers are on 24-hour call and often find themselves working long hours in the middle of the night at a distant location miles from everywhere. If something goes wrong with their complex electronic logging sondes, they are expected to deal with the problem. Because of this situation and because interpreting the wire-line logs that Schlumberger records can be a highly skilled job, the company established a database of employee skills. Schlumberger already had an employee directory on the Intranet; so it was a relatively modest step to add categories for this additional information. Some of these skills are technical, such as interpreting a specific wire-line tool in a particular geological environment, and others are more general, such as experience in a particular remote oil field.

When a Schlumberger team faces a particularly vexing problem, members can search these skill categories and locate an expert within the company, regardless of where in the world that individual is currently based. The search engine is from Excite Inc and was covered in the *Announcing Your Web Site to the World* chapter earlier in this book.

It comes as no surprise to hear that Schlumberger has developed an unusually keen Intranet awareness. People in the company look to the Intranet first rather than to traditional sources of information. Product centers no longer issue progress reports on paper; they post the report on the Web and send the URL to all interested parties.

Schlumberger still has problems, however, such as how to make older company documents available in a form suitable for posting on the Intranet and how to deal with the information avalanche this will unleash on the corporation. When everything is on the Intranet, simply finding the information you are looking for can become a time-consuming challenge.

Sun Microsystems

As you might imagine, the Intranet at Sun Microsystems plays an important role in several company operations, including training, and includes a journal of articles on several technical subjects, a searchable archive of technical e-mail messages, and a projects registry.

Sun has made training modules available on the Intranet as an alternative to classroom training, which is still available. Engineers can use the Web-based modules to access the information they need immediately, without waiting for a class to roll around on the schedule and without wading through material that they already know and understand. Training is provided in several formats, including plain text, interactive modules, and even some video, although video is used sparingly because of the high bandwidth requirements it places on the system. All training tools contain "hack" sections full of tips and tricks, often contributed by the engineers themselves.

Taco Bell Corporation

The Taco Bell Corporation, a division of PepsiCo, wanted a mechanism that would allow restaurant managers to share information on topics as varied as how to keep produce fresh and what to do when gang members assemble in the dining area.

Taco Bell technical staff looked at Lotus Notes, but decided against it because they had just standardized on Microsoft Office and did not want to go to a different proprietary system. With a network based on TCP/IP and Windows NT Server with Windows 95 on the desktop, using NT Server and the Internet Information Server seemed the best solution. Taco Bell also added the Verity TopicSearch search engine, described in the *Announcing Your Web Site to the World* chapter earlier in this book.

In the early days, questions were raised about security and restricting access to data. Now, restrictions are few, partly because of bandwidth concerns, partly because of the maintenance demands of keeping track of everything, but mostly because upper management decided that restrictions would defeat the purpose of using the Intranet in the first place, which was to energize the company around a common source of information.

Weyerhaeuser

You don't have to have an Intranet just because you have a Web presence on the Internet, or vice versa. One company, Weyerhaeuser of

Tacoma, Washington, has had an Intranet for more than a year, but is still debating the benefits of establishing an external Internet site. The company is not sure that a Web site would be a beneficial addition to the other communications mechanisms already in place.

Weyerhaeuser's Intranet provides up-to-date information about the company and offers one central place for policies such as how to use the company logo, safety information, company benefits, and disaster-recovery services. Weyerhaeuser also has a way to let some of its wholesale customers access parts of the system to list current prices and to place orders for paper.

Comptroller of Public Accounts, Texas

All the case studies we have looked at so far have been from the corporate world; let's close this section with an example from the State of Texas and the Comptroller of Public Accounts.

This agency is responsible for collecting state taxes, for managing the state's properties and assets, and for collecting sales taxes on behalf of more than 1,000 local government bodies and tax districts. Much of the information collected by the agency is contained on a selection of IBM 3270 mainframe systems.

Because a new interface on a legacy system can go a long way toward extending the useful life of that system, the agency decided to add a new graphical user interface and to consolidate some of the fragmented applications and integrate many of the scattered data repositories.

The agency looked at many products before deciding that a Web-based system was a good way to go. This approach requires a layer of software between the legacy back-end databases and the HTML front end, but gave the agency the most flexibility in designing methods to organize and deliver the data. With this division, the developers can take their time replacing the databases and can attack each side of the problem independently. First, they can add Web interface elements to improve access to the data, and then they can replace the underlying systems with better integrated solutions that will lead to less duplication of data.

Making the Most of Your Intranet

As the concept of the corporate Intranet matures, many changes and adjustments will be made. Here are some suggestions for getting the most out of this young and emerging technology:

- Let those people in your company who are most familiar with the content recommend what to post on your Intranet site. Management will have to OK their suggestions or provide guidelines in the case of restricted material, but the people on the ground are the ones who know the value of the information they control.

- Prepare a plan of what material will be posted along with a justification for posting it. After all, posting this information on your Web site is supposed to benefit the company in some way; so you need a good solid business reason to do it.

- Be sure that all material is easily identifiable and that users of your Web site know who posted what information. Always add a contact name, an e-mail address, and an extension number so that people can ask questions or make suggestions.

- Consider adding a FAQ section or organizing a question-and-answer forum so that experienced group members can share information with people from outside your department and with recent arrivals.

- Help others to help themselves. Post hints and tips that other departments can use when creating their sites. Add examples of how to use HTML effectively or how to use scripts to access a corporate database. Create "getting started" documents that show others what you did and how you did it.

- Apply the appropriate level of security, and restrict certain types of information by password access.

- Make your site as useful as possible. Add links to other sites when it makes good sense to do so, but don't do it just because the other sites exist within the company, and never link to a site still under construction.

The corporate Intranet is after all only a tool, and it is merely one of many that can be used to improve internal communications. Installing the hardware and the Internet Information Server is only a very small step in this companywide process.

Groupware and Your Intranet

Many large companies have invested much time and effort in installing and using *groupware*, software that lets people collaborate on the same project from many geographical locations. Companies such as FedEx, Domino's Pizza, and others have linked employees with existing packages such as Lotus Notes or Novell's GroupWise, but these packages can be expensive to buy and to maintain. Just what does Web technology mean for those companies, and what should they do about these legacy applications in light of all this emphasis on the Web?

One way to create a corporate Intranet is by combining groupware applications with Internet technology. Using Lotus InterNotes, for example, groups can track discussions and record conferences, as well as manage other collaborative endeavors. Attachmate's Open

Mind is a similar product; it uses Internet technology to publish documents and manage the requirements of information sharing. Let's take a moment to look at the impact an Intranet might have on a traditional Lotus Notes installation.

Lotus Notes versus an Intranet

The main differences between using a groupware application such as Lotus Notes, with its proprietary file structures and databases, and using an open system based on Web technology, are in philosophy and in cost.

Lotus Notes was originally designed during the early days of the move toward networking and uses proprietary database structures that replicate data and does not always allow for easy access to remote databases. A Web server such as IIS can support either an Internet Web site, an Intranet Web site, or both at the same time, but Lotus Notes is an internal application only.

According to a recent survey, the average cost of a Lotus Notes installation is on the order of $250,000, with an average expected payback time of two years. You will see estimates of what it costs to set up a Web site in the trade press, and many of these estimates are ridiculously low. One recent article suggested quite seriously that a major corporation could move its whole Lotus Notes application to a Web server for a one-time cost of $10,000. Perhaps that company should approach the writer of the article and say that it will pay the writer exactly that amount to make the conversion.

Even after the recent Lotus Notes price reductions, a complete implementation is still relatively expensive. The price of a Notes development client stayed the same at $275, but the Notes Desktop or run-time client price fell 55 percent from $155 to $69 in volume. On the other hand, the costs associated with setting up an Intranet continue to fall. Microsoft bundles both the Web browser software (Internet Explorer) and the Web server software (Internet Information

Server) free with Windows NT Server and has announced plans to integrate the Internet Explorer into the Windows 95 user interface. Both SCO and Hewlett-Packard have also announced plans to add Web support into their operating systems for free, and so the pressure on Lotus Notes continues to mount. Web browsers are available for all the major operating-system platforms; so if you run a mixed hardware/software environment, there is a very good chance that you will be able to find the right browser at the right price.

Mindful that this pressure from Microsoft and others may threaten its core business, Lotus is moving toward including at least some component of Web technology, rather than continue in direct competition; we'll take a look at one such offering, Lotus InterNotes, in the next section. There is no doubt whatsoever that these lower-cost Intranet solutions have caught the eye of many IS professionals and managers at many companies around the world. IS managers now must justify their decisions to invest in Notes rather than take advantage of this "free" Web technology. Lotus will face a long, hard, uphill struggle to regain its previously strong position.

And costs on the Intranet front? The truth is that many companies don't yet know what the true costs of setting up an Intranet are because the technology is so new to the corporate world; others may have spent more than they planned and may not want the world to know.

Using Lotus InterNotes

Lotus has addressed some of the concerns outlined in the last section with the release of Lotus InterNotes, one of the most significant additions in Lotus Notes version 4.2.

InterNotes is a connection between Notes and the Internet and performs two major functions: It retrieves information from the Internet, and it converts that information into Notes database format. Once in this format, the information is available to any Notes client, as is any Notes database.

Users interact with the InterNotes Web Navigator, which looks much like any other Notes database on the desktop. When you ask for a Web page, your request goes to the InterNotes server. If the page is already available on the server, it is loaded immediately at network speed. If the page is not on the server, it is loaded from the Internet. The page is then converted from HTML into Notes format, with all the graphics and links preserved intact.

This approach does have a drawback, in that you can't look at a document until the whole page has been converted into the Notes format; you don't see the text as it loads, and you don't see the graphics as they are painted. This means that you can't preview the text as the graphics are in the process of loading and then change your mind about viewing the page; once you start, you have to finish. The more complex the page, the longer and more frustrating the delay is likely to be, especially to people who have used traditional Web browsers in the past.

InterNotes supports HTML version 2.0 and does not include enhancements such as frames, tiled background images, blinking text, or multimedia support. Interlaced and noninterlaced GIF formats are supported as well as JPEG format files. Lotus promises to make a stream of enhancements as HTML and other extensions are finalized. Some of these changes will require upgrades to the basic Notes document architecture; they may not arrive quickly.

Because the Web pages are stored as Notes databases, you can use them in the same way that you use a normal Notes database. You can make full text searches of Web pages, you can embed a link to a site in an e-mail message so that the recipient can simply click on the name to look at the site, and you can even organize Web-based tours of your competitor's sites as a sales-training aid.

InterNotes also includes agents, which bring the power of a macro to Lotus Notes, and a set of LotusScript functions you can use to access Web data. InterNotes can convert Notes-format files into HTML version 2.0 format files complete with graphics, file attachments, table formatting, and document links. Notes forms become HTML forms, bitmap files in Notes documents become GIF files, and Notes doclinks become hypertext links. Find out more at: `http://www.internotes.lotus.com`.

Not all companies need the top-of-the-line tools that Notes has become and can use a more flexible and cheaper Intranet approach. If you don't need the collaborative work environment that Notes offers, but instead need a way to publish information on a large scale, the Intranet approach makes most sense. An Intranet is easier to set up, does not require a highly skilled and highly paid Notes staff, and has lower software and training costs.

The bottom line is that if your company is faced with deciding on which way to go today, the Web-based approach will undoubtedly be cheaper. If you already have a significant investment in Notes, including the highly skilled technical staff needed to configure and maintain a Notes installation, the decision is much more difficult. It all depends on your corporate goals and what you want to accomplish. To help you arrive at the right decision we'll look at some of the Intranet tools available in the next section.

Finding Intranet Products

The combined Internet/Intranet industry, estimated at $5 billion in 1995, is expected to grow to $42 billion by 1999 according to recent surveys. Most of that revenue is expected to come from developments in Intranet applications. After all, a company may only need to establish one or two Internet sites to serve its purpose, but may establish an unlimited number of Intranet sites.

Because the technical underpinnings for the Internet and Intranets are the same, it is not usually a big jump from one to the other. The growth we are seeing today is driven by the open environment and the ability to solve important problems that businesses face every day in an increasingly competitive world.

Some of the applications covered in this part of the chapter have been designed and written from scratch with the Intranet in mind. Other developers have added HTML front ends to existing legacy applications, allowing them to continue to exploit their features and add value to your Intranet.

Group Discussion Software on Your Intranet

In this section, we'll look at a number of group discussion packages that you can add to your Intranet and that can be accessed by your Web browser. In many ways, these products resemble legacy discussion products such as Collabra Share or Attachmate Corporation's Open Mind or even the group discussion features in Lotus Notes. All the products except one let you look at discussions in a threaded format, arranged by topic with responses indented.

FrontPage

Microsoft's FrontPage is a general-purpose tool for Web construction that happens to include a group discussion feature. Originally developed by Vermeer Technologies, which was later bought by Microsoft, FrontPage includes preprogrammed CGI scripts called WebBots that perform common functions.

To start a new discussion group, first select the Discussion Web Wizard, and then configure the Discussion WebBot parameters, including the name of the discussion and its location on the server. In the main view, you can see all the posts, with replies indented below each one. Once the page is activated and saved, anyone can participate in the discussion, create new topics, and reply to messages from others. Other than disk space, there are no limitations on the number of threads you can begin or on the number of responses to responses you can make; however, you cannot modify a posted message, nor can you attach a file to a message. All messages must be in plain text. For more on FrontPage, see the *Creating Your Web Site with FrontPage* chapter earlier in this book.

net.Thread

net.Thread, from the net.Genesis Corporation, provides simple discussion features, but lacks some of the more advanced features such as multiple message views and file attachments. You can create new discussion groups using a template, and these discussion groups can even be moderated, but to add bold, italic, or bulleted text or graphics to your messages, you must add the appropriate HTML tags yourself. There are no limits on the number of messages or responses you can post. For more information, check out the Genesis Web site at: `http://www.netgen.com/`.

Web Crossing

Web Crossing, from Lundeen and Associates, lets you create discussion groups, but presents each conversation topic as a single chronological list instead of a series of threads and responses. Special buttons such as Post, Edit, and Add Topic make it easy to create new messages. All the messages are stored in a proprietary format and are converted to HTML on the fly as they are needed. You can add bold and italic text using an HTML editor, but if you want to add a link to a file or add a graphic, you will have to do so by hand. You can edit your own messages for up to 30 minutes after you post them, and you can delete your own messages at any time. The Lundeen and Associates Web site contains a guided tour that demonstrates all the features of Web Crossing and also contains a sample discussion page. Take the tour at: `http://webx.lundeen.com/`.

Workgroup Web and Workgroup Web Forum

Workgroup Web and Workgroup Web Forum are both from the Digital Equipment Corporation (DEC). Workgroup Web is aimed at smaller discussion groups, and Workgroup Web Forum is a more fully featured product. Both products will run without any kind of Web server; however, you will need a Web browser, and you will have to install some proprietary client software from DEC to run Workgroup Web.

Workgroup Web

Workgroup Web is aimed at smaller discussion groups and would be fine for a small company or a single department. You don't need a Web server, and you don't have to use TCP/IP; Workgroup Web will operate over almost all the popular networking protocols.

Once a discussion folder has been opened, anyone can post messages and replies and can even insert pointers to documents in the current discussion folder. Although the discussions are threaded, you can only look at direct responses to each message on a single screen. Workgroup Web does not recognize HTML in the message fields; so you cannot add HTML tags to your messages.

You can search using keywords or phrases; Workgroup Web lists those that meet your search options in a separate page with links back to the original documents. There are no limits to the number of messages or replies, but users cannot modify or delete their messages once they have been posted to the group.

Workgroup Web Forum

Although Workgroup Web Forum is similar to Workgroup Web in many ways, it does not require the addition of proprietary software from DEC. All you need is a Web browser. Forum provides more power than the Workgroup Web, including more complex search options and the ability to search using Boolean operators. You can use HTML tags in your messages, but you must code them by hand. You can attach documents by uploading them to the Web server in their original format, and you can insert URL pointers to other Web servers.

Forum has a moderator feature; so you can look at messages before they are posted. It even has a feature for online voting on a topic that lets you chart the ballot results to show how users voted. You can find out more about both Workgroup Web and Workgroup Web Forum at the DEC Web site. Check into: `http://www.digital.com`.

And Still to Come

Several software developers have announced plans for exciting new Intranet products to ship in the near future. askSam Systems plans to make its popular flat-file database available to Intranet users with the forthcoming askSam Web Publisher, which can convert any askSam data file into HTML on the fly. For more information, see the askSam Web site at: `http://www.asksam.com`.

Attachmate is offering its Emissary Workgroup Emcee package, which you can use to create discussion groups, send and receive e-mail, and attach files to messages. Emcee is a new version of Attachmate's OpenMind collaboration package that now includes HTML and CGI. Find out more at: `http://attachmate.com`.

Novell's GroupWise now includes GroupWise Web Access, which allows any Web browser to access a GroupWise in-box via an Intranet. Using the Web browser, you will be able to send and receive e-mail, set up meetings, and view files and faxes. Web Access requires an existing GroupWise installation and access to a GroupWise Post Office server. Check out Novell's Web site at: `http://www.novell.com`.

Several companies have adapted their bulletin-board software to run on an Intranet, including Galacticomm Inc's Worldgroup and Searchlight Software's Spinnaker Web Server. For more information, contact: `http://www.gcomm.com` or `http://www.searchlight.com`.

Workflow Software on Your Intranet

Workflow software helps you to move and manage information, combining the functions of e-mail, imaging, and document-management software. A document moves through various stages of processing as it is edited, signed, or validated by members of the group, and each stage is orchestrated by the workflow software. For instance, a technical support help desk might use workflow software to track a design-change request on a piece of hardware or a bug fix to a software package. The change request is logged into the system and is then tracked as it proceeds from customer service to product management to design engineer to manufacturing engineer, to purchasing, and finally to manufacturing, where the change is made on the production line.

ActionWorkflow Metro

ActionWorkflow Metro from Action Technologies lets your employees and suppliers access workflow applications using a standard Web browser instead of a licensed proprietary application running on each desktop. This package is expensive, but also includes 20 complete example workflow applications you can use right out of the box for customer service and technical support, sales and marketing, finance and accounting, and human resources. If one of these bundled applications does not meet your requirements, Action Technologies also provides the Metro Development Center, which you can use to create your own custom workflow application. See the Action Technologies Web site at: `http://www.actiontech.com`.

Ultimus Workflow Starter Kit

The Ultimus Workflow Starter Kit with WebFlow includes Ultimus' engine, WebFlow, a forms designer and a graphical design interface that lets you specify workflow rules, and five client packages. Although Ultimus cannot track the workflow process, any user can initiate a workflow action using a Web browser. For more information, see: `http://www.ultimus1.com`.

Having Webbed Suites

The three major developers of software suites—Microsoft, Lotus, and now Corel (Corel bought most of the PerfectOffice Suite from Novell)—have all been busy adding Intranet features to their suites of programs and, no doubt, will add more features in the future. Let's take a look.

Microsoft Office

The applications in Microsoft Office suite all have a layer of software known as DocObjects, which is part of Microsoft's OLE (Object Linking and Embedding) strategy and which allows your Intranet and desktop applications to know about one another. For example, if you are looking at a Web page with Internet Explorer and you see a link to a Word document, the DocObjects technology automatically launches Word for you.

Microsoft also offers Internet Assistants for Excel, PowerPoint, and Word with which you can create HTML documents. These tools are available free from Microsoft's Web site, but they are not yet integrated into the full shipping product.

If you don't currently have the Office suite of programs, Microsoft offers a set of free stand-alone viewers for each of the Office applications so that you can view and print documents created in Excel, PowerPoint, or Word. These viewers are very easy to use. If you are browsing a page that contains a Word document, simply click on the document, and the viewer loads and displays the contents of the document. The viewers and Internet Assistants are all available from Microsoft's Web site at: `http://www.microsoft.com/msoffice/`.

Lotus SmartSuite

The latest version of Lotus SmartSuite was designed right from the start to allow users to share, access, and publish information on the Internet or on a local Intranet.

SmartSuite includes an HTML editor you can use with the WordPro and the Freelance Graphics applications; Word Pro can also function as a mini-browser by letting you open URLs. With Freelance Graphics, you can save presentations into linked HTML pages. You simply create the documents using standard text and graphics, and SmartSuite converts them to HTML format automatically. Find out more from the Lotus Web site at: `http://www.lotus.com`.

PerfectOffice

The PerfectOffice suite has had a checkered ownership history: Novell bought WordPerfect from the WordPerfect Corporation and bought the Quattro Pro spreadsheet from Borland International and combined them with other programs into a suite that Novell thought could rival Microsoft's Office suite. Novell has since sold the suite to the Corel Corporation, its current owners.

Corel has announced plans to make PerfectOffice Intranet and Internet aware. Both WordPerfect and Quattro will be able to create and save documents in HTML and save existing HTML documents. Each of the existing applications will include a URL linking feature that will launch a browser when you click on a Web address in a document; and in a Quattro Pro spreadsheet, you will be able to link formulas in cells to HTML documents.

The Future of Intranet Applications

More and more companies, government organizations, and nonprofit agencies are realizing the benefits of using a Web-based Intranet as the solution to all sorts of business problems. By adding a Web server to an existing TCP/IP network, organizations can distribute and update a huge variety of corporate information, while improving efficiency and reducing costs.

Web servers are based on open systems and as such represent a very different approach from proprietary systems such as Lotus Notes and other commercial collaborative software. The costs associated with implementing these open system solutions are much lower than the costs of designing, implementing, and managing a Lotus Notes installation.

As development tools increase in ability and complexity, Web sites will become more dynamic, and it will become much easier to build applications associated with Web servers that allow complex transactions against databases, legacy systems, and other important corporate information sources. Better authoring tools will allow people to create and publish multimedia Web pages rich in content much more easily. Better management tools will allow fewer people to support larger and larger installations without sacrificing control, and improved security systems will make sure that users are authorized to access the information they seek.

Proper installation of an Intranet certainly requires careful planning and a clear understanding of the corporate goals involved, but can bring a cost-effective and efficiency improvement in corporate communications across the entire enterprise.

CHAPTER

FIFTEEN

15

Putting Your
Intranet to Work

- Configuring TCP/IP on your workstations

- Security and your Intranet

- Looking at Peer Web Services on Windows NT Workstation

- Using Internet Explorer

- Configuring IIS with Internet Explorer

- Getting the most out of Index Server

Most corporate Intranets are based on Web servers made available to employees by the local area network or by dial-up access. By providing links to corporate databases, these Intranets provide information to people using a common interface, that of the Web browser, no matter where the data they are working with is actually stored. The corporate Intranet effectively provides a layer of data that is essentially independent of the underlying operating system; almost anyone running a Web browser on any hardware/software platform can access information using the same browser he or she uses to surf the Web. And as the Java programming language becomes more popular, this trend is likely to increase.

In the last chapter, we looked at the ways people are using Intranet technology to solve specific problems in the workplace. In this chapter, we'll look at some of the tools you can use to set up your Intranet. I'll go through the process of setting up your workstations to use the TCP/IP suite of protocols and then look at Intranet security concerns. I'll cover the Microsoft Web browser, the Internet Explorer, in detail, describe the new Peer Web Service included in NT Workstation 4, and then close out the chapter by taking a long look at Microsoft's search engine, Index Server.

Configuring TCP/IP on Your Workstations

One of the unanticipated costs of setting up a corporate Intranet is converting your network to the TCP/IP family of networking protocols. If your local area network already uses TCP/IP, you are home free; but converting can present both hardware and configuration problems.

If you don't want to adopt TCP/IP as your new standard, you can use one of several TCP/IP gateway products from companies such as Firefox or Performance Technologies. These gateways translate between TCP/IP and Novell's IPX (Internet Packet Exchange) or NetBIOS and help to reduce many of the startup problems associated with converting a local area network.

If you are using NT Server, there is a very good chance that you are also using either NT Workstation or Windows 95 as your workstation operating system. In the next two sections, we'll look at configuring TCP/IP for both these operating systems. Now that NT Server and NT Workstation are both using the familiar Windows 95 user interface, there are actually very few differences to note.

TCP/IP on Windows NT Workstation

Configuring TCP/IP on NT Workstation is much the same as configuring it on NT Server; so I'll review the process very quickly here:

1. Choose Start, choose Settings, and then open the Control Panel.

2. Double-click on the Network icon to open the Network dialog box.

3. In the Network dialog box, click on the Protocols tab, and then select Add.

4. In the Select Network Protocol dialog box, choose TCP/IP from the protocols in the list box and click on OK.

5. Back in the Network dialog box, select TCP/IP in the list box, and click on the Properties button.

6. The Microsoft TCP/IP Properties dialog box opens with the following tabs:

   - **IP Address.** Lets you set up an IP address for this computer.
   - **DNS.** Allows you to configure DNS name resolution.
   - **WINS Address.** Lets you configure the Windows Internet Naming Service.
   - **Routing.** Lets you enable IP forwarding.

7. Configure these settings and then click on OK.

8. In the Network dialog box, click on OK.

You should then shut down and restart Windows NT Workstation so that these new settings can all be loaded and configured for use. For more information on the TCP/IP configuration settings, see the *TCP/IP in a Nutshell* chapter.

TCP/IP on Windows 95

To install TCP/IP support on Windows 95, follow these steps:

1. Choose Start, Settings, Control Panel. In the Control Panel, double-click on the Network icon.

2. In the Network dialog box, as shown in Figure 15.1, click on the Add button.

3. In the Select Network Component Type dialog box, click on Protocol, and then click on Add.

4. In the Select Network Protocol dialog box, shown in Figure 15.2, choose Microsoft from the list in the Manufacturers list box, and select TCP/IP from the Network Protocols list box. Click on OK.

5. When the Configuration dialog box appears again, highlight the TCP/IP protocol and then click on the Properties button.

FIGURE 15.1:

The Network dialog box

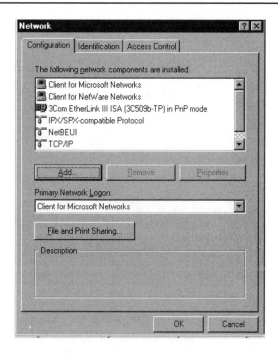

FIGURE 15.2:

The Select Network
Protocol dialog box

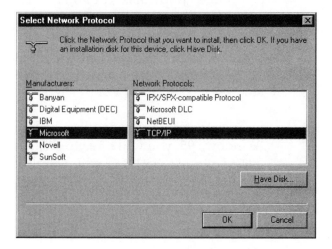

6. The TCP/IP Properties dialog box has a number of tabs across the top that you can use to configure your installation. All these configuration settings were described in detail in the *TCP/IP in a Nutshell* chapter, but to recap very quickly:

- **IP Address.** Lets you set up an IP address for this computer.
- **WINS Configuration.** Allows you to configure WINS name resolution.
- **DNS Configuration.** Allows you to configure DNS name resolution.
- **Gateway**. Lets you set up a gateway.
- **Bindings.** Lets you configure the protocol bindings that you will need.
- **Advanced.** Lets you set various protocol-specific parameters.

7. Click on OK when your configuration is complete to return to the Network dialog box, and then click on OK again to return to the Control Panel. Windows may ask you to load one or more floppy disks, or it may access your Windows 95 CD.

8. Close the Control Panel and restart Windows 95.

For more information on this and other Windows 95 topics, see Robert Cowart's excellent book *Mastering Windows 95*, available from Sybex.

Once the protocol is in place on both NT Workstation and Windows 95, you will have to create the appropriate accounts on NT Server for each user who wants access to your Intranet.

TCP/IP and Unix

The TCP/IP family of networking protocols originated in the Unix world; so you are unlikely to have any problems connecting

Unix workstations to your NT Server. Depending on the variety of Unix you are using, however, you may run into problems sharing files. The Unix world has long used NFS (Network File System), a distributed file system developed by Sun Microsystems more than a decade ago.

NFS is platform independent and runs on mainframes, minicomputers, RISC-based workstations, and PCs. NFS has been licensed and implemented by more than 300 vendors.

You should also note that Unix uses forward slashes (/) rather than backslashes (\) to separate file and directory names; that's another Unix feature.

Security and Your Intranet

In two earlier chapters, *Windows NT Server Operating System Security* and *External Security and Firewalls*, we looked at all the aspects of internal and external security and paid particular attention to maintaining security with your Internet connection. Your Intranet can provide all the benefits of using Internet technology without the risk of invasion by hostile intruders. Users access your private Intranet from the local area network or by dial-up connections; but without connections to the outside world of the Internet, you can operate in isolation. Your Intranet is an island that does not appear on any of the usual maps.

Because one of the objectives in establishing your Intranet was to give people access to information, you may see little need to secure it. As you saw in the *External Security and Firewalls* chapter, however, many intruders are actually employees too. Although much of the information on your Intranet may be accessible by all and sundry, some of it may require tighter control, particularly corporate financial information and personnel records.

In fact, you should think long and hard about the benefits of making this kind of information available, and weigh those benefits against the drawbacks. Certain kinds of information will always be better controlled by more traditional means—filing cabinets and locked doors. You, and only you, can specify the level of security needed on your Intranet.

Internet Information Server can help you manage the access function smoothly and efficiently, as you saw in the *Advanced Web Site Administration* chapter. You can use the Internet Service Manager to allow or deny access based on an IP address or by a username.

And on a final note, remember that CGI scripts can be a security hole in an Intranet just as they can on an Internet Web site. CGI scripts make the interactive forms on your Intranet actually work, but when writing them, never assume what data a user may actually enter into one of your forms. Even though a field on a form is labeled "e-mail" address, do not assume that you will get a valid e-mail address when you read this field.

People make accidental typographical errors, and they also enter the wrong information on purpose, just to see what might happen. Curious users may enter all sorts of characters, including wildcard characters such as * or ?, a pipe symbol (|), or a dollar sign, semicolon, or a colon in an attempt to gain access to a command prompt. Others may try to blow up your program by entering huge strings of letters or numbers. To be secure, your scripts must anticipate and then deal appropriately with unexpected input.

Other problems with CGI scripts include the following:

- Calling an external program that then opens up possible security holes that a malicious user can exploit
- Using include files (See the "Using Server Side Includes" section in the *Advanced Web Site Administration* chapter for more on this topic.)

Looking at Peer Web Services on Windows NT Workstation

Microsoft Peer Web Services is a smaller, personal Web server, optimized for use on Windows NT Workstation 4. You can create your own personal Web server running on Windows NT Workstation, and other network users can access your HTML files using their copy of Microsoft's Internet Explorer. You can even use Peer Web Services for developing and testing HTML content or ISAPI scripts that you plan to publish with IIS, using the Web, FTP, or Gopher services. The first task is to install Peer Web Services.

Installing Peer Web Services

Once you have installed NT Workstation 4, adding Peer Web Services is straightforward. Put your original NT Workstation 4 CD into your CD-ROM drive, and follow these steps:

1. Choose Start and then Settings, and open the Control Panel.
2. Double-click on the Network icon.
3. In the Network dialog box, select the Services tab, and then click on the Add button.
4. In the Select Network Services dialog box, choose Microsoft Peer Web Services in the list box and then click on OK.
5. Read the information in the Microsoft Peer Web Services Setup dialog box, and then click on OK to continue the installation.
6. In the Microsoft Peer Web Services Setup dialog box, select the Web services you want to install; all are checked by default. Click on OK to continue.

7. In the Publishing Directories dialog box, either accept the default directory names for Web, FTP, and Gopher publishing, or enter your own names. Click on OK to continue.

8. Setup copies files from your CD to your hard disk and tells you when the installation is complete. Click on OK to return to the Network dialog box, and then click on Close to return to the Control Panel.

When you return to the NT Workstation desktop, you will find that your Programs menu now contains an entry for Microsoft Peer Web Services, which in turn contains:

- **Internet Service Manager.** Starts the Internet Service Manager (ISM), which you use to monitor and control Microsoft Peer Web Services. ISM is described in detail in the *Advanced Web Site Administration* chapter.

- **Key Manager.** Gives you access to the Key Manager utility. For more information, see the "Using Key Manager" section in the *Advanced Web Site Administration* chapter.

- **Peer Web Setup.** Gives you access to the Setup program so that you can change your configuration or even remove Peer Web Services altogether.

- **Product Documentation.** A comprehensive online manual that you can access using the Topics selection in the ISM Help menu. You can also look at this documentation on your NT Workstation installation CD before you install Peer Web Services by using the Internet Explorer to see the files in `\inetsrv\htmldocs\inetdocs\inetdocs.htm`

The day-to-day operation of Peer Web Services is very similar to that of IIS. Let's take a look.

Configuring Peer Web Services

After you install Peer Web Services on your NT Workstation, you can look at and configure the various settings using the Internet Service Manager (ISM). ISM was described in detail in the *Advanced Web Site Administration* chapter, and the only differences you need to remember when using ISM with Peer Services are differences in scale. Internet Information Server is intended to run a major Web site supporting many hundreds of simultaneous Internet connections, and Peer Web Services is designed for use with only a few users accessing your own personal Web pages across a corporate Intranet. There are other smaller differences. Peer Web Services can log only to a file; so if you want the option of logging to a SQL or ODBC database, you must use IIS instead.

Using Internet Explorer

Microsoft was late in joining the browser game, but now that it is firmly committed to the race, it is releasing improved versions of the Internet Explorer at an astonishing rate. Windows NT includes version 2, but Microsoft is planning a whole series of upgrade releases for the immediate future.

Since employees can use their Web browser to access information on the Intranet, send e-mail, and access corporate databases, your training costs are reduced substantially, and employees feel much more comfortable using a single application for all major tasks rather than having to learn a new interface for each one.

Playing Tag

Internet Explorer gets very high marks indeed for being able to display almost all the HTML 2.0 specification tags, as well as many from

HTML 3.0, including most of the popular Netscape extensions such as tables, font colors, and background images.

The only important Netscape extensions that the Explorer cannot display are Netscape-style frames and the 3-D shading effect on table borders. Many of those sites that claim to be "best viewed with Netscape" actually look just fine when you use Explorer.

And it wouldn't be a Microsoft product if it didn't include a few new tags that (at least for the moment) only Internet Explorer can display. The most popular of these new tags is the marquee: a line of text that marches across the screen just like the displays in Times Square in New York.

The Internet Explorer can display Usenet newsgroup posts, but it does not allow you to look at posts by thread. It also does not contain a way to view encoded binaries.

Although the Explorer can go the distance when displaying static Web pages, it is still a long way behind when it comes to multimedia and animation. Many plug-ins are available for the Netscape Navigator, and very few are available for the Explorer; but this is bound to change in the very near future.

The Big Picture

There is close integration among all the desktop user interfaces across the Windows 95, Windows NT Desktop, and Windows NT Server line of products, and this is very well demonstrated in the Internet Explorer. Explorer and Microsoft Office applications look very similar and in fact share many screen, toolbar, and menu layouts. Once again, Microsoft is working with the assumption that you should only have to learn how to do something once and then be able to apply that knowledge in all your other applications.

Using Internet Explorer

To start the Internet Explorer, double-click on the Internet Explorer icon on the Windows NT desktop. You will see the main display shown in Figure 15.3.

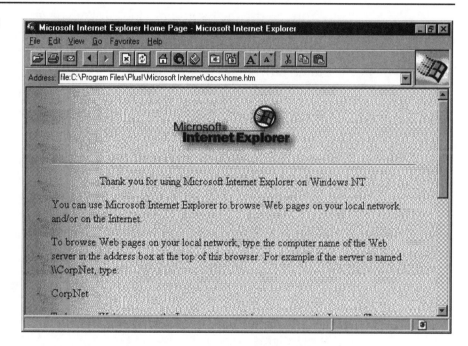

If you have used one of the other popular Web browsers or have used the Microsoft Office suite of products, this display will look familiar. Across the top of the main window you will see a line of menu selections, and then below them you will see the toolbar. Some of the functions contained in the menus are duplicated on the toolbar for convenience.

Next, you will see the Address box. If you are working on an Intranet, you enter the name of the Web server here; if you are working with the Internet, you enter the URL of the Web site that you want to access. The main part of the window is taken up by the area in which the material contained in the HTML files is actually displayed. The scroll bars on the sides of the display work as you expect, allowing you to scroll up or down through the document. You can open multiple documents in the Explorer, and you can use the selections in the Edit menu or the buttons on the toolbar to copy and paste data in all the usual ways.

You can use the Explorer to look at Web pages on the Internet (in which case you will need a direct connection or a connection via RAS to the Internet) or on a corporate Intranet. To look at HTML files stored on your own local area network, type the name of the computer that runs the Web server in the Address box at the top of the main Internet Explorer window just below the toolbar, and the home page or default document will be displayed.

You can also use the Open selection from the File menu to perform this task; either type the URL into the Address box, or click on Open File if you want to look at a local HTML file. Either way, once the file is downloaded from the server (irrespective of where the server is actually located), the HTML file is displayed in the main part of the window.

To locate a word in the document currently being displayed, choose Find from the Edit menu. Type the word you are looking for, and then click on Find Next; when Internet Explorer finds the word, it highlights the word in the text.

To save a copy of the current HTML file to your own hard drive choose File ➤ Save As.

Configuring Internet Explorer

Use the selections in the View menu to configure the Internet Explorer to your needs. You can check or clear the checkmarks opposite the first three items in the menu—Toolbar, Address Bar, and Status Bar—to turn these three window elements on or off. I suggest that you leave them on for the time being; you can turn them off when you are more familiar with the operation of the Explorer. When you do turn them off, the display real estate that they occupied is made available to the main display area of the window so that you can see more of the HTML document.

The Fonts choice lets you change the point size of the font used in the main display; this can be very useful on some sites that display text in tiny type. You can also use the two toolbar icons labeled with the large and small letter A to change the size of the type in the display window.

The next two options in the View menu are to help you manage the display process. Choose Stop to halt the loading of the current HTML page, and choose Refresh to redisplay the current page.

The Options selection in the View menu lets you set up many of the Internet Explorer's custom features; so we'll look at this selection a little more closely. Figure 15.4 shows the Options dialog box open at the Appearance tab.

The Options dialog box has the following tabs:

- **Advanced.** Lets you set cache parameters and history information.

- **Appearance.** Lets you select the proportional and the monospaced fonts to use when displaying a document and specify how you want to display shortcuts.

- **File Types.** Lets you look at existing or specify new file type associations for Internet Explorer. This is where you specify which application should load to display a specific non-Web file type such as a Word DOC file or a TIF image file.

- **News.** Lets you set up a Usenet news server so that you can read and post articles to Usenet newsgroups.

- **Security.** Lets you set up Internet Explorer security for both sending and receiving information.

FIGURE 15.4:

The Appearance tab of
the Options dialog box

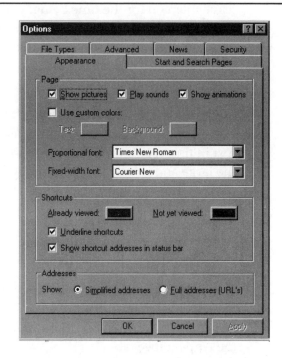

- **Start and Search Pages.** Lets you specify the Internet or an Intranet start page you want each Internet Explorer session to display first, and lets you specify the location of your favorite search engine. You will go directly to this search engine site when you click on the Search the Internet button on the toolbar. You can also use this tab to set both these sites back to their original default values after you have changed them.

Go through these tabs, setting the configuration parameters as you wish. Most will work just fine with their original default settings.

Finding Your Favorite Places

Internet Explorer lets you store the locations of your favorite sites as bookmarks so that you can load them quickly the next time you want to visit them. When you find a site that you think you might want to return to in the future, be sure that the site is displayed in the main Explorer window and then choose Add to Favorites from the Favorites menu or click on the Add to Favorites button on the toolbar.

The next time you want to visit this site, simply click on the Open Favorites button on the toolbar or select the Open Favorites selection from the Favorites menu and double-click on the site in the Favorites dialog box. You will also see that the name of the site is added to the bottom of the Favorites menu, and you can simply select it from the menu if you wish.

Speeding Up Internet Explorer

If you are more concerned with speed of access than with looking at all the graphics on a page when using the Internet Explorer, you can change a couple of settings to speed things up:

1. From the View menu, choose Options.

2. Select the Appearance tab.

3. Be sure that the Show Pictures, Play Sounds, and Show Animations boxes are not checked.

Turning off these options will make the Internet Explorer appear to operate much more quickly because it does not now have to load and process graphics, audio, or animation files. Running your Web browser in this mode is often called text mode. If images are still displayed even after you clear the Show Pictures checkbox, you can hide them by using Refresh from the View menu or by using the Refresh icon on the toolbar.

And even if the Show Pictures box is not checked, you can still look at an individual graphic if you right-click on the icon for the graphic and then click Show Picture.

If you want to browse previously viewed pages as quickly as possible and have lots of free space on your hard disk, move the slider in the Cache area of the Advanced tab to the right. Web pages that you have already looked at will now be loaded from the disk cache rather than from the Web site, saving you quite a lot of time. You can also check the Never checkbox to prevent Internet Explorer from updating the cache.

Looking into the Future

Windows NT 4 includes Version 2 of the Internet Explorer, but version 3 is being beta tested and is bound to be available shortly. And version 4 is already registering on the radar. The revision cycle for Web browsers is very short indeed, with the major players releasing significantly new versions of their products three and even four times a year. This can lead to major version trauma and to confusion on the part of users, not to mention increased training and administration costs.

Microsoft is still very much playing catch-up with Netscape in the browser market, and much of the new work on the Internet Explorer has been done under the hood. Version 3.0 allows you to view content created in Java and JavaScript and includes support for Netscape plug-ins, enabling more than 130 plug-ins written for the Netscape Navigator to run with the Internet Explorer browser.

You can also view Web pages created with Netscape HTML extensions, as well as content created using ActiveX and HTML 3.2 extensions. Internet Explorer includes a just-in-time Java compiler that speeds up Java applets by compiling them as native applications when they are downloaded. The really big question is whether Microsoft's ActiveX technology will catch on in a big way or will fizzle. If ActiveX draws the flood of application developers that Microsoft is hoping for, Internet Explorer version 3 will emerge as a serious challenger to Netscape Navigator.

Microsoft's ultimate goal is to merge the Internet Explorer and the Windows Explorer into one program that you can use to look at the contents of your local hard disk, a hard disk on your local area network, your corporate Intranet, or the Internet.

Configuring IIS with Internet Explorer

Throughout this book I have described how to use a Web browser as a front end so that users can learn one common interface and then apply what they have learned to different tasks. As a demonstration of just how effective a Web browser can be at performing user-interface tasks, Microsoft has provided a mechanism called the HTML Administrator that you can use to configure IIS functions. And to do this, all you need is a copy of the Internet Explorer browser. Here's how it works:

1. Install Internet Information Server on NT Server or install Peer Web Services on NT Workstation.

2. Be sure you are logged on as Administrator.

3. Use the Internet Explorer to open
   `computername/htmla/htmla.htm`.

4. When the Internet Explorer opens as Figure 15.5 shows, simply follow the instructions on the screen.

5. Select a service from WWW, FTP, or Gopher, and you will see that the HTML Administrator screens displayed using the Internet Explorer are very similar to the ISM Property sheets we looked at in the *Advanced Web Site Administration* chapter, although there are indeed some minor differences in style and layout.

FIGURE 15.5:

Using the Internet
Explorer to administer
Internet Services

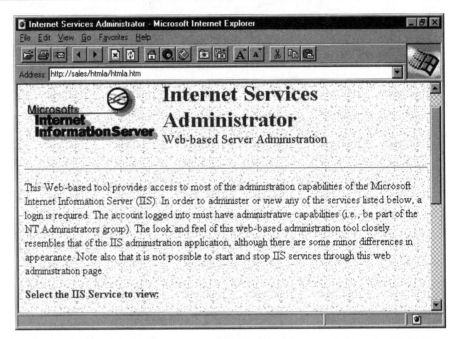

FIGURE 15.5:

Using the Internet Explorer to administer Internet Services

The one function that you cannot perform from within the HTML Administrator is halting or restarting one of the three services; for that task you must use the ISM or the Services applet in the Control Panel.

Several links provided in the HTML Administrator are actually shortcuts to Microsoft's own Web site on the Internet. If you are not connected to the Internet, you will see an Internet Explorer error message telling you the link could not be found when you click on one of these links. Connect to the Internet and try again, and your attempts will meet with success.

Getting the Most out of Index Server

Now that your Intranet is up and running and is loaded with content, someone asks an obvious question, How do we find stuff on the Intranet? Microsoft's Index Server is the answer.

Index Server is a search application, included with NT Server 4, that can search and index ASCII text files, HTML files, and files created by the Microsoft Office and BackOffice suites of products. In addition to full-text searches, you can also search for OLE document properties and HTML tags. Index Server, previously code named Tripoli and at one time called Search Server, is an element of Microsoft's Cairo technology that was released early and is tightly integrated with the NT file system for better efficiency.

Index Server can search across several Internet or Intranet servers running IIS and supports fairly advanced syntactical analysis; so you can find documents or properties based on grammatically correct variations of common nouns or verbs. Index Server also allows users to search through documents written in seven common languages: English (U.S. and International), Dutch, French, German, Italian, Spanish, and Swedish.

Designed for a "no maintenance" environment, Index Server requires that IIS or Peer Web Server run 24 hours a day, seven days a week. Once set up, however, all operations are automatic, including index updates and optimization—even crash recovery after a hardware problem or a power failure. Index Server requires NT Server 4 or Workstation 4; it will not run on NT 3.5 or 3.51 systems.

The Query Language

At the heart of Index Server is the query language that makes everything happen. The rules to follow when you create a query can be summarized as follows:

- All queries are case-insensitive; you can use upper- or lowercase, and the results of the search will be the same.

- A group of consecutive words is treated as a complete phrase and must appear in a document in the same order.

- You can search for any word in a document except those on the exception list. Common words such as *a*, *and*, and *as* are ignored to avoid creating thousands of unwanted matches.

- You can use the Boolean operators and, or, and not in a search.

- You can use the proximity operator near in a search.

- You can use a wildcard character to match words with a particular prefix.

- Common punctuation marks such as the period, comma, colon, and semicolon are ignored.

- To use punctuation marks that have a special meaning, enclose the whole query in quotation marks.

- You can also search on file attributes, values, and ActiveX attributes.

Let's take a look at how some of these search elements actually work, starting with free text queries.

Free Text Queries

You can use free text queries to find pages that contain a match for a word or a phrase that you specify by entering it into the search field.

If you enter multiple words, separate them with commas. This search:

```
rock, star
```

looks for all occurrences of the word *rock* and the word *star*. To combine these words into a phrase, enclose them in quotation marks:

```
"rock star"
```

and the results of the search will be very different indeed.

You can also make content searches. This is done by finding pages that match the meaning rather than those that match the exact wording of your query. Boolean, proximity, and wildcard query operators are ignored during a free text query, and all content queries must be prefixed with $contents.

To search for all the pages that mention saving files in Microsoft Word, you would use the following query:

```
$contents how do I save files in Microsoft Word?
```

Vector Space Queries

A variation on a free text query is the vector space query. This a complicated-sounding name for a search that ranks the results of a query according to a weighting system, in which the rank of each page indicates how well the result matches the query. Separate the individual components in a vector space query by using commas, and you can specify the weighting by adding a number in square brackets like this:

```
tulip[50], bulb[400]
```

Wildcard Queries

You can use wildcard queries to match words with a common prefix. For example, the query:

```
moth*
```

matches *moth, mother, mothball,* and *mother-in-law,* among others. You can also look for words with a common root. The query:

```
walk**
```

will find pages containing words based on the same root, such as *walking, walked, walker,* and so on.

Regular Expression Queries

Queries based on regular expressions are a little more complex. The term *regular expression* originated in the Unix world, and many popular Unix utilities use regular expressions.

A regular expression is a sequence of characters that can match a set of fixed-text strings used in searching text. Many of the characters only match themselves, and other characters have special meanings. Table 15.1 lists the characters that have a special meaning in Index Server queries.

The material in Table 15.1 looks rather gruesome, but it is really straightforward. A few examples will help clear up any lingering doubts. Here are some more rules to remember:

- Any character matches itself except for the special characters shown in the table. This means that an m matches an m, just as you might imagine.

- You must enclose regular expressions within quotes if they contain space characters.

So lets get on with the examples. To find all the uppercase letters, use:

```
[A-Z]
```

and to find all the other lowercase letters, characters, and numbers, use:

```
[^A-Z]
```

You can combine these characters and query options to create some very powerful and complex expressions to use in your queries.

TABLE 15.1:   Characters with a special meaning in Index Server queries

Character	Description
Single characters	
*	Matches any number of characters
.	Matches a period or the end of a sentence
?	Matches a single character
|	The escape character; gives a special meaning to characters that follow
Special meaning after an Escape character	
(	Opens a group; must be followed by a)
)	Closes a group; must be preceded by a (
[	Opens a character class; must be followed by a]
]	Closes a character class; must be preceded by a [
{	Opens a counted match; must be followed by a }
}	Closes a counted match; must be preceded by a {
,	Separates two OR clauses
*	Matches zero or more occurrences of the preceding expression
+	Matches one or more occurrences of the preceding expression
Special meaning between [and]	
^	Matches everything except the characters that follow; must be the first character following the [
—	Range separator
Special meaning between { and }	
|{m|}	Matches exactly m occurrences of the preceding expression, where m is between 0 and 256
|{m,|}	Matches at least m occurrences of the preceding expression, where m is between 1 and 256
|{m,n|}	Matches between m and n occurrences of the preceding expression, inclusive; m and n must be between 0 and 256

Boolean and Proximity Queries

Boolean queries let you use one of the three Boolean operators—and, or, not—and the proximity queries let you use a similar operator—near. You can write these queries out in full as in:

```
apples and oranges
```

or you can use symbols instead of the operators, as in:

```
apples & oranges
```

Table 15.2 summarizes these operators.

TABLE 15.2:   Boolean and proximity operators

Operator	Symbol
and	&
or	|
not	!
near	~

Here are some rules to bear in mind as you prepare your Boolean and proximity queries:

- If a Boolean or proximity query operator occurs in a free text query, enclose the whole query within quotes. This allows Index Server to look for pages containing the phrase "Laurel and Hardy" rather than the Boolean expression of Laurel and Hardy.

- The near proximity operator returns a match if the words specified in your query appear within 50 words of each other.

- You can use parentheses to nest expressions; the operators inside the parentheses will be evaluated first.

Property Value Queries

You can also search for ActiveX property values, including elements stored in the document summary files prepared by ActiveX-aware applications.

The two kinds of property value queries are:

- **Relational.** Always preceded by an @ symbol, these queries also contain a property name, a relational operator, and a property value. For example, to find all the files larger than 1K, use `@size > 1024.`

- **Regular Expression.** Always preceded by a # symbol, these queries also contain a property name and a regular expression for the property value. For example, to find all the HTML files, use: `#filename *.htm.`

Table 15.3 lists all the relational operators you can use in a property value query, and Table 15.4 lists all the property values you can use in your queries.

TABLE 15.3:   Relational operators

Operator	Description
<	Less than
<=	Less than or equal to
=	Equal to
!=	Not equal to
>=	Greater than or equal to
>	Greater than

TABLE 15.4: Property values

Property value	Description
Access	Time the file was last accessed
All	Matches any property
AllocSize	Size of file's disk allocation
Attrib	File attributes
Classid	Class ID of an object
Change	Time the file was last modified; includes changes to the file's attributes
Characterization	Abstract of document; created by Index Search
Contents	Main content of the file; does not support a relational operator. For example, @Contents billg will find documents containing the word billg; @Contents = billg will find none
Create	Time the file was created
DocAppname	Name of the application that owns the file
DocAuthor	Name of the author of the document
DocCharCount	Number of characters in the document
DocComments	Comments about the document
DocCreatedTime	Time the document was created
DocEditTime	Total time spent editing the file
DocKeywords	Document keywords
DocLastAuthor	Name of the person who worked on the document last
DocLastPrinted	Time the document was last printed
DocLastSavedTm	Time the document was last saved

TABLE 15.4: Property Values (continued)

Property Value	Description
DocPageCount	Number of pages
DocRevNumber	Present version number
DocSubject	Subject of the document
DocTemplate	Name of document template
DocThumbNail	Name of document thumbnail
DocTitle	Title of the document
DocWordCount	Number of words in the document
FileIndex	Unique file ID number
FileName	Name of the file
HitCount	Number of words matching the query in the file
HtmlHRef	Text of HTML HREF
Path	Complete path name, including the filename
Rank	Rank of row; larger numbers indicate better matches
SecurityChange	Time security on the file was changed
ShortFileName	MS-DOS–style filename
Size	File size in bytes
USN	Update Sequence Number on NTFS drives only
VectorProp	Vector properties
Vpath	Virtual path to file
Write	Time file was last written

Date and time values are in the form yyyy/mm/dd hh:mm:ss and are in GMT, and numeric values can be in decimal or, if preceded by 0x, in hexadecimal.

An Index Server Example

For a short tour of Index Server, open the Internet Explorer and use this URL:

```
http://computername/samples/search/query.htm
```

where *computername* is the name of your computer. You will see the search query shown in Figure 15.6 on your screen.

FIGURE 15.6:

An example Index Server query

Enter the query:

```
$contents IIS
```

and click on the Execute Query button. Index Server returns a numbered list of references for that query as Figure 15.7 shows, including item number, a short text abstract, the URL or location of the file, and the file size and time.

An example of Index Server query results

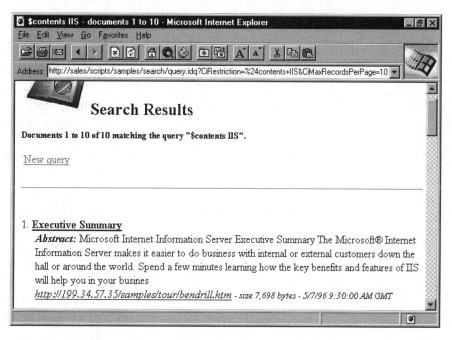

Index Server returns the results of the query in batches of 10; to see the next group, click on the Next Ten button. To start a new query, click on the Clear button and enter your new query. Index Server also includes several other demonstration queries, including:

- File Size Property
- File Modification Time Property
- File Author Property

Index Search is without doubt a convenient and easy-to-use search engine, and it is one you can use on your Intranet or on the Internet, as you please.

Monitoring Index Server Performance

Once you add Index Server to your system, several new counters appear in the Performance Monitor, including the following:

% Cache Hits	Percentage of queries found in the query cache
% Cache Misses	Percentage of queries not found in the query cache
Active Queries	The current number of running queries
Current Requests Queued	The number of pending requests
Queries per Minute	The number of queries processed each minute
Total Queries	The total number of queries processed since Index Server started to run

To prepare statistics on these new counters, choose Add to Chart from the Edit menu in the Performance Monitor. In the Add to Chart dialog box, select HTTP Content Index from the list of options in the Object list box.

CHAPTER
SIXTEEN

16

Future Directions
for the Web

- The future according to Microsoft

- Extensions to HTML

- The sun shines on Java

- Advances in multimedia

- The future of audio and video conferencing

- Advances in Intranets

- Virtual reality and 3-D

- Unleashing personal agents

- The future of Web commerce

- Communications advances

The commercial future of the World Wide Web will be shaped more by developments in back-end applications that run on Web servers than by new developments in browsers. These back-end applications might include order-processing software, financial and accounting applications, and other business-related packages, and they are the programs that will drive the continuing commercial use of the Internet.

One of the most interesting technical debates that will continue into the foreseeable future is between Sun Microsystems and Microsoft over Sun's Java and Microsoft's ActiveX technologies. One is an open approach to the problem, and the other is a more proprietary and closed approach. We'll take a look at the components in this debate later in this chapter.

The noisiest debate will surround the continuing battle between Microsoft and Netscape to dominate the Web browser business; Netscape is the current champion, and Microsoft is in the unusual position (for Microsoft) of being the challenger. This debate is mostly sound and fury, signifying nothing of significance for the continuing commercial development of the Web.

As technology advances, some improvements will be accepted very quickly, and others will take longer. We'll take a look at all these developments in this chapter. Be careful to apply the same evaluation of this technology that you would apply to any other new business strategy. The George Leigh Mallory mountaineer's justification of "Because it is there" is not a sufficient reason to chase after these advances. Ask the same questions you always ask: What is the payoff? What is the return on this investment? And be prepared to leave some of the flashiest glitz behind if you don't perceive a quantifiable benefit.

Some of the most cost-effective advances will be in areas that facilitate communications between the Web server and the corporate database. The large database developers have a long, long lead over Web server developers and are not likely to be caught. Look for advances from companies such as Oracle, Sybase, and the like in the areas of SQL (Structured Query Language), communications, and OLTP (online transaction processing).

Much of the technology we take for granted is still in its infancy, and changes that seem imminent may in fact be several years in the future. But no matter what you call it, change is coming. Let's take a peek at what it might look like.

The Future According to Microsoft

Microsoft came to the Internet late, but it has not lagged behind in recent developments; huge amounts of money and resources have been allocated to develop Microsoft's presence in this exploding market. Much of the current storm between Netscape and Microsoft is in terms of their two browsers and each company's version of several so-called standards.

Currently Netscape claims 80 to 90 percent of the browser market, and Microsoft wants to lower that number by promoting its own browser, the Internet Explorer.

Several important elements form Microsoft's plan of attack, with developments on many fronts, including Windows NT, the Internet Information Server, the Internet Explorer, proposed emerging standards such as ActiveX and ISAPI, additions to Windows 95, and the creation of HTML development tools and editors. Let's look at each of these in turn.

The Future of Windows NT

It must be very obvious to everyone by now that Windows NT has a great future. Microsoft is planning to promote both the server and the workstation editions heavily in the near term, and now that both these versions support the Windows 95 GUI, many previous differences in tools, device drivers, and so on will start to disappear. It was no accident that all Windows 95 applications also had to run on Windows NT to receive Microsoft's blessing and permission to use the "Windows 95 Compatible" logo on their packaging.

And Microsoft is in discussion with other major players to include clustering (several servers mirrored together to provide for fault-tolerant operations) support in Windows NT in the future. This would be a major step forward and would undoubtedly convince many major clients, including Fortune 1000 companies, to consider Windows NT as a platform for mission-critical applications.

Windows NT sales continues to increase in the networking world, previously dominated by Novell and now becoming a much more fragmented arena. Novell recently sold its rights to Unix to SCO (the Santa Cruz Operation), and SCO has announced plans to merge its Unix products with Novell's UnixWare and then work with Hewlett-Packard and other Unix vendors to create a single unified system.

Novell's plans for its own flagship network operating systems seem to lack direction and focus. At one time Novell could claim at least 70 percent of the network operating system business, but with all this uncertainty, that figure has started to fall. All this is good for sales of Windows NT, and Microsoft will take every competitive advantage it can get; there is no doubt whatsoever that Windows NT sales will rise at an astonishing clip over the next two years.

An element that is crucial for the development of any operating system is the availability of the right kinds of applications to run on the operating system. The broadening of the operating system platforms to combine Windows 95 and Window NT is bound to convince more and more third-party software developers that this is a market they cannot afford to ignore. In most cases, the software can be written to run identically on both operating systems.

The Internet Information Server

With Microsoft placing such emphasis on developing Internet and Intranet applications, we can expect a series of releases of the Internet Information Server and associated products over time to build more depth and strength into the product.

Microsoft has already announced that it is working on future releases, as well as products to add several important functions to the server, including a commerce server for secure transactions, links to other back-end products from Microsoft and from other companies, and several important security-related products.

Microsoft's Browser: Internet Explorer

One very visible part of the development effort for Microsoft is its Web browser, the Internet Explorer. Other companies active in the browser field have kept up a punishing schedule of beta software as well as actual releases, with new versions of browsers appearing every three months or so.

To be in the competition, and to catch up to the other major competitors, Microsoft must at least maintain this same pace. If it does not, it will be left behind in the dust—something that doesn't happen to Microsoft very often.

With the release of Internet Explorer 3.0, Microsoft added support for Netscape's HTML extensions, Navigator plug-ins, and Java (more on Java later in this chapter), as well as Microsoft's own new standards of ActiveX, which adapts objects (OCXs) for the Web and has support for ISAPI. Microsoft has also added its own HTML extensions, including the FACE parameter for the FONT tag, which lets designers control typography more closely by specifying a prioritized list of alternative fonts; the use of Cascading Style Sheets (CSS), a proposed standard to allow both author- and reader-defined fonts, spacing, and layout; and the use of background sounds, marquees that allow scrolling text, and watermarks.

But the most important announcement from Microsoft describes plans to integrate the Internet Explorer browser right into Windows 95 and replace the Windows 95 Explorer. This will not only make setup and configuration a breeze, but will further dilute the distinction between local files on your hard disk and remote files on a LAN server, on a corporate Intranet, or on the Internet itself.

The Web continues to evolve at an astonishing rate; remember that there was no such job as a Web page developer just a year or two ago. The rate at which all these innovations are accepted by Web-site developers will determine which of the proposed "standards" will emerge and be widely accepted and which will simply disappear.

Microsoft's ActiveX

Microsoft's answer to Sun Microsystem's object-oriented platform-independent Java programming language is the ActiveX specification, which consists of three main elements:

- ActiveX Controls, which function just like conventional OLE Controls (OLXs). They can be located on your browser or can be downloaded from the server and can be used for something as simple as a button all the way to something as complex as a whole report. ActiveX controls can also interact with one another.

- ActiveX Documents, which allow you to view active documents as well as HTML pages, thus presenting you with a common interface for several tasks.

- ActiveX Scripting, which allows you to coordinate ActiveX Controls on your Web site using the two available scripting languages, JavaScript and the Visual Basic-based VBScript. Eventually, we may even see ActiveX scripting implementations of Sun's JavaScript and of Perl. At this point, VBScript has a smaller run time module, at 50K compared with the 1.2MB needed for Java.

ActiveX controls are not completely incompatible with Java, and Microsoft has not only licensed Java from Sun, but has also agreed to provide a wrapper to make Java applets behave just like ActiveX objects.

And now that ISAPI is gaining ground, we will certainly see other additions to the Visual C++ and Visual Basic programming environments. Anyone serious about developing cutting-edge applications will certainly use the C++ programming language, but many small-to medium-sized organizations already have custom applications developed in Visual Basic that they want to keep or add to. Look for additions to the Microsoft Foundation Classes—a package that programmers use to develop Windows applications—in the future to make the Internet easily accessible to Visual C++ developers.

Microsoft has also announced a set of drop-in ActiveX controls for nonbrowser applications, including the following:

- FTP ActiveX Control, which lets applications use FTP

- HTML ActiveX Control, which lets applications launch their own simple Web browser

- HTTP ActiveX Control, which lets applications behave like simple Web servers

- NNTP ActiveX Control, which gives applications access to Usenet newsgroups and other NNTP news

- SMTP/POP3 ActiveX Control, which lets applications use e-mail without the need to start a separate program

- WinSock ActiveX Control, which provides an interface to the TCP/IP suite of protocols in Windows 95 and Windows NT

These controls are all contained in Microsoft's Internet Control Pack (ICP) and were jointly developed by NetManage Inc and Microsoft.

Nearly all the ActiveX technical papers, downloadable software, tips and tricks can be found on Microsoft's Web site, but you should also visit the ActiveX Gallery at:

```
http://198.105.232.6:80/ie/appdev/controls/
```

The ActiveX Gallery includes a library of ActiveX applications, as well as instructions for downloading the huge 12MB software development kit (SDK).

HTML Development Tools

Another element missing from Microsoft's package is a professional-strength HTML development environment, with editor, syntax checker, viewer, and associated utilities. The various add-ons to Microsoft Word such as Internet Assistant are certainly serviceable, but they lack essential features.

Microsoft's FrontPage works much like a desktop publishing tool to create HTML pages as we saw in the *Creating Your Web Site with FrontPage* chapter; a new release of this product is currently in the works. Internet Studio, which began its life as a content-creation tool for the Microsoft Network, will emerge as the professional HTML development tool, integrating ActiveX and Cascading Style Sheets with HTML extensions and VBScript, as well as collaborative Web development features.

Online Office

There is no doubt that in the near future, everyone's desktop will be seamlessly integrated with the Internet, and Microsoft has plans to secure its share of that future. The requirement that you know exactly where a specific resource is located will become much less important as the old distinctions between your local hard disk, local area network, Intranet, and the Internet become increasingly blurred.

Microsoft will continue to add such features to the Microsoft Office and BackOffice suites of products. Advances will include the ability to download a specialized dictionary for the Java-driven spelling checker to use on your latest technical paper and to collaborate on interoffice work easily over the Internet.

To see local and international news, you will access a collection of information that has been custom prepared for you according to your own biases and preferences, complete with online audio and video. Online magazines will proliferate, and the latest issue will be available as a link to a Web page, rather than as a collection of printed pages sent in the mail.

The direct consequence of all this is the pressure on the existing infrastructure of the Internet and the need for more and more bandwidth. I am not forecasting that the end of the Web is nigh, but toward the end of this chapter, we will take a look at some of the techniques we will be able to use to get around this communications crunch.

Users will begin to expect all servers to be available at all times, creating a need for very reliable hardware—computers and hard disks and perhaps some form of RAID (Redundant Array of Inexpensive Disks) protection.

Extensions to HTML

Undoubtedly, many extensions to HTML will be proposed as time goes on to add features that Web page designers think they need. As this process continues through the current proposals to extend HTML, it is becoming more and more evident that HTML is moving away from describing the structure of a document, which was the original intention behind its design, and is moving toward a page-description language.

Additions to the current VRML language standards (described later in this chapter) will give designers plenty to work with in the short term. The price for these additions will be the need for sympathetic design of Web pages and for increased bandwidth between browser and server. If you are working on a corporate Intranet, LAN speed is usually pretty good; but if you connect to the Internet through a relatively slow analog modem, that is a very different story indeed.

The Sun Shines on Java

Java is a serious programming language originally developed by Sun Microsystems and is not just a source of bad coffee-related jokes. With Java you can create absolutely any kind of software you can imagine that will work across the Internet. What this means to most users is that instead of browsing from site to site, you can now think of the Web as a giant hard disk that contains all the applications you could ever want. Java has the power to add dynamic, interactive content to your Web pages, sending static HTML pages the way of the dinosaurs.

Microsoft's Internet strategy, like that of many companies, has always been to try to impose its own standards on the rest of the industry, and this has usually been done by locking the customer into the set of Microsoft products. Sun, on the other hand, comes from the Unix world, where standards are traditionally much more open. Sun is trying to build Java into a broad, acceptable alternative to Microsoft. Microsoft may bundle products, and sometimes give products away as free promotions, but it would never have distributed Java in the way that Sun has done.

Almost all the popular Web browsers now support Java, and a small group of Java developers have created animated and interactive Web sites. Sun maintains that if you can write an application in C++ (and you can write almost any application in C++), you can write that same application in Java and distribute it across the Web.

Using Java Applets

Java requires a multithreaded operating system, which means that Windows 95 and NT are in and that Windows 3.1 is definitely out. A Java applet (an applet is a small application running under the control of another application, usually the Java-enabled Web browser) is downloaded from the server and executes under the control of the Java interpreter in the computer running the browser. Many early Java demos concentrated on sizzle rather than steak, but one of the major longer-term benefits of Java is the ability to manage new data types as soon as they are developed and to create distributed interactive applications.

Right now, you can't "play" a new type of data file until you find the appropriate helper or add-in application that knows how to manage and decode the data. With Java, an applet can contain the viewing mechanism along with the data, or alternatively, the Java applet can instruct the browser to collect the viewer from another Web site.

Another potentially large impact is in the area of interactive applications, created and managed until now by CGI or Perl scripts. Java will almost certainly displace CGI programming simply because it is both more efficient and more powerful. CGI scripts are host based and place overhead on the server for every script that runs; Java runs on the local processor in the computer running the Web browser.

Some of the early Java demos will not run until the whole Java program has been received from the server; the effect is rather like waiting for a large graphic to load. Until it arrives, the Web page you are viewing has a hole in it. Other demos require a large number of GIF files to present an animated image; in this case, the image files take longer to download than the animation itself takes to run. Most of these effects are because Java is still very young; once programmers start to optimize their code, and they invent the tips and tricks that are common in other languages, you will see some astonishing things done using Java.

Java and HTML

Java applets are opened by using an HTML link and the `APPLET` tag; so providing a Java effect on a Web page can be as simple as copying a Java file to your server and adding the HTML link. The HTML to do that might look like this:

```
<HTML>
<HEAD>
<TITLE>A Java applet </TITLE>
</HEAD>
<BODY>
<APPLET CODE="MYAPPLET">
</APPLET>
</BODY>
</HTML>
```

Note that no filename extension is used in the applet name. You can also use other modifiers with the `APPLET` tag to align the applet on your Web page, retrieve the applet from another URL, and so on.

Because Java is considered an interpreted language, there is a performance penalty when it is compared with a C++ compiled program. The Java program runs somewhere between 10 and 20 times slower than the equivalent compiled C++ program, but it is still much faster than most scripting languages. But Java is not a completely interpreted language and compromises by creating a byte-code so that the final Java interpreter has considerably less work to do than a normal stand-alone interpreter. When this byte-code file arrives in your computer, it provides 70 to 80 percent of the data needed to run the applet; the other 20 to 30 percent is provided by the Java runtime environment and tells the applet how to perform on that specific platform.

How Does It All Work?

So how does a Java applet get from the server to a Java-enabled Web browser? Here are the steps:

1. The Web browser requests an HTML page from the Web server.

2. The Web browser receives and displays the Web page.

3. The Web browser interprets the APPLET tag and sends a request to the server for the file specified in the tag.

4. The Web browser receives the specified file, verifies the byte code, and starts executing the Java applet on your system.

Any Web server can send out the Java file; no special requirements are placed on the server, and no modifications are required. And because execution takes place on the client computer, Java applets are largely unaffected by restrictions in bandwidth or by limitations in HTML.

The Java Programming Language

Java is an object-oriented programming language that is quite similar to C++ with a couple of major exceptions. To use Java effectively, you should have a background in C++ programming and wide experience in solving real time programming problems. This similarity to C++ is no accident; it ensures a huge population of professional programmers who already know how to use Java from their previous experience in writing C++ code.

Java, as it was originally conceived, is an interpreted language, although as we will see in the next section, some companies have taken a novel approach to the interpreter. A Java applet can define classes of objects that are acted on by a method; for example, an object can be a graphical image, and a method can be a set of instructions to place or move the graphic in a specific way.

Java programming is similar to C++, but is a little simpler in two important respects: There are no pointers in Java; and the interpreter, rather than the program, manages memory. This approach to memory management is also a useful security control; it means that an applet cannot get to the underlying operating system and violate Java's security model.

Java is also a major departure from the HTML that is used to prepare Web page content for display by a Web browser. Hypertext Markup Language is straightforward enough that you can learn how to code a Web page relatively quickly; C++ skills are much harder to come by and are usually the province of only very advanced amateurs and professional programmers.

Java is also designed to be platform independent; a Java applet can run on any hardware as long as a Java interpreter is available for that system. The practical application of this is that you can download the same Java applet to users that have all sorts of browsers, and the Java interpreter will take care of any site-specific differences. The Java programming language has been licensed by literally hundreds of software companies, including IBM and Microsoft, by all the makers of software development tools, by all the major database developers, and by all the network operating system companies; if a company is considered a major player in the software field, it has a Java license.

Security in Java

Inherent in the Java system are several important security aspects. Java downloads include a byte-code verification process; if the packet's size changes along the way, the transfer is aborted. The Java loader assumes that the data stream may have been tampered with and so checks very carefully to make sure that it has not changed en route. This is to protect against viruses or Trojan Horses being added in transit.

Once the Java applet is running on your system, the operations it can perform are strictly limited by the Web browser you are using. In general, Java applets do not read or write files, manipulate network connections (other than the connection to your Web site), run other applications on your system, make native function calls to the underlying operating system, or access memory directly. In some cases, a Java applet may be allowed to read files named on a read-access control list.

In Java version 1.1, you will find RSA's public-key encryption scheme to provide security for commercial and credit card transactions. Java will also be compatible with Netscape's Secure Sockets Layer (SSL) and with the Microsoft and Visa Private Communications Technology (PCT).

Java on Your Intranet

Software developers are not just interested in Java because it is new and interesting and can bring sparkle to their Web pages; they are interested in Java because it is hardware and operating system independent. Many developers will use Java because the applications they create will run on any platform, provided the user has a Java-enabled browser.

This single aspect of Java has many programmers—who face a company full of different kinds of hardware running several variations of different operating systems—smiling all the way back to their cubes. They can now write a Java applet to solve that nagging integration problem. If you are looking for a low-cost way to distribute applications across your enterprise, take a look at Java; it might just be the answer to your prayers.

Finding Java Toolkits

Until very recently, the greatest obstacle to efficient use of Java was the almost complete lack of any programming tools or integrated development environments (IDE). C++ programmers are familiar with IDEs that include source-code editors, code beautifiers, syntax checkers, make tools, debuggers, and compilers all under one roof.

That obstacle has changed, fortunately, and some excellent tools are now available. As Java consolidates its position, we will see a steady stream of more and better tools; for example, Informix Software Inc, Oracle Corporation, and Sybase Inc have promised that their next-generation database products will all support Java. Here are details of some of the early winners on the software development front.

The Java Developer's Kit

The Java Developer's Kit (JDK) from JavaSoft, an operating company of Sun Microsystems Inc, contains the Java compiler, runtime libraries for Windows 95 and NT, and several simple command-line utilities, including a debugger. There is no graphical software development environment yet, and the documentation is not searchable; you will also have to provide your own source-code editor and make utilities. Having said all this, the price is right. You can download it free from Sun's Java Web site at:

```
http://java.sun.com/
```

There is a fee for the Java Virtual Machine source code. You will also find an excellent tutorial on Java at:

```
http://java.sun.com/tutorial/
```

which will help you get started quickly.

JavaSoft has announced plans to release Java Workshop, which will be a complete IDE, in the near future.

JavaScript

JavaScript, jointly developed by Sun Microsystems and Netscape, is designed to allow users to dynamically script the behavior of objects running on either the server or the client computer. For more information, see:

```
http://www.sun.com/
```

or

```
http://home.netscape.com/
```

JavaScript is available now.

Symantec Café

Symantec's Café is a stand-alone development environment based on Symantec's well-constructed and popular C++ product and includes the JDK from JavaSoft. With Café, you organize source-code files in separate windows and navigate by file or by class. The editor is tightly integrated with the compiler and with the help system so that when a compile-time error is detected, you can jump right from the error message in the compile window to the offending line in your source code. Café's compiler is fast, and the Java runtime environment has also been optimized for speed. More than 80 royalty-free applets are included with Café, and you may find that you can simply modify one of them to meet your needs. For more information, check out:

```
http://cafe.symantec.com/
```

Symantec has also announced that it plans to release a just-in-time Java compiler for Café that transforms Java code into native executable files; this will give Java a considerable boost in speed, and it is already 4 times faster than Visual Basic.

Borland's C++ Development Suite and Borland's Latte

The new Borland C++ Development Suite is a complete IDE that includes a set of Java add-on tools. Borland's programming tools have always been excellent and well liked by programmers, and this product is no exception; however, this is not a stand-alone Java development environment. For more information, see:

```
http://www.borland.com/
```

Borland has also announced plans for Latte, which will be a complete Java IDE with integrated graphical debugger, a just-in-time compiler, class browsers, and wizards to help automate complex operations. This product will probably be made available in pieces; the just-in-time compiler and graphical debugger are available now, and the other components will ship later.

Others Waiting in the Java Cafeteria

With the ever-increasing popularity of Java, it should come as no surprise that many other companies have announced Java products, including the following.

Authorware and Director Authorware and Director, both from Macromedia, let users with little or no programming experience add Java support to their applications. Find out more at:

```
http://www.macromedia.com/
```

CodeWarrior Metrowerks plans to add Java and JavaScript support to its CodeWarrior products. Contact Metrowerks at:

```
http://www.metrowerks.com/
```

Connection for Java Connection for Java from Open Horizon is a middleware product that allows Java developers to connect their applets with remote databases, transaction-processing systems, and pre-existing legacy business applications. Find Open Horizon at:

```
http://www.openhorizon.com/
```

FutureTense Texture FutureTense Texture from FutureTense Inc is a Web-authoring and Java applet-viewing product with which graphics designers can create interactive publications. For more information, check out:

```
http://www.futuretense.com/
```

Jakarta Jakarta is the codename for Microsoft's Java and ActiveX IDE, which are based on its Blackbird technology. Check out:

```
http://www.microsoft.com/devonly/
```

NetCraft NetCraft, from SourceCraft Inc, is a visual development tool that works with JavaSoft's JDK to generate Java code. It is available now. For more details, contact:

```
http://sourcecraft.com/
```

Optima++ Optima++ from PowerSoft Corporation is an IDE used for developing C++ and Java applications. See:

```
http://www.powersoft.com/
```

Spider Spider, from Spider Technologies Inc, is a development tool that links Web pages to databases and that can drop Java applets into HTML page templates. Contact Spider Technologies at:

```
http://www.w3spider.com/
```

Web Element Web Element, from Neuron Data, is a development kit with which users can embed Web browsers into mission-critical applications; support for Java and JavaScript will be added shortly. For more information, contact:

```
http://www.neurondata.com/
```

WebC WebC, from Maximum Information Inc, is a development tool for creating applications that run on Web servers. It supports Java and VRML and is available now. See it at:

```
http://www.maxinfo.com/
```

WebObjects WebObjects, from Next Software Inc, is a development tool for creating applications that run on Web servers. It will work with Java and JavaScript, allowing Java applets to access databases, as well as legacy business systems. Check it out at:

```
http://www.next.com
```

Java Enhancements

What Java can't do today, it will probably be able to do tomorrow; so just be patient. Sun only finalized the release of Java 1.0 in January 1996 and has already announced plans for extensions and improvements to the language and its class libraries. So you now have to keep up to date on extensions to HTML as well as watch out for more announcements of Java enhancements.

At the 1996 Internet World trade show, 9 operating-system vendors, including Apple Computer, Hewlett-Packard, IBM, Microsoft, Novell, and SCO, announced plans to embed Java into their operating systems.

Sun has announced a small Java operating system called Kona that will open the way for Java use on noncomputing devices—TV set-top boxes, cellular phones, CD players, and digital cameras—devices for which Java was originally designed. Kona provides the interface layer between the hardware and Java applications.

Sun has also announced a set of 6 new class libraries for Java, detailed in Table 16.1. These new class libraries will allow programmers to create even more complex Java applets, adding audio, video, electronic payment services, and many other features needed for mainstream business use.

TABLE 16.1 :   Java Class Library by function

Class Library	Function
Applet	Interapplet communications; developed with Netscape
Commerce	Electronic commerce and financial transactions
Connect	Remote applet functions
Crypto	Digital certificates
Media	Audio, video, telephony, 2- and 3-D animation
Serverle	Applet integration into Internet servers

Also announced recently, JavaOS is a small operating system designed to run on the Internet appliances being developed by several companies to allow very low cost hardware to access the Internet. These Internet appliances have no disk storage space, and some of them use a TV rather than the usual monitor. Experts are divided on whether these Internet appliances will be snapped up by an eager public (especially when AST and other companies continue to cut mainstream PC prices to the bone) or whether they will be a complete financial disaster.

Should You Use Java?

Is Java the answer on your Web site? As always, it all depends. If your Web site's content is simple and can be presented in text and simple graphics, the answer is probably no, you don't need Java. You should also look at the programming skills you can draw on in support of your site. If programming in C++ gives you the mother of all headaches, again, the answer is probably no, you don't need Java.

Also, keep in mind the type of communications link that the majority of your users can access. If they all use 14.4Kbps modems, they will be spending a lot of time waiting as more and more stuff is downloaded from your site. If you run a fast corporate Intranet, bandwidth may be less an issue, and you may find you can use Java to add a little spice to your Web pages.

Java may actually be the best thing since sliced bread, but it is also a topic that attracts a great deal of overstatement and inflated claims when discussion turns to what will happen to the Web in the future. Don't use it just because it is there; use it because it fills a well-defined need on your Web site. It will prove to be a good way to add multimedia to your site and will make game-playing a totally new experience.

Advances in Multimedia

You will be hearing a lot about using multimedia on your Web site as more and more audio, animation, and video technologies converge to constitute a toolkit of genuinely useful products. One of the continuing problems is that of available network bandwidth; multimedia applications can generate large files that simply gobble up bandwidth. Here are two common approaches to this problem:

- Encapsulated multimedia consists of the appropriate data segments in a file that is transferred as a single large entity and "played" after the download is complete. This approach is becoming less and less popular.

- Live multimedia consists of the data streams sent over the network to allow audio and video to be "played" in real time so that the person using the browser can interact with the data stream. Most current products use this approach.

Live multimedia components are often called streaming or continuous-delivery audio and video to differentiate them from encapsulated multimedia. We'll look at these two technologies in a moment, and then we'll look at some experimental aspects of this kind of data transmission over the Internet. But we'll begin with a quick look at how you can assess the case for using multimedia on your Web site in the first place.

Using Multimedia on Your Web Site

As you saw in some earlier chapters in this book, I am always concerned that you evaluate the return on your Web site investment. Therefore, before describing these new technologies in detail, let's ask a few questions about what you hope to achieve by using audio or video on your Web site:

- Why are you providing a multimedia service? What are you trying to accomplish? Is there some specific part of the message you want to get across that can only be presented using audio or video, or could you use some other, less intensive method?

- What is the value to your company of a multimedia presentation, and how will you quantify the returns on this investment?

- What is the value to your customers of a multimedia presentation? Can they access your site using a communications link that is fast enough to get the benefits, or will they just find it enormously frustrating as they wait, and wait, and wait?

- Can you condense the message you want to get across to one simple but direct statement and use multimedia to enhance that message while leaving the rest of your site as a more traditional combination of text and graphics?

Other important questions to ask include: How soon do you need to add this element to your Web site? What will be the consequences for the current server hardware and software? Do you need to upgrade?

If so, at what anticipated cost? Remember that other essential services, such as e-mail and DNS, must continue to receive support and bandwidth.

Evaluating Transmission Mechanisms: TCP, UDP, and IP Multicasting

The TCP/IP family of protocols was originally designed to deliver files over the network reliably, but with some measure of allowable delay, and so is generally unsuitable for applications that require continuous realtime data. For streaming audio or streaming video to work, compromises have to be made in the transmission mechanism. Currently, three mechanisms are in use: TCP, UDP, and IP multicasting.

Most corporate firewalls will pass through TCP-transported information, but some will not pass information transported by UDP. This is not a security issue, but it may have an impact on your ability to receive information from beyond the firewall.

TCP

TCP (Transmission Control Protocol) is probably the most common protocol in use on the Internet. It is used to transmit large packets of information and to guarantee delivery of those packets. TCP also includes flow-control mechanisms that ensure that it does not saturate the communications link. (For detailed information, see the *TCP/IP in a Nutshell* chapter.)

A drawback from the audio-video point of view is that TCP retransmits a packet that is lost. This introduces a gap in the data, which is quite noticeable and which usually interrupts playback until the errant packet is retransmitted and received successfully. Even with these concerns, TCP is a good all-purpose solution to transmitting audio-video data over the Internet.

UDP

UDP (User Datagram Protocol) is a maintenance protocol that can transmit a large number of small packets very quickly at a high priority but that cannot guarantee packet delivery. The receiving application must manage this potential for dropped packets in some way. Using UDP in this way can also saturate communication links; you should, therefore, not use it without some flow-control mechanism to manage the link. User Datagram Protocol is well suited to transitory applications such as Internet phones.

IP Multicasting

In IP multicasting, a host group is created, and all members of the groups receive every IP datagram. Membership is dynamic. You join that group when you start receiving audio-video data, and you leave the group when you stop. IP multicasting is a good solution when you need to send the same audio-video information simultaneously to a group of people.

Creating the Files

The steps you take to prepare audio, animation, or video for transmission are essentially the same:

1. Digitize the audio or video source using a sound card, a video frame grabber, or both. Given that much of the processing still to be done to these raw data files will result in a loss of quality, do as much as you can to make them as good as possible.

2. Encode and compress the raw data. Each type of technology uses a different lossy compression algorithm.

3. Code the appropriate HTML tags into your Web page so that browsers can find the encoded files on your server.

4. Load the multimedia files onto your server. The server registers the filename extension as a MIME type.

You must download and install the appropriate add-in application or browser before trying to play a file from a Web site. All the encoding technologies are slightly different; so be sure you get the right one.

Now when you select a media link, your browser sends a message to the server; the server returns a token file that tells your browser which add-in application (player or viewer) to open. Once this application is running, it sends a request to the server, which transmits the file to the player; after a few seconds wait as the file is buffered, playback begins.

Streaming Audio

The main bottleneck in receiving audio information from a Web site is capacity of the communications link from the browser to the Internet. Table 16.2 lists some common connection types and indicates the quality of audio you might expect.

TABLE 16.2: Connection type and sound quality

Connection type	Speed	Audio quality
Dial-up modem	9.6 to 14.4Kbps	8 kHz (mono or AM radio)
Dial-up modem	28.8Kbps	16 or 22 kHz (mono)
Frame Relay/ISDN	56 to 64Kbps	16 or 22 kHz (stereo) or 44 kHz (mono)
ISDN	128Kbps	44 kHz (stereo)
T1	1.544Mbps	VHS quality stereo

Streaming audio not only allows a browser or add-in application to play the file as it arrives, but with it, you (the user) can manipulate the data by fast forwarding, rewinding, or pausing the data stream. You can also seek for a specific packet of data. Prerecorded data can be compressed before it is sent, something that is all but impossible to do with live audio.

Streaming audio products for NT are available from a variety of sources, including RealAudio from Progressive Networks Inc (find it at `http://www.realaudio.com/`) and StreamWorks from Xing Technology Inc (located at `http://www.xing.com/`).

Streaming Video

Streaming video places demands on the Web server that are more stringent than those of any other Web content type, with the possible exception of interactive video. Consequently, its development is a little behind that of streaming audio. Products are available from several sources, including StreamWorks from Xing Technology Inc (located at `http://www.xingtech.com/`) and VDOLive from VDOnet Corporation (find it at `http://www.vdolive.com/`).

Mbone

Mbone, the abbreviation for multicast backbone, is an experimental technology used to transmit digital video over the Internet. Even at relatively modest data-sampling rates, a video broadcast can easily saturate an ISDN circuit or a fractional T1 link; so imagine the likely effects on the owner of a 14.4Kbps modem.

Mbone requires the creation of another Internet backbone service using special hardware and software to accommodate the high data rate transmissions needed for digital video. Mbone has been used to transmit concerts and conferences to a limited number of people for some time.

The Internet protocol committees are currently working to add support for broadcast modes to the next version of IP (known as

IPng), and support for multimedia and multicasting is seen as a key requirement for this new protocol.

Video Cameras on the Web

A surprising number of Web sites include 24-hour-a-day video images. These sites have been called cam pages, office cams, cube cams, or spy cams, as well as other, less polite names. Most of them feature static interior or exterior shots, and traffic is strictly one way. A few sites are beginning to offer two-way communications so that you can move the camera to look at a specific aspect of the view or to send the site a greeting e-mail message.

Some sites use top-of-the-line video cameras or surveillance cameras; others use cheaper, readily available cameras such as Sony Handicams. The video image is fed into a video frame-grabber board in a computer, which automatically generates a digital version of the video image. Software then converts this digital image into a GIF or JPEG format file on a hard disk, which is then displayed by a simple HTML tag, such as:

```
<IMG SRC=YOURCAM.GIF>
```

The Future of Audio and Video Conferencing

Are you fed up with running around trying to organize people to attend face-to-face meetings? Or trying to get the production manager to go over the schedule with the sales rep in San Francisco? It is not easy to get everyone in the same place at the same time. With video conferencing, people can stay at their desks and participate; they don't have to all be in the same place.

Conferencing Applications

Several collaborative technologies for Web users are emerging—including text-based conferencing, video conferencing, and whiteboard (or chalkboard) applications—in which several participants can work on the same project at the same time, and everyone can immediately see the effects of changes made by one member of the group. Most of the packages support basic drawing tools, including pen, underline, and annotation tools, and some allow you to show a conference the output from another application running on your system. One such program even lets you pass control of an application running on your machine to another conference participant. A status line at the bottom of the screen usually shows the names of the conference participants.

Administrative utilities accessible from within a Web browser allow system administrators to create conferences, establish access controls and security options, and add or remove users from the conferencing system.

Some of these packages organize the discussion into a series of threads, rather like Usenet newsgroups, and let you search the threads by author, date, subject, or message text. Other applications add facilities to append files to threads or to conversations and allow participants to vote on significant issues.

Microsoft's NetMeeting

The recently released NetMeeting conferencing application from Microsoft allows people working in different locations to collaborate simultaneously on the same project, using any Microsoft-compatible program to edit documents. NetMeeting can also support audio conferencing over the Internet. You can download a free version of NetMeeting from Microsoft's own Web site.

Internet Phones

Another development is the use of Internet phones, which so far are restricted to point-to-point connections among users who have the same software, and the quality of the connections has been far from that of "hearing a pin drop." Speakers also experience unnerving one to two second delays, rather like those of the first satellite phone connections. You must also have a full duplex sound card for simultaneous two-way conversation. Still, the price is right—you pay no long-distance charges.

Advances in Intranets

Any of the advances described in this chapter that apply to the World Wide Web and to the Internet also apply to corporate Intranets. Browser enhancements, additions to HTML, the addition of sound and video, virtual reality, and 3-D rendering will all add to the capabilities of an Intranet. Each company must decide whether to embrace the new technology, and plenty of signs indicate they will do so with great gusto and imagination.

Virtual Reality and 3-D

VRML (Virtual Reality Modeling Language) is an open, platform-independent language for building 3-D worlds on the Web that was developed by the same people who brought you HTML. A VRML document (with the filename extensionWRL, an abbreviation of the word *world*) is a blueprint for a 3-D world in which you can walk around if you have a VRML browser or a VRML plug-in for an HTML browser; it's all a bit like being inside a DOOM screen.

A History of VRML

The origins of VRML can be traced to the first annual World Wide Web conference held in Geneva, Switzerland, in March 1994. Tim Berners-Lee—creator of the World Wide Web and one of the developers of HTML—and David Raggett convened a session on virtual reality and the Web. At the time, VRML was the abbreviation for Virtual Reality Markup Language; this was subsequently changed to the current Virtual Reality Modeling Language. Attendees laid out the beginning requirements for a 3-D version of HTML, which at the next World Wide Web conference in October 1994 became the draft specification for VRML 1.0.

Rather than invent a new language, interested parties decided to base VRML on a subset of an existing standard, the Open Inventor ASCII File Format, which was developed by Silicon Graphics Inc and is used in the 3-D Open Inventor modeler. Gavin Bell from SGI adapted the format for VRML and, with input from other interested parties, added Web-specific commands to create links to other VRML sites on the Web. Silicon Graphics allowed the format to be used in the open market and even placed a VRML parser into the public domain to help VRML gain momentum.

Version 1.0 of VRML was unveiled in April 1995, but the developers had to leave a few holes in the definition in the interest of getting version 1.0 up and running as quickly as possible. The specification is available on the Internet at:

```
http://www.hyperreal.com/~mpesce/vrml.tech/vrml110-3.html
```

Version 1.1 of VRML corrects some of the deficiencies of version 1.0 and adds support for basic audio and video capabilities.

Version 2.0 will transform VRML into a fully interactive multiuser environment, in which objects will be able to define their own behavior and participants in the VRML world will be able to see one another on the screen. The specifications call for 4 principle enhancements:

- **Interactivity.** In an interactive VRML world, you can open doors slowly to see what lies behind them; you can even pet your VRML dog before you leave for your VRML job. Interactivity is likely to force a considerable increase in world file sizes

- **Behaviors.** Behaviors allow objects to take on a life of their own and, along with interactivity, allow two or more objects to work together in the same world. Objects will be animated and will be able to move; imagine two fighter jets in a duel or knights jousting.

- **Sound.** The introduction of sound adds a whole new level of complexity to your virtual world. Even adding simple sounds increases the intensity of the virtual experience.

- **Multiuser capability.** The addition of multiuser capability will change VRML in all sorts of unanticipated ways. It will also increase the server overhead because it will have to track who is here, who has left, and who turned into a vampire by someone or something breaking his or her Internet connection.

Several other important issues to be resolved in VRML version 2.0 include the addition of the forms and tables currently available in the HTML extensions.

The VRML Language

Virtual Reality Modeling Language is scriptlike. Its documents, or scene graphs as they are known, are plain ASCII text documents. They consist of "nodes" that define objects in a scene and also describe certain properties of those objects, including size, color, and surface texture. Nodes also define lighting effects such as directional, point-source, and spot lighting, and camera modes define either orthographic or perspective projections. In VRML, as in most 3-D graphics systems, coordinates are given in the *x-y-z* system and can be rotated, translated, or scaled using the transformation nodes.

What You Will Need

To look at a VRML Web page, you will need either a Web browser that supports VRML or an add-in to your normal HTML browser that supports VRML. Some VRML-enabled browsers or add-ins come with simple VRML worlds that you can use to get accustomed to the navigation commands before you access a world on the Internet.

The 3-D worlds displayed by VRML require a large number of supporting files, sometimes 20 or more; a visitor's browser screen stays blank until all these files are downloaded from the server. In many ways this adds up to the need for more hard-disk space on the server, a faster network, and a faster processor in both the server and the visitor's browser.

The VRML browser downloads these files in the same way that an HTML browser downloads HTML files that contain page descriptions. The browser interprets the scene descriptions and renders the scene on the screen. During rendering, you appear to be looking through the lens of a virtual camera, and you navigate the scene by opening doors that lead from one room to another inside a virtual building.

Authoring Tools and Converters

Creating a VRML world from scratch might teach you a great deal about how to use VRML, but there is a good chance that it will also drive you loopy as you try to keep track of your 3-D world. To make life simpler, you can use 2 types of tools: VRML authoring tools and converters.

Most VRML authoring tools are just emerging from beta testing. These software-development environments do for VRML what HTML authoring tools do for the creators of conventional Web pages: They let you assemble and then examine your 3-D world.

You use converters to transform conventional CAD (computer-assisted design or computer-assisted drafting) files into VRML format. One problem with the currently available converters is that they are not optimized and thus create very large, unwieldy files. Another problem is that these files may not be true VRML, but a variant that does not display the way that your browser expects.

Some developers have created Perl scripts that go some way toward optimizing converted files. One technique cuts the number of decimal places, but this technique can produce unexpected results if you anticipate a certain level of precision in the placing of objects in your VRML world.

Unleashing Personal Agents

As the number of sites on the Web continues to grow, your ability to find information by simply surfing the Web diminishes. The popularity of the search engines we look at in the *Announcing Your Web Site to the World* chapter is a testament to this. Another aspect of this problem is that a Web site such as Yahoo uses categories that it developed in-house, and those categories may not be the ones you want to use.

A solution is to use special programs called *intelligent agents*, which will automatically monitor important sites for you and inform you when a significant change occurs. By using an agent, you can reduce the amount of time you spend making keyword searches on several of the most popular search engine sites, leaving you free to work with the information that you have located. An agent can monitor a site and, based on information that you specify, can alert you to changes that require your attention. Other agents can comparison shop for you so that you can find the best price on a networked printer or even on an automobile, saving you a vast amount of time and effort.

Windows 95 and NT users can configure an agent from Surflogic, called Surfbot (an acronym created from *surfing robot*), that will regularly visit your bookmarked sites and burrow down through the linked pages looking for any changes. This program can also run keyword and concept searches for you using the conventional search engine Web sites. You can schedule the Surfbot to access the Web at any time, day or night, and you can use a wizard to help you configure the agent and to specify your download criteria.

Surflogic posts an "Agent of the Week" on its Web site at:

```
http://www.specter.com/
```

to demonstrate just how many ways you can configure Surfbot and how many different kinds of tasks you can automate by using it on your system.

The future will bring more and more intelligent agents, and the OSF (Open Software Foundation), a consortium of computer companies with the goal of establishing open standards and open software environments, is already establishing interfaces and other standardsfor intelligent agents, including a utility called WebWare, available from the Web site:

```
http://www.osf.org/
```

WebWare's modular extensions can create indexes of all the sites you visit to be used in subsequent keyword or context searches, can discover changes in documents of interest, and can gauge the freshness of information based on your browsing habits.

Research into more complex agents continues at universities and in corporate laboratories; we will undoubtedly see the release of even more capable agents that can perform ever more complex tasks for us in the years ahead.

The Future of Web Commerce

With consumers still wary about presenting information about their credit cards to online merchants, the impact of Internet commerce on traditional retailing is still too small to be measured with any confidence. A recent survey indicates that only 7 percent of Internet users have ever bought anything over the Web.

Questions such as, What is the future of electronic cash? are difficult to answer, given the current laws concerning money laundering and large international transfers of cash and the incompatible tax laws of various countries. Banking has always been a conservative industry, and the banks have been slow to support this emerging technology.

Improving Secure Electronic Transactions

Considering the volume of transactions that the credit card companies manage daily all over the world right now, establishing standards for use on the Internet should not be a Herculean task, but one that they are well qualified to perform. One thing we can say is that the Web is a very efficient way to connect retailers and customers, and over time, there is a good chance that merchandise purchased over the Internet will attract a price advantage that is not available to shoppers in a traditional mall. When standards are widely accepted by the banks and by the merchants and when consumers have a trusted mechanism for online transactions, more companies will offer their goods and services online, and more buyers will take advantage of this availability.

Improvements in security and the emergence of a solid foundation for Internet commerce have certainly led to some interesting projections. One recent survey indicates that worldwide revenues from Internet commerce increased to $240 million in 1994 and to $350 million in 1995—slow beginnings indeed. Revenues are estimated to reach $6.9 billion by the end of the decade. To put this into context, the 1995 revenues from only one company in the computer industry, Intel, were well over $11 billion.

Removing the Middle Man

Some companies, offering very specific services, may find that they can use the Web to remove the middle man and market directly to the consumer. Imagine a tailor or a dressmaker taking your measurements over his or her Web site and sending you a custom-made garment in only a few days. This approach allows the businesses to keep costs and inventory as low as possible; they no longer have the clothing racks to fill. Of course, some goods and services will never be sold over the Web; it is still really hard to get a good haircut or a perfect espresso from a Web site.

Industries that have traditionally employed large sales organizations may find that they can use their Web sites to do much the same job. Imagine filling in a Web form for your health insurance or automobile insurance and then asking the site to find you the best deal.

And then there are PC software sales. The distribution channel is already in place, and anyone buying software presumably already has a computer and is familiar with how it operates. Almost all computers sold these days include a modem, and Internet access is becoming more and more common. Selling software online is a natural. Other businesses lend themselves to online access: Music CDs are available from a growing number of Web sites, and the book world already has Amazon.com, a business we looked at in an earlier chapter.

The Web's Impact on Advertising

No assessment of the future of the Web can be complete without considering the advertising world. Slowly but surely, as the number of people connected to the Web grows, advertising on the Web will take its place alongside the traditional channels of broadcast and print. Even though numbers are increasing rapidly in terms of the people around the world who can access the Web and the hours they spend online, these numbers are still very small in comparison with the number of people who watch television.

Initially, Web advertising had the same look and feel as print advertising, but as the degree of interactivity increases, Web advertising will diverge from the print world of static pages and find its own place in the scheme of things. Innovations such as Java and ActiveX will help this process and produce some truly inspired ads. Companies on the Web will be able to create individualized ads on a huge scale without the need for the huge advertising budgets of times past. By carefully using Web technology, small companies can create polished and professional Web sites every bit as attractive and useful as those of the giant corporations.

Using Web technology, companies can also collect information about visitors to their sites, as catalog companies do now with frequent purchasers, but Web advertisers do it quickly and easily and in a way that lets them apply that information. Web advertisers can do the following:

- Track the exact information accessed by a visitor to their sites.
- Present information to a repeat visitor based on his or her previous purchasing history.

- Inform customers about special purchases or discounts. If you bought flowers last year for an anniversary or a birthday, the Web site could remind you that it is time to place another order.

- Develop customer profiles for regular visitors.

When the Web server identifies a repeat customer, it can assemble a dynamic page containing only new or updated links likely to be of particular interest to that customer, based on his or her past history.

Some Web sites are already doing some of these things. For example, Amazon.com will suggest new titles you might like based on your previous book purchases; and Firefly, a virtual record store on the Web (find it at `http://www.ffly.com/`), uses artificial intelligence techniques to analyze your taste in music and to recommend purchases.

In the past, advertising has concentrated on selling a single message to a mass audience; in the future, Web advertising at its best will be a two-way, interactive exchange between a merchant and a potential customer. Small niche companies will have as much presence on the Web as large multinational corporations; and if some of the big companies don't change, they will slowly wither and die.

The Web and the World of Publishing and Journalism

Many major magazines and book publishers are busy creating a Web presence, usually for one of two purposes:

- To put their current book catalog in front of as many people as possible and to sell books.

- To publish articles or parts of articles that have previously appeared in print, either as an online version or as a way to induce people to buy the print edition after reading the online version. The idea of paying for an online subscription to a print magazine has not met with great success to date, and it is not clear whether publishers of online editions are making any money from their efforts.

Some magazines can offer online editions specifically tailored to your requirements; they will include news only on the list of topics you choose. This may well work efficiently in certain technical areas to reduce the volume of material, but one of the most interesting aspects of reading a real newspaper or magazine is the article on a subject that you didn't know you were interested in until you read about it. Some of the most illuminating insights into the human condition appear in small snippets from the news services.

Microsoft entered this fray in June with the publication of the first issue of *Slate*, an online magazine edited by Michael Kinsley, liberal TV pundit and former editor of the *New Republic*. *Slate* is written by professional journalists, attempts to maintain traditional professional standards, and just happens to be published on the Web. Each issue opens with an editorial, followed by feature articles; there is even a virtual back of the book that has theater, book, and film reviews. Plenty of Web flash will be incorporated into the magazine, such as poetry that can read itself out loud, but the main question is: Will readers slog their way through a long complex article on their monitors? If people are willing to read only 500-word short pieces, the magazine will fail.

The second major question concerns subscription rates for online magazines. *Slate* will certainly carry advertising on its virtual pages and will be free for a trial period. After that, readers will have to pay to continue their subscriptions. Plans are to distribute a certain number of copies on floppy disk to reach potential subscribers who don't have a link to the Web. None of the high printing and distribution costs associated with a conventional magazine will be associated with *Slate*, but Microsoft will have to meet salaries and other fixed costs. Circulation goals target 100,000 subscribers after 3 years. We will just have to wait and see.

Other current Web publications worth checking out are listed in Table 16.3.

TABLE 16.3   Web magazines and theri URLs

Web magazine	URL
Feed	http://www.feedmag.com
HotWired	http://www.wired.com
Salon	http://www.salon1999.com
Suck	http:/www.suck.com
Word	http://www.word.com

One aspect of publishing that is going from strength to strength on the Web and that is expected to grow in the future is micropublishing, or the creation of relatively small, single-topic newsletters.

The Virtual Company

The Web will also have a huge effect in shaping the way that certain kinds of companies do business. A virtual company does not have a large permanent staff or headquarters building in a prestigious part of town. It is created to meet a single, well-defined market need and then folds when that need is met. Individual staff members may never meet in person, but communicate by e-mail and by video conferencing. As a business model this is a perfect fit for companies producing products as varied as software, computer games, or large-format coffee table books.

Large corporations will adopt this strategy when assembling teams for a special project. With the old limitations of geography removed, members can actually work at their own desks in different states or even in different countries, but can bring their collective experience to bear on the project at hand. When the work is done and the report has been written and distributed, the team is disassembled, and team members move on to new projects as members of a new virtual team.

Communications Advances

All the developments and improvements to the Internet and to Internet services described in this chapter will place a severe strain on the Internet infrastructure, the actual communications circuits that move the data packets from one computer to the next. So how do we evaluate new communications technologies? Here are some issues to consider:

- Unit hardware, installation, and operating costs.

- Available bandwidth and impact of potential bottlenecks.

- Security and privacy.

- Restrictions in geographical or time-zone availability.

- Degree of interactivity. Can both directions handle data at the same speed?

- Suitability to the types of information currently available: graphics, animation, audio-video, virtual reality.

The system still has plenty of capacity; an analog phone line can be upgraded to an ISDN circuit, an ISDN circuit to a fractional T1, a fractional T1 to a T1, and so on. But let's take a look at some of the new communications technology that will be available in the relatively near future.

ADSL

ADSL (Asymmetric Digital Subscriber Line), a service soon to be offered by local telephone companies and long-distance carriers, can provide faster and cheaper service connections than those of ISDN. ADSL was originally designed to serve as the delivery system for interactive television, an idea that fortunately went nowhere.

ADSL can provide download connection speeds ranging from 1.6Mbps to 6Mbps over existing copper telephone wire, but upload speed (from you to the service provider) is only 64Kbps, or half the speed of ISDN. This may not be a big deterrent if you don't need to transmit huge amounts of data.

One problem with ADSL is that it can operate only over short distances; if you are more than two miles from the phone company's switching systems, you could be out of luck. Miles measured along the telephone wires are much longer than those measured by crow flight; so ADSL coverage is distinctly limited. And you have to use an ADSL-specific modem compatible with the one the phone company is using.

Cable Modems

Two-way digital cable service will appear in the United States slowly during the next decade or so, although several companies are already providing full commercial services in other countries such as Canada. Many technical problems remain to be overcome, not to mention the various layers of regulation that companies will have to navigate.

The cable TV companies are not known for the quality or the reliability of their signals or their technical support, and they are currently just a one-way service. Both long- and short-term service drop-outs are common, and the current systems are prone to damage by wind and rain. A TV set showing a moving picture is a very low resolution display device, and when short-term signal drop-outs do occur, the human eye quickly fills in the missing detail. A large download from the Web will not be anywhere near as forgiving. Also, cable companies have experienced problems in sustaining communications speed as the number of simultaneous users increases. A network might start out delivering 10Mbps, but as thousands of other users access the system, rates can fall precipitously.

The potential is certainly there, because cable modems can provide high-speed connections equivalent to Ethernet speeds at 10Mbps or more, depending on the features built in to the modem. The cable companies, however, face considerable costs in upgrading their one-way systems into two-way, in overcoming a distinct lack of applicable standards, and in dealing with several competing technologies. You will find a cable modem FAQ at:

```
http://www.cox.com/modemfaq.html
```

You can think of a cable modem as a router with a 10BaseT Ethernet connection on one end and a proprietary connection to the cable on the other. You connect the Ethernet adapter in your PC to the 10BaseT connection, and away you go. You will probably be able to lease the cable modem from the same company that provides your cable TV service, in much the same way that you lease a set-top box now. The major players in this market include AT&T, DEC, General Instrument, Hewlett-Packard, Intel, Motorola, and Zenith.

Satellite Links

Several companies are offering high-speed data services using the same DSS (Digital Satellite System) satellites that can bring your favorite TV channels into your home. The DirecPC system from Hughes Network Systems uses a 24-inch dish (only slightly larger than DSS) with a special receiver mounted on an ISA card. This one-way system gives a download speed of about 400Kbps. Your uploaded data must travel through a V.34 modem using a dial-up line, which limits your outgoing speed to 28.8Kbps.

PART V

World Wide Web
Resource Guide

World Wide Web and
Windows NT Resources
Available on the Internet

This appendix includes a selection of the many and various World Wide Web and Windows NT resources available on the Internet, including a number of sites of interest to Web authors, script developers, system administrators, and those pursuing answers to technical questions relating to TCP/IP protocols, ISDN modems, and other communications issues.

Web sites and Usenet newsgroups come and go with time, but the sites listed in this appendix will provide a series of jumping-off points for your own explorations.

Introduction to the World Wide Web

The World Wide Web Frequently Asked Questions (FAQ) list, maintained by Thomas Boutell, is at:

```
http://www.boutell.com/faq/
```

You will find Web subject guides and resources at the World Wide Web Consortium. This site is low on flashy graphics and high on good solid content, including official and draft specifications for the different versions of HTML, as well as the specification for HTTP:

```
http://www.w3.org/
```

For a listing of World Wide Web servers based on geographical region, see:

```
http://www.w3.org/pub/DataSources/WWW/Servers.html
```

and for a list based on subject, see:

`http://www.w3.org/hypertext/DataSources/bySubject/Overview.html`

For background information on the Internet, try one of the following sites:

`http://www.cs.indiana.edu/docproject/zen/zen-1.0_toc.html`

`http://lcweb.loc.gov/global/internet/history.html`

`http://www.rpi.edu/Internet/Guides/decemj/text.html`

`http://slacvx.slac.stanford.edu:80/misc/internet-services.html`

`http://www.ncsa.uiuc.edu/SDG/Software/Mosaic/StartingPoints/NetworkStartingPoints.html`

`http://info.cern.ch/hypertext/WWW/Provider/Style/Overview.html`

`http://www.pbs.org/internet`

Search Engines

The Yahoo site offers keyword searching of more than 200,000 Web sites and a well-organized, cross-referenced hierarchical subject guide that has more than 20,000 categories. Other features include Web Launch, a service you can use to announce your new Web site to the world; a directory of the Web's most popular sites; and Yahoo's own list of the Web's coolest pages. Yahoo is at:

`http://www.yahoo.com/`

The Lycos search engine at Carnegie Mellon University is used by more than 500,000 people every week and catalogs almost 20 million Web pages, FTP sites, and Gopher sites:

`http://lycos.cs.cmu.edu/`

The Web Crawler, a free service from America Online, gives you fast access to a 200MB database of 2 million indexed World Wide Web documents:

http://webcrawler.com/

The World Wide Web Worm won the Best of the Web award in 1994, and it lets you search URLs, titles, or hypertext entries of indexed documents:

http://www.cs.colorado.edu/www

The AltaVista search engine is sponsored by the Digital Equipment Corporation. AltaVista processes more than 2.5 million search requests every day and has cataloged more than 30 million Web pages, but no FTP or Gopher sites. Check it out at:

http://www.altavista.digital.com/

InfoSeek is a full-text search system that lets you search Web pages, Usenet newsgroups, computer magazines, news wires and press releases, and even technical-support databases. Some services are free; others incur a charge:

http://www2.infoseek.com/

The Galaxy search engine not only lets you search the Galaxy listings, but also lets you search Gopherspace and Telnet services:

http://galaxy.einet.net/search.html

Excite contains the full text to about 1.5 million Web pages, as well as Usenet newsgroups, and is at:

http://www.excite.com/

Open Text contains the full text to about 1.5 million Web pages, as well as FTP and Gopher sites, at:

http://www.opentext.com/

For more general information on Internet robots, consult:

`http://web.nexor.co.uk/mak/doc/robots/robots.html`

and for information on a proposed (and often used) method of preventing robots from accessing your Web site, see:

`http://info.webcrawler.com/mak/projects/robots/robots.html`

For more information on spiders, consult:

`http://www.december.com/net/tools/index.html`

Yellow Page Listings

Many listing services are on the World Wide Web, including the following sites. Some of these sites are searchable, and others are not.

The Big Yellow listing from Nynex Information Technologies contains more than 16 million entries, at:

`http://bigyellow.com/`

BizWeb, at:

`http://www.bizweb.com/`

Open Market's list of sites, at:

`http://www.directory.net/`

Pointcom, at:

`http://www.pointcom.com/`

McKinley's Magellan Internet Directory, at:

`http://magellan.mckinley.com/`

Apollo, at:

`http://apollo.co.uk`

LinkStar, at:

`http://www.linkstar.com`

The World Wide Yellow Pages, at:

`http://www.yellow.com/`

and the Virtual Yellow Pages, at:

`http://www.vyp.com/`

You will find Starting Point at:

`http://www.stpt.com/`

and Tribal Voice at:

`http://www.tribal.com/search.html`

The WWW Virtual Library is at:

`http://www.w3.org/hypertext/DataSources/bySubject/Overview.html`

You will find The Yellow Pages at:

`http://theyellowpages.com/`

and Yahoo at:

`http://www.yahoo.com/Economy/Business/Corporations/`

Metasearch Web Sites

A metasearch Web site lets you send a single query to several databases at the same time.

SavvySearch can perform parallel searches on as many as 5 databases simultaneously, and the results are retrieved and combined onto one page, with all duplicates removed. You can find SavvySearch at:

```
http://cage.cs.colostate.edu
```

The All-in-One search page has more than 200 basic search forms on a single Web site, and searches are performed individually. Find them at:

```
http://www.albany.net/allinone/
```

The Internet Sleuth has one of the largest collections of searchable databases on the Net, more than 900 of them, covering all sorts of subjects from the Civil War to carnivorous plants. See this site at:

```
http://www.intbc.com/sleuth
```

Doing Business on the Web

Electronic commerce is becoming more and more important as the Web evolves; you may not need these features on your Web site this year, but chances are, you will need them by next year. Some companies and sites to watch include the following.

First Virtual Holdings Inc, a broker for secure Web transactions and electronic payment systems similar to a credit card system is at:

```
http://www.fv.com/
```

The Digicash Corporation develops and licenses technology for electronic payments based on its Electronic Data Interchange system and is at:

```
http://www.digicash.com/
```

CheckFree is one of the largest companies in electronic commerce, serving businesses, customers, and financial and banking institutions. Check its site at:

```
http://www.checkfree.com/
```

CommerceNet is a nonprofit organization backed by the U.S. government's Technology Reinvestment Project, which supports and promotes electronic commerce on the Internet:

```
http://www.commerce.net/
```

The Electronic Commerce Association is a voluntary organization that provides a forum for discussion topics including electronic data exchange (EDI), electronic funds transfer, e-mail, smart cards, and so on. Find it at:

```
http://www.globalx.net/eca/
```

Financial Services Technology Consortium (FSTC) is a collection of financial service providers, universities, and government agencies who sponsor and participate in noncompetitive research and development on interbank technical projects. Look at:

```
http://www.fstc.org
```

The Internet Society is a nongovernment organization for coordination of the Internet and Internet technologies and applications. Its Web site is at:

```
http://www.intsoc.com/
```

The Internet Group has an online business center containing information about doing business on the Web, lists of companies already using Web sites, discussions about marketing and security, and statistics and demographics. Find it at:

```
http://www.tig.com/
```

CyberCash provides a link between the Internet and the more traditional banking system, with emphasis on privacy and security. This Web site is rather light on technical information:

```
http://www.cybercash.com/
```

NetCash is another electronic payment system. Find it at:

```
http://www.netbank.com/~netcash/
```

NetChex offers a virtual checking account that is an extension of a customer's existing checking account. See this site at:

```
http://www.netchex.com/
```

The Secure Electric Payment Protool (SEPP) defines secure credit-card transactions on the Internet. SEPP is under development by several companies, including MasterCard, CyberCash, IBM, and Netscape. See:

```
http://www.mastercard.com/set/set.htm
```

Premenos is a provider of electronic data exchange (EDI) software and has an extensive list of EDI and EC organizations, at:

```
http://www.premenos.com/
```

And then there are the Web sites of interest to all business people, including the Small Business Administration, at:

```
http://www.sba.gov
```

U.S. government information on the Internet, at:

```
http://www.wcs-online.com/usgovdoc/
```

The Better Business Bureau, at:

```
http://www.bbb.org/bbb/
```

The U.S. Department of Commerce, at:

`http://www.doc.gov/`

The U.S. Chamber of Commerce, at:

`http://www.uschamber.org/chamber/`

The American Marketing Association, at:

`http://www.ama.org`

The Foundation for Enterprise Development, at:

`http://www.fed.org/fed/`

NAFTAnet, at:

`http://www.nafta.net/`

Online Malls

There are also many malls and online markets, including the following sites. Shop D Net, a list of virtual marketplaces from Blake and Associates, at:

`http://www.neosoft.com/citylink/blake/malls.html`

Sofcom at:

`http://www.sofcom.com.au/`

Security and Firewalls

You will find the home page of the Internet Engineering Task Force for World Wide Web security at:

`http://www-ns.rutgers.edu/www-security/`

For some excellent Web security information, check out:

```
http://www.genome.wi.mit.edu/WWW/faqs/www-security-faq.html
```

or

```
http://www.commerce.net/information/services/security/
inet.security.html
```

For information on S-HTTP, try one of these sites:

```
http://www.eit.com/creations/s-http/
```

```
http://www.commerce.net/information/standards/
```

For information on the Pretty Good Privacy (PGP) public-key encryption scheme created by Phil Zimmermann, see:

```
http://www.mantis.co.uk/pgp/pgp.html
```

The Telstra Corporation (previously maintained by Telecom Australia) World Wide Web page contains many links to other sites concerned with Internet security:

```
http://www.telstra.com.au/info/security.html
```

You will also find excellent information at the COAST (Computer Operations, Audit, and Security Technology) site:

```
http://www.cs.purdue.edu/coast/coast.html
```

For a description of the Secure Hypertext Transfer Protocol, see:

```
http://www.eit.com/projects/s-http/
```

The Secure Sockets Layer is a definition of how Web servers and browsers can communicate without someone being able to eavesdrop on the conversation:

```
http://www.netscape.com/newsref/std/SSL.html
```

For information on the Shen Protocol, see:

`http://www.w3.org/hypertext/WWW/Shen/ref/security_spec.html`

Creating Hypertext Documents

The original HTTP specification:

`http://www.w3.org/hypertext/WWW/MarkUp/MarkUp.html`

HTML 2.0 Document Type Definition (DTD):

`http://www.halsoft.com/sgml/html-2.0/DTD-HOME.html`

HTML 3.0 Document Type Definition (DTD):

`http://www.halsoft.com/sgml/html-3.0/DTD-HOME.html`

Netscape extensions to HTML; remember that using these tags will not help the appearance of your Web pages when viewed from a non-Netscape browser:

`http://www.netscape.com/assist/net_sites/html_extensions_3.html`

HTML specifications, including the Internet Engineering Task Force draft for HTML 3.0:

`http://www.w3.org/hypertext/WWW/MarkUp/html3/CoverPage.html`

Information on using tables from Netscape:

`http://home.netscape.com/assist/net_sites/tables.html`

Information on creating dynamic documents from Netscape:

`http://www.netscape.com/assist/net_sites/pushpull.html`

For an explanation of Netscape's version of HTML3 backgrounds, access the following:

```
http://www.netscape.com/assist/net_sites/bg/
```

MIME (Multipurpose Internet Mail Extensions) RFC1341:

```
http://www.w3.org/hypertext/WWW/Protocols/rfc1341/
```

and for information on MIME type suffixes, consult:

```
http://www.w3.org/hypertext/WWW/Daemon/User/Config/
Suffixes.html
```

For URL specifications and listings, try one of the following sites:

```
http://www.w3.org/hypertext/WWW/Adressing/Adressing.html
```

```
http://www.ncsa.uiuc.edu/demoweb/url-primer.html
```

```
http://www.netspace.org/users/dwb/url-guide.html
```

```
http://www.yahoo.com/Computers/World_Wide_Web/
```

```
Programming/URLs_Universal_Resource_Identifiers/
```

For information on how to compose good HTML, consult one of these sites:

```
http://www.access.digex.net/~werbach/home.html
```

```
http://www.hypermall.com/tk/basic.html
```

```
http://www.ncsa.uiuc.edu/demoweb/html-primer.html
```

```
http://www.ncsa.uiuc.edu/General/Internet/WWW/HTMLPrimer.html
```

```
http://www.cs.cmu.edu/~tilt/cgh/
```

```
http://www.ziff.com/~eamonn/crash_course.html
```

You will find the HTML Writer's Guild at:

`http://www.hwg.org/`

and the comprehensive reference site, at:

`http://webreference.com/`

And finally, here's the How'd They Do That With HTML site, with tips and tricks and links to many related Web sites:

`http://www.nashville.net/~carl/htmlguide/index.html`

Web Authoring Tools

For an up-to-date list of HTML editors, consult:

`http://www.yahoo.com/Computers/World_Wide_Web/HTML_Editors/`

The Internet Assistant is a free Microsft Word add-on that creates HTML documents (and also acts as a rather slow browser):

`http://www.microsoft.com/msoffice`

HTML Syntax Checkers and Converters

Microsoft Word for Windows converters are available from these sites:

`http://www.cuhk.hk/csc/cu_html/cu_html.htm`

`ftp://ftp.einet.net/einet/pc/ANT_DEMO.ZIP`

or from:

```
http://infolane.com/nice/nice.html
```

Cyberleaf is a commercial converter from Interleaf that can convert from a variety of formats, including Word, to HTML. For information, see:

```
http://www.ileaf.com/cyberleafds.html
```

Web Site Design Guides

For a selection of online style guides, consult one or more of these sites:

```
http://www.w3.org/hypertext/WWW/DesignIssues/Overview.html
```

```
http://frazier.cit.cornell.edu/style/style.html
```

```
http://www.dsiegel.com/tips/tips_home.html
```

```
http://www.links.net/webpub/style.html
```

Clip Art, Icons, and Graphics Resources

Literally hundreds of Web sites offer free or low-cost images you can use on your Web pages; just be sure you understand your usage rights if an image carries a fee.

For a listing of graphical icon archive sites, check:

```
http://www.yahoo.com/Computers/World_Wide_Web/
Programming/Icons/
```

And for sources of clip art and icons, try one of the following sites:

http://www.w3.org/hypertext/WWW/Icons/

http://www.jsc.nasa.gov/~mcoy/Icons/index.html

http://www.wit.com/mirrors/ibmpc/simtel/deskpub/

http://hyperarchive.lcs.mit.edu/HyperArchive/Abstracts/
gst/grf/HyperArchive.html

http://www.nsca.uiuc.edu/General/Icons/

http://www.cs.yale.edu/homes/sjl/clipart.html

http://www.infi.net/~rdralph/icons/

For stock photographs that you can search through, pay for, and download from the Web, check out Photodisc at:

j695
http://www.photodisc.com/

and for more information on photographers, check out:

http://www.photographers.com/

For information on and sources for World Wide Web page backgrounds, check out these sites:

http://www.yahoo.com/Computers/World_Wide_Web/
Programming/Backgrounds/

http://drizzle.stanford.edu/~achille/images/misc/backgrounds/

http://home.netscape.com/home/bg/backgrounds.html

http://home.netscape.com/assist/net_sites/bg/index.html

For information on imagemaps and how to create and use them, see:

http://www.stars.com/Vlib/Providers/Imagemaps.html

http://www.hway.com/ihip/

http://www.kosone.com/people/nelsonl/image.htm

Perl and CGI Programming

The Perl scripting language is a popular choice for writing CGI applications. Perl has its roots in the Unix world, but has been ported to many other operating systems, including Windows NT. Check out the following sources of Perl wisdom:

```
http://www.perl.com/
```

```
http://www.worldwidemart.com/scripts/
```

```
http://www.oac.uci.edu/indiv/ehood/perlWWW/
```

```
http://www.charm.net/~web/Vlib/Providers/Perl.html
```

```
http://www.metronet.com/perlinfo/perl5.html
```

```
http://www.ee.pdx.edu/~rseymour/perl/
```

```
http://www.yahoo.com/Computers/Languages/Perl/
```

WebLint is a Perl syntax checker you can use to check your Web pages. It is free from:

```
http://www.khoros.unm.edu/staff/neilb/weblint.html
```

For an overview of CGI programming, with lots of links to other important documents, see one of these sites:

```
http://hoohoo.ncsa.uiuc.edu/cgi/overview.html
```

```
http://hoohoo.ncsa.uiuc.edu/cgi/interface.html
```

```
http://www.yahoo.com/Computers_and_Internet/Internet/
World_Wide_Web/CGI/Common_Gateway_Interface/
```

```
http://www.cyserv.com/pttong/cgiprog.html
```

```
http://www.Catch22.com/Clickables/
```

```
http://www.cisc.com/src/demo.html
```

```
http://www2.best.com/~wooldri/tools/tools.html

http://www.w3.org/pub/WWW/CGI/

http://www.w3.org/pub/WWW/Tools/Overview.html

http://www.stars.com/Vlib/Providers/CGI.html

http://www.best.com:80/~hedlund/cgi-faq/new/faq.1-basic.html

http://www.genome.wi.mit.edu/WWW/faqs/www-security-faq.html
```

Java Programming

For information about Java, Sun's new programming language, use a Java-enabled browser to check out Sun Microsystems site at:

```
http://www.sun.com/
```

or Sun's Java site at:

```
http://java.sun.com/
```

Check out the Java User Resource Network, at:

```
http://www.nebulex.com/URN/home.html
```

See Infinite Data Source's The Java Developer, at:

```
http://www.idsonline.com/digitalfocus/faq
```

and the Virtual Rendezvous' Club Java, at:

```
http://rendezvous.com/java/
```

John December's Java information sources, at:

```
http://www.rpi.edu/~decemj/works/java/info.html
```
and *JavaWorld Magazine*, at:

```
http://www.javaworld.com/
```

You will find a FAQ list from this newsgroup at:

```
http://sunsite.unc.edu/javafaq/javatutorial.html
```

And to check out what developers have created so far, look at the Gamelan collection of more than 100 Java applets at:

```
http://www.gamelan.com/
```

then look at a site run by an advertising agency for a demonstration of how you can use these exciting new graphical applets:

```
http://dimensionx.com/
```

and then check out a site featuring animated text from the staff at *HotWired*:

```
http://www.hotwired.com/java/
```

You will find more Java information at the following sites:

```
http://www.yahoo.com/Computers_and_Internet/Languages/Java/
```

```
http://reality.sgi.com/employees/shiffman_engr/Java-QA.html
```

```
http://www.entmp.org/cgi-bin/lwgate/STRONG-JAVA/
```

```
http://java.sun.com/doc/programmer/
```

Audio and Video Resources

For collections of audio clips, consult one of the following sites:

```
http://www.yahoo.com/Computers/Multimedia/Sound/Archives/
```

```
http://www.music.indiana.edu/music_resources/
```

```
http://www.eecs.nwu.edu/~jmyers/other-sounds.html
```

For video collections, consult one of the following sites:

```
http://www.yahoo.com/Computers/Multimedia/Video/Archives/
```

```
http://www.arc.umn.edu/GVL/Software/mpeg.html
```

```
http://www.eeb.ele.tue.nl/mpeg/
```

```
http://sunsite.unc.edu/pub/multimedia/animation/mpeg/
berkeley-mirror/
```

```
http://nbn.nbn.com/footage/
```

Real Audio is a high-quality, real-time audio system for the Web. The server used to provide Real Audio is not free. The helper application is available free at:

```
http://www.realaudio.com/
```

For information on MBONE, check out:

```
http://www.research.att.com/mbone-faq.html
```

All Things Virtual

For general information, resources, and links for Virtual Reality Modeling Language (VRML), access one of these sites:

```
http://VRML.wired.com/
```

```
http://www.caligari.com/
```

```
http://www.vrml.org/
```

```
http://www.eit.com/vrml/
```

```
http://www.lightside.com/3dsite/cgi/VRML-index.html
```

```
http://cedar.cic.net/~rtilmann/mm/vrml.htm
```

The version 1.0 specification for VRML is at:

`http://www.hyperreal.com/~mpesce/vrml/vrml.tech/vrml10-3.html`

and a VRML-enabled version of the specification is at:

`http://www.virtpark.com/theme/vrml/`

To check out the Lawrence Livermore National Laboratory's VRML test page, use:

`http://dsed.llnl.gov/documents/WWWtest.html`

To see the San Diego Supercomputing Center's VRML repository, check out:

`http://www.sdsc.edu/vrml/`

A VRML FAQ is maintained at:

`http://www.oki.com/vrml/VRML_FAQ.html`

and you can access the WebMaster Inc site for information on a variety of Web-based applications focusing on VRML technologies, at:

`http://www.webmaster.com/`

For VRML helper applications, check out Vrweb at:

`http://www.iicm.tu-graz.ac.at/Cvrweb`

or InterVista's WorldView VRML browser at:

`http://www.intervista.com/`

Paper Software's WebFX at:

`http://www.paperinc.com/webfx.html`

Template Graphics Software WebSpace browser at:

`http://www.tgs.com/~template/`

and Silicon Graphics' WebSpace at:

`http://webspace.sgi.com/`

For demonstrations of just what VRML can do, take a flight over New York at:

`http://www.sony.co.jp/TechnoGarage/VRML_sample.html`

or San Francisco at:

`http://www.hyperion.com/planet9/vrsoma.htm`

Two of the most elaborate sites are at:

`http://vrml.arc.org/gallery95/index2.html`

and

`http://www.cgrg.ohio-state.edu/~mlewis/Gallery/vrml.htm`

Intranet Resources

To read *PC Magazine*'s news and reviews of Intranet software, go to:

`http://www.zdnet.com/pcmag/IU/iuser.htm`

To see Process Software Corporation's Intranet white paper, visit:

`http://www.process.com/news/intrawp.htp`

To look at Netscape's Intranet white paper, customer profiles, and demos, go to:

`http://home.netscape.com/comprod/at_work/index.html`

To access BES/Internet Services *Intranet Journal* for information and discussion groups on Intranets, check out:

`http://www.brill.com/intranet/`

And to read Zona Research's Intranet report, check out:

`http://www.zonaresearch.com/Pubs/inet.html`

New from Wordmark Associates is a site containing a glossary, white papers on Intranet construction, and an online primer, at:

`http://webcom.com/wordmark/sem_1.html`

For more information on Intranets, see one of the following:

`http://www.intranet.co.uk/intranet/intranet.html`

`http://www.lochnet.com//client/smart/intranet.htm`

`http://wwwstrom.com/pubwork/intranetp.html`

For Intranet tools, see the Open Text Corporation's site at:

`http://www.opentext.com/livelink/`

or the Hummingbird Communications site at:

`http://www.hummingbird.com/`
`j713`

Modem and Communications Information

For information on ISDN modems, check one of the sites in this next section.

3Com Corporation:

`http://www.3com.com/`

Boca Research:

http://www.boca.org/

Farallon Computing:

http://farallon.com/

Motorola Information Systems Group:

http://www.mot.com/mims/isg/

Racal:

http://www.racal.com/

U S Robotics:

http://www.usr.com/

ZyXEL:

http://www.zyxel.com/

You will find an ISDN FAQ at:

http://rtmf.mit.edu/pub/usenet/news.answers/isdn.html

and PacBell's ISDN User's Guide at:

http://www.pacbell.com/isdn/Book/

The California ISDN User's Group is at:

http://www.ciug.org/

and you will find Dan Kegel's ISDN Page at:

http://alumni.caltech.edu/~dank/isdn

You can also complete an ISDN worksheet that takes you through the often confusing process of specifying and ordering ISDN services at Microsoft's site:

http://www.microsoft.com/windows/getisdn/

or at the Motorola site:

http://www.mot.com/isdn/

For communications information, check one or more of these sites:

http://www.yahoo.com/Computers/Internet/Connectivity/

http://www.yahoo.com/Computers/Networks_and_Data_Communication/

http://www.modem.com/

http://www.teleport.com/~curt/modems.html

http://intellinet.com/Customer-Service/FAQ/AskMrModem/

http://www.ee.manitoba.ca/~blight/telecom.html

http://wwwhosts.ots.utexas.edu/ethernet/ethernet-home.html

http://galaxy.einet.net/Reference-and-Interdisciplinary-Information/Internet-and-Networking.html

http://netlab.itd.nrl.navy.mil/Internet.html

http://www.pacbell.com/isdn/isdn_home.html

http://www.ipps.lsa.umich.edu/telecom-info.html

For lists of Internet service providers, check out one of these URLs:

http://thelist.com/

http://www.cybertoday.com/cybertoday/isps/

http://wings.buffalo.edu/world/

Windows NT Resources

This section includes a listing of Web sites where you will find more information on Microsoft products, including NT, and begins with Microsoft's main Web site at:

`http://www.microsoft.com/`

You will find Microsoft's Gopher site at:

`gopher://gopher.microsoft.com`

Digital Equipment Corporation maintains an NT site at:

`http://www.windowsnt.digital.com/`

and you will find Windows NT shareware at:

`http://spectrum.ece.jhu.edu/shrindex.htm`

and NT tools at:

`http://digital.com/www-swdev/pages/Home/TECH/software/sw-wnt.html`

For native Alpha NT tools and utilities, check out:

`http://www.garply.com/tech/comp/sw/pc/nt/alpha.html`

And for general information about NT, check out one or more of the following sites:

`http://www.bhs.com/winnt/`

`http://infotech.kumc.edu/winnt/`

`http://rmm.com/nt/`

`http://ms-nic-gsfc.nasa.gov/Titles/WinNT.html`

`http://emwac.ed.ac.uk/`

`http://www.yahoo.com/Computers/Operating_Systems/Windows_NT/`

Microsoft's Web Site

The Microsoft site is one of the busiest on the Web, and it holds a vast amount of information. Here are some suggested starting points for your explorations.

The main Web site address is:

`http://www.microsoft.com/`

For NT Server information, check out:

`http://www.microsoft.com/ntserver/`

For NT Workstation information, check out:

`http://www.microsoft.com/ntworkstation/`

To check IIS information, see:

`http://www.microsoft.com/infoserv/`

For BackOffice information, see:

`http://www.microsoft.com/backoffice/`

For Exchange information, see:

`http://www.microsoft.com/exchange`

For Visual Basic Scripting information, see:

`http://www.microsoft.com/vbscript/`

For Internet Explorer information, check:

`http://www.microsoft.com/ie/`

and for SQL Server information, see:

`http://www.microsoft.com/sql/`

You can also get information on Microsoft Press books at:

`http://www.microsoft.com/mspress/books/b.htm`

For the Microsoft Windows NT Hardware Compatibility list, that list of computer systems and peripherals which have passed strict compatibility testing, see:

`http://www.microsoft.com/BackOffice/ntserver/`

You can also get this information by FTP from this site:

`ftp.microsoft.com\bussys\winnt\winnt-docs\hcl`

You will find information on Microsoft training and certification schemes at:

`http://www.microsoft.com/train_cert/`

Other Windows NT Internet Servers

You can download many of these Internet servers (which may take some time, depending on the speed of your connection) for a free trial before you buy the product. You can also get them through the normal supply channels.

The Microsoft Internet Information Server:

`http://www.microsoft.com/infoserv/`

The EMWAC (European Microsoft Windows NT Academic Centre at Edinburgh University Computing Services) Internet server:

`http://emwac.ed.ac.uk/html/internet_toolchest/https/contents.htm`

The WebSite Internet server, from O'Reilly & Associates, at:

`http://www.ora.com/`

The Purveyor server, from Process Software, at:

`http://www.process.com/`

The WebStar 95/NT server, from Quarterdeck Corp, at:

`http://www.quarterdeck.com`

The WebQuest server, from Questar Microsystems Inc, at:

`http://www.questar.com`

The Spry Web Server, from Compuserve's Internet Division, at:

`http://server.spry.com`

The Spyglass Server, from Spyglass Inc, at:

`http://www.spyglass.com/`

IntraNet Server, from NetManage Inc, at:

`http://www.netmanage.com/`

For a detailed look at many servers, check out this site; it contains pointers to all the servers mentioned:

`http://www.proper.com/www/servers-chart.html`

Secure Web servers are available from the following vendor sites.

Netscape's Commerce Server for NT at:

`http://home.netscape.com/`

O'Reilly and Associates WebSite Professional at:

`http://website.ora.com/`

Commerce Builder, from the Internet Factory, at:

`http://www.artisoft.com/ifact/inet.html`

Process Software's Purveyor WebServer for Windows NT at:

`http://www.process.com/`

CompuServe Internet Division's Spry SafetyWeb Server for NT at:

`http://server.spry.com/`

America Online's GNN-Server at:

`http://www.tools.gnn.com/`

Frontier Technologies Corporation's SuperWeb at:

`http://www.frontiertech.com/`

NaviSoft Inc's NaviServer at:

`http://www.navisoft.com/`

Mustang Software Inc's Wildcat Web Server at:

`http://www.mustang.com/`

Esplanade Secure Web Server, from FTP Software, designed primarily for Intranets, at.

`http://ftp.com/`

For a review of two secure NT Internet servers, the Netscape Commerce Server and the Commerce Builder from the Internet Factory, consult:

`http://www.zdnet.com/~pcweek/sr/1030/tserv.html`

Internet Browsers

In this section you will find information on the most popular Web browsers; some are free, others are bundled with other products from the same company, and many are only available through normal retail channels.

Cyberjack, from the Delrina Group, Symantec Corporation, at:

`http://www.delrina.com/`

Emissary, from the Wollongong Group, at:

`http://www.twg.com/`

Explore Anywhere, from FTP Software, at:

`http://ftp.com/`

Microsoft Internet Explorer, from Microsoft Corporation, at:

`http://www.microsoft.com/`

Mosaic in a Box, from CompuServe, at:

`http://www.spry.com/`

NCSA Mosaic at:

`http://www.ncsa.uiuc.edu/`

Netscape Navigator, from Netscape Communications Corporation, at:

`http://www.home.netscape.com/`

PowerBrowser, from Oracle Corporation, at:

`http://oracle.com/`

Quarterdeck InternetSuite, from Quarterdeck Corporation, at:

`http://www.qdeck.com/`

Spyglass Mosaic, from Spyglass Technologies, at:

`http://www.spyglass.com/`

WebExplorer, from IBM, at:

`http://www.raleigh.ibm.com/`

WebExplorer Mosaic, from IBM Networking Software Division, at:

`http://www.raleigh.ibm.com/`

WebSurfer, from NetManage Inc, at:

`http://www.netmanage.com/`

And for reviews of individual browsers and how well they perform, including how they display different HTML examples, check one of these sites:

`http://www.colosys.net/~rscott/barb.htm`

`http://www.browserwatch.com/`

`http://www.threetoad.com/main/Browser.html`

`http://www.w3.org/hypertext/WWW/Clients.html`

`http://www.cen.uiuc.edu/~ejk/bry1.html`

Specialty Web Browsers

In this section you will find information on Web browsers that meet a specific additional need.

Accent Multilingual Mosaic provides Web access in more than 30 languages and is at:

`http://www.accentsoft.com/`

Ariadna, from Advanced Multimedia System Design in Russia, is at:

`http://www.amsd.ru`

Cello, from Cornell Law School Legal Information Institute, was one of the first Web browsers ever released and is at:

`http://www.law.cornell.edu/cello/`

CyberSearch, from Frontier Technologies Corporation, includes an off-line search engine from Lycos and is at:

`http://www.frontiertech.com/`

HotJava, from Sun Microsystems, was the first Java-enabled browser and is at:

`http://www.javasoft.com/`

InterGo, from TeacherSoft Inc, includes educational resources and KinderGuard so that you can screen out certain sites and is at:

`http://www.teachersoft.com/`

Mariner for Windows, from Network Computing Devices Inc, lets you organize information collected from the Web and is at:

`http://www.mariner.ncd.com/`

Mathbrowser, from MathSoft Inc, handles Mathcad documents and is at:

`http://www.mathsoft.com/browser`

MultiNet for Windows, from TVG Inc, offers secure transactions support for the corporate user and is at:

`http://www.tvg.com/`

NetCruiser, from Moon Valley Software Inc, is the proprietary browser for NetCom, a leading ISP, and is at:

`http://www.moonvalley.com/`

NetShark, from InterCon Systems Inc, is a leading 32-bit Mac browser:

```
http://netshark.inter.net/
```

Pythia, from Appian Interactive Corporation, targets large businesses with security features, live database access, and multimedia and is at:

```
http://pythia.com/
```

SlipKnot, from MicroMind Inc, won *PC Magazine*'s 1995 Shareware Award and is at:

```
http://plaza.interport.net/slipknot/slipknot.html
```

Video On Line Browser, from Video On Line, one of the largest of the European online services, offers a version of their browser in more than 18 languages at:

```
http://www.vol.it/US/EN/
```

Web Browser Plug-ins

For information on Web browser plug-ins, programs you can link into your broswer that add special additional features to the browser, check:

```
http://home.netscape.com/products/navigator/
```

You can also locate individual plug-ins at the following sites.

Acrobat Reader, from Adobe Systems, lets you view, navigate, and print files in PDF (Portable Document Format), commonly used by government agencies, including the IRS, and is at:

```
http://www.adobe.com/Acrobat/
```

Shockwave, which lets you watch animation and play some games, is at:

`http://www.macromedia.com/Tools/Shockwave`

Crescendo, which lets you play music, is at:

`http://www.liveupdate.com/`

You can find KEYview, which allows you to view files in more than 200 formats, including Microsoft Word, Microsoft Excel, and WordPerfect, at:

`http://www.ftp.com/mkt_info/keyv2.html`

RealAudio, which lets you listen to news reports, sports broadcasts, and music via the Internet without having to launch the RealAudio helper application, is at:

`http://www.realaudio.com/`

Internet Wave audio player, another audio helper, is at:

`http://www.vocaltec.com/`

TrueSpeech Player, from The DSP Group, plays high-quality streaming audio. Find it at:

`http://www.dspg.com/`

CyberGate, from Black Sun Interactive, is a virtual reality plug-in, and you will find it at:

`http://wwwblacksun.com/`

You can get Microsoft's VRML plug-in for the Internet Explorer at:

`http://www.microsoft.com/`

VisNet, a very fast VRML plug-in from Superscape, is available at:

`http://www.superscape.com/`

WIRL, a plug-in from VREAM Inc, is at:

`http://www.vream.com/`

Legal Information

For information on copyrights, consult the U. S. Copyright Office:

`gopher://marvel.loc.gov/11/copyright/`

If you see an image in a magazine or other publication that you would like to use on your Web site, you can look up the name of the photographer in the Copyright Holders Database at:

`http://chd.com/`

Usenet Newsgroups

You can subscribe to large number of Usenet newsgroups covering system administration topics, including:

`comp.admin.policy`

`comp.protocols.tcp-ip`

`comp.risks`

`comp.security.announce`

`comp.security.misc`

A group of `alt` newsgroups is also devoted to security issues, including:

`alt.2600`

`alt.security`

`alt.security.index`

```
alt.security.keydist

alt.security.pgp

alt.security.ripem
```

A large number of Usenet newsgroups are devoted to various World Wide Web and Intranet topics, including the following:

```
comp.groupware

comp.infosystems.www

comp.infosystems.www.advocacy

comp.infosystems.www.authoring.cgi

comp.infosystems.www.authoring.misc

comp.infosystems.www.browsers.ms-windows

comp.infosystems.www.servers.ms-windows

comp.infosystems.www.servers.misc

comp.infosystems.www.authoring.html

comp.infosystems.www.authoring.cgi

comp.infosystems.www.authoring.images

comp.infosystems.www.authoring.misc

comp.infosystems.www.misc

comp.infosystems.www.providers

comp.infosystems.www.users

comp.infosystems.www.servers.ms-windows
```

The newsgroups devoted to programming languages include:

```
comp.lang.java

comp.lang.perl
```

and there is even a newsgroup devoted to ISDN:

```
comp.dcom.isdn
```

And then there are the newsgroups devoted to Windows NT and
NT Server:

```
comp.os.ms-windows.nt.admin.misc
```

```
comp.os.ms-windows.nt.admin.networking
```

```
comp.os.ms-windows.nt.advocacy
```

```
comp.os.ms-windows.nt.misc
```

```
comp.os.ms-windows.nt.pre-release
```

```
comp.os.ms-windows.nt.setup
```

```
comp.os.ms-windows.nt.setup.hardware
```

```
comp.os.ms-windows.nt.setup.misc
```

```
comp.os.ms-windows.nt.software.backoffice
```

```
comp.os.ms-windows.nt.software.compatibility
```

```
comp.os.ms-windows.nt.software services
```

```
comp.os.ms-windows.programmer.nt.kernel-mode
```

Finally, some of the Windows newsgroups also relate to Windows NT,
particularly with respect to networking and remote access topics,
including:

```
comp.os.ms-windows.networking.ras
```

```
comp.os.ms-windows.networking.tcp-ip
```

```
comp.os.ms-windows.networking.win95
```

```
comp.os.ms-windows.networking.windows
```

```
comp.os.ms-windows
```

Electronic Newsletters

You can subscribe to Microsoft's automatic *WinNT* electronic newsletter by filling out a questionaire at:

```
http://www.bhs.com/microsoft.winntnews/
```

or by sending an e-mail message to:

```
winntnews-admin@microsoft.bhs.com
```

with the command:

```
subscribe winntnews your-real-name
```

as the first line of your e-mail message. Once you are registered, you will receive the newsletter by e-mail.

Similarly, you can subscribe to the *Microsoft BackOffice News* electronic newsletter by filling out the questionaire at:

```
http://www.bhs.com/microsoft.backofficenews
```

or by sending an e-mail message to:

```
backofficenews-admin@microsoft.bhs.com
```

with the command:

```
subscribe backofficenews your-real-name
```

as the first line of your e-mail message, where *your-real-name* is your name and not an alias; many mailing lists do not accept subscription requests from aliases. Again, once you are registered, you will receive the newsletter by e-mail. The Beverly Hills Software Resource Center runs other mailing lists too, including the NT Consultants list (send e-mail to `list@bhs.com` with `subscribe nt consult` as the first line of the message).

The Firewalls mailing list, maintained by Great Circle Associates, is one of the main forums for system administrators who want to know about the design, construction, maintenance, and operation of Internet filewalls. To subscribe, send an e-mail message to:

```
majordomo@greatcircle.com
```

with the message:

```
subscribe firewalls your-real-name
```

as the first and only line in the message. As this is a fairly high-volume mailing list, you might want to set your subscription to digest mode so that you receive one large digest consisting of many messages, rather than hundreds of smaller, individual e-mail messages.

The WWW-Security mailing list is devoted to the discussion of security for World Wide Web clients and servers. Send an e-mail message to:

```
majordomo@nsmx.rutgers.edu
```

containing the line:

```
subscribe www-security your-real-name
```

To subscribe to the copyright issues discussion group, send an e-mail message to:

```
listproc@cni.org
```

containing the line:

```
subscribe cni-copyright your-real-name
```

To subscribe to an HTML authoring discussion group, send an e-mail message to:

```
listserv@netcentral.net
```

containing the line:

```
subscribe html-list your-real-name
```

And to subscribe to a World Wide Web developers discussion group, send an e-mail message to:

```
listserv@listserv.unb.ca
```

containing the line:

```
subscribe wwwdev your-real-name
```

Glossary of Windows NT and World Wide Web Terms

This appendix contains definitions of some of the new terms, acronyms, and abbreviations you may encounter during your travels on the Internet or in Windows NT Server and in setting up Microsoft Internet Information Server.

SYMBOLS

@ symbol
In an e-mail address the @ symbol (pronounced "at symbol") is often used to separate the user ID from the domain name of the computer used for mail. *See also* domain name; e-mail.

10/100
A term used to indicate that a network device can support both Ethernet (at a data-transfer rate of 10 Mbps) and Fast Ethernet (at a data-transfer rate of 100 Mbps). *See also* Ethernet; Fast Ethernet.

10Base2
An Ethernet standard that uses thin coaxial cable; also known as thinnet. *See also* Ethernet.

10Base5
An Ethernet standard that uses thick coaxial cable; also called thicknet. *See also* Ethernet.

10BaseF
An Ethernet standard that defines the use of Ethernet over fiber-optic cable. *See also* Ethernet; fiber-optic cable.

10BaseT
An Ethernet standard that uses Category 3 unshielded twisted-pair telephone cable. *See also* Category 1-5; Ethernet.

A

Access
A desktop database program developed by Microsoft; a run-time version of the database engine is included with Microsoft Visual Basic.

access server
A computer that provides access to remote users who dial into the system and access network resources as though their computers were connected to the network directly.

ActiveX
A programming specification from Microsoft used by programmers for performing back-end applications previously accomplished by use of CGI scripts. *See also* Common Gateway Interface; Java.

Address Resolution Protocol
Abbreviated ARP. A protocol within the TCP/IP family of protocols that allows a host to find the physical address of a node on the same network when it only knows the target's logical address. *See also* protocol; Transmission Control Protocol/Internet Protocol.

Under ARP, a network interface card contains a table (known as the address resolution cache) that maps logical addresses to the hardware addresses of nodes on the network. When a node needs to send a packet, it first checks the address resolution cache to see if the physical address information is present. If it is present, that address is used, and network traffic is reduced; otherwise a normal ARP request is made to determine the address.

American Standard Code for Information Interchange

Abbreviated ASCII. A standard coding scheme that assigns values to letters, numbers, punctuation marks, and control characters to achieve compatibility between computer systems. In ASCII, each character is represented by a unique integer value composed of 7 bits. The values from 0 to 31 are used for nonprinting control characters, and the values from 32 to 127 are used to represent the letters of the alphabet, numbers, and common punctuation marks.

All computers that use ASCII can understand the Standard ASCII Character Set. It is used to represent everything from source code to written text and is used when exchanging information between computers.

anonymous FTP

A method used to access an Internet host with FTP that does not require you to have an account on the target computer system. Simply log on to the Internet computer with the username *anonymous* and use your e-mail address as your password. This access method was originally provided as a courtesy so that system administrators could see who had logged on to their systems, but now it is often required to gain access to an Internet computer that has FTP service. *See also* File Transfer Protocol.

You cannot use anonymous FTP with every computer on the Internet—only with those that have been set up to offer the service. The system administrator decides which files and directories will be open to public access, and the rest of the system is considered off limits and cannot be accessed by anonymous FTP users. Some sites only allow you to download files from them; as a security precaution, you are not allowed to upload files to them. All this aside, the world open to anonymous FTP users is enormous; you can access tens of thousands of computers, and you can download hundreds of thousands of files.

anchor

A hypertext link in the form of text or a graphic that, when you click on it, takes you to the linked file. An anchor may be at the source or the destination of the hypertext link. *See also* hypertext; link.

answer mode

A function that allows a modem to answer an incoming call, detect the protocol being used by the calling modem, and then synchronize with that protocol. *See also* modem; protocol.

API

See application programming interface.

application layer

The seventh, or highest, layer in the ISO/OSI networking model. This layer uses services provided by the lower layers but is completely insulated from the details of the network hardware. It describes how applications interact with the network operating system, including database management, e-mail, and terminal emulation programs. *See also* International Standards Organization/Open System Interconnection model.

application programming interface

Abbreviated API. The complete set of operating system functions that an application can use to perform such tasks as managing files and displaying information.

An API provides a standard way to write an application, and it also describes how the application should use the functions that it provides. Using an API is quicker and easier than developing functions from scratch and helps to ensure some level of consistency to all applications developed on a specific operating system.

Archie

A system used on the Internet to locate files available by anonymous FTP. Archie was written by students and volunteers at McGill University's School of Computer Science in Montreal, Canada, and is available on servers worldwide.

You can use an Archie client on your system, log on to an Archie server using Telnet, or send e-mail to an Archie server.

When you ask Archie to look for a file, it looks in a database rather than searching the whole Internet; once Archie finds the file, you use anonymous FTP to retrieve it.

archive file

A single file that contains one or more files or directories that may have been compressed to save space. Archives are often used to transport large numbers of files across the Internet.

An archive file created by the Unix operating system may have the filename extension TAR (for tape archive); those created with DOS, OS/2, and Windows systems may have the filename extension ZIP from the PKZIP program. Archive files created on the Macintosh will probably have the extension SAE or SIT created by the StuffIt program.

An Internet host that provides access to a large number of archive files is usually known as an archive site.

ARP

See Address Resolution Protocol.

ASCII

See American Standard Code for Information Interchange.

Asynchronous Transfer Mode

Abbreviated ATM. A method used for transmitting voice, video, and data over high-speed local area networks. ATM uses continuous bursts of fixed-length packets called cells to transmit data. The basic packet consists of 53 bytes, 5 of which are used for control functions and 48 for data.

ATM is a connection-oriented protocol, and two kinds of connections are possible: permanent virtual circuits (PVCs), in which connections are made manually; and switched virtual circuits (SVCs), in which the connections are made automatically. Also known as cell relay.

asynchronous transmission

A method of data transmission that uses start bits and stop bits to coordinate the flow of information so that the time intervals between individual characters do not have to be equal. Parity is often used to check the accuracy of the data received. *See also* parity.

ATM

See Asynchronous Transfer Mode.

attribute

A quantity that defines a special property of an HTML element. An attribute is defined within the start tag. *See also* element; Hypertext Markup Language; tag.

auditing

The process of scrutinizing network security-related events and transactions to ensure that they are accurate, particularly reviewing attempts to create, access, and delete files and directories. Records of these events are stored in the event log, which can only be examined by the system administrator. *See also* system administrator.

audit trail

An automatic feature of certain programs or the operating system that creates a running record of all transactions. An audit trail allows you to track a piece of data from the moment it enters the system to the moment it leaves and to determine the origin of any changes to that data.

authentication

In a network or multiuser operating system, the process that validates a user's log on information. Authentication usually involves comparing the username and password to a list of authorized users and their passwords. If a match is found, the user can log on and access the system in accordance with the rights or permissions assigned to his or her account.

authorization

The provision of rights or permissions based on identity. Authorization and authentication go hand in hand in networking; your access to services is based on your identity, and the authentication processes confirms that you are who you say you are.

B

Baby Bells

A slang term for the Regional Bell Operating Companies (RBOC) formed when AT&T was broken up in 1984. Includes Ameritech, Bell Atlantic, Bell-South, NYNEX, Pacific Telesis, Southwestern Bell, and Bell Labs.

backbone

That portion of the network that manages the bulk of the traffic. The backbone may connect several locations or buildings, and other smaller networks may be attached to it. A backbone often uses a higher-speed communications system than the individual LAN segments. *See also* local area network.

bandwidth

The transmission capacity of a communications channel, usually stated in megabits per second (Mbps). For example, Ethernet has a bandwidth of 10 Mbps, and FDDI has a bandwidth of 100 Mbps. *See also* fiber-distributed data interface.

bandwidth on demand

A feature of WANs that allows the user to dial up additional bandwidth as the application demands. Most network traffic does not flow in steady and easily predictable streams, but in short bursts, separated by longer periods of inactivity. This pattern makes it very difficult to predict peak loads. Bandwidth on demand allows the user to pay only for the bandwidth used. *See also* wide area network.

bang path

From the Unix world, a bang is an exclamation point, and a bang path is a series of host names used to direct e-mail from one user to another. *See also* e-mail.

baseband network

A technique for transmitting signals as direct current pulses rather than as modulated signals. The entire bandwidth of the communications channel is used by a single digital signal; so computers in a baseband network can only transmit when the channel is not busy. Ethernet is an example of a baseband network. *See also* Ethernet.

baseline

The process of determining and documenting network throughput and other performance information when the network is operating under what is considered a normal load.

Basic Rate ISDN

Abbreviated BRI. An ISDN service that offers two bearer channels: a 64Kbps bandwidth used for data transfer, and a data-link 16Kbps channel used for signaling and control information.

bastion host

A computer system that is the main connection to the Internet for users of a local area network. A bastion host is usually configured in such as way as to minimize the risk of intruders gaining access to the main LAN. It gets its name from the fortified projections on the outer walls of medieval European castles. *See also* firewall; proxy server.

BISDN

See Broadband Integrated Service Digital Network.

bits per second

Abbreviated bps. The number of bits transmitted every second during a data-transfer procedure.

bps

See bits per second.

BRI

See Basic Rate ISDN.

Broadband Integrated Service Digital Network

Abbreviated BISDN. A high-speed communications standard for WANs that handles high-bandwidth applications, such as voice, video, data, and graphics.

SMDS and ATM are two BISDN services that can provide huge bandwidth for WANs. *See also* Asynchronous Transfer Mode; Switched Multimegabit Data Services; wide area network.

broadband network

A technique for transmitting a large amount of information, including voice, data, and video, over long distances using the same communications channel. Sometimes called wideband transmission, it is based on the same technology as cable television. The transmission capacity is divided into several distinct channels that can be used concurrently by different networks, normally using FDM. The individual channels are protected from one another by guard channels of unused frequencies. *See also* frequency-division multiplexing.

browser

A program used to explore Internet resources. A browser lets you wander from site to site without regard for the technical details of the links between the nodes or the specific methods used to access them and presents the information—text, graphics, sound, or video—as a document on the screen. Most people use the Netscape browser or the browser from Microsoft known as the Internet Explorer.

C2

A discretionary level of operating system security as defined by the NCSC that requires a user to log in to a system using a password. *See also* National Computer Security Center; password.

callback modem

Also known as a dialback modem. A special modem that does not answer an incoming call, but instead requires the caller to enter a code and then hang up so that the modem can return the call. As long as the entered code matches a previously authorized number, the modem dials the number. Callback modems are used in installations for which communications lines must be available for remote users but data must be protected from intruders. *See also* modem.

Category 1–5

The Electronics Industry Association/ Telecommunications Industry Association (EIA/TIA) standards for cabling.

- Category 1. Unshielded twisted-pair telephone cable suitable for voice but not for data transmissions.

- Category 2. Unshielded twisted-pair cable for use at speeds of up to 4Mbps; similar to IBM Cabling System type 3 cable.

- Category 3. Unshielded twisted-pair cable for use at speeds of up to 10Mbps. Category 3 is the minimum requirement for 10BaseT. The cable has four pair of conductors and three twists per foot.

- Category 4. The lowest grade of cable acceptable for use with 16Mbps Token Ring networks.

- Category 5. 100-ohm four-wire twisted-pair copper cable for use at speeds of up to 100Mbps with Ethernet or ATM. This cable is low capacitance and exhibits low crosstalk when installed according to specifications.

CDDI

See Copper Distributed Data Interface.

cell

Any fixed-length packet. For example, Asynchronous Transfer Mode (ATM) uses 53-byte cells. *See also* Asynchronous Transfer Mode; packet.

cell relay

A form of packet transmission used in BISDN networks that uses a fixed-length, 53-byte cell over a packet-switched network. Also known as ATM. *See also* Asynchronous Transfer Mode; Broadband Integrated Service Digital Network; packet switching.

Centre Européen pour la Recherche Nucléaire

Abbreviated CERN. The European laboratory for particle physics where the concept of the World Wide Web first originated in 1989.

Centrex

A contraction formed from Central Exchange. Services provided to a company by the local telephone company. Because all the switching takes place at the telephone company's central office rather than at the customer site, Centrex services are easy to expand.

CERN

See Centre Européen pour la Recherche Nucléaire.

CERT

See Computer Emergency Response Team.

CGI

See Common Gateway Interface.

Channel Service Unit

Abbreviated CSU. A device that functions as a certified safe electrical circuit, acting as a buffer between the customer's equipment and a public carrier's WAN equipment. *See also* wide area network.

A CSU prevents faulty CPE, such as DSUs, from affecting a public carrier's transmission systems and ensures that all signals placed on the line are properly timed and formed. All CSU designs must be approved and certified by the FCC (Federal Communications Commission). *See also* customer premises equipment; Data Service Unit.

client

An application that uses information or services provided by a server. Many of the common Internet tools, including Gopher, FTP, and the Web browsers, are all client applications interacting with the appropriate server. *See also* client-server.

client-server

A network model that distributes processing between the client (or front end) and the server (or back end) on the network. Clients, including many popular Internet tools—such as Gopher, FTP, and the Web browsers—request information from the servers. The servers store data and programs and provide network-wide services to clients. *See also* client; server.

collaboration software

A set of network-based applications that let users share information quickly and easily.

common carrier

A communications company such as MCI, AT&T, or ITT that provides data and voice telecommunications services to the general public.

Common Gateway Interface

Abbreviated CGI. A standard way that programs can interface with Web servers and allow them to run applications such as search engines and to access databases and other back-end applications. *See also* search engine.

Common Object Request Broker Architecture

Abbreviated CORBA. A standard from the OMG, whose members include IBM and Sun Microsystems, that enables communications between distributed objects.

Computer Emergency Response Team

Abbreviated CERT. Founded in 1988 in response to the infamous "Internet worm" incident, CERT works with the Internet community to increase awareness of security issues; it conducts research into improving existing systems and provides a 24-hour technical assistance service for responding to security incidents. You can reach CERT by e-mail at cert@cert.org or by telephone at (412) 268-7090.

congestion

A condition that occurs when the load exceeds the capacity of a communications circuit. You may see a very slow response from a server, or you may see a message telling you that no ports are available for the service or host you are requesting.

connection-oriented

A term that describes a communications model that goes through three well-defined stages: establishment of the connection, transfer of the data, and release of the connection. TCP is a connection-oriented protocol. *See also* protocol; Transmission Control Protocol.

connectionless

A term that describes a communications model in which the source and destination addresses are included in each packet so that a direct connection between nodes is not required for communications. *See also* node; packet.

Copper Distributed Data Interface

Abbreviated CDDI. A version of the FDDI standard designed to run on shielded and unshielded twisted-pair cable rather than on fiber-optic cable. *See also* fiber-distributed data interface.

CORBA

See Common Object Request Broker Architecture.

CPE

See customer premises equipment.

cracker

An unauthorized person who breaks into a computer system planning to do harm or damage or with criminal intent. The popular press often portrays crackers as programmers with exceptional talent, and some of them are, but most of them use a set of well-worn tricks to exploit common security weaknesses in the systems they target. *See also* hacker.

CSU

See Channel Service Unit.

customer premises equipment

Abbreviated CPE. Communications equipment, either leased or owned, used at a customer site.

D

daemon

A background program that runs unattended, collecting information or performing administrative tasks. The Microsoft Internet Information Server uses several daemonlike programs to run the Internet server. The term comes from the Unix world.

data communications equipment

Abbreviated DCE. In communications, a device that connects a computer or a terminal to a communications channel or public network. The most familiar DCE device is a modem. *See also* modem.

Data Encryption Standard

Abbreviated DES. A standard method of encrypting and decrypting data, developed by the U.S. National Bureau of Standards. DES works by a combination of transposition and substitution. It is used by the U.S. government and most banks and money-transfer systems to protect all sensitive computer information.

data-link layer

The second layer of the seven-layer ISO/OSI networking model. The data-link layer validates the integrity of the flow of data from one node to another by synchronizing blocks of data and controlling the flow of data. *See also* node; International Standards Organization/Open System Interconnection model.

data packet

One unit of information transmitted as a discrete entity from one node on the network to another. More specifically, in packet-switched networks, a packet is a transmission unit of a fixed maximum length that contains a header, a set of data, and error-control information. *See also* node.

Data Service Unit

Abbreviated DSU. A device that connects DTE to digital communications lines. A DSU formats the data for transmission on the public carrier WAN and ensures that the carrier's requirements for data formats are met. *See also* data terminal equipment; wide area network.

data terminal equipment

Abbreviated DTE. In communications, any device such as a terminal or a computer, connected to a communications device, channel, or public network.

DCE

See data communications equipment.

D-channel

The data channel in ISDN used for control signals and customer data. In BRI, the D-channel operates at 16Kbps; in PRI, it operates at 64Kbps. *See also* Base Rate ISDN; bits per second; Integrated Services Digital Network; kilobits per second; Primary Rate ISDN.

DCOM

See Distributed Common Object Model.

dedicated line

A communications circuit used for one specific purpose and not used by or shared between other users. You need only dial a dedicated line to restore service after an unscheduled interruption. Also known as a dedicated circuit or a direct connection. An ISDN connection to the Internet qualifies as a dedicated line. *See also* direct connection; Integrated Services Digital Network.

demand priority

A technique used in Fast Ethernet to arbitrate access to the network and avoid collisions. Demand priority replaces CSMA/CD used in slower Ethernet networks. *See also* Ethernet; Fast Ethernet.

Demand priority can also prioritize certain specific network traffic such as video and other time-critical data, giving it a higher precedence; when multiple requests are received, the highest priority is always serviced first.

DES

See Data Encryption Standard.

dial-up line

A nondedicated communications channel in which a connection is established by dialing the destination code and is then broken once the call is complete.

digital signature

A unique value associated with a transaction that is used to verify the identity of the sender as well as the origin of the message. Digital signatures cannot be forged.

direct connection

A communications circuit used for one specific purpose and not used by or shared between other users. You need only dial a dedicated line to restore service after an unscheduled interruption. Also known as a dedicated circuit or a direct line. An ISDN connection to the Internet qualifies as a direct connection. *See also* dedicated line; Integrated Services Digital Network.

Distributed Common Object Model

Abbreviated DCOM. A specification from Microsoft that enables communications between distributed objects.

DNS

See Domain Name Service.

DNS alias

A host name that the DNS server knows points to another host. Computers always have one real name, but they can also have several aliases. DNS aliases are sometimes called CNAMEs or canonical names. *See also* Domain Name Service.

DNS name server

A server containing information that is part of the DNS distributed database which makes computer names available to client programs querying for name resolution on the Internet. *See also* Domain Name Service.

document database

A carefully organized collection of related documents; for example, a set of technical support bulletins.

document instance

In SGML, the text component of a document as distinct from the structure of the document. *See also* document type definition; Standard Generalized Markup Language.

document root

On an Internet server, a directory that contains the files, images, and data you want to present to all users who access the server with a browser. *See also* browser.

document type definition

Abbreviated DTD. In SGML, the structural component of a document as distinct from the actual data or content of the document. *See also* document instance; Standard Generalized Markup Language.

domain

A description of a single computer, a whole department, or a complete site, used for naming and administrative purposes. Top-level domains must be registered to receive e-mail from outside the organization; local domains have meaning only inside their own enterprise. Depending on the context, domain can have several slightly different meanings:

- On the Internet, a domain is part of the Domain Name Service.

- In Windows NT, a user can log on to the local computer and be authenticated to access just that one system or can log on to a domain and be authenticated to access other servers within that domain.

domain name

In DNS, an easy-to-remember name that identifies a specific host, as opposed to the hard-to-remember numeric IP address. *See also* Domain Name Service; IP address.

Domain Name Service

Abbreviated DNS, and sometimes referred to as Domain Name System. The distributed database system used to map host names to numeric IP addresses. DNS lets you use the Internet without having to remember long lists of cryptic numbers. *See also* IP address.

download

In communications, to transfer a file or other information from the server to another computer over a network link or via modem. *See also* upload.

DSU

See Data Service Unit.

DTE

See data terminal equipment.

DTD

See document type definition.

E

element

A unit of structure in HTML. Some elements have start and stop tags; others have only a single tag. Certain elements can contain other elements. *See also* Hypertext Markup Language; tag.

e-mail

Also called electronic mail. The use of a network to transmit text messages, memos, and reports. Users can send a message to one or more individual users, to a predefined group, or to all users on the system. When you receive an e-mail message, you can read, print, forward, answer, or delete it.

An e-mail system can be implemented on a variety of computers. E-mail is by far the most popular Internet application, with more than 80 percent of all Internet users taking advantage of this service.

E-mail has several advantages over conventional mail systems, including:

- E-mail is fast; very fast when compared with conventional mail.

- If something exists on your computer as a file, you can probably send it as e-mail, including text, graphics, even sound and video.

- E-mail is very extensive; you can now send e-mail to well over half the countries in the world.

The problems with e-mail are similar to those associated with online communications in general, such as security (always assume that your e-mail is not private) and the legal status of documents exchanged via e-mail.

encapsulation

The process of inserting the header and data from a higher-level protocol into the data frame of a lower-level protocol. *See also* protocol.

encryption

The process of encoding information in an attempt to make it secure from unauthorized access. The reverse of this process is known as decryption.

The two main encryption schemes in common use are:

- Private (Symmetrical) Key Schemes. An encryption algorithm based on a private encryption key known to both the sender and the recipient of the information. The encrypted message is unreadable and can be transmitted over nonsecure systems.

- Public (Asymmetrical) Key Schemes. An encryption scheme based on using the two halves of a long bit sequence as encryption keys. Either half of the bit sequence can be used to encrypt data, but the other half is required to decrypt the data.

encryption key

A unique and secret number used to encrypt data to protect it from unauthorized access.

enterprise

A term used to encompass an entire business group, organization, or corporation, including all local, remote, and satellite offices.

enterprise network

A network that connects every computer in every location of a business group, organization, or corporation and runs the company's mission-critical applications.

In many cases, an enterprise network includes several types of computers running several operating systems.

Ethernet

A popular network protocol and cabling scheme with a transfer rate of 10Mbps, originally developed by Xerox in 1976. Ethernet uses a bus topology, and network nodes are connected by thick or thin coaxial cable, fiber-optic cable, or twisted-pair cabling.

Ethernet uses CSMA/CD (Carrier Sense Multiple Access/Collision Detection) to prevent network failures or collisions when two devices both try to access the network at exactly the same moment.

The advantages of Ethernet include:

- It's easy to install at moderate cost.

- The technology is available from many sources and is well known and understood.

- It offers a variety of cabling options.

- It works well in networks with only occasional heavy traffic.

Disadvantages of Ethernet include:

- Heavy traffic can slow the network down

- A break in the main cable can bring down large chunks of the network, and troubleshooting a bus topology can sometimes be very difficult.

Ethernet address

The address assigned to a network interface card by the original manufacturer. This address identifies the local device address to the rest of the network and allows messages to find the correct destination. Also known as the MAC (media access control) address or the hardware address.

Eudora
A widely used e-mail system. *See also* e-mail.

Exchange
A groupware product from Microsoft that allows users to discuss corporate-wide issues, set up meetings, and send e-mail containing links to pages on the World Wide Web. Exchange competes with Lotus Notes from IBM and with GroupWise from Novell.

F

FAQ
Abbreviation for frequently asked questions. Originally a Usenet document that contained the answers to the questions that new users ask when they first subscribe to a newsgroup. Recent use has spread beyond Usenet, although the concept remains the same: to distribute answers to questions that the seasoned users have grown tired of answering. An FAQ is often an excellent introduction to a technically difficult subject. *See also* newsgroup; Usenet.

Fast Ethernet
A version of the Ethernet standard that permits data-transfer rates of 10Mbps or 100Mbps or both and uses CSMA/CD access methods. *See also* Ethernet.

FDDI
See fiber-distributed data interface.

FDM
See frequency-division multiplexing.

fiber-distributed data interface
Abbreviated FDDI. A specification for a fiber-optic network running at speeds of as much as 100Mbps over a dual, counter-rotating, token-ring topology.

fiber-optic cable
A transmission technology that sends pulses of light along specially manufactured optical fibers. Each fiber consists of a core, thinner than a human hair, surrounded by a sheath with a much lower refractive index. Light signals introduced at one end of the cable are conducted along the cable as the signal reflects from the sheath.

Fiber-optic cable is lighter and smaller than traditional copper cable, is immune to electrical interference, offers better security, and has better signal-transmitting qualities. It is, however, more expensive than traditional cables and is more difficult to repair. Fiber-optic is often used for high-speed backbones, but as prices drop, we may even see fiber-optic cable run to the desktop.

File Transfer Protocol
Abbreviated FTP. The TCP/IP protocol used to log on to a computer, list files and directories, and transfer files. FTP supports a range of file-transfer types and formats, including ASCII, EBCDIC, and binary. *See also* American Standard Code for Information Interchange; Transmission Control Protocol/Internet Protocol.

firewall
A barrier established in hardware or in software, or sometimes in both, that allows traffic to flow only one way: outward from the protected network. A firewall is a device commonly used to protect a network from unwanted intruders.

FORM

An HTML element that allows users to complete information in fill-in-the-blanks boxes, checklists, or other formats and then submit that data as an application to be processed. The FORM element is specified in level 2 HTML. *See also* Hypertext Markup Language.

FQDN

See fully qualified domain name.

fractional T1

One portion of a T1 circuit. A T1 circuit has a capacity of 1.544Mbps, the equivalent of twenty-four 64 Kbps channels. Customers can lease as many of these 64Kbps channels as they need; they do not have to lease the entire 1.544Mbps circuit.

frame relay

A standard for a packet-switching protocol, running at speeds of up to 2Mbps, that also provides for bandwidth on demand. Frame relay is less robust than X.25 but provides better efficiency and higher throughput. *See also* packet; packet switching.

frequency-division multiplexing

Abbreviated FDM. A method of sharing a transmission channel by dividing the bandwidth into several parallel paths, defined and separated by guard bands of different frequencies. FDM is often used in analog transmissions, such as in communications over a telephone line or on a baseband network. *See also* statistical multiplexing; time-division multiplexing.

FTP

See File Transfer Protocol.

ftp

The command used to invoke FTP.

fully qualified domain name

Abbreviated FQDN. A host name with the appropriate domain name appended. For example, on a host with the host name `wallaby` and the DNS domain name `my-company.com`, the FQDN is `wallaby.my-company.com`. *See also* domain name; Domain Name Service.

G

gateway

A shared connection between a LAN and a larger system, such as the Internet. *See also* local area network.

GIF

See Graphics Interchange Format.

global group

User accounts granted server and workstation rights in their own and other domains whose security systems allow access. Global groups are a means of providing rights and permissions to resources inside and outside the domain to a group of users within a single domain. *See also* domain; local group.

Gopher

A popular client/server application that presents Internet resources as a series of menus, shielding the user from the underlying mechanical details of IP addresses and different access methods. Developed at the University of Minnesota, home of the Golden Gophers. *See also* client-server; IP address.

Gopherspace

A collective term used to describe all the Internet resources accessible using Gopher.

groupware

Network software designed for use by a group of people all working on the same project or needing access to the same data.

Graphics Interchange Format

Abbreviated GIF. A graphics file format, originating on CompuServe, that results in relatively small graphics files. A graphic in this format can be used as an inline image in an HTML document. Two other graphics file formats can also appear inline in an HTML document: X-Bitmaps (filename extension XBM) and X-Pixelmaps (filename extension XPM). *See also* Hypertext Markup Language; inline image.

hacker

In the programming community, where this term originated, a hacker is a person who pursues knowledge of computer systems for its own sake—someone willing to "hack through a problem." More recently, particularly in popular culture, the term has come to mean a person who breaks into other people's computers with malicious intent (what programmers call a "cracker"). *See also* cracker.

helper

A program launched or used by a Web browser to process a file that the browser cannot handle. A helper may view a JPEG file, play a sound file, or expand compressed files. Sometimes called a plug-in. A helper that deals with video, graphics, or animation is called a viewer; a helper that deals with sound files is called a player. *See also* Joint Photographics Expert Group; player; viewer.

hit

A hit on a Web page occurs whenever you access any file, whether it is an HTML document, a graphic, a CGI script, or an audio or video clip on that page. If you access three files on an HTML page, you generate three hits. This means that a hit is not usually a good estimate of the number of individual people visiting a site because the number of hits simply reflects the number of files accessed. *See also* Common Gateway Interface; Hypertext Markup Language.

home page

An initial starting page on the World Wide Web. A home page may be associated with a single person, a specific subject, a corporation, a non-profit organization, or a school and is a convenient jumping-off place for links to other pages or Internet resources.

host

The central or controlling computer in a networked environment, providing services that other computers or terminals can access via the network.

A large system accessible on the Internet is also known as a host. Sometimes known as a *host system* or a *host computer*.

HotJava

An interactive Web browser from Sun Microsystems. HotJava is the browser related to Java, the programming language designed to create small executable programs that can be downloaded quickly and run in a small amount of memory. *See also* Java.

HTML
See Hypertext Markup Language.

HTTP
See Hypertext Transfer Protocol.

hypertext
A method of presenting information so that it can be viewed by the user in a nonsequential way, regardless of how the topics were originally arranged.

Hypertext was designed to make a computer respond to the nonlinear way that humans think and access information—by association rather than by the linear organization of film, speech, or books.

In a hypertext application, you can browse through the information with considerable flexibility, choosing to follow a new path each time you access the information. When you click on a hot spot, you activate a link to another hypertext document, which may be located on the same Internet host or can be on a completely different system thousands of miles away. The utility of these links depends entirely on the care that the document originator used when assembling the document; unfortunately, many links turn into dead ends.

Hypertext Markup Language
Abbreviated HTML. A language with which World Wide Web documents are formatted. HTML defines the appearance and placement of HTML elements, including fonts, graphics, text, hypertext links to other sites, and many more details. HTML is a subset of SGML.

See also hypertext; Standard Generalized Markup Language.

Hypertext Transfer Protocol
Abbreviated HTTP. The protocol used to manage the links between one hypertext document and another. *See also* hypertext; link.

HTTP is the mechanism that opens the related document when you select a hypertext link, no matter where that related document happens to be located.

I

IAB
See Internet Architecture Board.

ICMP
See Internet Control Message Protocol.

ICP
See Internet Content Provider.

IETF
See Internet Architecture Board.

imagemap
A graphical inline image on an HTML page that potentially connects each region of the image with a Web resource; you can click on the image to retrieve the resource. *See also* inline image; Hypertext Markup Language.

inline image
An image merged with text displayed on an HTML page. The process of placing the image is

known as inlining. *See also* Hypertext Markup Language.

Integrated Services Digital Network

Abbreviated ISDN. A standard for a worldwide digital communications network intended to replace all current systems with a completely digital, synchronous, full-duplex transmission system. Computers and other devices connect to ISDN via simple, standardized interfaces. When complete, ISDN systems will be capable of transmitting voice, video, and data all on the same line—a task that currently requires three separate connections.

International Standards Organization/Open System Interconnection model

Abbreviated ISO/OSI model. A network reference model defined by the ISO that divides computer-to-computer communications into seven connected layers. Such layers are known as a protocol stack.

Each successively higher layer builds on the functions provided by the layers below, as follows:

- Application layer 7: The highest level of the model. It defines the manner in which applications interact with the network, including database management, e-mail, and terminal-emulation programs.

- Presentation layer 6: Defines the way in which data is formatted, presented, converted, and encoded.

- Session layer 5: Coordinates communications and maintains the session for as long as it is needed, performing security, logging, and administrative functions.

- Transport layer 4: Defines protocols for structuring messages and supervises the validity of the transmission by performing some error checking.

- Network layer 3: Defines protocols for data routing to ensure that the information arrives at the correct destination node.

- Data-link layer 2: Validates the integrity of the flow of data from one node to another by synchronizing blocks of data and controlling the flow of data.

- Physical layer 1: Defines the mechanism for communicating with the transmission medium and the network-interface hardware.

internet

Short for internetwork. Two or more networks using different networking protocols, connected by means of a router. Users on an internet can access the resources of all connected networks.

Internet

The world's largest computer network, consisting of millions of computers supporting tens of millions of users in more than 100 countries. The Internet is growing at such a phenomenal rate that any size estimates are quickly out of date.

The Internet was originally established to meet the needs of the U.S. defense industry, but it has quickly grown into a huge global network serving universities, academic researchers, commercial interests, and government agencies, both in the United States, and overseas.

The Internet uses TCP/IP protocols, and Internet computers run many operating systems, including several variations of Unix, Windows NT, and VMS.

Internet Activities Board

See Internet Architecture Board.

Internet Architecture Board

Abbreviated IAB. The coordinating committee for management of the Internet. IAB has two main subcommittees:

- The Internet Engineering Task Force (IETF) specifies protocols and recommends Internet standards.
- The Internet Research Task Force (IRTF) researches new technologies and refers them to the IETF.

Previously, the abbreviation stood for Internet Activities Board.

Internet Content Provider

Abbreviated ICP. A company that will design and deliver content for your Web site.

Internet Control Message Protocol

Abbreviated ICMP. That portion of TCP/IP that provides the functions used for network layer management and control. *See also* International Standards Organization/Open System Interconnection model; Transmission Control Protocol/Internet Protocol.

Internet Engineering Task Force

See Internet Architecture Board.

Internet NFS

A TCP/IP-based protocol from Sun Microsystems used for sharing and accessing files remotely over the Internet. *See also* Network File System.

Internet Packet Exchange

Abbreviated IPX. Part of Novell NetWare's protocol stack, used to transfer data between the server and the workstations on the network. IPX packets are encapsulated and carried by the packets used in Ethernet and by the frames used in token ring networks. *See also* Ethernet.

Internet Protocol

Abbreviated IP. The TCP/IP session-layer protocol that regulates packet forwarding by tracking Internet addresses, routing outgoing messages, and recognizing incoming messages. IP does not guarantee the delivery of a packet, nor does it specify the order of delivery. *See also* packet; Transmission Control Protocol/Internet Protocol.

Internet Research Task Force

See Internet Architecture Board.

Internet Server API

Abbreviated ISAPI. An Internet Information Server programming interface for back-end applications developed by Microsoft and Process Software Corporation. *See also* Netscape Server API.

Internet Service Provider

Abbreviated ISP. The company that provides you or your organization with access to the Internet via a dial-up or a dedicated connection. An ISP will normally have several servers and a high-speed connection to an Internet backbone. *See also* backbone; dedicated line; dial-up line.

InterNIC

The organization that maintains unique addresses for all the computers on the Internet by means of DNS. *See also* Domain Name Service.

Intranet

A private corporate network that uses Internet software and TCP/IP protocol standards. Many companies use Intranets for tasks as simple as distributing a company newsletter and for tasks as complex as posting and updating technical support bulletins to service personnel worldwide. An Intranet does not always include a permanent connection to the Internet. *See also* Internet; Transmission Control Protocol/ Internet Protocol.

intruder

An unauthorized user of a computer system, usually a person with malicious intent.

IP

See Internet Protocol.

IP address

A set of 4 numbers (4 bytes, or 32 bits), separated by dots, that specifies the actual location of a computer on the Internet or other TCP/IP-based network. These numbers are difficult for most people to remember; so humans tend to refer to Internet computers by their domain names instead. *See also* domain name; Transmission Control Protocol/Internet Protocol.

IPX

See Internet Packet Exchange.

IRTF

See Internet Architecture Board.

ISAPI

See Internet Server API.

ISDN

See Integrated Services Digital Network.

ISO/OSI model

See International Standards Organization/ Open System Interconnection model.

ISP

See Internet Service Provider.

J

Java

An object-oriented programming language developed by programmers at Sun Microsystems, designed to create distributed, executable applications for use with special Web browsers. Java technology has been licensed by many companies, including Microsoft, IBM, Adobe Systems, Oracle, Borland, Symantec, and other companies developing Web applications. *See also* ActiveX, HotJava.

Joint Photographic Experts Group

Abbreviated JPEG. An image-compression standard and file format that defines a set of compression methods for high-quality images such as photographs, single video frames, or scanned pictures; JPEG does not work very well when compressing text, line art, or vector graphics.

JPEG uses lossy compression methods that result in some loss of original data; when you decompress the image, you don't get exactly the same image you originally compressed, although JPEG was specifically designed to discard information not easily detected by the human eye. JPEG can store 24-bit color images in as many as 16 million colors; files in GIF format can only store a maximum of 256 colors. *See also* Graphics Interchange Format; lossy compression.

JPEG
See Joint Photographic Experts Group.

K

Kbps
See kilobits per second.

key
An entry in the Windows NT Registry Editor that contains an element of configuration information.

kilobits per second
Abbreviated Kbps. The number of bits transmitted every second, measured in multiples of 1024 bits per second; used as an indicator of transmission rates.

L

LAN
See local area network.

leased line
A communications circuit or telephone line reserved for the permanent use of a specific customer; also known as a dedicated line. *See also* dedicated line.

legacy system
A computer system that has been in use for a long time, either in a corporation (in the case of a mainframe computer) or in a home or small office (in the case of an older PC system). The problem of backward compatibility with legacy systems is always thorny, because these systems often perform essential functions that cannot be disrupted.

link
In a hypertext document, a connection between one element and another in the same or in a different document. *See also* hypertext.

listserver
Often shortened to listserv. An automatic mailing system on the Internet. An individual sends an e-mail message to the server, which in turn sends it to all the other subscribers. Several other automatic mailing programs exist, including `mailserv`, `majordomo`, and `almanac`.

local area network
Abbreviated LAN. A group of computers and associated peripheral devices connected by a communications channel, capable of sharing files and other resources between several users. *See also* wide area network.

local disk
A disk attached to your workstation rather than to the network file server; also known as a local drive.

local group
In Windows NT, a group granted rights and permissions to adjust the resources on the servers of its own domain. *See also* domain; global group.

lossless compression
Any data-compression method that compresses a file by re-recording the data it contains in a more compact fashion. With lossless compression, no original data is lost when the file is decompressed. Lossless compression methods are used on program files and on images such

as medical X rays, where data loss cannot be tolerated. *See also* lossy compression.

lossy compression

Any data compression method that compresses a file by discarding any data that the compression method decides is not needed. Original data is lost when the file is decompressed. Lossy compression may be used to shrink audio or images files if absolute accuracy is not required and if the loss of some data will not be noticed. *See also* lossless compression.

mailing list

On the Internet, a group of people who share a common interest and who automatically receive all the mail posted to the listserver or mailing list management program. Contributions are sent as e-mail to the server and then are automatically distributed to all subscribers. *See also* listserver.

MBONE

See multicast backbone.

Mbps

See megabits per second.

megabits per second

Abbreviated Mbps. A measurement of the amount of information moving across a network or communications link in one second, measured in multiples of 1,048,576 bits.

Microsoft BackOffice

A powerful software suite from Microsoft that consists of Windows NT Server, SQL Server, Exchange Server, the Internet Information

Server, SNA Server, and Systems Management Server (SMS).

MIME

See Multipurpose Internet Mail Extensions.

modem

Contraction of modulator/demodulator; a device that allows a computer to transmit information over a telephone line.

The modem translates between the digital signals used by the computer and the analog signals suitable for use by the telephone system. When transmitting, the modem modulates the digital information onto a carrier signal on the telephone line. When receiving, the modem performs the reverse process to demodulate the data from the carrier signal.

Mosaic

A World Wide Web client program or Web browser, originally written by the National Center for Supercomputing Applications (NCSA) at the University of Illinois. There are several excellent commercial versions of Mosaic, the most common being Netscape Navigator from Netscape Communications. *See also* browser; Web browser.

Motion Picture Experts Group

Abbreviated MPEG. An image compression standard and file format that defines a compression method for desktop audio, animation, and video.

MPEG is a lossy compression method that results in some data loss when a video clip is decompressed. *See also* lossy compression.

MPEG
See Motion Picture Experts Group.

multicast backbone
Abbreviated MBONE. An experimental method of transmitting digital video over the Internet in real time.

The TCP/IP protocols used for Internet transmissions are unsuitable for real time audio or video; they were designed to deliver text and other files reliably, but often with some delay. MBONE requires the creation of another backbone service with special hardware and software to accommodate video and audio transmissions. *See also* Transmission Control Protocol/Internet Protocol.

Multipurpose Internet Mail Extensions
Abbreviated MIME. An Internet specification that allows users to send multiple-part and multimedia messages rather than simple ASCII-text messages. A MIME-enabled e-mail application can send PostScript images, binary files, audio messages, and digital video over the Internet. *See also* American Standard Code for Information Interchange.

National Center for Supercomputing Applications
Abbreviated NCSA. At the University of Illinois at Urbana-Champaign, NCSA is credited with the creation of Mosaic, the first graphical Web browser. *See also* Mosaic; Web browser.

National Computer Security Center
Abbreviated NCSC. A branch of the U.S. National Security Agency that defines security for computer products. The Department of Defense Standard 5200.28, also known as the Orange Book, specifies several levels of increasingly complex security measures.

NCSA
See National Center for Supercomputing Applications.

NCSC
See National Computer Security Center.

Netscape Server API
Abbreviated NSAPI. A programming specification used by Netscape servers when performing back-end applications. *See also* ActiveX; Internet Server API.

network drive
A disk drive located on a computer other than the one currently being used, which is also available to users on the network.

Network File System
Abbreviated NFS. A distributed file-sharing system developed by Sun Microsystems more than 10 years ago that has been licensed and implemented by more than 300 vendors.

network layer
The third of seven layers of the ISO/OSI model for computer communications. The network layer defines protocols for data routing to ensure that the information arrives at the correct destination node and manages communications errors. *See also* International Standards Organization/Open System Interconnection model; protocol.

network news transfer protocol

Abbreviated NNTP. A protocol used for posting and retrieving news articles on Usenet newsgroups. *See also* newsgroup; protocol; Usenet.

newsgroup

A Usenet e-mail discussion group devoted to a single topic. Subscribers to the newsgroup post articles that can be read by all the other subscribers. *See also* Usenet.

Newsgroup names fit into a formal structure in which each component of the name is separated from the next by a period. The leftmost portion of the name represents the category of the newsgroup, and the name gets more specific from left to right.

The major top-level newsgroup categories are:

- `alt`: Newsgroups outside the main structure outlined below.

- `comp`: Computer science and related topics, including information about operating systems and hardware, as well as more advanced topics such as artificial intelligence and graphics.

- `misc`: Anything that does not fit into one of the other categories.

- `news`: Information on Usenet and newsgroups.

- `rec`: Recreational activities such as hobbies, the arts, movies, and books.

- `sci`: Discussion groups on scientific topics including math, physics, and biology.

- `soc`: Groups that address social issues and different cultures.

- `talk`: Groups that concentrate on controversial subjects such as gun control, abortion, religion, and politics.

newsreader

An application used to read the articles posted to Usenet newsgroups. Newsreaders are of two kinds: *threaded* newsreaders group the posts into threads of related articles; *unthreaded* newsreaders present the articles in their original order of posting. Of the two, threaded newsreaders are much easier to use. *See also* newsgroup; Usenet.

NFS

See Network File System.

NNTP

See network news transfer protocol.

node

Any device attached to the network capable of communicating with other network devices.

NSAPI

See Netscape Server API.

NT file system

Abbreviated NTFS. The file system native to Windows NT and Windows NT Server. There are several advantages to using NTFS, including long filenames, reduced file fragmentation, improved fault tolerance, and much better recovery after a system crash.

NTFS

See NT file system.

O

octet

The Internet's own term for 8 contiguous bits, or a byte. Some computer systems attached to the Internet used a byte with more than 8 bits, hence the need for this term.

ODBC

See open database connectivity.

ODSI

Abbreviation for Open Directory Services Interface. A standard from Microsoft that enables client software to query Internet directories, by providing a common API for naming.

Open Database Connectivity

Abbreviated ODBC. A programming interface developed by Microsoft that allows clients to access many types of database and file formats. *See also* client; client-server.

P

packet

A block of data sent over a network. Each packet contains sender, receiver, and error control information in addition to the actual message. Packets may be fixed- or variable-length and are reassembled if necessary when they reach their destination.

packet filtering

A process that limits protocol-specific network traffic to one segment of the network, isolates

e-mail domains, and performs other traffic-control functions.

packet-switched network

A network that consists of a series of interconnected circuits that route individual data packets over one of several possible routes, offering both flexibility and reliability. *See also* packet.

packet switching

A data-transmission method that simultaneously routes and transmits data packets from many customers over a communications channel or telephone line, thus optimizing the use of the line.

An addressed packet is routed from node to node until it reaches its destination, although related packets may not all follow the same route to that destination. Because long messages may be divided into several packets, packet sequence numbers are used to reassemble the original message at the destination node. *See also* node; packet.

page

A single file of text in HTML. *See also* Hypertext Markup Language.

parity

In communications, a simple form of error checking that uses an extra or redundant bit after the data bits but before the stop bit or bits. Parity may be set as follows:

- Odd parity: Indicates that the sum of all the 1 bits in the byte plus the parity bit must be odd. If the total is already odd, the parity bit is set to zero; if it is even, the parity bit is set to one.

- Even parity: If the sum of all the 1 bits is even, the parity bit must be set to zero; if it is odd, the parity bit must be set to one.

- Mark parity: The parity bit is always set to one and is used as the eighth bit.

- Space parity: The parity bit is set to zero and is used as the eighth bit.

- No parity: If the parity is set to none, there is no parity bit and no parity checking is done.

The parity settings used in both computers involved in exchanging data over a communications link must be the same.

password

A security method that identifies a specific, authorized user of a computer system or network by a specific string of characters. In general, passwords should be a mixture of upper- and lowercase letters and numbers and should be longer than 6 characters. Passwords should be kept secret and changed often. The worst passwords are the obvious ones—people's names or initials, place names, birth dates, and anything to do with computers or Star Trek.

PCT

See Private Communication Technology.

PDF

See Portable Document Format.

PEM

See privacy enhanced mail.

Perl

An acronym formed from Practical Extraction and Report Language or Pathologically Eclectic Rubbish Lister, depending on who you believe.

A scripting language written by Larry Wall with which you can write powerful data and text manipulation routines quickly and easily. For this reason, Perl has become a popular language for writing CGI applications. Perl does not suffer from the arbitrary limitations that plague other languages; lines can be of any length, arrays can be of any size, variable names can be as long as you care to make them, and binary data does not cause any problems. *See also* Common Gateway Interface.

permanent virtual circuit

Abbreviated PVC. A fixed communications circuit, created and maintained even when no data is being transmitted. A PVC has no setup overhead and gives improved performance for periodic transmissions that require an immediate connection.

permissions

In Windows NT, the ability of a user to access certain system resources, including files and directories. Permissions are based on the rights granted to user accounts by the system administrator. *See also* system administrator.

PGP

Abbreviation for Pretty Good Privacy. A popular shareware public-key encryption program, written by Phil Zimmermann and available at no cost from certain Internet sites. *See also* encryption.

physical layer

The first and lowest of the seven layers in the ISO/OSI model for computer communications. The physical layer defines the physical, electrical, mechanical, and functional procedures used to connect the equipment. *See also* International Standards Organization/Open System Interconnection model.

player

A program launched or used by a Web browser to process a file that the browser cannot handle. A player is a program that deals with sound files. *See also* helper; plug-in; viewer.

plug-in

A small program that you link in to your browser to add a special capability. Plug-ins are available from a variety of companies, usually free, including:

- Acrobat Amber Reader from Adobe Systems, with which you can view, navigate, and print files in PDF (Portable Document Format), commonly used by U.S. government agencies, including the IRS

- Shockwave, with which you can watch animation and play some games

- Crescendo, with which you can play music

- KEYview, with which you can view files in more than 200 formats, including Microsoft Word, Microsoft Excel, and WordPerfect

- RealAudio, with which you can listen to news reports, sports broadcasts, and music via the Internet, without having to launch the RealAudio helper application

Point-to-Point Protocol

Abbreviated PPP. A TCP/IP protocol used to transmit over serial lines and telephone connections. PPP allows a user to establish a temporary direct connection to the Internet via modem and to appear to the host system as if it were an Ethernet port on the host's network. PPP also provides an automatic method of assigning an IP address so that mobile users can connect to the network at any point. *See also* Ethernet; IP address; protocol; Transmission Control Protocol/Internet Protocol.

Point-to-Point Tunneling Protocol

Abbreviated PPTP. A proprietary networking protocol from Microsoft that supports virtual private networks, allowing remote users to access NT Server systems across the Internet without compromising security.

point of presence

Abbreviated POP. A connection to the telephone company or to long-distance carrier services.

POP

See point of presence.

Portable Document Format

Abbreviated PDF. A file-format standard that was developed by Adobe Systems and others. A file in this format usually has PDF as the filename extension.

port number

The default input/output location identifier for an Internet application.

For example, FTP, Gopher, HTTP, and Telnet are all assigned unique port numbers so that the computer knows how to respond when it is contacted on a specific port; Gopher servers usually talk at port 70, HTTP servers use port 80, and SMTP e-mail is always delivered to port 25. You can override these defaults by specifying different values in a URL. *See also* File Transfer Protocol; Hypertext Transfer Protocol; simple mail transfer protocol; Telnet; Uniform Resource Locator.

PPP

See Point-to-Point Protocol.

PPTP
See Point-to-Point Tunneling Protocol.

presentation layer
The sixth of the seven layers that make up the ISO/OSI model of computer communications. The presentation layer defines the way in which data is formatted, presented, converted, and encoded. *See also* International Standards Organization/Open System Interconnection model.

PRI
See Primary Rate ISDN.

Primary Rate ISDN
Abbreviated PRI. An ISDN service that provides 23 B (bearer) channels capable of speeds up to 64Kbps, and a D (data) channel, also capable of 64Kbps. The combined capacity of 1.544Mbps is equivalent to one T1 channel. *See also* Integrated Services Digital Network; kilobits per second; megabits per second.

privacy enhanced mail
Abbreviated PEM. An e-mail system that uses RSA encryption to provide a confidential method of authentication. *See also* RSA.

Private Communication Technology
Abbreviated PCT. A standard for transmitting secure data of all types, rather than only financial information, developed by Microsoft and Visa. PCT employs some of the algorithms used in the Microsoft/Visa secure transaction technology (STT). *See also* secure transaction technology.

Private Key Scheme
See encryption.

protocol
In networking and communications, the formal specification that defines the procedures to follow when transmitting and receiving data. Protocols define the format, timing, sequence, and error checking used on the network.

protocol stack
A layered set of protocols that work together to provide a set of network functions. Internet and Intranet computers use a TCP/IP stack. *See also* protocol; Transmission Control Protocol/Internet Protocol.

proxy server
A program running on a server positioned between your LAN or Intranet and the Internet. This program filters all outgoing connections so that they all appear to come from the same machine, in an attempt to conceal the underlying network structure from any intruders. A proxy server will also forward your request to the Internet, intercept the response, and then forward the response to you at your network node. A system administrator can also regulate the outside points to which the LAN users may connect. *See also* Internet; Intranet; local area network; node; system administrator.

Public Key Scheme
See encryption.

PVC
See permanent virtual circuit.

Q

query language

In a database management system, a programming language that allows a user to extract and display specific information from a database. SQL is an international database query language that allows the user to issue high-level commands or statements, such as SELECT or INSERT, to create or modify data or the database structure. *See also* Structured Query Language.

R

RAS

See Remote Access Service.

RealAudio

Technology developed by Progressive Networks that lets you play audio files as they are in the process of being downloaded rather than waiting until the complete file has arrived. This gives a much faster response.

redirection

The mechanism that reroutes clients attempting to access a specific URL to a different URL, either on the same or on a different server. This can be a convenient way of avoiding dead-ends if you change to a different ISP. *See also* Internet Service Provider; Uniform Resource Locator.

registry

In Windows NT, the system database that contains information on hardware, software, and users on the system.

remote access

A workstation-to-network connection, made using a modem and telephone circuit, that allows data to be sent or received over large distances. Also known as remote connection.

Remote Access Service

Abbreviated RAS. A Windows NT function that allows users to log on from a remote location.

remote connection

See remote access.

replication

The process of synchronizing data stored on two or more computers.

Request for Comments

Abbreviated RFC. A document or set of documents in which proposed Internet standards are described or defined. For example, the rules to follow for e-mail message composition are specified in the document RFC822.

resource

In HTML, any URL, directory, or application that the server can access and send to a requesting client. *See also* Hypertext Markup Language; Uniform Resource Locator.

RFC

See Request for Comments.

rights

The privileges granted to a user or a group of users by the system administrator and that determine the operations you can perform on the system. *See also* permissions; system administrator.

RIP

See Routing Information Protocol.

robot

A World Wide Web application that automatically locates and collects information about new Web sites. Robots are most often used to create large databases of Web sites.

rot-13

A simple encryption scheme used to scramble posts to Usenet newsgroups and that makes the text unreadable until it is decoded. Rot-13 is often used when the subject matter might be considered offensive. *See also* encryption; newsgroup; Usenet.

Routing Information Protocol

Abbreviated RIP. A widely used protocol that distributes routing information on TCP/IP networks. *See also* protocol; Transmission Control Protocol/Internet Protocol.

RSA

A public-key, or asymmetric, encryption scheme, invented by and named after three mathematicians—Ron Rivest, Adi Shamir, and Len Adlemen. *See also* encryption.

S

search engine

A special Web server that lets you perform keyword searches to locate interesting Web pages. The AltaVista, Yahoo, and WebCrawler Web sites each contain examples of different search engines.

Secure HTTP

Abbreviated S-HTTP. A nonproprietary extension of HTTP used for authentication and encryption between a server and a browser. *See also* encryption; Hypertext Transfer Protocol.

secure sockets layer

Abbreviated SSL. An interface developed by Netscape that provides an encrypted data transfer between client and server applications over the Internet. *See also* client-server.

secure transaction technology

Abbreviated STT. A definition of secure credit-card transactions on the Internet, under development by Microsoft and Visa.

Serial Line Internet Protocol

Abbreviated SLIP. A protocol used to run IP over serial lines or telephone connections using modems. SLIP allows you to establish a temporary direct connection to the Internet via modem and appear to the host as though you were using a port on the host's network. SLIP is slowly being replaced by PPP. *See also* Internet Protocol; modem; protocol; Point-to-Point Protocol.

server

Any computer that makes access to files, printing, communications, and other services available to users on the network. On a small network, one single server may perform all these tasks; on larger networks, individual servers tend to specialize in a particular function. *See also* client.

server root

A directory on an Internet server that contains the server program as well as configuration and information files.

service

In Windows NT, an executable object installed in the NT Registry database that can be started on demand or started automatically when the system starts running. Only one instance of a service can run at a time. *See also* registry.

session layer

The fifth of the seven layers of the ISO/OSI model for computer communications. The session layer coordinates communications and maintains the session for as long as it is needed, performing security, logging, and administrative functions. *See also* International Standards Organization/Open System Interconnection model.

SGML

See Standard Generalized Markup Language.

S-HTTP

See Secure HTTP.

simple mail transfer protocol

Abbreviated SMTP. The TCP/IP protocol for exchanging e-mail on the Internet. *See also* e-mail; protocol; Transmission Control Protocol/Internet Protocol.

simple network management protocol

Abbreviated SNMP. A standard protocol, part of the TCP/IP suite, used to manage and monitor nodes on a network. *See also* node; protocol; Transmission Control Protocol/Internet Protocol.

SLIP

See Serial Line Internet Protocol.

SMDS

See Switched Multimegabit Data Services.

SMTP

See simple mail transfer protocol.

sniffer

A small program loaded onto your system by an intruder, designed to monitor specific traffic on the network. The sniffer program watches for the first part of any remote logon session that includes logon ID, password, and host name of a person logging on to another machine. Once this information is in the hands of the intruder, he or she can log on to that system at will. One weakly secured network can therefore expose not only other local systems, but also any remote systems to which the local users connect.

SNMP

See simple network management protocol.

spider

A World Wide Web application that automatically locates and collects information about new Web sites. Spiders are most often used to create large databases of Web sites that in turn are accessed by search engines responding to user requests for information. *See also* search engine.

SQL

See Structured Query Language.

SSL

See secure sockets layer.

Standard Generalized Markup Language

Abbreviated SGML. A standard that defines the management and structure of electronic documents. HTML, used in many World Wide Web documents on the Internet, is a part of SGML. *See also* Hypertext Markup Language.

statistical multiplexing

In communications, a method of sharing a transmission channel by using statistical methods to allocate resources. A statistical multiplexor can analyze traffic density and dynamically switch to a different channel pattern to optimize the transmission. At the receiving end of the communications circuit, the different signals are merged into their individual data streams. *See also* frequency-division multiplexing, time-division multiplexing.

Structured Query Language

Abbreviated SQL. A query language developed by IBM originally for use in its mainframe database applications, but now available for use on a wide variety of platforms. SQL contains about 60 commands and is used to create, modify, query, and access data organized in tables. It can be used as an interactive interface or as embedded commands in an application. Microsoft BackOffice includes an SQL server.

STT

See secure transaction technology (STT).

subnet

A logical network created from a single IP address. A mask is used to identify bits from the host portion of the address to be used for subnet addresses. *See also* IP address.

SVC

See switched virtual circuit.

Switched Multimegabit Data Services

Abbreviated SMDS. A high-speed metropolitan area network (MAN) service based on the IEEE (Institute of Electrical and Electronics Engineers) 802.6 standard for use over T1 and T3 circuits.

switched virtual circuit

Abbreviated SVC. A connection that exists for only as long as it is in use; the connection is broken when the transmission is complete. *See also* permanent virtual circuit.

system administrator

The person charged with the responsibility of managing a computer system; often abbreviated to SA. In a very large installation, the system administrator may actually be several people or even a small department. The tasks performed by the system administrator include:

- Starting up and shutting down the system
- Setting the system time and date
- Assigning and changing passwords
- Adding and removing users and groups
- Monitoring system security
- Installing, updating, and removing software packages and installing operating system upgrades
- Backing up the system, storing archives off location, and restoring files from the archives when needed
- Installing and configuring hardware such as printers, terminals, modems, routers, gateways, and firewalls
- Monitoring system performance and making tuning adjustments as needed
- Running system diagnostics as needed to track down and isolate hardware problems

T

T1

A long-distance point-to-point circuit, providing 24 channels of 64Kbps, giving a total bandwidth of 1.544Mbps. The standard T1 frame is 193 bits long and consists of twenty-four 8-bit voice samples and one synchronization bit. It transmits 8000 frames per second. When a T1 service is made available in single 64Kbps increments, it is known as fractional T1. *See also* kilobits per second; megabits per second.

In Europe, the comparable circuit is known as E-1, and it has a speed of 2.054Mbps.

T2

A long-distance point-to-point communications service, providing a maximum of 4 T1 channels.

T2 offers 96 channels of 64Kbps, for a total bandwidth of 6.3Mbps. T2 is not available to commercial users, although it is used within telephone company networks. *See also* kilobits per second; megabits per second.

T3

A long-distance point-to-point communications service, providing a maximum of 28 T1 channels.

T3 can carry a maximum of 672 channels of 64Kbps, for a total bandwidth of 44.736Mbps and is usually available only over fiber-optic cable. T3 is used almost exclusively by AT&T and the regional telephone operating companies, although certain large private corporations are using T3 with digital microwave or fiber-optic networks. *See also* kilobits per second; megabits per second.

T4

A long-distance point-to-point communications service, providing a maximum of 28 T1 channels.

T4 can carry 4032 channels of 64Kbps, for a total bandwidth of 274.176Mbps. T4 can be used for both digitized voice and data transmission. *See also* kilobits per second; megabits per second.

tag

An element in HTML used to annotate a document. A tag is text enclosed by less than and greater than symbols that tells the browser what each part of the document means. For example, the tag ⟨H1⟩ indicates the start of a level one heading, and the tag ⟨/H1⟩ marks the end of a level one heading. *See also* element; Hypertext Markup Language.

T-carrier

A digital communications service from a common carrier for voice or data transmission. The 4-level time-division multiplexed specification for the U.S. telephone system allows the bit stream of the smaller carriers to be multiplexed into the larger ones.

TCP

See Transmission Control Protocol.

TCP/IP

See Transmission Control Protocol/Internet Protocol.

Telnet

A terminal emulation protocol, part of the TCP/IP suite of protocols, that provides remote terminal-connection services. *See also* protocol; tn3270; Transmission Control Protocol/Internet Protocol.

time-division multiplexing

Abbreviated TDM. A method of sharing a communications channel by dividing the available time equally between competing stations. At the receiving end, the different signals are merged into their individual data streams. *See also* frequency-division multiplexing; statistical multiplexing.

TFTP

See Trivial File Transfer Protocol.

top-level domain

The highest category of hostname, which either signifies the type of institution or the country of its origin. The most common top-level domains in the United States are:

- com: a commercial organization
- edu: an educational establishment
- gov: a branch of the U.S. government
- int: an international organization such as NATO
- mil: a branch of the U.S. military
- net: a network organization such as InterNIC
- org: a nonprofit organization

Most countries (except the United States) also have unique domains named after their international abbreviations; for example, ca represents Canada, uk represents the United Kingdom, and jp represents Japan. *See also* domain; domain name; Domain Name Service.

tn3270

A special version of the Telnet program, specifically designed for use with large IBM computers using 3270 and 327*x* series terminals. *See also* Telnet.

Transmission Control Protocol

Abbreviated TCP. The connection-oriented, transport level protocol used in the TCP/IP suite of protocols. *See also* protocol.

Transmission Control Protocol/Internet Protocol

Abbreviated TCP/IP. A set of communications protocols first developed by the Defense Advanced Research Projects Agency (DARPA) in the late 1970s. The TCP/IP protocols encompass media access, packet transport, session communications, file transfer, e-mail, and terminal emulation. *See also* e-mail; packet; protocol.

TCP/IP is supported by a large number of hardware and software vendors and is available on many computer systems, from PCs to mainframes. Many corporations, universities, and government agencies use TCP/IP, and it is also the basis for the Internet. *See also* Internet.

transport layer

The fourth of seven layers of the ISO/OSI model for computer communications. The transport layer defines protocols for message structure and supervises the validity of the transmission by performing some error checking. *See also* International Standards Organization/Open System Interconnection model; protocol.

Trivial File Transfer Protocol

Abbreviated TFTP. A simplified version of the TCP/IP File Transfer Protocol that does not include password protection or user-directory capability. *See also* File Transfer Protocol; Transmission Control Protocol/Internet Protocol.

U

UDP

See User Datagram Protocol.

unauthorized access

To gain entry to a computer system using stolen or guessed passwords. *See also* password.

Unicode

A 16-bit character code, defined by the Unicode Consortium and by the ISO 10646 standard, that supports a maximum of 65,536 unique characters rather than the 256 characters available in the current ASCII character set. *See also* American Standard Code for Information Interchange.

Uniform Resource Locator

Abbreviated URL. A method of accessing Internet resources.

URLs contain information about both the access method to use and the resource itself and are used by Web browsers to connect you directly to a specific document or home page on the World Wide Web, without your having to know where that resource is physically located. *See also* browser; home page; World Wide Web.

uninterruptible power supply

Abbreviated UPS. An alternative power source, usually consisting of a set of batteries, used to power a computer system if the normal power service is interrupted or falls below acceptable levels.

upload

In communications, to transfer a file or other information from your computer to the server over a network link or via modem. *See also* download.

UPS

See uninterruptible power supply.

URL

See Uniform Resource Locator.

Usenet

A contraction formed from User Network. An international, noncommercial network, linking many thousands of sites. Although Usenet and the Internet are closely related, they are not the same thing by any means. Not every Internet computer is part of Usenet, and not every Usenet system can be reached from the Internet. Like the Internet, Usenet has no central governing body; it is run by the people who use it. With well over 10,000 newsgroups, Usenet is accessed by millions of people every day, in more than 100 countries.

Usenet newsgroups

The individual discussion groups within Usenet. Most newsgroups are concerned with a single subject; the range of subjects is phenomenal—there are more than 10,000 newsgroups from which to choose. If people are interested in a subject, you are sure to find a newsgroup for it somewhere. *See also* newsgroup.

user account

A security mechanism that is used to control access to a network, established and maintained by the system administrator. Elements of a user account include password information, rights, and information about the groups to which the user belongs. *See also* password; system administrator.

User Datagram Protocol

Abbreviated UDP. The connectionless, transport-level protocol used in the TCP/IP suite of protocols, usually bundled with IP-layer software. Because UDP does not add overhead, as does connection-oriented TCP, UDP is often used with SNMP applications. *See also* Internet Protocol; protocol; simple network management protocol; Transmission Control Protocol/Internet Protocol.

V

viewer

An application launched by a Web browser to view a file that the browser cannot handle by itself. Sometimes called a helper application.

A viewer displays video clips and animation files.

virtual circuit

A temporary shared communications path that appears to the user as a dedicated connection. A virtual circuit is maintained only for as long as the customer needs a connection; the next time a call is placed, a completely different virtual circuit may be used. *See also* dedicated line.

virtual data network

A method used to provide full interconnection of all LAN segments without the use of dedicated circuits so that the customers pay only for the services they actually use. Also known as a virtual LAN. *See also* dedicated line; local area network.

Virtual Reality Modeling Language

Abbreviated VRML. A draft specification for three-dimensional rendering used in conjunction with Web browsers. *See also* browser; Web browser.

VMS

A multiuser multitasking virtual memory operating system from Digital Equipment Corporation (DEC) for the popular VAX line of computers and workstations.

VRML

See Virtual Reality Modeling Language.

W

WAN

See wide area network.

Web browser

A World Wide Web client application that you use to look at hypertext documents and follow links to other HTML documents on the Web. *See also* browser; hypertext; Hypertext Markup Language; World Wide Web.

Web page

Information placed on a Web server for viewing with a Web browser. A Web page may contain text, graphics, audio or video clips, and links to other Web pages. *See also* browser; Web browser.

Web server

A hardware and software package that provides services to Web clients. *See also* client; client-server; server.

wide area network

Abbreviated WAN. A network that connects users across large distances, often crossing the geographical boundaries of cities or states. *See also* local area network.

WinCGI

A Common Gateway Interface for Windows applications.

workflow software

Software that allows users to move and manage information among themselves, combining the functions of e-mail, imaging, and document management. A document moves through various stages of processing as it is edited, signed, or validated by the various members of the workgroup. *See also* workgroup; e-mail.

workgroup

A group of individuals who work together and share the same files and databases over a LAN. Special software coordinates the workgroup and allows users to edit and exchange files and update databases as a group. *See also* local area network.

World Wide Web

Abbreviated WWW, W3, or simply the Web. A huge collection of hypertext pages on the Internet. Web traffic is growing faster than most other Internet services, and the reason for this becomes obvious when you try out a capable Web browser; it is very easy and a lot of fun to access World Wide Web information. *See also* browser; hypertext; Internet.

APPENDIX
C

Bibliography

This appendix includes a selection of books available from bookstores and libraries covering some of the more technical areas of communications and computer operations, security and the use of firewalls, as well as books on the Internet and on Windows NT.

General Internet and World Wide Web

Albitz, Paul, and Cricket Liu. *DNS and Bind*. O'Reilly and Associates, Inc., 1994.

Cady, Glee Harrah, and Pat McGregor. *Mastering the Internet*. Sybex, 1996.

Cronon, Mary. *Doing More Business on the Internet*. Van Nostrand Reinhold, 1995.

Eddy, Sandra E. *The Internet Business-to-Business Directory*. Sybex, 1996.

Ellsworth, Jill and Matthew. *Marketing on the Internet: Multimedia Strategies for the World Wide Web*. John Wiley, 1995

Estrada, Susan. *Connecting to the Internet*. O'Reilly and Associates, Inc. 1993

Falk, Bennett. *The Internet Roadmap*. Sybex, 1996.

Hoffman, Paul. *The Internet Instant Reference*. Sybex, 1996.

Kroll, Ed. *The Whole Internet User's Guide and Catalog*. O'Reilly and Associates, 1994.

Lui, Cricket, Jerry Peek, Russ Jones, Bryan Buus, and Adrian Nye. *Managing Internet Information Systems*. O'Reilly and Associates, Inc., 1994.

Internet Commerce

Godin, Seth. *Presenting Digital Cash*. Macmillan Computer Publishing, 1996.

Kalakota, Ravi, and Andrew Whinston. *Frontiers of Electonic Commerce*. Addison-Wesley, 1996.

Lynch, Daniel. *Digital Money, the New Era of Internet Commerce*. John Wiley, 1996.

Tapscott, Don. *The Digital Economy*. McGraw-Hill, 1995.

Wayner, Peter. *Digital Cash, Commerce on the Net*. Ap Professional, 1995.

Security and Firewalls

Chapman, Brent, and Elizabeth Zwicky. *Building Internet Firewalls*. O'Reilly and Associates, Inc., 1993.

Cheswick, Bill, and Steve Bellovin. *Firewalls and Internet Security*. Addison-Wesley, 1994.

Cooper, Frederic, and Chris Goggans, et al. *Implementing Internet Security*. New Riders, 1995.

Garfinkel, Simson. *PGP: Pretty Good Privacy*. O'Reilly and Associates, Inc., 1995.

Russell, Deborah, and G. Gangemi. *Computer Security Basics*. O'Reilly and Associates, Inc., 1991.

Stallings, William. *Network and Internetwork Security*. Prentice Hall, 1994.

TCP/IP and Networking

Cromer, Douglas. *Internetworking with TCP/IP, Volume 1: Principles, Protocols, and Architecture*. Prentice Hall, 1991.

Dyson, Peter. *The Network Press Dictionary of Networking*. Sybex, 1995.

Feibel, Werner. *The Network Press Encyclopedia of Networking*. Sybex, 1996.

Halsall, Fred. *Data Communications, Computer Networks, and OSI*. Addison-Wesley, 1994.

Handel, Rainer, and Manfred Huber. *Integrated Broadband Networks*. Addison-Wesley, 1991.

Hunt, Craig. *Networking Personal Computers with TCP/IP*. O'Reilly and Associates, Inc., 1995.

Hunt, Craig. *TCP/IP Network Administration*. O'Reilly and Associates, Inc., 1992.

Huitema, Christian. *Routing in the Internet*. Prentice-Hall, 1995.

Piscitello, David, and Lyman Chapin. *Open Systems Networking: TCP/IP and OSI*. Addison-Wesley, 1993.

Stevens, W Richard. *TCP/IP Illustrated, Volume 1: The Protocols*. Addison-Wesley, 1995.

Stevens, W Richard. *TCP/IP Illustrated, Volume 2: The Implementation.* Addison-Wesley, 1995.

Stevens, W Richard. *TCP/IP Illustrated, Volume 3: TCP for Transactions.* Addison-Wesley, 1996.

ISDN

Hopkins, Gerald. *The ISDN Literacy Book.* Addison-Wesley, 1995.

Motorola. *The Basic Book of ISDN.* Addison-Wesley, 1992.

Pacific Bell. *ISDN; A Users Guide to Services, Applications, and Resources in California.* Pacific Bell, 1994.

Sapien, Mike, and Greg Piedmo. *Mastering ISDN.* Sybex, 1996.

HTML and Web Site Design

Aronson, Larry. *HTML Manual of Style.* Ziff-Davis, 1994.

Dornfest, Asha. *Easy Web Publishing with Word.* Sybex, 1996.

Dornfest, Asha. *Do-It-Yourself Web Publishing with PageMill.* Sybex, 1996.

Graham, Ian. *The HTML Sourcebook.* John Wiley, 1995.

Jaworski, James. *Easy Web Publishing with HoTMetaL.* Sybex, 1996.

McCoy, John. *Mastering Web Design.* Sybex, 1996.

Morris, Mary. *HTML Authoring for Fun and Profit.* Prentice Hall, 1995.

Musciano, Chuck, and Bill Kennedy. *HTML: The Definitive Guide.* O'Reilly and Associates, 1996.

Niederst, Jennifer, and Edie Freeman. *Designing for the Web*. O'Reilly and Associates, 1996.

Internationalization

Axtel, Roger. *Do's and Taboos Around the World*. John Wiley & Sons, 1993.

Axtel, Roger. *Do's and Taboos of Using English Around the World*. John Wiley & Sons, 1993.

Hoft, Nancy. *International Technical Communication: How to Export Information about High Technology*. John Wiley & Sons, 1995.

Horton, William. *The Icon Book*. John Wiley & Sons, 1994.

Horton, William. *Illustrating Computer Documentation*. John Wiley & Sons, 1991.

IBM Corporation. *National Language Support Reference Manual; Volume 2*. IBM Corporation, order number SE09-8002.

Jones, Scott, Cynthia Kennellyijn, and Claudia Mueller. *Developing International User Information*. Digital Press, 1992.

O'Donnell, Sandra. *Programming for the World: A Guide to Internationalization*. Prentice Hall, 1994.

Java

Arnold, Ken, and James Gosling. *The Java Programming Language*. Addison-Wesley, 1996.

Bartlett, Neil, Alex Leslie, and Steve Simkin. *Java Programming Explored*. Corialis Group, 1996.

Campione, Mary, and Kathy Walrath. *The Java Language Tutorial: Object-Oriented Programming for the Internet.* Addison-Wesley, 1996.

Daconta, Michael. *Java for C++ Programmers.* John Wiley, 1996.

December, John. *Presenting Java.* Macmillan Computer Publishing, 1996.

Flanagan, David. *Java in a Nutshell.* O'Reilly and Associates, 1996.

Fraise, Scott, Chris Laurel, and Ryan Watkins. *Programming Java Applets.* Ziff-Davis, 1996.

Gosling, James, Bill Joy, and Guy Steele. *The Java Language Specification.* Addison-Wesley, 1996.

Gosling, James. *The Java Application Programming Interface.* Addison-Wesley, 1996.

Hoff, Arthur van, and Sami Shaio. *Hooked on Java.* Addison-Wesley, 1996.

Lemay, Laura, and Charles Perkins. *Teach Yourself Java in 14 Days.* Macmillan Computer Publishing, 1996.

Mangan, Mark, Edith Au, Jonathon Wallace, Ellick Quach, and Michael Wei. *Java Basics.* MIS Press, 1996.

Pew, John. *Instant Java.* SunSoft Press, 1996.

Purcell, Lee. *Fast Track to Java Script.* Sybex, 1996.

Vanhelse, Laurence. *Mastering Java.* Sybex, 1996.

Perl and CGI Programming

Deep, John. *Developing CGI Applications with Perl*. John Wiley, 1995.

Gundavaram, Shishir. *CGI Programming on the World Wide Web*. O'Reilly and Associates, 1996.

Shwartz, Randal. *Learning Perl*. O'Reilly and Associates, 1993.

Vromans, John. *Perl 5 Desktop Reference*. O'Reilly and Associates, 1996.

Wall, Larry, and Randal Shwartz. *Programming Perl*. O'Reilly and Associates, 1991.

Audio and Video

Dean, Damon. *A Pocket Tour of Multimedia on the Internet*. Sybex, 1996.

Harrel, William D. *The Multimedia Authoring Workshop*. Sybex, 1996.

Varchol, Douglas J. *The Multimedia Scriptwriting Workshop*. Sybex, 1996.

VRML

Ames, Andrea, David Nadeau, John Moreland, and Robert Russ. *The VRML Sourcebook*. John Wiley, 1995.

Pesce, Mark. *VRML—Browsing and Building Cybersapce*. New Riders, 1995.

Windows NT and Windows NT Server

Microsoft Press. *Windows NT Resource Guide*. Microsoft Press, 1993.

Minasi, Mark, Christa Anderson, and Elizabeth Creegan. *Mastering Windows NT Server 4.0*. Sybex, 1996.

Minasi, Mark. *Mastering Windows NT X Workstation*. Sybex, 1996.

Russel, Charles. *The ABCs of Windows NT X Workstation*. Sybex, 1996.

Walters, Boyd. *Fast Track to NT Server*. Sybex, 1996.

INDEX

Note to the Reader: Throughout this index **boldface** page numbers indicate primary discussions of a topic. *Italicized* page numbers indicate illustrations.

B

D

G

H

I

J

N

Q

R

S

T

U

Y

Z

Java Resources on the Internet

Name	URL
Sun Microsystems	`http://www.sun.com/`
Sun's Java Site	`http://java.sun.com/`
Java User Resource Network	`http://www.nebulex.com/URN/home.html`
The Java Developer	`http://www.idsonline.com/digitalfocus/faq`
Virtual Rendezvous' Club Java	`http://rendezvous.com/java/`
JavaWorld Magazine	`http://www.javaworld.com/`
Gamelan	`http://www.gamelan.com/`
DimensionX	`http://dimensionx.com/`
HotWired	`http://www.hotwired.com/java/`
Yahoo	`http://www.yahoo.com/Computers_and_Internet/Languages/Java/`
SGI	`http://reality.sgi.com/employees/shiffman_engr/`